TRANSPARENCY IN HEALTH AND HEALTH CARE IN THE UNITED STATES

Transparency is a concept that is becoming increasingly lauded as a solution to a host of problems in the American health care system. Transparency initiatives show great promise, including empowering patients and other stakeholders to make more efficient decisions, improve resource allocation, and better regulate the health care industry. Nevertheless, transparency is not a cure-all for the problems facing the modern health care system. The authors of this volume present a nuanced view of transparency, exploring ways in which transparency has succeeded and ways in which transparency initiatives have room for improvement. Working at the intersection of law, medicine, ethics, and business, the book goes beyond the buzzwords to the heart of transparency's transformative potential, while interrogating its obstacles and downsides. It should be read by anyone looking for a better understanding of transparency in the health care context.

Holly Fernandez Lynch, JD, MBE, is the John Russell Dickson, MD Presidential Assistant Professor of Medical Ethics at the University of Pennsylvania's Perelman School of Medicine. She focuses her scholarly research on issues at the intersection of law, bioethics, and health policy, in particular the ethics and regulation of research with human subjects and conflicts of conscience in health care.

I. Glenn Cohen, JD, is the James A. Attwood and Leslie Williams Professor of Law and Faculty Director of Petrie-Flom Center for Health Law, Biotechnology & Bioethics at Harvard Law School. He is one of the world's leading experts on the intersection of bioethics and the law, as well as health law. He is the author of more than 110 articles in venues like the New England Journal of Medicine, JAMA, Nature, and the Harvard Law Review, and the author, editor, or co-editor of 12 books.

Carmel Shachar, JD, MPH, is the Executive Director of the Petrie-Flom Center for Health Law Policy, Biotechnology, and Bioethics at Harvard Law School. Carmel's scholarship focuses on law and health policy, in particular the regulation of access to care for vulnerable individuals, health care anti-discrimination law and policy, and the use of all-payer claims databases in health care research. Carmel is also a Lecturer at Law on Harvard Law School, where she co-teaches a course on "Health Care Rights in the Twenty-First Century."

Barbara J. Evans, PhD, JD, LLM, is the Mary Ann and Lawrence E. Faust Professor of Law, Professor of Electrical and Computer Engineering, and Director of the Center for Biotechnology & Law at the University of Houston. Her research interests include data privacy and access, regulation of emerging biotechnologies and machine-learning software, and genomic civil rights.

Transparency in Health and Health Care in the United States

LAW AND ETHICS

Edited by

HOLLY FERNANDEZ LYNCH
University of Pennsylvania, Perelman School of Medicine

I. GLENN COHEN
Petrie-Flom Center, Harvard Law School

CARMEL SHACHAR
Petrie-Flom Center, Harvard Law School

BARBARA J. EVANS
University of Houston Law Center

CAMBRIDGE
UNIVERSITY PRESS

University Printing House, Cambridge CB2 8BS, United Kingdom

One Liberty Plaza, 20th Floor, New York, NY 10006, USA

477 Williamstown Road, Port Melbourne, VIC 3207, Australia

314–321, 3rd Floor, Plot 3, Splendor Forum, Jasola District Centre, New Delhi – 110025, India

79 Anson Road, #06–04/06, Singapore 079906

Cambridge University Press is part of the University of Cambridge.

It furthers the University's mission by disseminating knowledge in the pursuit of education, learning, and research at the highest international levels of excellence.

www.cambridge.org
Information on this title: www.cambridge.org/9781108470995
DOI: 10.1017/9781108658867

© Cambridge University Press 2019

This publication is in copyright. Subject to statutory exception and to the provisions of relevant collective licensing agreements, no reproduction of any part may take place without the written permission of Cambridge University Press.

First published 2019

Printed and bound in Great Britain by Clays Ltd, Elcograf S.p.A.

A catalogue record for this publication is available from the British Library.

ISBN 978-1-108-47099-5 Hardback
ISBN 978-1-108-45693-7 Paperback

Cambridge University Press has no responsibility for the persistence or accuracy of URLs for external or third-party internet websites referred to in this publication and does not guarantee that any content on such websites is, or will remain, accurate or appropriate.

Every effort has been made in preparing this book to provide accurate and up-to-date information which is in accord with accepted standards and practice at the time of publication. Although case histories are drawn from actual cases, every effort has been made to disguise the identities of the individuals involved. Nevertheless, the authors, editors and publishers can make no warranties that the information contained herein is totally free from error, not least because clinical standards are constantly changing through research and regulation. The authors, editors and publishers therefore disclaim all liability for direct or consequential damages resulting from the use of material contained in this book. Readers are strongly advised to pay careful attention to information provided by the manufacturer of any drugs or equipment that they plan to use.

I. Glenn Cohen – To Daniel Segal, bright light and dark matter; To Vik Joshi, a subway ride and trips not taken

Holly Fernandez Lynch – To Cristine Hutchison-Jones, my Type-A comrade

Carmel Shachar – To I. Glenn Cohen and Holly Fernandez Lynch for drawing me back into the PFC family

Contents

List of Contributors	*page* xi
Acknowledgments	xv
Introduction Carmel Shachar, I. Glenn Cohen, Holly Fernandez Lynch, and Barbara J. Evans	1

PART I: TRANSPARENCY IN HEALTH AND HEALTH CARE: THEMATIC ISSUES — 13

Introduction to Part I
Abigail R. Moncrieff — 15

1 Smashing into Windows: The Limits of Consumer Sovereignty in Health Care
 Barry R. Furrow — 17

2 The Interplay of Privacy and Transparency in Health Care: The HIPAA Privacy Rule as a Case Study
 Barbara J. Evans — 30

3 Transparency Trade-offs: Priority Setting, Scarcity, and Health Fairness
 Govind Persad — 44

4 Slightly Hazy: Transparency and the Costs of Too Much Information
 Oliver J. Kim — 58

PART II: TRANSPARENCY AND INFORMED CONSENT   69

Introduction to Part II   71
Luke Gelinas

5   Transparency versus Informed Consent: The Patient/Consumer Paradigms   75
Craig J. Konnoth

6   Transparency and Financial Conflicts: The Uncertain Case for Sunshine   88
Richard S. Saver

7   Making Religion Transparent: The Substance, Process, and Efficacy of Disclosing Religious Restrictions on Care   103
Elizabeth Sepper

PART III: TRANSPARENCY AND ECONOMICS: HEALTH CARE COSTS AND BILLING   115

Introduction to Part III   117
Kristin M. Madison

8   Transparency on Prescription Drug Research Expenditures: A Lever for Restraining Pricing?   121
Ameet Sarpatwari, Jerry Avorn, and Aaron S. Kesselheim

9   Is Pharmaceutical Price Transparency an Effective Means to Reduce High Prices and Wide Variations?   132
Marc A. Rodwin

10   Price Transparency: A Contracts Solution   153
Wendy Netter Epstein

11   Solving Surprise Medical Bills   165
Mark A. Hall

PART IV: TRANSPARENCY AND INNOVATION   179

Introduction to Part IV   181
Holly Fernandez Lynch

12   Increasing the Transparency of FDA Review to Enhance the Innovation Process   185
Rachel E. Sachs and Thomas J. Hwang

13	Transparency and Clinical Trial Data Sharing: Legal and Policy Issues Barbara E. Bierer, Mark Barnes, and Rebecca Li	196
14	The European Medicines Agency's Approach to Transparency Stefano Marino and Spyridon Drosos	210

PART V: TRANSPARENCY AND OUTCOMES: PROMOTING HEALTH AND SAFETY 227

Introduction to Part V 229
Gregory Curfman

15	The Role of Transparency in Promoting Healthy Behaviors: Pros, Cons, and Perils of Information Sharing to Foster Personal Responsibility in Health Care Anthony W. Orlando and Arnold J. Rosoff	233
16	The Role of Transparency in Patient Safety Improvement Michelle M. Mello, David M. Studdert, Brahmajee K. Nallamothu, and Allen Kachalia	244
17	Personal Health Records as a Tool for Transparency in Health Care Sharona Hoffman	260
18	Nontransparency in Electronic Health Record Systems Jim Hawkins, Barbara J. Evans, and Harlan M. Krumholz	273
19	Transparency Challenges in Reproductive Health Care Dov Fox	286

PART VI: CHALLENGES IN PROMOTING AND MEASURING TRANSPARENCY IN HEALTH CARE 297

Introduction to Part VI 299
I. Glenn Cohen

20	ERISA as a Barrier for State Health Care Transparency Efforts Erin C. Fuse Brown and Jaime S. King	301
21	Transparency and Data Sharing in Clinical Research and Big Pharma Jennifer E. Miller	314

22 Promoting IRB Transparency: About What, To Whom,
    Why, and How?   329
    Holly Fernandez Lynch

23 Using Disclosure to Regulate PBMs: The Dark Side
    of Transparency   343
    David A. Hyman and William E. Kovacic

Contributors

Jerry Avorn, MD Chief, Division of Pharmacoepidemiology and Pharmacoeconomics, Brigham and Women's Hospital; Professor of Medicine, Harvard Medical School, Boston, MA, USA

Mark Barnes, JD, LLM Partner, Ropes & Gray, LLP, Boston, MA, USA; Visiting Lecturer in Law, Yale Law School, New Haven, CT, USA

Barbara E. Bierer, MD Senior Physician, Brigham and Women's Hospital; Faculty Director, the Multi-Regional Clinical Trials Center of Brigham and Women's Hospital and Harvard; Professor of Medicine (Pediatrics), Harvard Medical School, Boston, MA, USA

Erin C. Fuse Brown, JD, MPH Associate Professor of Law and Faculty Member of the Center for Law, Health and Society, Georgia State University College of Law, Atlanta, GA, USA

I. Glenn Cohen, JD James A. Attwood and Leslie Williams Professor of Law; Faculty Director, Petrie-Flom Center for Health Law Policy, Biotechnology, and Bioethics, Harvard Law School, Cambridge, MA, USA

Gregory Curfman, M.D. Deputy Editor, JAMA, Chicago, IL, USA

Spyridon Drosos, LLM Legal Adviser at the European Medicines Agency, London, UK; Visiting Lecturer at the Catholic University of Lille, Paris, France

Wendy Netter Epstein, JD Professor of Law and Faculty Director of the Mary and Michael Jaharis Health Law Institute, DePaul University College of Law, Chicago, IL, USA

Barbara J. Evans, PhD, JD, LLM Mary Ann and Lawrence E. Faust Professor of Law, Director of the Center for Biotechnology & Law; Professor of Electrical and Computer Engineering, the University of Houston, Houston, TX, USA

Dov Fox, LLM, JD, DPhil Professor of Law and Director of the Center for Health Law, Policy & Bioethics, University of San Diego School of Law, San Diego, CA, USA

Barry R. Furrow, JD Professor of Law and Director of the Health Law Program, Kline School of Law, Drexel University, Philadelphia, PA, USA

Luke Gelinas, PhD Chairperson, Advarra IRB, Columbia, MD, USA

Mark A. Hall, JD Fred & Elizabeth Turnage Professor of Law and Public Health; Director, the Health Law and Policy Program, Wake Forest University School of Law, Winston-Salem, NC, USA

Jim Hawkins, JD Professor of Law and George Butler Research Professor of Law, University of Houston Law Center, Houston, TX, USA

Sharona Hoffman, JD, LLM, SJD Edgar A. Hahn Professor of Law, Professor of Bioethics, and Co-Director of the Law-Medicine Center, Case Western Reserve University School of Law, Cleveland, OH, USA

Thomas J. Hwang, AB Associate Researcher, Program on Regulation, Therapeutics, and Law (PORTAL), Division of Pharmacoepidemiology and Pharmacoeconomics, Brigham and Women's Hospital and Harvard Medical School, Boston, MA, USA

David A. Hyman MD, JD Professor of Law, Georgetown Law Center, Washington, DC, USA

Allen Kachalia, MD, JD Associate Professor of Medicine, Harvard Medical School; Chief Quality Officer, Brigham Health, Boston, MA, USA

Aaron S. Kesselheim, MD, JD, MPH Director, Program on Regulation, Therapeutics, And Law (PORTAL), Division of Pharmacoepidemiology and Pharmacoeconomics, Brigham and Women's Hospital and Harvard Medical School; Associate Professor of Medicine, Harvard Medical School, Boston, MA, USA

Oliver J. Kim, JD, LLM President, Mousetrap Consulting, Washington, DC, USA; Adjunct Professor of Law, University of Pittsburgh Law School, Pittsburgh, PA, USA

Jaime S. King, JD, PhD Associate Dean and Faculty Director of the UCSF/UC Hastings Consortium on Science, Law and Health Policy, Professor of Law, and Bion M. Gregory Chair in Business Law, University of California, Hastings College of the Law, San Francisco, CA

Craig J. Konnoth, MPhil, JD Associate Professor of Law, University of Colorado School of Law, Denver, CO, USA

Harlan M. Krumholz, MD, SM Harold H. Hines, Jr. Professor of Medicine (Cardiology); Professor in the Institute for Social and Policy Studies, of Investigative Medicine and of Public Health (Health Policy); Director, Center for Outcomes Research and Evaluation, Yale-New Haven Hospital; Co-Director, Robert Wood Johnson Foundation Clinical Scholars Program, Yale University, New Haven, CT, USA

Rebecca Li, PhD Executive Director, Vivli; Senior Advisor, the Multi-Regional Clinical Trials Center of Brigham and Women's Hospital and Harvard; Instructor, Harvard Medical School, Boston, MA, USA

Holly Fernandez Lynch, JD, MBe John Russell Dickson, MD Presidential Assistant Professor of Medical Ethics, Perelman School of Medicine, University of Pennsylvania, Philadelphia, PA, USA

Kristin M. Madison, JD, PhD Professor of Law and Health Sciences, School of Law and the Bouvé College of Health Sciences, Northeastern University, Boston, MA, USA

Stefano Marino, Head of Legal Department at the European Medicines Agency, London, UK

Michelle M. Mello, JD, PhD, MPhil Professor of Law, Stanford Law School; Professor of Health Research and Policy, Stanford University School of Medicine, Stanford, CA, USA

Jennifer E. Miller, PhD Assistant Professor, Yale University School of Medicine, New Haven, CT, USA; Founder, Bioethics International, USA

Abigail R. Moncrieff, JD Visiting Scholar in the Law School and Graduate Student in Government at University of Texas, Austin

Brahmajee K. Nallamothu, MD, MPH Professor of Internal Medicine, University of Michigan Cardiovascular Center, Ann Arbor, MI, USA

Anthony W. Orlando, MSc, MPW, PhD Assistant Professor, Finance, Real Estate, and Law Department, California State Polytechnic University, Pomona, College of Business Administration, Pomona, CA, USA

Govind Persad, JD, PhD Assistant Professor, University of Denver Sturm College of Law, Denver, CO, USA

Marc A. Rodwin, JD, PhD Professor of Law, Suffolk University Law School, Boston, MA, USA

Arnold J. Rosoff, JD Professor Emeritus of Legal Studies and Health Care Management, Wharton School; Senior Fellow, Leonard Davis Institute of Health

Economics and Center for Public Health Initiatives, University of Pennsylvania, Philadelphia, PA, USA

Rachel E. Sachs, JD, MPH Associate Professor of Law, Washington University in St. Louis, St. Louis, MO, USA

Ameet Sarpatwari, JD, PhD Assistant Director, Program on Regulation, Therapeutics, And Law (PORTAL), Division of Pharmacoepidemiology and Pharmacoeconomics, Brigham and Women's Hospital and Harvard Medical School; Instructor in Medicine, Harvard Medical School, Boston, MA, USA

Richard S. Saver, JD Arch. T. Allen Distinguished Professor of Law, University of North Carolina School of Law; Professor (secondary appointment), University of North Carolina School of Medicine; Adjunct Professor, University of North Carolina Gillings School of Global Public Health, Chapel Hill, NC, USA

Elizabeth Sepper, JD, LLM Professor of Law, Washington University School of Law, St. Louis, MO, USA

Carmel Shachar, JD, MPH Executive Director, Petrie-Flom Center for Health Law Policy, Biotechnology, and Bioethics, and Lecturer on Law, Harvard Law School, Cambridge, MA, USA

David M. Studdert, LLB, ScD, MPH Professor of Law, Stanford Law School; Professor of Medicine, Stanford University School of Medicine, Stanford, CA, USA

Acknowledgments

A book like this is the result of the hard work of many. We thank our student line editors Joseph Ruckert (lead line editor), John Hylton, Gali Katznelson, Rohit Rajan, Nate Szyman, and Grace Wallack for their meticulous work. We are also grateful to Cristine Hutchison-Jones and Justin Leahey for their administrative support in putting on the conference that gave rise to this book, and Cristine in particular for her hard work shepherding all the many pieces of this manuscript. We also thankfully acknowledge the Petrie-Flom Center for Health Law Policy, Biotechnology, and Bioethics at Harvard Law School, with support from the Oswald DeN. Cammann Fund, for conference sponsorship. Finally, of course, we thank the contributors for their thoughtful and important scholarly contributions.

Introduction

Carmel Shachar, I. Glenn Cohen, Holly Fernandez Lynch, and Barbara J. Evans

In some ways, transparency is a relatively new concept to the world of health and health care, considering that just a few decades ago we were still in the throes of a "doctor-knows-best" model. Today, however, transparency is front and center on almost every list of solutions to a variety of health policy problems, ranging from conflicts of interest to rising drug costs to promoting efficient use of health-care resources, and more. Doctors are now expected to be transparent about patient diagnoses and treatment options, hospitals are expected to be transparent about error rates, insurers about policy limitations, companies about prices, researchers about data, and policymakers about priorities and rationales for health policy intervention.

Despite the newfound popularity of transparency initiatives, a number of important legal and ethical questions remain. For example, what exactly does transparency mean in the context of health, who has a responsibility to be transparent and to whom, what legal mechanisms are there to promote transparency, and what legal protections are needed for things like privacy, intellectual property, and the like? More specifically, when can transparency improve health and health care, and when is it likely to be nothing more than platitude?

The purpose of this volume is to better articulate the role that transparency can play in the American health-care landscape. We asked our contributors to use their work to: (1) describe the routine and special ways transparency manifests itself in American health policy, and why it has emerged in these spaces; (2) understand when, where, how, and why transparency may be a useful policy tool in relation to health and health care, what it can realistically be expected to achieve, and when it is unlikely to be successful, including limits on how patients and consumers utilize information even when we have transparency; (3) assess the legal and ethical issues raised by transparency in health and health-care, including obstacles and opportunities; and (4) learn from comparative examples of transparency, both in other sectors and outside the United States. In sum, we hope that this volume allows for a better understanding of transparency in the health-care context, so that this health policy buzzword can be used as a solution to pressing health policy issues where appropriate, while recognizing its true limitations.

The first theme interwoven in this volume is an understanding that transparency for its own sake is *not* the final goal. The universe of health-care data and information has been experiencing a 'big bang' of sorts over the last decade. The health-care data generated by the U.S. system is now measured by yottabytes (10^{24} gigabytes).[1] By contrast, five exabytes (10^{18} gigabytes) of data would contain all the words spoken on earth. Too much information can hamper decision making by patients, providers, and other health-care entities, by creating information overload that leads to anxiety, an inability to focus on key details, and other challenges.[2] For example, patients are frequently inundated with information, especially if they choose to supplement their physician's advice with internet sleuthing, and may find additional information paradoxically less helpful and more confusing for their decision making process. The risk of adopting transparency merely for its own sake is that these initiatives will only contribute flotsam and jetsam and add to the information overload that with which virtually all health-care stakeholders struggle. In this way, thoughtlessly implemented transparency initiatives may have the counterintuitive effect of muddying the waters rather than providing clarity.

The authors of this volume suggest two important considerations to prevent transparency from becoming counterproductive. The first is to be mindful of the true end goals of transparency initiatives. Time and time again, the true intent of the initiatives studied in these chapters is not transparency for its own sake. Rather, the purposes of these initiatives span the gamut of health-care policy goals. Regulation requiring pharmaceutical companies to publish their research and development costs has the immediate goal of allowing stakeholders to better understand the current pricing of drugs and the ultimate goal of bringing down pharmaceutical pricing. The purpose of the Sunshine Act is to empower patients to better understand when their health-care providers may have a conflict of interest resulting in biased advice or services. Federal and state bills requiring transparency around whether a provider is in or out of network for an insured patient express the ultimate goal of reducing or eliminating financially devastating surprise medical bills. In each of these cases transparency is a means to an end rather than an end in itself.

The second important consideration is that while overly broad transparency can often miss the mark, targeted initiatives can have positive impacts on the health-care goals they are intended to influence. For example, there are many websites and apps that list the retail drug prices from a variety of pharmacies. While these listings may increase overall transparency for drug pricing, a service that compiled all the relevant prices and presented them in a concise manner to consumers might ultimately have a greater impact on consumers' spending choices, even if that service presented less information overall than the aggregation of the websites and

---

[1] Wullianallur Raghupathi and Viju Raghupathi, Big Data Analytics in Healthcare: Promise and Potential, 2 Health Information Science and Systems 3 (2014).

[2] David Bawden and Lyn Robinson, The Dark Side of Information: Overload, Anxiety, and Other Paradoxes and Pathologies, 35 J. of Information Science 2, 180–191 (2008).

apps currently existing. Likewise, for transparency intended to facilitate informed consent, targeted disclosure of the materials facts designed to facilitate dialogue with the patient may ultimately lead to a better outcome than merely providing all the information possible, regardless of relevance. There have been attempts to embrace this idea of smarter disclosure, such as the revised Common Rule's new requirement that informed consent forms must "begin with a concise and focused presentation of the key information that is most likely to assist a prospective subject or legally authorized representative in understanding the reasons why one might or might not want to participate in the research."[3] But how do we determine when we are being transparent about the right information and when selected transparency becomes too paternalistic? Moreover, *who* makes the decisions and what are the distributive consequences of favoring transparency that caters only to some information communities? Throughout this volume, the contributors illustrate examples of the ways in which transparency initiatives can become smarter, more focused, or otherwise better suited to achieve their ultimate policy goals. While there is no bright-line rule to help us distinguish between overly broad, "just right," and too narrow transparency initiatives, these explorations of transparency can help us better identify the happy medium for which to aim.

Another theme that emerges from this volume is the complicated relationship between transparency and privacy. Privacy, especially around health-care data, is another important value and buzzword in health care.[4] At first glance, transparency and privacy seem opposed. After all, if certain data is deemed to be private or sensitive, it perhaps should not be available for transparency initiatives. In some cases, the assumption that transparency and privacy are in a zero-sum relationship is true. For example, sharing deidentified data sets may help advance science, but as technology progresses, there is also some risk that these data could be correlated with other data sets to reidentify patients. Companies are also pushed to be transparent about their clinical trial results or billing patterns, which could lead to competitors utilizing disclosed information to achieve competitive advantages or even dampen incentives for knowledge creation. In the public policy context, an overemphasis on transparency, in tandem with privacy requirements, can prevent agencies from carrying out their ultimate purposes. For example, the Environmental Protection Agency (EPA) in early 2018 proposed a policy change that would prevent it from considering scientific research unless the underlying data is made public for other scientists and industry groups to evaluate.[5] This potential policy would prevent the EPA from being able to consider important environmental health studies that are

---

[3] 45 C.F.R. § 46.116 (a)(5)(i) (2018).
[4] For an exploration of privacy in the context of health care big data, see I. Glenn Cohen, Holly Fernandez Lynch, Urs Gasser, and Effy Vayena (eds.), Big Data, Health Law, and Bioethics (2018).
[5] Lisa Friedman, The E.P.A. Says It Wants Research Transparency. Scientists See an Attack on Science, N.Y. Times (Mar. 26, 2018) www.nytimes.com/2018/03/26/climate/epa-scientific-transparency-honest-act.html.

based on personal health information, because of the heightened privacy requirements and expectations around that data. This dilemma, caused by the interaction of transparency initiatives and privacy considerations, relates directly back to our previously discussed theme that transparency must be considered within the context of broader goals rather than pursued solely for its own sake. As demonstrated by the dilemma facing the EPA, there can be a cost to transparency, and several chapters in this volume attempt to balance privacy interests of stakeholders against the potential of transparency to change the health-care landscape.

On the other hand, several contributors to this volume make the points that transparency and privacy are not mutually exclusive values, and that transparency initiatives can often support the privacy interests of health-care stakeholders. Transparency around the use of health-care data, for example, can better empower patients to understand the flow of health information and to set appropriate boundaries on the use of their own data. Increased transparency around the workings of the health-care system can allow for stakeholders to make more informed choices about the use of their information, empowering individuals to take steps that enhance privacy protection.

Altogether, this volume presents a sense of the exciting potential that transparency has to improve the American health-care system. At the same time, it cautions against an unqualified embrace of transparency. Transparency is not a panacea, and not all transparency initiatives will achieve their intended effects. The works in this volume create a framework for designing and evaluating transparency initiatives in the health-care context. In that sense, this collection should be read as an open invitation for further research, collaboration, and discourse among a broad range of stakeholders as they continue to implement transparency initiatives in diverse health-care settings.

The book is divided into six parts. Part I, introduced by Abigail R. Moncrieff, provides a big picture overview of the state of transparency initiatives in the American health-care landscape. Strikingly, all of these contributions frame healthcare information as a market good, to be facilitated by transparency initiatives, rather than an intrinsic right. As a result of this framing, these chapters highlight the importance of remembering the end goals of transparency initiatives – that the information gleaned from these policies results in better-informed decisions that more closely reflect the goals of the decision makers. Additionally, these chapters remind us that transparency comes at a cost and all transparency initiatives should be assessed for their cost–benefit trade-offs.

Barry R. Furrow, in his chapter, "Smashing into Windows: The Limits of Consumer Sovereignty in Health Care," identifies significant barriers to improving medical decision making through increased information to patients, such as physician control over the information, hospital circumvention of consent rules, and patient irrationality. Furrow suggests that there is reason to be optimistic that these challenges may be overcome by new technologies and initiatives such as social media platforms, health coaches, and virtual tools. He does caution, however, that we must carefully consider the costs and benefits of each transparency tool as we attempt to empower consumers' medical decision making.

Barbara J. Evans, in her chapter, "The Interplay of Privacy and Transparency in Health Care: The HIPAA Privacy Rule as a Case Study," argues that transparency and privacy need not be seen as mutually exclusive. In health-care settings, transparency has many aspects that serve different goals, and some policies that promote transparency – such as granting individuals a right of access to their own data – simultaneously enhance privacy protections.

Govind Persad, in "Transparency Trade-offs: Priority Setting, Scarcity, and Health Fairness," explicitly explores the distribution of a certain type of healthcare transparency, information about the benefits and burdens of health-related products, including pharmaceuticals, medical devices, and food. He argues that transparency initiatives must be designed with distributive consequences in mind because trade-offs between the benefits and burdens of these programs will vary widely between individuals.

Finally, Oliver J. Kim, in "Slightly Hazy: Transparency and the Cost of Too Much Information," focuses on the costs of transparency initiatives. Kim cautions that too much information, one of the potential results of increased transparency, may overwhelm consumers. This may lead to consumers making suboptimal medical decisions. Thus, Kim shies away from promoting transparency initiatives wholeheartedly, instead recommending a more paternalistic regulatory approach to help guide patient decisions.

Part II of this volume, introduced by Luke Gelinas, focuses on transparency and informed consent. At first glance, the relationship between transparency and informed consent is clear – in order for true informed consent to be given, researchers and health-care providers must be transparent about the purpose, method, drawbacks, and other aspects of a particular intervention. Without sufficient transparency it is impossible for individuals to provide "informed" consent to any intervention. Nevertheless, the three chapters in Part II illustrate that the relationship between transparency and informed consent is more nuanced than our initial assumptions. What is the appropriate level of disclosure necessary to meet our goal of facilitating informed consent? What must we disclose in order to achieve informed consent? How transparent must transparency be in this context? All three authors in this part conclude that broad and thoughtless disclosure will not in and of itself result in true informed consent. Rather, thought must be given to ensure that the patient is empowered to make decisions reflecting his or her values.

In the first chapter of this part, "Transparency versus Informed Consent: The Patient/Consumer Paradigms," Craig J. Konnoth distinguishes between informed consent and transparency, noting that the former is a concept typically applicable to patients, while the latter is applicable to consumers, and that use of either term is indicative (and potentially determinative) of social roles and expectations. The chapter traces the evolution of transparency relative to informed consent, noting the ways in which the consumer model has taken hold – and where it has not. According to Konnoth, "[i]nformed consent and transparency conceive of autonomy in different ways," with the former demanding the provision of resources and status to promote autonomy, and the latter assuming that the individual already has the necessary resources, and must only be provided with information and then have his or her decisions respected. The chapter concludes by suggesting that informed consent and transparency ought to be viewed on a spectrum, with some clinical circumstances calling for a patient role, and others that of a consumer.

Richard S. Saver, in "Transparency and Financial Conflicts: The Uncertain Case for Sunshine," addresses a paragon of health-care transparency: the Physician Payments Sunshine Act and its associated Open Payments Database. The law is intended to deter inappropriate financial relationships and avoid bias in medical decision making through reporting, but Saver notes a number of downsides to the law's requirement for transparency. For example, it may crowd out more substantial regulation of physician payments, result in information overload for patients, and paradoxically, lead to greater trust in physicians receiving such payments and higher payments in order to compensate for any detrimental reputational effects. Saver does note some high points, indicating that the law's real value will be to regulators, who can utilize reported payment information to "better inform evidence-based regulation of industry's promotional activities [and] enforce the existing health-care fraud and abuse laws by revealing unknown financial ties or outliers that warrant further scrutiny."

Elizabeth Sepper, in "Making Religion Transparent: The Substance, Process, and Efficacy of Disclosing Religious Restrictions on Care," scrutinizes the argument that transparency about religious restrictions will help resolve informational asymmetry and allow consumers to make informed choices in light of their health-care needs, noting that transparency is not the equivalent of access to services that have been restricted. This poses a challenge to the consumer model of care and suggests that referral – not just transparency – will be important. Sepper adds an additional rationale for transparency in this context: democratic engagement regarding mergers and acquisitions that may curtail access to care in light of the application of religious restrictions. The chapter concludes by addressing the role of transparency regarding such restrictions in the context of informed consent, asking whether mere disclosure without options or control really satisfies the goals of informed consent at all.

Part III, introduced by Kristin M. Madison, addresses transparency and economics, in particular health-care costs and billing. The chapters in this part attempt to articulate transparency's potential to reduce health-care costs while being mindful of its limitations as a solution to the problem of rising health-care costs. Transparency has the potential to curtail wasteful medical spending and to promote competition that can lower prices on goods and services. Nevertheless, as the contributions to this section discuss, realizing the full potential of transparency to address health-care costs is very challenging. The contributors to this part all make the argument that transparency must be smart or targeted in order to achieve its intended effect.

Ameet Sarpatwari, Jerry Avorn, and Aaron S. Kesselheim, in "Transparency on Prescription Drug Expenditures: A Lever for Restraining Pricing?" examine the impact that greater transparency may have on pharmaceutical drug pricing. Sarpatwari and his coauthors dissect the potential impact of laws requiring the disclosure of pharmaceutical companies' research and development costs on drug pricing, arguing that these laws will likely not produce the intended benefits. The authors then propose alternative disclosure requirements that would shine better light onto the current structure of the pharmaceutical markets as being more effective at reducing drug pricing.

Marc A. Rodwin, in "Is Pharmaceutical Price Transparency an Effective Means to Reduce High Prices and Wide Price Variations?" likewise argues that transparency initiatives in the retail market for prescriptive drugs have not achieved their intended effect on drug pricing. His empirical analysis of the retail drug market demonstrates that significant price variation persists, even when drug prices are available to consumers online or via special apps. Rodwin argues that that there are limitations to transparency as a means to counter high prices and price variations due to other market imperfections that allow drug firms to price discriminate.

Wendy Netter Epstein, in her chapter, "Price Transparency: A Contracts Solution," looks at provider costs and the proper outcome when patients and providers have failed to discuss price. Epstein draws upon contract law and scholarship to suggest that a penalty default rule could help promote transparency for provider charges by encouraging courts to recognize a price of zero when providers have failed to meaningfully disclose their prices to consumers. This suggestion again reminds us of the need to promote thoughtful transparency, in ways that would empower the consumer to make better choices, rather than to simply provide information overload through an almost impenetrable hospital chargemaster, or a long list of service prices.

Mark A. Hall, with his contribution, "Solving Surprise Medical Bills," concludes this part by examining the problem of when an insured patient discovers, after the fact, that a provider responsible for some part of his or her care was not in-network, leading to much higher payments for care. Hall posits that increased transparency could help in some, but not all, of these situations. He recognizes that for transparency to prevent this problem, the patient must not be in an emergency situation, must not be faced with an unduly complex web of provider relationships, and must have the meaningful opportunity to locate another provider. Thus, Hall also argues that only targeted or thoughtful transparency, rather than transparency for its own sake, will help address wasteful medical spending.

Part IV, introduced by Holly Fernandez Lynch, focuses on transparency and innovation. Transparency in pharmaceutical product development is especially challenging because of the expectation that "confidential commercial information" must be protected to avoid conferring an advantage to potential competitors. Nevertheless, the contributors to this section make a strong argument that greater transparency in this area must be encouraged to help foster innovation. The authors of the chapters in this part also highlight where initial steps, however small, have been taken to encourage transparency.

Rachel E. Sachs and Thomas J. Hwang open this section with their chapter, "Increasing the Transparency of FDA Review to Enhance the Innovation Process." They take issue with the lack of transparency in FDA communications with the sponsors of pharmaceutical research and marketing applications, arguing that the agency has greater authority than it currently uses to disclose limited information to the public regarding regulated products as they wind their way through the approval process. This secrecy has serious repercussions for patients and their caregivers, as well as research participants, and is also detrimental to innovation, preventing sponsors from learning from each other's experiences in ways that could maximize both efficiency and safety. To address this problem, Sachs and Hwang recommend adopting at least a system of limited disclosure, in which the FDA discloses to the public "at a minimum, 1) the existence of particular events, including the sending of a complete response letter, the placement of a clinical hold, a meeting between the agency and a sponsor and 2) a general categorization of their substance."

Barbara E. Bierer, Mark Barnes, and Rebecca Li pick up many of these threads in their chapter, "Transparency and Clinical Trial Data Sharing: Legal and Policy Issues." Here, they provide a robust overview of the value of transparency regarding individual-level clinical trial data, highlighting efforts to promote such transparency as well as legal barriers and protections in both the United States and Europe. They acknowledge the importance of privacy interests and autonomy regarding individual-level trial data, but argue that on balance, its public health value is paramount. Thus, individuals should not be permitted to refuse the disclosure of their deidentified or anonymous data, but a number of safeguards should be implemented, including better education about the utility of the data, notice regarding how data is used, and enhanced protections against its inappropriate use.

Stefano Marino and Spyridon Drosos close Part IV with their chapter, "The European Medicines Agency's Approach to Transparency." They begin with a normative rationale for transparency regarding information held by the EMA, including accountability in the approval process, advancing the interests of patients and healthcare professionals, and maximizing the utility of clinical trial data. They then go on to explore both "reactive" and "proactive" transparency, i.e., how the EMA complies with EU requirements to provide information upon request and requirements to spontaneously disclose information, including clinical data submitted with applications for marketing authorization. In particular, the chapter explores the tension between legal requirements for transparency and legal requirements for the protection of confidential commercial information and personal privacy, describing progress in the EMA's approach, and remaining areas of debate. Each chapter in this section considers the impact that the lesser or greater embrace of transparency will have on incentivizing developing and bringing to market new pharmaceutical products and applications.

Gregory Curfman introduces Part V, which focuses on the impact that transparency initiatives can have on promoting health and safety. This section acknowledges the trend to have patients become more personally involved in their own health care and the expectation that medical decision making will be shared decision making between the patient and provider. The patient can only occupy this increasingly central role to medical decision making through increased transparency and better information. As such, transparency initiatives are vital for promoting better medical decision making and improving outcomes. The chapters in this section also remind us, however, about the tension between increased transparency and patients' privacy interests.

Anthony W. Orlando and Arnold J. Rosoff open this part with their chapter, "The Role of Transparency in Promoting Healthy Behaviors: Pros, Cons, and Perils of Information Sharing to Foster Personal Responsibility in Health Care," which focuses on health information sharing in employee wellness programs. They are concerned that these programs pose a significant risk to employees' privacy because they encourage employees to participate in health risk assessments and share that information with their employers. Orlando and Rosoff's work cautions that we should not blindly embrace transparency for all aspects of health information, even when increased transparency might encourage healthier behaviors, but should remain mindful that privacy concerns also must be addressed.

Michelle M. Mello, David M. Studdert, Brahmajee K. Nallamothu, and Allen Kachalia, in their chapter, "The Role of Transparency in Patient Safety Improvement," document a wide range of initiatives intended to improve patient safety and experiences. They argue that these initiatives, while not strictly transparency focused, may reinforce transparency-focused initiatives by influencing the availability of information for patients to use to make medical decisions. Thus, this chapter encourages us to remember that transparency initiatives exist in a broader health-care ecosystem.

Sharona Hoffman, in her chapter, "Personal Health Records as a Tool for Transparency in Health Care," expresses a concern about the proper balancing between transparency and privacy. Hoffman examines the use of personal health records (PHRs), especially in the context of promoting health-care transparency. Hoffman acknowledges the benefits of PHRs, such as allowing patients to store and access their own information, while also remaining concerned about the increased risk to privacy, such as an increased risk of hacking. While Hoffman does not argue against the use of PHRs, she reminds us that more work must be done to refine these technologies to maximize their transparency benefits while minimizing their privacy concerns. This concern echoes the worries put forth by Orlando and Rosoff earlier in Part V.

Jim Hawkins, Barbara J. Evans, and Harlan M. Krumholz, in "Nontransparency in Electronic Health Record Systems," focus on the interaction between transparency and patient safety. They describe various nontransparent business practices – such as gag clauses that prevent frank discussion of safety incidents involving electronic health record systems – that may adversely affect patients' physical safety. They also explore how other nontransparent business practices, such as allowing deidentified health data to be shared without informing patients, can expose patients to privacy and dignitary harms.

Dov Fox closes Part V with his chapter, "Transparency Challenges in Reproductive Health Care." Fox is concerned that a significant information gap exists in the assisted reproductive technology (ART) field, which is generally unregulated. Fox believes there should be increased transparency for "never events," such as mishandling, misinformation, and misconception, potentially crowd sourced from previous patients. Data about these often devastating ART events is not currently being collected, so patients cannot adequately evaluate the quality of each provider. Fox's chapter is a good reminder that there exist many corners of the health-care industry that remain shockingly nontransparent and prevent patients from being able to determine which health-care provider will provide them with the best, safest, or most appropriate outcomes.

Part VI, "Challenges in Promoting and Measuring Transparency in Health Care," with an introduction by I. Glenn Cohen, casts a wide net over the topic of transparency. Nevertheless, these chapters all document the challenges to successfully implementing transparency initiatives, such as financial costs, federal preemption of state programs, and noncompliance. These chapters are also concerned with the political dimensions of transparency in health care.

Erin C. Fuse Brown and Jaime S. King, in their chapter, "ERISA as a Barrier for State Health-Care Transparency Efforts," look at how state efforts to promote consumer health-care transparency, such as adopting all-payers claim databases, have been stymied by the broad application of the federal Employee Retirement Income Security Act (ERISA). Recent Supreme Court jurisprudence, especially *Gobeille* v. *Liberty Mutual*, have dramatically broadened ERSIA's preemption reach to block state efforts to increase health-care price transparency. Fuse Brown and King argue that the federal government must address the newly expanded reach of ERISA to facilitate and support state efforts to use transparency to improve health-care costs.

Jennifer E. Miller, in "Transparency and Data Sharing in Clinical Research and Big Pharma," focuses on the promotion of transparency around clinical trials and their results. Miller notes that there are no clear best practices when it comes to clinical trial transparency, which can make implementation of transparency very challenging for stakeholders, especially those in the pharmaceutical industry. She reviews three categories of prominent definitions for clinical trial transparency that have emerged in practice and guidance documents. Miller argues that an independent third-party governance system is needed to help set and disseminate industry standards. In particular, she highlights the fact that setting industry standards, especially through a third party, would also allow for improved dialogue around the ethics of clinical trial transparency.

Holly Fernandez Lynch picks up some of these concerns in "Promoting IRB Transparency: About What, To Whom, Why, and How?" She critiques Institutional Review Boards (IRBs) as "largely opaque" and argues that they should also be pushed toward greater transparency to a variety of stakeholders about a range of activities. This could occur through regulatory change, but since that is unlikely, Lynch suggests that IRBs voluntarily accept transparency as an important value that will help advance human subjects' protections and procedural fairness for regulated research. Contrasted to many of the other chapters in this volume, which deal with health-care systems that have already attempted some transparency initiatives, this chapter is an interesting exploration into a system that has not yet meaningfully incorporated transparency as a central goal.

Lastly, David A. Hyman and William E. Kovacic address the need for increased transparency in the work of pharmacy benefit managers (PBMs) in "Using Disclosure to Regulate PBMs: The Dark Side of Transparency." PBMs play an increasingly important role in the delivery of pharmaceuticals, handling purchasing, rebates, creation of formularies, and other key tasks. Nevertheless, they are relatively unregulated and often can operate in the shadows between pharmaceutical companies and insurers. Hyman and Kovacic make the point that transparency initiatives can have significant anticompetitive consequences, especially around pharmaceutical pricing, that hurt consumers. Hyman and Kovacic forcefully argue that, while transparency is needed in this area, state regulators have used transparency initiatives as a weaker substitute for the more politically unpalatable but necessary direct regulation of this industry.

CONCLUSION

Transparency is a concept that is becoming increasingly lauded as a solution to a host of problems in the American health-care system. Transparency initiatives show great promise, including empowering patients and other stakeholders to make more efficient decisions, improving resource allocation, and better regulating the health-care industry. Nevertheless, transparency is not a cure-all for the problems facing the modern health-care system. The authors of this volume present a nuanced view of transparency, exploring ways in which transparency has succeeded and ways in which transparency initiatives have room for improvement. We invite readers to explore transparency by diving into this volume while keeping the thematic issues raised, such as the ultimate purpose of transparency and the interplay between transparency and privacy, in mind.

PART I

Transparency in Health and Health Care: Thematic Issues

Introduction to Part I

Abigail R. Moncrieff

As the title suggests, the opening section of this volume tackles broad themes of transparency in health and health care markets. Indeed, all four of this section's chapters note considerable uncertainty in the concept of transparency itself, especially as applied to health care. Beyond their common recognition of conceptual uncertainty though, the chapters appear to be quite disparate, reflecting the diversity of themes and topics covered in the volume. Govind Persad's chapter focuses on broad ethical challenges in the distribution of information while Barbara J. Evans centers her analysis on a single regulatory case study. Barry R. Furrow and Oliver J. Kim take a completely different approach, each tackling the limits of transparency-based health care policy. But Furrow and Kim seemingly disagree on whether calibration of the information flow will suffice to empower consumers.

Considered more broadly, though, the four chapters have an important commonality: the consideration of health care information as a good that the market might either overprovide or underprovide. All four chapters ask whether and when information might improve consumers' decision making, and although they approach the question from different angles, they all highlight important cost–benefit tradeoffs in transparency-based approaches to health care regulation.

Persad is the most self-conscious of these four authors in his treatment of health care information as a good, explicitly shifting his discussion away from the treatment of health care information as a right. He then narrows his discussion to one kind of health care transparency – information about the benefits and burdens of health-related products, from pharmaceuticals and medical devices to food and beverages – and highlights the interpersonal and intrapersonal tradeoffs that necessarily occur in the market's provision of that information. For instance, calorie labels at restaurants might help wealthy consumers who are trying to maintain healthy weight, but there is some evidence that they harm lower-income consumers who try to maximize calories per dollar – and end up eating less nutritious foods. Noting these tradeoffs between and among consumers (and within single consumers over time) and drawing on insights of distributive justice, Persad argues that transparency regimes ought to be designed with their distributive consequences in mind, at least until personalized medicine has advanced enough to eliminate interpersonal problems. Throughout the discussion, Persad explicates the understanding of transparency as a good, like any other, that is subject to resource constraints and that therefore must be optimized.

Evans uses the Privacy Rule enacted under the Health Insurance Portability and Accountability Act (HIPAA) of 1996 as a case study to examine tradeoffs between transparency and privacy. Throughout her examination, she emphasizes the importance of understanding transparency instrumentally: as a good that serves regulatory purposes, promotes efficiency, creates public benefits, and empowers consumers. Once understood in these instrumental terms, Evans argues, transparency need not be as antagonistic to privacy as it first seems. Indeed, transparency rules, if carefully crafted like the HIPAA Privacy Rule, can complement the motivating values of privacy, especially patient autonomy and empowerment. Evans thus focuses on a core set of cost–benefit tradeoffs in the dissemination of health care information and their interaction with the values of patient autonomy and privacy.

Kim's chapter offers a straightforward caution against overprovision of transparency, arguing that consumers will soon feel overwhelmed if the market inundates them with information. Like Persad and Evans, Kim explicitly treats information as a good that the market could either underprovide or overprovide relative to consumer demand and efficient use. For health care markets in particular, Kim argues that sometimes less is more. Ultimately, Kim seems to take a pessimistic view of transparency approaches to health care regulation, favoring the more paternalistic regulatory approaches that guide rather than merely inform patient decisions.

Furrow similarly addresses the limits of information as a tool for improving patients' choices, but he ends on a more optimistic note than does Kim for the future of transparency-based regulation. Furrow notes three significant barriers to improving medical decision making through information provision: physician control over the information, hospital avoidance of consent rules, and patient irrationality. He then argues that the most recent generation of patient-empowering tools – social media platforms, behavioral interventions, health coaches, and virtual tools – could surmount those barriers more successfully than did their predecessors. Furrow's focus, then, is on strategies for maximizing the empowerment of consumers through careful consideration of the costs and benefits of transparency.

All four of these authors take the somewhat controversial step of treating health care information as an ordinary market good – not subject to rights constraints on the side of either the speaker or the listener. And all four engage in wide-ranging consideration of the costs and benefits of information for both consumers and providers in the market. The disagreements among the authors as to the potential of transparency-based regulatory approaches make for a lively introduction to this important topic.

1

Smashing into Windows

The Limits of Consumer Sovereignty in Health Care

Barry R. Furrow*

A movement is afoot to improve decision making for health care consumers. One current example is the Clear Choices Campaign, a group of "leading patient, consumer, employer, physician, and insurer organizations" that seeks ways to improve health care outcomes and reduce costs by "empowering consumers to make better health choices."[1] The Campaign's goal is to build an arsenal: "[b]*etter tools* for consumers and employers to make informed decisions; [m]*ore and better data* in the hands of more experts to power consumer tools; and [m]ore *competitive markets* where consumers can use comparative tools."[2]

This flowering of consumerism in medicine imagines model patients – skeptical, aggressive, and self-reliant. These "new sick" patients can manage their own illness, process all information, and partner with the doctor.[3] They will "own" their illnesses, operating as equal decision makers with their physicians, weaning themselves from "free" decisions as they share risk and cost with providers, and are nudged or dragged toward self-direction by providers and their world of treatment tools. This idealization of patient choice requires close examination – is real patient autonomy possible?[4]

This chapter will consider some of the structural, legal, and behavioral barriers to such an ideal model of patient choice, and some possible solutions. I will consider physician-driven constraints, hospitals' lack of responsibility, and patient limits because of bounded rationality. I will then examine the evolution of consent models

---

* I want to thank the Brocher Foundation for providing me with the space and time for work on this project as a Brocher Fellow in the summer of 2015; the Petri-Flom Center for its support; and Barbara Evans for her helpful editorial suggestions.

[1] Clear Choices: A Movement for Informed Health Care, www.clearchoicescampaign.org (last visited Nov. 17, 2017); see also Joel White, Promoting Transparency and Clear Choices in Health Care, Health Affairs Blog, June 9, 2015, www.healthaffairs.org/do/10.1377/hblog20150609.048337/full/, archived at https://perma.cc/6U9X-3MVW.

[2] Clear Choices: A Movement for Informed Health Care, www.clearchoicescampaign.org/ (last visited Nov. 17, 2017).

[3] See Eric Topol, The Patient Will See You Now: The Future of Medicine is in Your Hands 5–12 (2015).

[4] Stefan Schwarzkopf, The Political Theology of Consumer Sovereignty: Towards an Ontology of Consumer Society, 28 Theory, Culture & Soc'y 106, 106–29 (2011).

from a first generation (*Gen1*) legal model of "informed consent" to a second generation model (*Gen2*) of sophisticated decision aids that move beyond informed consent forms. Finally, generation three (*Gen3*) models will be considered, including behavioral incentive reforms, structural changes such as a focus on patient engagement in accountable care organizations (ACOs), and finally technologies such as virtual tools and social media to improve patient decision making.

I. GOALS OF MEDICAL TRANSPARENCY

Medical transparency has a range of goals. Transparency means creating a health care environment of "full" information about health care services and products. Given such information, understandable and accessible to patients, transparency will promote patient autonomy by improving patients' health care choices; improve provider medical decision making; improve quality of care; and reduce costs – all at the same time.[5]

A. *Promoting Patient Autonomy Through Practice*

Autonomy is, in Kant's words, "the ground of the dignity of human nature and of every rational nature."[6] Autonomy as applied to health care is grounded in the individual's right and ability to make choices based on full information.[7] Informed consent – the process of communication between a patient and physician that results in the patient's authorization to undergo a specific medical intervention – is grounded on patient autonomy manifested in choice.[8] The problem is that more information may not always promote better patient choice, but instead can impede the process of choosing.[9]

B. *Improving Medical Decision Making and Quality of Care*

Patient involvement in medical decision making arguably forces providers to sharpen their diagnostic awareness and reconsider their prognoses.[10] Preference-sensitive treatments require patient input as to risks attached to alternative procedures, such as those available in the treatment of prostate cancer. Tools such as the

---

[5] I will not examine the role of information in lowering health care costs in this chapter.
[6] Immanuel Kant, Groundwork of the Metaphysics of Morals 4: 436 (Mary Gregor trans. and ed., 1997).
[7] Gerald Dworkin, The Theory and Practice of Autonomy 6 (1988).
[8] Vikki A. Entwistle et al., Supporting Patient Autonomy: The Importance of Clinician-Patient Relationships, 25 J. Gen. Intern. Med. 741, 741 (2010).
[9] Mark Schlesinger & Brian Elbel, Bounded Rationality and the Conceptual Underpinnings of Health Policy: A Rationale and Roadmap for Addressing the Challenges of Choice in Medical Settings 3 (2006), www.researchgate.net/publication/237462004.
[10] See generally Yves Longtin et. al., Patient Participation: Current Knowledge and Applicability to Patient Safety, 85 Mayo Clin. Proc. 53 (2010).

OpenNotes program can help patients detect physician errors through access to their medical records and physician notes, including errors that clinicians missed.[11] Such tools also enhance patients' trust of their physicians, and help them focus on compliance with complex treatment regimens. Quality of care is expected to improve when patients are engaged in their own care.[12]

II. LIMITS ON PATIENT HEALTH CARE CHOICES

Transparency is an attractive goal in the current health care environment. As patients, we face a treatment environment that is often deeply flawed, for at least three reasons. First, many treatments are unnecessary. Medical practice variation[13] and medical uncertainty create barriers to accurate communication of treatment necessity and risk assessment. Providers too often offer care that is not "trustworthy" – that is, it is of uncertain and therefore questionable value.[14]

Second, many treatments are of low quality. Americans receive appropriate evidence-based care when they need it only around half the time.[15] All Americans are at risk of receiving poor care – regardless of where they live, how much money they have, or their race, education, or health insurance.[16] Tens of thousands of Americans die each year as a result of preventable hospital errors.[17] Legally driven conversations between doctor and patient hardly begin to address the preexisting problems of unnecessary and poor-quality treatments offered by providers.

Third, too many treatments are unaffordable. Patient care is often denied because of high cost.[18] Many drug therapies and most dietary supplements are wasteful of

---

[11] Sigall K. Bell, Tom Delbanco & Jan Walker, OpenNotes: How the Power of Knowing Can Change Health Care, NEJM Catalyst (2016), http://catalyst.nejm.org/opennotes-knowing-change-health-care/, archived at https://perma.cc/9URS-NE3U; Joel S. Weissman et al., Comparing Patient-Reported Hospital Adverse Events with Medical Record Review: Do Patients Know Something That Hospitals Do Not?, 149 Ann. Intern. Med. 100, 100 (2008).

[12] Angela Coulter, Suzanne Parsons & Janet Askham, Where Are the Patients in Decision-Making About Their Own Care?, WHO Policy Brief (2008), www.who.int/management/general/decisionmaking/WhereArePatientsinDecisionMaking.pdf, archived at https://perma.cc/FFR3-VL3S.

[13] See generally John E. Wennberg, Variation in Use of Medicare Services Among Regions and Selected Academic Medical Centers: Is More Better?, Commonwealth Fund Pub. No. 874 (Dec. 2005).

[14] Id at 4.

[15] Elizabeth A. McGlynn et al., The Quality of Health Care Delivered to Adults in the United States, 348 New Eng. J. Med. 2635, 2643 (2003).

[16] See generally National Committee for Quality Assurance, The Essential Guide to Health Care Quality, www.ncqa.org/Portals/0/Publications/Resource%20Library/NCQA_Primer_web.pdf. (last visited Oct. 1, 2018).

[17] See John T. James, A New, Evidence-Based Estimate of Patient Harms Associated with Hospital Care, 9 J. Patient Safety 122, 127 (2013)(estimating 210,000 to 400,000 deaths a year associated with medical errors among hospital patients); see also Martin Makary & Michael Daniel, Medical Error – The Third Leading Cause of Death in the U.S., 353 BMJ 2 (2016).

[18] Murray v. UNMC Physicians, 806 N.W.2d 118, 123–25 (Neb. 2011) (describing a failure to administer Flolan therapy because of its cost).

resources and without proven benefit.[19] Even beneficial treatments may be too costly for either patient or insurer to pay for.

Even if full evidence-based information helps to reduce poor quality or unnecessary care, transparency is thwarted by further impediments to full information flow between patients and providers. Other barriers to such information run the gamut from provider power to direct patient decisions, all the way to patient cognitive limitations when processing complex information.

A. Provider Power: Thwarting Patient Decisions

1. **Doctors Direct Patient Decisions.** Knowing behavioral psychology creates tools: doctors may frame the risks as an 80 percent survival rate rather than a 20 percent mortality rate; overstate the benefits of a particular treatment; overstate their experience with a procedure; or intimidate patients through a range of psychological devices. Doctors are often frustrated with patient ignorance or stubbornness, and doctors do often know the best treatment. But tricking patients violates their autonomy rights and denies them real choice.
2. **Doctors Misuse Consent Forms.** Consent forms are complex and incoherent and they fail readability standards for many patients. The formality of legal compliance protects providers while obfuscating risks and alternatives. The disclosures fail to give patients the kind and range of information needed for truly informed decisions, while medical providers pretend that a brief discussion and a patient signature are enough.
3. **Doctors Communicate Poorly.** Doctors often fail to give patients the kind and range of information needed for truly informed decisions.[20] Even life-and-death decisions are made without proper information, with patients failing to grasp the statistics about survival rates and disease recurrence.[21] Doctors often lack empathy, are poor listeners, are rushed in their clinical encounters, and have distaste for – or unconscious biases against – certain classes of patients.[22] Doctors need institutional support to improve their patient communication.
4. **Doctors Are Bribed to Prescribe Brand Name Drugs and Devices.** Physician drug-prescribing patterns can be influenced by skillful pharma strategies. Studies of the Physician Payment Sunshine Act have found that a fifteen-dollar sandwich

---

[19] Tracy Rupp & Diana Zuckerman, Quality of Life, Overall Survival, and Costs of Cancer Drugs Approved Based on Surrogate Endpoints, 177 JAMA Internal Med. 276, 277 (2017).
[20] Clarence H. Braddock III et al., Informed Decision Making in Outpatient Practice: Time to Get Back to Basics, 282 JAMA 2313, 2315 (1999).
[21] For a critical perspective on mandated disclosures in health care and other domains, see generally Omri Ben-Shahar & Carl E. Schneider, The Failure of Mandated Disclosure, 159 U. Pa. L. Rev. 647 (2011) (noting that doctors fail to disclose full information, forms are poorly written, and patients fail to understand or remember even clearly described choices).
[22] Nirmal Joshi, Doctor, Shut Up and Listen, N.Y. Times, Jan. 4, 2015.

given for free by a drug or device manufacturer to a doctor changes prescribing patterns, and the more costly the sandwich, the bigger the change.[23]

5. **Physicians Resist Disclosure of Error Rates and Personal Performance Data.** Disclosure to a patient of a medical error that has resulted in serious harm is considered a bioethical imperative that informs patients about the particular risks that a doctor may pose.[24] Yet full error disclosures are rare, with limited disclosures without apology the most common approach in many settings.[25] Self-protective motivations are often the reason for nondisclosures or limited disclosures. However, patient choice evaporates in the face of lack of information about provider-generated risks.

B. Hospital Avoidance of Consent Obligations

Hospitals have no legal duty to obtain a patient's consent to surgery, nor to conduct any kind of inquiry into the quality of the patient's consent.[26] Hospitals are supposed to help their independent medical staffs use consent forms[27] but typically such forms are little more than a ritual, without a real conversation between provider and patient about risks. These hospital consent forms are treated in many states as presumptively valid consent to treatment, with the burden on the patient to rebut the presumption.[28]

The time pressures on patient care in hospitals and the lack of clear responsibility for obtaining consent leads in practice to staff avoidance of responsibility for serious conversations with patients. Hospitals lack motivation because they are largely immune from liability risks for consent failures; their medical staffs are independent contractors who bear sole responsibility for obtaining patient consent.[29] Even the adoption of a hospital requirement that physicians must obtain informed consent is not sufficient to shift the burden of obtaining such consent from the physician to the institution.[30]

---

[23] Physician Payment Sunshine Act, 42 U.S.C.A § 1128G(a)(1)(A)(vi) (2010). See also Colette DeJong et al., Pharmaceutical Industry–Sponsored Meals and Physician Prescribing Patterns for Medicare Beneficiaries, 176 JAMA Internal Med. 1114, 1120 (2016).

[24] Stephanie P. Fein et al., The Many Faces of Error Disclosure: A Common Set of Elements and a Definition, 22 J. Gen. Internal Med. 755, 760 (2007).

[25] Id. at 755; A. Rani Elwy et al., Surgeons' Disclosures of Clinical Adverse Events, 151 JAMA Surgery 1015 (2016); Kathleen Mazor et al., Primary Care Physicians' Willingness to Disclose Oncology Errors Involving Multiple Providers to Patients, 25 BMJ Quality & Safety 787 (2016)(finding that the majority of primary care physicians given two hypothetical scenarios involving diagnosis of cancer would not fully disclose a harmful medical error).

[26] See, e.g., Winters v. Podzamsky, 621 N.E.2d 72, 76 (Ill. App. Ct. 1993) ("Any inadequacy of the physician's explanation cannot be imputed to the hospital.").

[28] See West's Fla. Stat. Ann. § 766.103(4); Ga. Code Ann. § 88–2906.1(b)(2); Idaho Code § 39–4305.

[29] See generally Barry R. Furrow et al., Health Law: Cases, Materials and Problems (8th ed. 2018), 283.

[30] Kelly v. Methodist Hospital, 664 A.2d 148, 151 (Pa. Super. Ct. 1995).

A second constraint on informed consent in hospitals comes from a climate of cost sensitivity, where time is money in terms of staff time spent per patient. Respectful conversation takes time, and the payoff may be viewed by administrators as too subtle to justify substantial changes in the way medical staff relate to patients.

C. Patient Capacity Limits: Bounded Rationality

The problem of bounded rationality distorts health care decisions, perhaps more than decisions in other areas.[31] Our normal decision making when confronted with hard choices is subject to a wide range of behavioral constraints.[32] When we become ill, we are further debilitated in our ability to process risks and make decisions about our care.[33]

1. **Patients Struggle to Process Medical Information.** Average functional health literacy and numeracy in the United States are extremely low; patients are typically unable to understand or choose between treatment options with different risks, likelihoods of success, and morbidity and mortality consequences.[34] Moreover, social class and income level affect rational decision making.[35] Health information is hard to process even when providers make serious attempts to communicate.[36] Most patients neither understand nor remember information even when well communicated to them.[37]
2. **Patients Refuse Treatments Because of Belief Structures.** Patients who refuse treatments are predominantly legally competent but may have religious beliefs, phobias, or psychological conditions that lead them to refuse "rational" treatments. Patients may be anxious about effective treatments for irrational reasons such as fears of the knife or phobic feelings about diseases such as cancer.
3. **Disclosure Does Not Matter to Patients.** Studies suggest that risk information will go unused in any event, since patients rarely change their minds. Patients also tend to make one-reason decisions when considering treatment options for serious ailments, where multiple factors should be considered.[38]

---

[31] See generally Mark Schlesinger and Brian Elbel, supra note 9.
[32] See id. at 14–19.
[33] Mark A. Hall & Carl E. Schneider, Patients as Consumers: Courts, Contracts, and the New Medical Marketplace, 106 Mich. L. Rev. 643, 650–51 (2008).
[34] Russell Korobkin, Comparative Effectiveness Research as Choice Architecture: The Behavioral Law and Economics Solution to the Health Care Cost Crisis, 112 Mich. L. Rev. 523, 539 (2014).
[35] Bruce W. Sherman, Teresa B. Gibson, Wendy D. Lynch & Carol Addy, Health Care Use And Spending Patterns Vary By Wage Level In Employer Sponsored Plans, 36 Health Affs. 250, 254 (2017).
[36] Margaret L. Schwarze et al., Exploring Patient Preferences for Infrainguinal Bypass Operation, 202 J. Am. C. Surgeons 445, 450 (2006).
[37] David A. Herz et al., Informed Consent: Is It a Myth?, 30 Neurosurgery 453, 455 (1992).
[38] Carl E. Schneider, The Practice of Autonomy: Patients, Doctors, and Medical Decisions 94–95 (1998).

4. **Patients as Consumers Are Seduced by Powerful Marketing.** Vendors of drugs, supplements, and medical devices market to circumvent patient rationality.[39] Vendors market to doctors as agents of patients, and sometimes they sell doctors a bill of goods. Direct-to-consumer advertising of drugs causes patients to demand the advertised drugs, pressuring doctors to prescribe unnecessarily.[40]

III. THE EVOLUTION OF PATIENT DECISION MAKING

Legal doctrine and practice innovations are forces in improving transparency goals, albeit slowly and erratically. Three generations of reforms provide the underpinnings of real improvements in transparency.

A. *Generation 1 (Gen1): Informed Consent and the Doctor–Patient Relationship*

The law of informed consent has moved medical practice away from a paternalistic approach toward patients. The common law and some state statutes require that physicians disclose and discuss material risks of a medical treatment and alternatives to it, which are perhaps the most important pieces of information for a patient to consider.[41]

Probabilities of various risks must be disclosed by physicians in a fashion that accurately informs the patient.[42] Some courts have moved beyond a rote compliance with informed consent procedures, holding physicians responsible for providing more sophisticated and accurate information.[43] This may include disclosure of reliable tests to rule out a patient's condition, even if unrelated to the final diagnosis.[44] Researchers have also developed concepts of stratified risk disclosure, with only the most important risks disclosed to patients.[45]

Gen1 informed consent has clearly advanced the art of giving information to promote patient choices. It also suffers from a range of practical limitations. First, effective modes of communication have proved difficult. The universal consent

---

[39] Joseph Heath, The Irrational Consumer, National Post, Apr. 16, 2014, http://news.nationalpost.com/opinion/joseph-heath-the-irrational-consumer ("[A]dvertising seeks to bypass the consumer's rationality completely ... Language is the vehicle of rational thought, so if you want to bypass reason, cut out the language and stick to pictures.").

[40] Food & Drug Admin., The Impact of Direct-to-Consumer Advertising, www.fda.gov/Drugs/ResourcesForYou/Consumers/ucm143562.htm, archived at https://perma.cc/PBA7-G63Y (noting that benefits of drugs are overstated and risks obscured, creating pressure on doctors to prescribe when patients mention DTC ads).

[41] *Harbeson v. Parke Davis*, 746 F.2d 517, 522 (9th Cir. 1984).

[42] *Korman v. Mallin*, 858 P.2d 1145, 1149–50 (Alaska 1993).

[43] See, e.g., *Distefano v. Bell*, 544 So. 2d 567, 571 (La. Ct. App. 1989).

[44] *Jandre v. Wis. Injured Patients & Families Comp. Fund*, 813 N.W.2d 627, 636 (Wis. 2012).

[45] Baruch Fischhoff & Sara L. Eggers, Questions of Competence: The Duty to Inform and the Limits to Choice, in The Behavioral Foundations of Public Policy 223–24 (Eldar Sharif ed., 2013).

forms are often complex, incoherent, and fail readability standards.[46] Documents used to record informed decisions are often too difficult for the average patient to understand, and patients are unlikely to grasp important elements of alternative medical interventions. Patients are unlikely to do a very good job of making efficient medical care decisions at the point of treatment, and the current ritualistic process for obtaining informed consent and the related forms are little help.[47] The nature of bounded rationality, discussed in Section II.C., compounds the problem.

B. Generation 2 (Gen2): Decision Aids and Preference-Sensitive Care

Informed consent approaches have evolved. John Wennberg and others have long argued for the use of decision aids to help patients decide whether or not to have procedures that are "preference based," such as prostate surgery or treatments for heart disease.[48] Decision Aids (DAs) are decision support tools that provide patients with detailed and specific information on options and outcomes, help them clarify their values, and guide them through the decision-making process.[49]

Decision aids are part of "shared medical decision making," defined by Jaime Staples King and Benjamin Moulton as "a process in which the physician shares with the patient all relevant risk and benefit information on all treatment alternatives and the patient shares with the physician all relevant personal information that might make one treatment or side effect more or less tolerable than others. Both parties then use this information to come to a mutual medical decision."[50] When decision aids (such as brochures, DVDs, or online tools) are available to patients and they have the opportunity to participate in medical decision making with their physician, the evidence is that patient-physician dialogue and patient well-being both improve.[51]

Decision aids help patients become better informed and more aware of their own personal values; they have the greatest impact among patients uncertain about which option to choose. They complement – but do not replace – counseling by

---

[46] See Michael K. Paasche-Orlow et al., Readability Standards for Informed-Consent Forms as Compared with Actual Readability, 348 New Eng. J. Med. 721, 724 (2003).
[47] See John Hsu et al., Unintended Consequences of Caps on Medicare Drug Benefits, 354 New Eng. J. Med. 2349, 2356 (2006).
[48] John E. Wennberg & Philip G. Peters, Unwanted Variations in the Quality of Health Care: Can the Law Help Medicine Provide a Remedy/Remedies?, 37 Wake Forest LRev. 925, 925–41 (2002).
[49] See, e.g., Elie A. Akl et al., A Decision Aid for COPD Patients Considering Inhaled Steroid Therapy: Development and Before and After Pilot Testing, 7 BMC Med. Informatics Decision Making 12, 13 (2007).
[50] Jaime Staples King & Benjamin Moulton, Rethinking Informed Consent: The Case for Shared Medical Decision-Making, 32 Am. J. L. & Med. 429, 431 (2006).
[51] See Michael J. Barry, Health Decision Aids to Facilitate Shared Decision Making in Office Practice, 136 Annals Internal Med. 127, 127 (2002).

practitioners.[52] Decision aids are beginning to be adopted by some health plans as an improvement over traditional informed consent requirements.[53] Mixed models use decision aids combined with enhanced support tools such as trained health coaches.[54]

Decision aids can also be designed to help physicians better communicate the relative size of the material risks compared to other life risks, such as driving or drinking. The concept of micromorts, developed by Ronald Howard, is an application of decision analysis adapted to health care. Howard suggests a scale for risks, using the concept of a microprobability, or the chance of one in one million, to help patients understand medical risks compared to other life risks.[55]

C. Generation 3 (Gen3): Patient Engagement and Chronic Disease

Patient health outcomes improve if patients are fully involved in understanding their treatments and their illnesses, and in managing their own treatments to a greater extent. Gen3 tools begin with the application of behavioral incentives to improve both patient and provider decision making. Second, the expansion of accountable care organizations provides a more robust model of "patient engagement."[56] Such engagement creates patient capacity to manage care if the health care organization has the culture to support such engagement and providers can work with patients to design, manage, and achieve positive health outcomes.[57] The use of new technologies, such as virtual provider–patient contacts and health coaches, add further tools to help patients engage with their treatments. These approaches will improve patient compliance and hopefully better outcomes (and often lower costs) will be the result.[58]

1. Behavioral Interventions. Researchers have found that patients' bounded rationality limits can be compensated for; for example, "incentive programs that offer

---

[52] Dawn Stacey et al., Decision Aids for People Facing Health Treatment or Screening Decisions, 1 Cochrane Database of Systematic Revs. 7 (2014).
[53] Washington State adopted decision aids in Wash. Rev. Code. § 7.70.060 (2012). See generally David Arterburn, et al., Introducing Decision Aids at Group Health was Linked to Sharply Lower Hip and Knee Surgery Rates and Cost, 31 Health Affs. 2094 (2012).
[54] David Veroff, Amy Marr & David E. Wennberg, Enhanced Support for Shared Decision Making Reduced Costs of Care for Patients with Preference-Sensitive Conditions, 32 Health Affs. 285, 286 (2013).
[55] Ronald A. Howard, Microrisks for Medical Decision Analysis, 5 Int'l J. Tech. Assessment Health Care 357, 358 (1989).
[56] Kristin L. Carman et al., Patient and Family Engagement: A Framework for Understanding the Elements and Developing Interventions and Policies, 32 Health Affs. 223, 224 (2013).
[57] Athenahealth, Five Elements of a Successful Patient Engagement Strategy (2014),, archived at https://perma.cc/8BHX-DG45.
[58] Julia James, Health Policy Brief: Patient Engagement, 1, 3, Health Affairs, Feb. 14, 2013, www.healthaffairs.org/do/10.1377/hpb20130214.898775/full/ (finding that people actively involved in their health and health care tend to have better outcomes and even lower costs).

people small, frequent payments for behaviors of benefit to them – such as medication adherence – can, as a result of people's overweighting of immediate costs and benefits, have a disproportionate impact on behavior."[59] Strategies using incentives to change behavior include using smaller levels of incentives with a distinct reward format, staged benefit instead of single threshold and payment (to overcome mental accounting bias), automated hovering and frequent engagement (frequency/recency bias), and enhanced active choice (status quo bias).[60] The use of behavioral modifications can surmount patient limits of bounded rationality.

2. Accountable Care Organizations.[61] The Affordable Care Act has made patient engagement and shared decision making two central components of both Stage 2 meaningful-use requirements and the Medicare Shared Savings Program.[62] *Medical Homes* also emphasize patient engagement. Provider-driven *Gen3* models such as ACOs use patient engagement as a central feature of health plan design, with metrics designed to measure such engagement and make it part of the reimbursement structure. The goal is to improve information at all levels, from patient understanding to physician access to best evidence information.[63]

In an ACO, a group of primary care physicians, specialists, and other health professionals (or hospitals) agree to accept joint responsibility for the quality and cost of care provided to their patients.[64] If the ACO meets certain targets, its members receive a financial bonus.[65] The ACO model is built on a concept of patient engagement and "patient centeredness."[66] This patient focus facilitates patient buy-in and sets a high benchmark for patient engagement.[67]

Such an approach encounters several barriers to easy use: "overworked physicians, insufficient provider training, and clinical information systems that failed to track

[59] George Loewenstein, David A. Asch & Kevin G. Volpp, Behavioral Economics Holds Potential to Deliver Better Results for Patients, Insurers, and Employers, 32 Health Affs. 1244, 1248 (2013).
[60] Id. at 1248.
[61] See generally Furrow et al., supra note 29, at s. 8–17.
[62] See Centers for Medicare & Medicaid Services, Medicare Program; Medicare Shared Savings Program: Accountable Care Organizations, Person and Family Engagement Strategy, S. 5.2–5.5.1 (discussing the promotion of patient engagement), www.cms.gov/Medicare/Quality-Initiatives-Patient-Assessment-Instruments/QualityInitiativesGenInfo/Downloads/Person-and-Family-Engagement-Strategy.pdf.
[63] See The Nat'l Patient Safety Found., Lucian Leape Inst. Report of the Roundtable on Consumer Engagement, Safety Is Personal: Partnering with Patients and Families for the Safest Care (2014).
[64] See Timothy L. Greaney, Accountable Care Organizations – The Fork in the Road, 364 New Eng. J. Med. e1(1), e1(1)–(2) (2011) (discussing the benefits and concerns surrounding the implementation of ACO reform measures).
[65] See Mark McClellan et al., A National Strategy to Put Accountable Care into Practice, 29 Health Affs. 982, 983 (2010) (discussing different ACO payment models).
[66] Michael L. Millenson, Building Patient-Centeredness in the Real World: The Engaged Patient and the Accountable Care Organization, Health Quality Advisors (2012), www.nationalpartnership.org/research-library/health-care/building-patient-centeredness-in-the-real-world.pdf, archived at https://perma.cc/BPE5-6BUK.
[67] Stephen M. Shortell et al., An Early Assessment of Accountable Care Organizations' Efforts to Engage Patients and Their Families, 72 Med. Care Res. Rev. 580, 582 (2015).

patients throughout the decision-making process."[68] Engagement is costly and financial incentives may be needed to make the strategy work.[69]

Some plans are considering next generation portals to enable patients to become partners in their own care. These portals will include e-visits or e-consultations, interoperability across multiple providers, health evaluation and coaching, and televisits. Critics note however that such portals may do little to help manage chronic disease or give patients the resources to develop healthy behaviors.[70]

3. Virtual Forms of Provider-Patient Contact.[71] The technologies of the digital world also offer a *Gen3* approach to improve patient choice. Patients can benefit from live and computer-based approaches such as patient navigators, medical avatars, video games, and mobile apps. Hospitals may hire Chief Cognitive Officers.[72] Gen3 tools therefore may not only be institutional, such as ACOs but also virtual, such as avatars, remote coaching through the telephone or applications for phones, or use of virtual reality environments to reduce pain and increase attention.[73] They may also provide effective "hovering," using mobile apps, virtual coaches, or plain old phone contacts on a frequent basis to improve patient compliance.[74]

Virtual humans (VHs) have been developed to improve clinical interviews. Patients are more willing to disclose truthful information to such avatars than they are to human interviewers.[75] VHs can have high social skills that increase feelings of connection and rapport. Such VHs can better standardize users' experiences than

---

[68] Mark W. Friedberg et al., A Demonstration of Shared Decision Making in Primary Care Highlights Barriers to Adoption and Potential Remedies, 32 Health Affs. 268, 271 (2012)

[69] James, supra note 58, at 1; Kevin Volpp & Namita S. Mohta, Patient Engagement Survey: Technology Tools Gain Support – But Cost Is a Hurdle, NEJM Catalyst, Jan. 26, 2017.

[70] Rajiv Leventhal, Survey: Portals Aren't Enough for Successful Patient Engagement, Healthcare Informatics, Apr. 8, 2015, www.healthcare-informatics.com/news-item/himss-analytics-survey-portals-aren-t-enough-engage-patients, archived at https://perma.cc/N8RG-6E55.

[71] See generally Patrick Kenny et al., Virtual Humans for Assisted Health Care, PETRA (2008); Albert Rizzo et al, An Intelligent Virtual Human System for Providing Healthcare Information and Support, 163 Stud. Health Tech. Informatics 503 (2011).

[72] Dan Housman, The Rise of the Chief Cognitive Officer, The Health Care Blog, May 12, 2016, http://thehealthcareblog.com/blog/2016/05/12/the-rise-of-the-chief-cognitive-officer/ ("The CCMO should focus on how to help and introduce changes for the physician to do their work as much as on helping the computer do its component of medical work. The physician and computer would, in essence, be training each other by transferring scale expertise from computer into the human one case at a time and with the human pushing back decisions and nuances about the case or documentation that only the physician can enrich through their specific perspective and undocumented knowledge.").

[73] Ike Swetlitz, Swedish Clinics Use Virtual Reality to Reduce the Sting of Shots, STAT, Oct. 27, 2016, www.statnews.com/2016/10/27/virtual-reality-pain-app/, archived at https://perma.cc/8UVV-YDDL; see Ryan Basen, Could Virtual, Augmented Reality Augment Medicine?, MedPage Today, Mar. 29, 2017.

[74] Veroff, Marr & Wennberg, supra note 54, at 1247.

[75] Gale M. Lucas et al., It's Only a Computer: Virtual Humans Increase Willingness to Disclose, 37 Computers Hum. Behav. 94, 98 (2014).

can human beings, and can provide a "safe" environment to encourage learning or provide honest disclosure of critical information.[76]

4. Health Coaches. Health coaching has been found to improve patients' "physiological, behavioral and psychological conditions ... Statistically significant results revealed better weight management, increased physical activity and improved physical and mental health status."[77] Health coaching is effective for chronic diseases, a proven tool to shape and support long-term behaviors in patients with chronic disease. Such coaching can also be used virtually for remote reinforcement of coaching, using phone, email, text, or video conference.[78]

5. Social Media Platforms. Facebook, Twitter, and YouTube disseminate information about health care issues – in the form of texts, images, audio, and videos. Such social media are subject to a range of problems – examples include celebrity boosting of products and patient groups that lack a scientific basis. Such media do however provide a range of tools that present reams of information to patients. *Facebook* allows its users to access health advice, disease prevention ideas, and treatment options, and to share knowledge interactively among connected friends. *Facebook* can promote direct doctor-patient interaction and allow providers can keep their page followers medically updated, thereby creating easy access to the platform via smartphones and portable devices.[79]

Twitter has the potential through microblogs to allow health information to flow from provider to patients to promote health education and compliance.[80]

Finally, *YouTube* contains much useful health care data.[81] It hosts health-related videos ranging from communications by lay health consumers to public service announcements. While *YouTube* contains a lot of junk information posted by for-profit companies and individuals with idiosyncratic health beliefs, some posted information is trustworthy – for example, interviews with patients about their medical conditions and health care experiences posted by health care organizations, which can help patients to understand their conditions and treatments.[82]

---

[76] Id. at 94.
[77] Kirsi Kivela et al., The Effects of Health Coaching on Adult Patients with Chronic Diseases: A Systematic Review, 97 Patient Educ. & Counseling 147, 150 (2014).
[78] Chase Hensel, With Health Coaching at Their Fingertips, People Can Better Manage Chronic Disease, STAT, Mar. 24, 2017, www.statnews.com/2017/03/24/health-coaching-chronic-disease/, archived at https://perma.cc/99KM-2AZ6.
[79] Nor Azura Adzharuddin & Norazmie Mohd Ramly, Nourishing Healthcare Information over Facebook, 172 Procedia – Soc. and Behav. Sci. 383, 386 (2015).
[80] C. Lee Ventola, Social Media and Health Care Professionals: Benefits, Risks, and Best Practices, 39 Pharmacy & Therapeutics 491, 493 (2014).
[81] Kapil Chalil Madathil et al., Healthcare Information on YouTube: A Systemic Review, 21 Health Informatics J. 173, 193 (2015).
[82] Id.

Some *Gen3* approaches improve the flow of information and thereby meet transparency goals, while other *Gen3* ideas motivate patients to act on the information they already have, improving compliance as a result.

IV. CONCLUSION

We can see improvements over time in both legal and reimbursement structures that improve the flow of health care information and its use by patients in decision making. *Gen1* tools have fostered transparency by forcing the disclosure of accurate risk and benefit information by physicians to patients. *Gen2* tools provide a more three-dimensional approach to integrating information with patient preference to improve decision making. *Gen 3* moves beyond simple models of transparency, since it is clear that full information, even if understood, may not improve patient health if patients are struggling to manage chronic diseases rather than making specific surgical decisions. Information is critical, but so are strategies that help patients act on information that is now available in transparent and improved delivery models.

Patient choice in health care is critical. Substantial resources will be needed – using all available tools of social media, psychology, technology, behavioral economics, and caring – to produce true patient engagement and real choice. Ultimately, physicians will have to take more time with their patients and develop better skills of listening and communicating, using an expanded range of tools within new models of health care delivery. Systems will also have to foster patient compliance through a variety of engagement and contact tools. If not, patients and providers will keep smashing into windows in the difficult and elusive quest for transparency in health care decision making.

2

The Interplay of Privacy and Transparency in Health Care

The HIPAA Privacy Rule as a Case Study

Barbara J. Evans

I. INTRODUCTION

At first glance, the values of privacy and transparency in health care seem irreconcilable: What is a privacy breach, if not an excess of transparency? On closer inspection, transparency has "many faces"[1] and "serves many goals,"[2] and the relationship of privacy to transparency is not a simple one. The two often are in conflict yet, sometimes, transparency enables privacy and, other times, transparency depends on privacy for its very existence. An example is patients' right to inspect and obtain copies of their own health records. Access to one's own data promotes transparency, but it also is a "fundamental aspect of protecting privacy"[3] because people's "confidence in the protection of their information requires that they have the means to know what is contained in their records."[4] Strong and trusted privacy protections, in turn, foster transparency by encouraging patients to make frank disclosures to clinicians. Stefano Marino and Spyridon Drosos acknowledge the potential conflicts between privacy and transparency (Chapter 14), yet the two values are "closely tied"[5] in subtle ways and, at times, are mutually reinforcing and defy easy dualism.

This chapter briefly sifts through the many faces of transparency to identify several concepts relevant to health care. It then explores the interplay of privacy and transparency in a major health information privacy regulation of the United

---

[1] Padideh Ala'i, The Many Faces of Transparency, 109 Am. Soc'y Int'l L. Proc. 319, 319 (2015).
[2] Frederick Schauer, Transparency in Three Dimensions, 2011 U. Ill. L. Rev. 1339, 1343 (2015).
[3] Standards for Privacy of Individually Identifiable Health Information, 64 Fed. Reg. 59,918, 59,980 (proposed Nov. 3, 1999) (to be codified at 45 C.F.R. pts. 160, 164).
[4] Standards for Privacy of Individually Identifiable Health Information, 65 Fed. Reg. 82,462, 82,606 (Dec. 28, 2000) (to be codified at 45 C.F.R. pts. 160, 164) (citing National Committee for Quality Assurance and the Joint Commission on Accreditation of Healthcare Organizations, Protecting Personal Health Information: A Framework for Meeting the Challenges in a Managed Care Environment 25 (1998)).
[5] 64 Fed. Reg. 59,918, 59,980.

States, the Health Insurance Portability and Accountability Act of 1996[6] (HIPAA) Privacy Rule.[7] The Privacy Rule was first promulgated in December 2000[8] but rests on a foundation of other federal laws, dating back to the 1970s, that addressed privacy and transparency in non-health care settings. After minor revisions in 2002,[9] the Privacy Rule took effect on a phased schedule during 2003–2004. Amendments in 2013[10] and 2014[11] extended the Privacy Rule's protections to genetic information – even when genetic test results lack clinical significance and thus are not *health information* in a true sense – and expanded the Privacy Rule's already-existing right for individuals to inspect and receive copies of their own data that is stored at HIPAA-regulated facilities such as clinics, hospitals, insurers, and laboratories[12] [hereinafter the "HIPAA access right"]. The Privacy Rule offers a useful case study in the interplay between privacy and transparency in health care – useful as a reminder that the two are not always antagonistic and, at times, work together to serve shared goals.

II. THE AIMS OF TRANSPARENCY IN HEALTH CARE

Transparency is touted as an antidote for many problems. It is said to support due process, rule of law, citizen participation in public and corporate decision making, accountability, anticorruption efforts, economic efficiency, human rights, and many other values[13] with more or less pertinence to health care. Frederick Schauer summarized the aims of transparency using four categories[14] that, with minor adaptations, are helpful to this discussion of transparency in health care.

In Schauer's scheme, "transparency as regulation" empowers the recipient of information to regulate, monitor, or control the information provider.[15] As David Hyman and Kovacic note in their chapter in this volume (Chapter 23), policymakers

---

[6] Health Insurance Portability and Accountability Act of 1996, Pub. L. No. 104-191, 110 Stat. 1936 (codified as amended in scattered sections of 18, 26, 29 and 42 U.S.C.).
[7] 45 C.F.R. pts. 160, 164.
[8] Standards for Privacy of Individually Identifiable Health Information, 65 Fed. Reg. 82,462 (Dec. 28, 2000) (to be codified at 45 C.F.R. pts. 160, 164).
[9] Standards for Privacy of Individually Identifiable Health Information, 67 Fed. Reg. 53,182, 53,182 (Aug. 14, 2002) (to be codified at 45 C.F.R. pts. 160, 164).
[10] See U.S. Dep't of Health and Human Servs., Modifications to the HIPAA Privacy, Security, Enforcement, and Breach Notification Rules Under the Health Information Technology for Economic and Clinical Health Act and the Genetic Information Nondiscrimination Act; Other Modifications to the HIPAA Rules, 78 Fed. Reg. 5566, 5568 (Jan. 25, 2013) (to be codified at 45 C.F.R. pts. 160, 164) (amending the Privacy Rule to protect genetic information as defined by GINA).
[11] U.S. Dep't of Health and Human Servs., CLIA Program and HIPAA Privacy Rule; Patients' Access to Test Reports, 79 Fed. Reg. 7290 (Feb. 6, 2014) (to be codified at 42 C.F.R. pt. 493 and 45 C.F.R. pt. 164).
[12] 45 C.F.R. § 164.524.
[13] Ala'i, supra note 1, at 320.
[14] Schauer, supra note 2, at 1347–50.
[15] Id. at 1347.

often – sometimes too often, and not always effectively – embrace transparency as a regulatory tool in health care, where it offers a compromise between those who favor command-and-control regulation and those who favor no regulation at all. Richard S. Saver's chapter on the Physician Payments Sunshine Act (Chapter 6), which requires physicians to report potentially conflicting payments from drug manufacturers, and Mark A. Hall's chapter on disclosure of excessive billing for out-of-network care insured patients receive (Chapter 11), portray transparency as a tool of regulation while acknowledging its potential to supplant more direct (and possibly more effective) regulatory approaches to the underlying problems.

Schauer's second concept, "transparency as efficiency," views information flows as instrumental to efficient markets[16] and corresponds, in the health care setting, to activities like sharing information to aid billing and health care operations. This type of transparency has many manifestations in health care, as exemplified in Wendy Netter Epstein's chapter on transparency about the pricing of health care services (Chapter 10), in Marc A. Rodwin's discussion of drug price reporting as a tool to effectuate competition (Chapter 9), and in Sharona Hoffman's discussion of the role personal health records can play in improving data accuracy and the efficiency of provider response to patient needs (Chapter 17).

Schauer recognized a third and closely related concept, "transparency as epistemology,"[17] in situations where access to information supports the creation of nonmarket and public goods[18] like scientific discovery, public health, health care quality improvements, or the capacity of courts to find the truth. This chapter refers to this last concept as transparency for public benefit. The chapter by Bierer, Barnes, and Li offers the example of clinical trial data sharing, which not only informs sound clinical and regulatory decision making but promotes ongoing discovery and quality improvement by moving data into beneficial secondary uses (Chapter 13).

The first three of Schauer's concepts portray information flows as delivering broad benefits to society as a whole. An individual whose data are caught up in those flows may reap a portion of the benefits but many of the benefits, presumably, go to others. Privacy and transparency may come into conflict.

Schauer identified a fourth concept, "transparency as democracy," which enables the governed to monitor and manage their government, not merely to facilitate better governmental decisions (which is a form of transparency as regulation of the government, by the people), but also to embody public control as an end in itself.[19] The term is awkward because the health care system is in a power relationship – but not a governance relationship – with its patients and research participants.

---

[16] Id. at 1350.
[17] Id.
[18] See generally Brett M. Frischmann, Infrastructure: The Social Value of Shared Resources (2012) (describing the role of infrastructure, including data infrastructure, in creating public and non-market goods).
[19] Schauer, supra note 2, at 1349.

The underlying values served by this form of transparency closely resemble the bioethical values of respect for autonomy/respect for persons and informed consent (mandated disclosures)[20] that promote accountability of the health care system to individuals, address imbalances of power between laypeople and experts in the health care and research settings, and enable patient control as an end in itself. The term "transparency as respect for autonomy" is better suited to health care. This form of transparency is on display in several chapters in this volume, such as Barry R. Furrow's chapter on the promise and limitations of transparency to promote patient sovereignty (Chapter 1); in Orlando and Rosoff's chapter about empowering people to make healthy decisions (Chapter 15); and in Sharona Hoffman's remarks about the dual role that personal health records play, not only as a market facilitator but also as a tool to enhance patient autonomy and empowerment (Chapter 17). As explored below, the Privacy Rule enables all four types of transparency but gives special weight to this final type of transparency.

III. ENABLING TRANSPARENCY FOR REGULATION, EFFICIENCY, AND PUBLIC BENEFIT

The HIPAA Privacy Rule is arguably misnamed. It protects transparency as well as privacy, sometimes to the chagrin of privacy advocates. Concern about protecting transparency was evident even before the Privacy Rule was proposed. The HIPAA statute[21] required the U.S. Department of Health and Human Services (HHS), by 1997, to submit recommendations to Congress on health data privacy. The statute envisioned that Congress would separately enact national health privacy legislation by August 21, 1999,[22] based on these recommendations. HIPAA authorized HHS to promulgate a Privacy Rule only if Congress failed to legislate,[23] which, as events unfolded, is what happened.

The 1997 HHS recommendations[24] accepted, as their starting point, that transparency offers benefits that, at times, must take precedence over individuals' desire for privacy:

---

[20] See, e.g., Office of the Sec'y, U.S. Dep't of Health, Educ.& Welfare, Nat'l Comm'n for the Prot. of Human Subjects of Biomedical and Behavioral Research, Ethical Principles and Guidelines for the Protection of Human Subjects of Research, pt. B (Apr. 18, 1979) [hereinafter "Belmont Report"], www.hhs.gov/ohrp/regulations and-policy/belmont-report/index.html [https://perma.cc/7UHH-UMZN] (listing "respect for persons" as the first of three "basic bioethical principles").

[21] Health Insurance Portability and Accountability Act of 1996, Pub. L. 104–191, 110 Stat. 1936 (August 21, 1996) § 264(a), (b).

[22] Id. at § 264(c).

[23] Id.

[24] See U.S. Dep't of Health & Human Servs., Confidentiality of Individually-Identifiable Health Information: Recommendation of the Secretary of HHS Pursuant to Sec. 264 of the Health Insurance Portability and Accountability Act of 1996 § I.I (Sept. 11, 1997) (available at Healthcare Compliance Rep. (CCH) ¶ 100,001, 1997 WL 354007170.

A Federal health privacy law should permit limited disclosures of health information without patient consent for specifically identified national priority activities. We have carefully examined the many uses that the health professions, related industries, and the government make of health information, and we are aware of the concerns of privacy and consumer advocates about these uses. The allowable disclosures and corresponding restrictions we recommend reflect a balancing of privacy and other social values.[25]

In addition to disclosures for treatment and payment purposes, these national priority activities included (1) regulatory oversight of the health care system (including audit, investigation, quality assurance, and licensure); (2) public health and disclosures in emergencies affecting life or safety; (3) health research; and (4) uses authorized by other laws or court orders for law enforcement, state health data systems, and court proceedings.[26] The mention of treatment and payment purposes evokes efficiency aims: information flows are "grease" for a well-running health care system. The first numbered item evokes Schauer's concept of transparency as regulation, while the other three items support the provision of various public benefits.

The 1997 recommendations gave individuals no right to block these forms of transparency. People's privacy would instead be protected through other mechanisms. HHS recommended that federal privacy legislation should incorporate "safeguards, including restrictions on re-disclosure, to ensure that individual subjects are not harmed."[27] For example, unconsented research uses of data should require an institutional review board (IRB) to determine that the research involves "no more than minimal risk, that the absence of consent will not harm the participants, and that the research would be impracticable if consent were required."[28] Even in research settings, people should have access to their own records with only narrow exceptions.[29] HHS viewed access to one's own data as an ethical necessity and as an important tool for protecting people's rights when their data are used without consent (see discussion later). Above all, privacy should be respected by placing limitations on *how much* data could be disclosed without a person's consent, as discussed in the next section.

When Congress failed to pass privacy legislation by 1999, HHS began work on the HIPAA Privacy Rule. The regulation incorporated HHS's 1997 recommendations, with two notable exceptions. The first exception is that the Privacy Rule offers little protection against downstream reuse, reidentification, and redisclosure of data by third parties who receive people's data, often without their consent, pursuant to the

[25] Id.
[26] Id.
[27] Id.
[28] Id.
[29] Id.

regulation's transparency-enhancing provisions. The HIPAA statute only allows HHS to regulate the so-called HIPAA-covered entities – basically, providers, insurers, and other entities in the health care payment chain. Transparency requires sharing data with many entities that are not HIPAA-covered – for example, many research facilities fit this description – and HHS has no power to constrain their redisclosure of data. In its 1997 recommendations, HHS urged Congress to enact further legislation that would extend HHS's jurisdiction to regulate all the entities that would receive data in service of transparency. Congress's failure to do so left HHS with inadequate jurisdiction to manage the impacts that transparency imposes on people's privacy. The second exception is that the Privacy Rule has always provided an individual access right, but this right did not provide access to laboratory-held data until 2014. Moreover, the Privacy Rule has never – then or now – allowed individual access to data stored by non-HIPAA-covered entities.

As a result, the Privacy Rule affords people whose data are disclosed for the sake of transparency less privacy protection than HHS, in 1997, recommended they should receive. The 1997 recommendations envisioned a balance between privacy and transparency that would honor transparency by relaxing the requirement for individual consent, while supplying an alternative set of privacy protections including individual access rights and limits on downstream reuse, reidentification, and redisclosure of people's data. The transparency materialized, but the alternative privacy protections did not. Without further Congressional action, HHS lacked the jurisdiction it needed to strike the balance it felt was necessary. The Privacy Rule that HHS promulgated was a substantial derogation from the principles that HHS, in its 1997 recommendations to Congress, proposed. This has left the Privacy Rule haunted, today, by an ongoing lack of public trust.

A final point is that the Privacy Rule merely enables transparency in service of the national priority activities HHS identified: it permits covered entities to disclose information for these activities but does not require them to do so. Thus, a hospital may disclose information without individual consent in response to a state public health statute or a court order, without violating the Privacy Rule. Whether the hospital is required to make the disclosure depends on external law (that is, law other than the Privacy Rule), such as the public health statute or the court order. For activities corresponding to Schauer's "transparency as regulation" or "transparency as efficiency," such external laws often exist, as discussed in several other chapters in this volume. In contrast, there are few external laws requiring covered entities to share their data for activities, such as research, that correspond to Schauer's notion of "transparency as epistemology." The Privacy Rule leaves such sharing to the discretion of the entity that holds the data. This creates a potential for our society to underproduce the nonmarket and public goods that transparency, in the form of broad data sharing, can provide.

IV. NUANCING PRIVACY PROTECTIONS IN THE FACE OF TRANSPARENCY

The Privacy Rule acknowledges that transparency has many different manifestations that provide different levels of societal and individual benefit. No single approach to balancing privacy and transparency is appropriate in every context.

The Privacy Rule's baseline requirement – conceptually, its "first tier" of privacy protection – is that individuals can control access to their data by signing or refusing to sign "authorizations"[30] (HIPAA's name for consents) allowing specific uses and disclosures. Individuals also have a right of access to their own stored data,[31] which they then can use or distribute as they wish. In both cases, the individual decides how much or how little data will be released, to whom, and for what purposes. This first tier of privacy protection corresponds to most people's hopes about health data privacy.

The Privacy Rule enables transparency by listing specific exceptions to its individual authorization requirement, corresponding to the national priority activities that HHS identified in its 1997 recommendations to Congress. Individuals have no right to block uses or disclosures of their data for these activities, and alternative privacy protections apply. As Table 1 shows, the alternative protections vary, resulting in three additional tiers of privacy protection (Tiers 2–4) under the Privacy Rule.[32]

The Privacy Rule's "minimum necessary" standard[33] is the principal privacy protection people receive in Tier 2. Tier 2 encompasses a list of specific activities[34] that promote efficiencies and public benefits – for example, health care billing, research that uses data subject to an IRB-approved waiver of individual authorization,[35] public health activities,[36] and health care quality improvement activities.[37]

The minimum necessary standard is conceptually simple: when HIPAA-covered entities use, request, or disclose people's private health data for Tier 2 activities, they must limit themselves to the least amount of information that is "reasonably necessary" to achieve the purpose of the intended data use.[38] The Health Information Technology for Economic and Clinical Health or

---

[30] 45 C.F.R. § 164.508.
[31] 45 C.F.R. § 164.524.
[32] See generally Barbara J. Evans & Gail P. Jarvik, Impact of HIPAA's Minimum Necessary Standard on Genomic Data Sharing, Genetics in Med., published online ahead of print, Sept. 14, 2017, doi:10.1038/gim.2017.141; Nat'l Comm. on Vital and Health Statistics, Recommendation on the HIPAA Minimum Necessary Standard 15–19 (Nov. 9, 2016), www.ncvhs.hhs.gov/recommendation-on-the-hipaa-minimum-necessary-standard/[https://perma.cc/YB2S-NZQA].
[33] See 45 C.F.R. § 164.502(b)(1).
[34] 45 C.F.R. § 164.506 and §§ 164.512 (a), (b), (d), (g), (h), (i), (j), (k), (l).
[35] 45 C.F.R. § 164.512(i).
[36] 45 C.F.R. § 164.512(b).
[37] 45 C.F.R. § 164.506.
[38] 45 C.F.R. § 164.502(b)(1); 45 C.F.R. § 164.514(d)(3)(i), (d)(4)(i).

TABLE 1 *HIPAA's Four Tiers of Privacy Protection*

Tier	Values Served	Method of Protecting Privacy
1	**Privacy** • Any data use that an individual has authorized • Individuals' access to and use of their own data under HIPAA's individual access right	**Individual control** Individuals control the use and disclosure of their data, including how much data can be disclosed.
2	**Transparency for efficiency and public benefit, with some respect for privacy** These uses include ten enumerated data uses[39] that provide public benefits like scientific discovery and public health. Information can also be disclosed to support an efficient health care system. For example: • Research uses of data under an IRB-approved waiver of individual authorization • Public health uses of data • Health care billing and operations, including quality improvement activities	**Limits on the amount of data disclosed** Individuals do not control access to their data (individual authorization is not required). The Privacy Rule's minimum necessary standard limits how much data can be requested, used, or disclosed.
3	**Transparency for efficiency and public benefit in law enforcement/judicial settings, with some respect for privacy** • Reporting of abuse, neglect, and domestic violence • Data required for judicial and regulatory proceedings • Data requested by law enforcement agencies	**Limits on the amount of data disclosed** Individuals do not control access to their data (individual authorization is not required). The minimum necessary standard also does not apply, but HIPAA recognizes other limits on how much data can be requested, used, or disclosed (for example, it looks to other laws or court orders to define the scope of permissible disclosure).
4	**Transparency for regulation and to support patient care, with no restrictions to protect privacy** • Disclosures of existing data to health care providers for use in treating patients • Uses of data by covered entities and HHS to ensure compliance with the Privacy Rule	**HIPAA offers no privacy protections and relies on external protections** Individuals do not control access to their data, and HIPAA sets no limits on how much data can be requested, used, or disclosed. Disclosures to HHS are subject to the 1974 Privacy Act, which governs governmental databases, and disclosures to health care providers are protected by professional standards and state medical privacy law.

[39] 45 C.F.R. § 164.506 and §§ 164.512 (a), (b), (d), (g), (h), (i), (j), (k), (l).

"HITECH" Act[40] makes clear that hospitals, insurers, and other entities that are asked to supply the data bear ultimate responsibility to comply with the minimum necessary standard. How much data is "necessary," however, is measured relative to the *data user's* intended purpose.[41] This means that, before disclosing data, a data supplier must inquire into the requester's proposed use and refuse requests that seek more data than are reasonably necessary. There is, however, no inquiry into whether the user's asserted purpose actually offers a public benefit. Here, once again, the Privacy Rule strays from the principles on which it rests. In its 1997 recommendations, HHS cited with favor a report[42] by the Privacy Protection Study Commission (PPSC).[43] The PPSC acknowledged that unconsented research uses of data can, at times, be ethically justified, but only subject to a public benefit standard to ensure that "the importance of the research or statistical purpose ... is such as to warrant the risk to the individual from additional exposure of the record or information."[44] The Privacy Rule, without discussion or explanation, dropped the public benefit requirement, but did retain the minimum necessary requirement.

When developing the Privacy Rule, HHS observed that the "minimum necessary" concept had long existed in professional codes of ethics.[45] Storing health information electronically increases privacy risks overall, but makes it easier to cull records to isolate the minimum necessary data – a process that often had been too labor intensive to do in the days of paper records.[46] Even with the help of modern data processing, HHS estimated that the costs of implementing the minimum necessary standard would account for one-third of the total costs regulated entities would incur to comply with the Privacy Rule.[47] Despite the standard's high cost, HHS believed it was essential to place strict limits on the amount of information disclosed without individual authorization. The European Union's 1995 Data Protection Directive[48] and the General Data Protection

---

[40] Div. A, Title XIII, and Div. B, Title IV, of Pub. L. 111–5, American Recovery and Reinvestment Act, 123 Stat. 115, at 226; see privacy provisions at Sec. 13001, codified at 42 U.S.C. § 17921 et seq.
[41] 45 C.F.R.§ 164.514(d)(3)(i).
[42] Privacy Prot. Study Comm'n, Personal Privacy in an Information Society (1977), www.epic.org/privacy/ppsc1977report [https://perma.cc/U6GQ-GY7T].
[43] U.S. Dep't of Justice, Overview of the Privacy Act of 1974: Role of the Privacy Protection Study Commission (July 16, 2015), www.justice.gov/opcl/role-privacy-protection-study-commission [https://perma.cc/Y29V-NB68].
[44] Privacy Protection Study Commission, supra note 42, at ch. 7, sec. 10(c); Barbara J. Evans & Eric Meslin, Biospecimens, Commercial Research, and the Elusive Public Benefit Standard, in Specimen Science: Ethics and Policy Implications 107, 112 (Holly Fernandez Lynch, Barbara E. Bierer, I. Glenn Cohen & Suzanne M. Rivera, eds. 2017).
[45] 65 Fed. Reg 82,462, 82,763.
[46] Id. at 82,545.
[47] Id. at 82,761.
[48] EU Data Protection Directive (95/46/EC), Article 6 (Oct. 24, 1995).

Regulation[49] that will supersede it in 2018 similarly require data access not to be "excessive" and to be "limited to what is necessary" in relation to the purposes for which data are collected.

Tier 3 includes data disclosures for judicial and law-enforcement uses.[50] These are not subject to the minimum necessary standard. Requiring data suppliers to block excessive law enforcement and judicial data requests could subject them to liability for obstructing justice. Instead, HIPAA relies on other mechanisms to limit disclosures and instill public trust, such as requiring a court to subpoena the data.

Tier 4 surprises many people: the Privacy Rule allows a person's stored data to be shared without authorization and with no constraint on the amount of data shared. Fortunately, Tier 4 includes only a short list of activities: uses and disclosures of a person's data for an institution's own HIPAA compliance activities and for HHS regulatory oversight[51] (both examples of Schauer's transparency as regulation), and disclosures of data to a health care provider for treatment purposes.[52] In these instances the data flow to privacy-protected environments (a privacy regulator or another regulated health care provider), so there is little incremental privacy risk. Moreover, the disclosures generally benefit the people whose privacy is burdened. The most controversial issue in Tier 4 is that the Privacy Rule allows one person's data to be disclosed to aid the treatment of another person.[53] The Privacy Rule implicitly assigns a high value to transparency that serves patient care: transparency trumps privacy when human lives may be at stake.

To summarize, the Privacy Rule, at the outset, identified a list of national priority data uses that warrant transparency. HIPAA-covered entities that store people's health information can disclose it without individual authorization for these national priority uses, but they must respect privacy by carefully managing how much information is disclosed. The minimum necessary standard acts as a throttle that dials the level of transparency up or down in response to privacy concerns, in situations where at least some transparency is warranted. This approach is noteworthy if only as a rejection of balancing analysis in a context where the competing interests are ultimately incommensurable.

---

[49] General Data Protection Regulation (Regulation (EU) 2016/679), Article 5 (Apr. 27, 2016).
[50] 45 C.F.R. § 164.512(c), (e), and (f).
[51] 45 C.F.R. § 164.502(b)(2)(iv),(vi).
[52] 45 C.F.R. § 164.502(b)(2)(i).
[53] U.S. Dep't of Health and Human Servs., Does the HIPAA Privacy Rule Permit Doctors, Nurses, and Other Health Care Providers to Share Patient Health Information for Treatment Purposes without Patient Authorization? (Nov. 3, 2003), www.hhs.gov/hipaa/for-professionals/faq/481/does-hipaa-permit-doctors-to-share-patient-information for-treatment-without-authorization/index.html [https://perma.cc/H52T-XRD5] (emphasis added).

V. TRANSPARENCY AS RESPECT FOR AUTONOMY

The preceding discussion neglected one crucial form of transparency: the one Schauer called "transparency as democracy" which, in the health care setting, is more aptly named "transparency as respect for autonomy." The Privacy Rule protects this form of transparency by granting individuals a legally enforceable right to inspect and receive copies of their stored health information.[54] One of the mysteries of the Privacy Rule is that it protects this form of transparency above all others. The Privacy Rule's other transparency-enabling provisions – those discussed earlier, which offer many benefits to society – are merely permissive; they allow but do not require data disclosures. HIPAA's access right is mandatory, although there have been ongoing complaints about lax compliance with, and enforcement of, HIPAA's right for individuals to access their own data. This right needs to be enforced because it is, as a former HHS Secretary once said, the "cornerstone of the Privacy Rule."[55]

HIPAA's individual right of access to one's own data follows a legal tradition established in other post-1970 federal laws to protect individuals in an age of electronic data storage. The Fair Credit Reporting Act of 1970[56] gave people a right to obtain data about themselves stored by consumer credit-reporting agencies.[57] Inspired by this example, a 1973 Code of Fair Information Practices for health data declared, "There must be a way for an individual to find out what information about him is in a record and how it is used."[58] The Privacy Act of 1974,[59] which regulates privacy in governmental databases (including, significantly, Medicare data) embraced this recommendation and provided a broad individual access right. Unfortunately, this left most Americans with uncertain access to their own health data, because the United States relies heavily on private-sector providers and payers that are not subject to the Privacy Act. In 1977, the PPSC called for individual access to medical data held by nongovernmental health care providers, insurers, and other organizations.[60] Two decades later, HIPAA provided the opportunity, at last, to implement this recommendation.[61]

---

[54] 45 C.F.R. § 164.524.
[55] See HHS Announces New Rule That Gives Patients Direct Access to Lab Test Results, CMA News (Feb. 06, 2014), www.cmanet.org/m/news/detail.dT/hhs-announces-new-rule-that-gives-patients [https://perma.cc/3R3B-T3T9] (quoting then-HHS Secretary Kathleen Sebelius).
[56] 15 U.S.C. § 1681.
[57] Fed. Trade Comm., A Summary of Your Rights Under the Fair Credit Reporting Act, www.consumer.ftc.gov/articles/pdf-0096-fair-credit-reporting-act.pdf [https://perma.cc/9A3G-X3PV].
[58] See U.S. Dep't of Health & Human Servs., supra note 24, at § II.C.2. (quoting U.S. Dep't of Health, Educ. & Welfare, Secretary's Advisory Committee on Automated Personal Data Systems, Records, Computers, and the Rights of Citizens 41 (1973)).
[59] 5 U.S.C. § 552(a)(d).
[60] Privacy Prot. Study Comm'n, supra note 42, at ch. 7.
[61] U.S. Dep't of Health & Human Servs, Standards for Privacy of Individually Identifiable Health Information; Proposed Rules, 64 Fed. Reg. 59,918, 59,980–982 (Nov. 3, 1999) (explaining, in the

HIPAA's access right, on casual inspection, simply empowers patients to monitor their health care providers and promotes patient control and autonomy as ends in themselves. HHS cited these rationales when promulgating and amending HIPAA's access right: access helps patients detect instances of misdiagnosis and medical malpractice.[62] It helps them understand their health status and treatment options.[63] It promotes health-reform concepts including personalized medicine, participatory medicine, and disease management and prevention.[64]

Yet these aims, instrumental to providing good health care, are not the only rationales HHS cited. Individual access is, in fact, HHS's response to the central dilemma of reconciling society's interest in transparency with the individual's interest in privacy. The central dilemma is that individuals have strong and widely acknowledged ethical claims for their health data to be kept strictly private and under their own control, yet honoring those claims – for example, through regulations that block unauthorized disclosures of people's health data – would inflict unbearable social costs in the form of scientific discoveries foregone,[65] harms to the public's health, health care system inefficiencies, sexual predators and child abusers eluding detection, court cases wrongly decided, and many other public "bads." Ethical protection of the person is not necessarily good for the people. The central dilemma of privacy regulation is that it can never truly protect privacy.

The PPSC recognized this dilemma in its 1977 report, which recognized that there may be compelling reasons to share people's data without their consent. The PPSC cautioned, however, that if a person's data – including research records – cannot be "totally protected against the possibility that individually identifiable information in them will be disclosed for any other purpose, the individual's concern is obvious and his access right highly relevant."[66] Individual access is ethically justified not merely because it is instrumental to better clinical health care. It is ethically necessary in contexts where people's data privacy is imperfectly protected – which is to say, in all health care and biomedical research contexts.

The purpose of strong data privacy protections is ultimately to protect people's civil rights – for example, to protect them from discrimination

preamble to the originally proposed HIPAA Privacy Rule, that HIPAA's access right was modeled on the similar provisions of the Privacy Act of 1974).

[62] See 79 Fed. Reg. 7290, 7293 (citing statistics that clinicians fail to inform patients of abnormal test results seven percent of the time).

[63] See id. at 7290 (noting, in preamble to final rule on laboratory data access, that barriers to individual data access "prevent[] patients from having a more active role in their personal health care decisions.").

[64] Id.

[65] I. Glenn Cohen, Is There a Duty to Share Health Data?, in Big Data in Health and Health Care 209 (I. Glenn Cohen et al. eds., 2018).

[66] Id.

they may suffer if their private data fall into other people's hands. One way to protect people would be to give them ironclad control over all uses, disclosures, and redisclosures of their data. Then, individuals could protect their own civil rights by limiting access to their data. This strategy fails, however, because the needed level of individual control carries an unacceptable cost in terms of national priority data uses foregone. Any rational privacy policy must allow considerable transparency for regulation, efficiency, and public benefit. This transparency poses a threat to the individual's civil rights.

In this dilemma, HIPAA's individual access right – transparency as respect for autonomy – supplies an essential fallback mechanism. Empowered by access to their own data, individuals can identify forms of health or genetic discrimination to which they may be susceptible. Access also enables their exercise of various other federally protected civil rights, including their First Amendment-protected rights to assemble and to petition the government for redress of grievances.[67] Individuals can assemble social networks of people who share their health and genetic characteristics to resist discrimination or promote research to understand, and hence destigmatize, the underlying medical cause. Precision medical scholar Matt Might has published how-to instructions for assembling social networks of people who share genetic variants associated with rare diseases.[68] Sharon Terry, President and CEO of the Genetic Alliance, adds that access to genetic test information aids the formation of social networks among people who share particular gene variants.[69] In a world where privacy is imperfectly protected, individual data access arms people with alternative tools to protect their civil rights.

Other rationales HHS cites for HIPAA's individual access right are, first, that it forces entities that store people's data to respect their autonomy;[70] and second, access strengthens privacy protections in an environment where privacy cannot, because of its social costs, be protected perfectly. Storing and sharing of people's health information contributes to their reidentification risk, the risk that stored data could be hacked and cross-correlated with deidentified data stored elsewhere to reidentify the person.[71] In an age of data transparency, reidentification is a growing

[67] U.S. Const. amend. I (protecting "the right of the people peaceably to assemble, and to petition the Government for a redress of grievances.").
[68] Matt Might, Discovering New Diseases with the Internet: How to Find a Matching Patient, matt.might.net/articles/rare-disease-internet-matchmaking/ [https://perma.cc/D7VA-BN25].
[69] Sharon F. Terry, The Tension Between Policy and Practice in Returning Research Results and Incidental Findings in Genomic Biobank Research, 13 Minn. J.L. Sci. & Tech. 691, 714 (2012).
[70] 65 Fed. Reg. 82,462, 82,606.
[71] See Nat'l Comm. for Vital Health Statistics, Letter to the Honorable Thomas E. Price, Secretary of Health and Human Services, Recommendations on De-identification of Protected Health

privacy threat that the Privacy Rule does little to address. The Privacy Rule allows HIPAA-covered entities to release data to others without individual consent to promote various transparency aims. Covered entities have little duty to account to the individuals for these disclosures, which have "expanded exponentially" in recent years.[72] Because of limits to HHS's regulatory jurisdiction, data released to non-HIPAA-regulated data aggregators, analytics companies, and health applications businesses can be reidentified and redisclosed in fully identified form.[73] The Privacy Rule does not protect against these risks, but its access right at least empowers people to understand the risks.

CONCLUSION

In the context of health care and biomedicine, privacy is highly valued. Transparency is also valued, setting up an inevitable dilemma of how to reconcile the two. The HIPAA Privacy Rule displays an attempt to do so – an attempt that ultimately fell short because HIPAA's jurisdiction is inadequate to regulate all the entities that receive, store, use, and redisclose a person's data under a transparency-promoting policy. The Privacy Rule's lessons can be summarized as follows: transparency in health care settings should be promoted not as a good in itself, but as an instrument to serve carefully defined, specifically enumerated aims. Out of respect for privacy, policymakers should encourage only the "minimum" level of transparency that is "necessary" to accomplish those aims. It may make sense to reject the balancing of public and privacy interests, because the interests in the balance are incommensurable. Above all, transparency that offers social benefits must be leavened with transparency that respects individual autonomy. The Privacy Rule's framers understood that the social value of transparency requires less-than-complete protection of individual privacy and that the Privacy Rule's gaps in privacy protection would subject individuals to various risks to their civil rights. Individual access is an essential tool to empower people to try to protect their civil rights, when privacy law cannot do so.

Information under HIPAA 5 (February 23, 2017), www.ncvhs.hhs.gov/wp-content/uploads/2013/12/2017-Ltr-Privacy-DeIdentification-Feb-23 Final-w-sig.pdf [https://perma.cc/KPS9-YT67] ("Even data properly de-identified under the Privacy Rule may carry with it some private information, and, therefore, poses some risk of re-identification, a risk that grows into the future as new datasets are released and as datasets are combined.").

[72] Id. at 5, 7.
[73] Id. at 5, 9–10.

3

Transparency Trade-offs

Priority Setting, Scarcity, and Health Fairness

Govind Persad[*]

I. INTRODUCTION

Legal and ethical arguments for transparency, including transparency in health care and policy, frequently frame transparency as a civil right of broad value to all. According to this view, transparency may conflict with other values such as privacy, but there are no interpersonal trade-offs: offering transparency to some individuals does not preclude or conflict with offering it to others.

In contrast, this chapter argues that we should understand transparency in a different way. Rather than viewing transparency as a right, we should regard it as a finite resource whose allocation involves trade-offs. It then argues that those trade-offs should be resolved by using a multiprinciple approach to distributive justice that incorporates values of welfare, autonomy, and priority to the least advantaged. Even those who are not persuaded by the second thesis may find the first thesis and the frameworks for evaluating those trade-offs valuable.

The chapter proceeds as follows: Part II provides a definition of transparency. It also distinguishes several categories of transparency – benefit/burden transparency, procedural transparency, and personal transparency – and clarifies that the chapter's focus will be on benefit/burden transparency. Part III defends the claim that efforts to achieve benefit/burden transparency inevitably involve trade-offs, because interests in receiving information vary across time and context within the same individual, and also vary between individuals. Part IV discusses several different approaches to resolving these trade-offs, drawing on existing work on distributive justice. These approaches include maximizing welfare, maximizing autonomy, and giving priority to the worst off. It argues that benefit/burden transparency should be apportioned using a multiprinciple approach that incorporates several distributive

---

[*] Thanks to Barbara Evans for her detailed comments on an earlier draft of this chapter, to Kristen Miller for her assistance with the references, and to Amy Saltzman for discussion regarding food labeling.

values. Part V examines some of the implications for law of recognizing the trade-offs presented by transparency proposals.

II. DEFINING AND CATEGORIZING TRANSPARENCY

Before making the case that pursuing transparency involves trade-offs, it is crucial to define transparency, yet much work on the topic curiously bypasses this first step. Transparency is a difficult term to define, and has typically not been defined clearly. Angus Dawson complains that

> despite its ubiquity in contemporary bioethics, I'm not sure what the term transparency means. After all, transparency is just a metaphor suggesting that we make things visible. It is not, in itself, either a moral principle or a key part of any substantive moral theory; so it is hardly a surprise that the invocation of transparency offers us only modest help in moral disputes.[1]

What do we want from a definition of transparency? For transparency to merit its status as a topic of interest for bioethics and law, it must be defined in a way that captures some aspect of what we care about. However, Dawson is right that transparency is unlikely to be a value of fundamental importance. Even if we are pluralists about what is valuable, rather than transparency being an object of value in itself, transparency is more likely to serve as a means to achieving valuable ends, such as better health or improved patient autonomy.

One reason to define transparency is that a good definition can ensure that transparency is distinct from other frequently discussed values. This resembles the value of avoiding redundancy when interpreting legal language. If a proposed definition rendered transparency identical to some other already-discussed value, that would be a point against it.

What the metaphor inherent in the concept of transparency suggests is clarity: transparency involves simple access rather than concealment or obscurity. Accordingly, I will define transparency as *easy access to relevant information*. This definition resembles the definitions offered by several scholars. Vaccaro and Madsen, in a business ethics context, define transparency as "the degree of completeness of information ... provided by each company to the market concerning its business activities"[2]; Vishwanath and Kaufmann define transparency as the "increased flow of timely and reliable economic, social and political information"[3]; and Fred Schauer defines transparency as information, processes,

---

[1] Angus Dawson, Transparency, Accountability, and Vaccination Policy, 35 J. Med. Ethics 274, 274 (2009).
[2] Antonino Vaccaro & Peter Madsen, Corporate Dynamic Transparency: The New ICT-Driven Ethics? 11 Ethics & Info. Tech. 113, 117 (2009).
[3] Tara Vishwanath & Daniel Kaufmann, Toward Transparency: New Approaches and Their Application to Financial Markets, 16 World Bank Res. Observer 41, 42 (2001).

or facts being "open and available for examination and scrutiny."[4] A recent article focusing on health care claims that transparency involves "making available to the public, in a reliable and understandable manner, information on the health care system's quality, efficiency and consumer experience with care."[5]

The provision of health care and the promotion and protection of health involve numerous types of information. As a shorthand, I will call the dimension of transparency on which I focus *benefit/burden* transparency, since it involves access to information about the health benefits and burdens of various interventions. Examples of these interventions are products and services that promote or threaten health. The clearest category of products that promote health are pharmaceuticals and medical devices. Many foods, beverages, and consumer goods also serve to promote health. Meanwhile, food and drink, as well as consumer goods and household and industrial chemicals, can also jeopardize health. The most important services that promote health are those of physicians, nurses, and other health care providers.

Efforts to promote benefit/burden transparency include calls for improved product labeling, and other information provision, on foods, beverages, pharmaceuticals, and medical devices.[6] Transparency principles have been proposed for health services as well as health-related products – for instance, some have suggested "report cards" for hospitals or health care providers that describe patient outcomes in absolute and/or comparative terms.[7]

Many other aspects of health provision, health care, and public health also raise issues of transparency. One frequently discussed issue is *procedural* transparency – that is, transparency regarding how private and public governance decisions are made. (There can even be "transparency transparency" – that is, procedural transparency about decisions regarding benefit/burden transparency.) Some have argued that procedural transparency requires that the bases for decision making, including evidence employed by decision makers, be made clear and open to all.[8]

Information about individuals' health status also presents important questions, which frequently contrast transparency with personal privacy or concealment. Discussions around data sharing and stored samples in biomedical research, as well as familiar public health debates around contact tracing, involve questions of what I will call *personal* transparency.

---

[4] Frederick Schauer, Transparency in Three Dimensions, 2011 U. Ill. L. Rev. 1339, 1343 (2011).
[5] Zahava R.S. Rosenberg-Yunger & Ahmed M Bayoumi, Transparency in Canadian Public Drug Advisory Committees, 118 Health Pol'y 255, 255 (2014).
[6] E.g., Andrea Freeman, Transparency for Food Consumers: Nutrition Labeling and Food Oppression, 41 Am. J. L. &. Med. 315, 317–21 (2015).
[7] See Steven D. Findlay, Consumers' Interest in Provider Ratings Grows, and Improved Report Cards and Other Steps Could Accelerate Their Use, 35 Health Aff. 688, 693–95 (2016).
[8] E.g., Ross E.G. Upshur, Principles for the Justification of Public Health Intervention, 93 Can. J. Pub. Health 101, 102 (2002).

While procedural and personal transparency are important for health, my focus in what follows will be on benefit/burden transparency.

III. TRANSPARENCY AS A FINITE RESOURCE

My first core claim is that efforts to promote benefit/burden transparency inevitably involve trade-offs, both between the informational interests of the same individuals in different contexts and between the interests of different individuals. This is because benefit/burden transparency typically involves choosing to highlight specific information about a given intervention, and a given piece of information is more helpful for some individuals and in some contexts than it is for other individuals and in other contexts.

Potential trade-offs between transparency and other values are widely recognized. Some, for instance, worry that transparency threatens privacy and trust.[9] My focus, in contrast, will be on the existence of trade-offs *internal* to transparency.

One way of understanding the existence of trade-offs within transparency is to consider the contrast between rights and goods. In a famous essay, Jurgen Habermas explores the distinction between these two concepts: goods promote interests or values and can be distributed among individuals, whereas rights are constraints on the distribution of goods – as Habermas puts it, rights "cannot be assimilated to distributive goods without forfeiting their deontological meaning."[10] The existence of trade-offs within transparency suggests that transparency should not be understood as a deontological right, but instead as a good or interest. A recent scholarly article argues that understanding transparency as an interest helps in adjudicating trade-offs:

> Among the reasons to prefer an instrumentalist position on transparency rights is that it allows the interests protected by transparency rights to be weighed against losses created by these protections in a familiar consequentialist fashion. By conceiving of transparency rights instrumentally, we can also distinguish in principle between relevant and irrelevant disclosures of information in a fashion that rights to know founded in the intrinsic value of knowledge or autonomy cannot easily accommodate.[11]

An instrumental understanding of transparency not only helps in distinguishing relevant from irrelevant information, but also in weighing the benefits of a given transparency policy for some against the benefits of a different policy for others.

---

[9] See, e.g., Sandrine Baume & Yannis Papadopoulos, Transparency: From Bentham's Inventory of Virtuous Effects to Contemporary Evidence-based Skepticism, Critical Rev. Int'l Soc. & Pol. Phil. 1, 11–14 (2015).

[10] Jurgen Habermas, Reconciliation Through the Public Use of Reason: Remarks on John Rawls's Political Liberalism, 92 J. Phil. 109, 114 (1995).

[11] John Elia, Transparency Rights, Technology, and Trust, 11 Ethics & Info. Tech. 145, 146 (2009).

Some transparency trade-offs will be interpersonal: a choice that improves transparency for some people could reduce transparency for others. Consider an analogy, likely familiar to many: in choosing the strength of a prescription for eyeglasses, providers cycle through numerous lenses, asking which provides the best view. The lens that provides the clearest view to me will rarely be the type that provides the clearest view for you. Transparency also presents trade-offs that are intrapersonal rather than interpersonal, because ways of presenting information that are transparent in some contexts may not be equally so in others. Again, consider eyeglasses. In some contexts, individuals want to see close-up detail; in others, they want to see far away. Similarly, in some contexts, individuals want to be shaded from the sun, and in others they want every last glimpse of light.

One might object that the analogy with eyeglasses indicates the *absence* of a trade-off. Typically, eyeglasses can be personalized to suit each person's needs and preferences: you will rarely need to look through my glasses. However, transparency in health care typically cannot be personalized in this way. Foods, drugs, and pharmaceuticals do not display personalized labels to different consumers, but instead have a single label. Even if different patients can ask their doctors different questions, the framing and presentation of an initial interaction cannot typically be individualized. Transparency typically involves presenting a set of information to all comers, even if different individuals may focus on different parts of that information, rather than presenting different initial information to different individuals.

That transparency cannot be perfectly suited at once to all individuals' interests presents an inevitable trade-off. We have limited space and time to present information, and must choose which information to make prominent and accessible. Some people may be very interested in the financial costs of using a service or product. Others may be more interested in the medical risks and benefits; among this group, different individuals will be interested in different medical risks and benefits. Yet all these individuals will be purchasing the same product or using the same service, which means that the product's labeling (for example) typically will be the same, even though different consumers have different informational needs.[12] Furthermore, fulfilling some individuals' interests in knowing about health care products and services will frequently compete with fulfilling other individuals' interests.

Many of the questions raised by informational and transparency policies resemble those raised in debates over "nudges." Like nudges, transparency efforts do not straightforwardly subsidize or proscribe certain choices. However, informational transparency efforts – like nudges – will tend to systematically favor certain options and individuals over others. Accordingly, they will pose some of the same questions

[12] Michelle Meyer discusses the problems that heterogeneous interests pose for safety, rather than transparency, regulations in her Regulating the Production of Knowledge: Research Risk-benefit Analysis and the Heterogeneity Problem, 65 Admin. L. Rev. 237 (2013).

of distributive justice that nudges inevitably do.[13] Transparency does not simply serve as an overlay that preserves existing patterns of distribution, but shifts those patterns in specific directions. Unless transparency is explicitly designed to preserve the distributive status quo, it will change that status quo in a variety of ways.

One source of trade-offs is the scarce space available for presenting information. Labels on medicines, or on foods and drinks, are scarce real estate that can only present a limited amount of text.[14] Furthermore, even within this scarce real estate, certain positions are more valuable than others: people are more likely to attend to items at the top or middle of a label than items at the bottom, and more likely to pay attention to information or warnings that are larger or placed on the front of a product than on the back.[15] Similarly, informed consent processes typically only present a limited range of the imaginable costs and benefits of an intervention – in order to avoid the problem of a consent form that is interminably long, certain risks and benefits must be foregrounded.

Moving from space to content, it is challenging to make the presentation of information neutral between different individuals' interests. Merely presenting information creates inferences that the information in question is relevant or important – otherwise, why would it be presented? The relative prominence of different types of information may affect judgments about the importance of that information. Achieving expert agreement about what information is correct and important can also be challenging. These challenges are exacerbated by the fact that information provision typically involves questions of values as well as questions of purely technical fact.

Another trade-off reflects the fact that some individuals have a preference not to know about some features of products.[16] For instance, calorie labeling can change the enjoyment of a meal or even encourage some individuals with eating disorders to make unwise choices, even as it provides valuable information to others.[17] Forced disclosure of information to decision makers who have already made their minds up – as occurs in some reproductive choice contexts – can also be contrary to some

[13] See Matthew A. Smith & Michael S. McPherson, Nudging for Equality: Values in Libertarian Paternalism, 61 Admin. L. Rev. 323, 328 (2009).
[14] See *Robinson v. McNeil Consumer Healthcare*, 615 F.3d 861, 869 (7th Cir. 2010); *Finn v. G.D. Searle & Co.*, 677 P.2d 1147, 1153 (Cal. 1984).
[15] See, e.g., John Grishin et al., Improving Food Labels for Health and Safety: Effects of Ingredients List Placement on Search Times, 60 Proc. of the Hum. Factors and Ergonomics Soc'y Ann. Meeting 1637, 1641 (2016); Gyorgy Scrinis & Christine Parker, Front-of-Pack Food Labeling and the Politics of Nutritional Nudges, 38 L. & Pol'y 234, 237–38 (2016).
[16] Cf. Suzanne M. Miller, Monitoring and Blunting: Validation of a Questionnaire to Assess Styles of Information Seeking Under Threat, 52 J. Personality & Soc. Psychol. 345, 351 (1987).
[17] On threats to enjoyment, see, e.g., Nicolas Cornell, The Aesthetic Toll of Nudging, 14 Geo. J.L. & Pub. Pol'y. 841, 852–54 (2015); on eating disorders, see, e.g., Ann F. Haynos & Christina A. Roberto, The Effects of Restaurant Menu Calorie Labeling on Hypothetical Meal Choices of Females with Disordered Eating, 50 Int'l J. Eating Disorders 275, 278–80 (2017).

individuals' informational interests.[18] Similarly, a medical report card or information about side effects might provide valuable facts to some patients but lead others to become fearful and avoid treatments that would be substantively beneficial.[19] The Food and Drug Administration has, in amicus briefs and its own guidance documents, taken the position that excessive warnings could discourage the use of a drug by patients who are likely to benefit.[20]

Questions about transparency and information presentation arise not only for regulatory authorities, but also for manufacturers, retailers, and health care providers. Particularly under a regime where regulatory intervention is weak – as in the United States – manufacturers, retailers, and providers face ethical decisions about what sort of transparency to provide about product ingredients and likely effects.

I will use food labeling as an example of the numerous trade-offs involved in transparency. A simple can of food includes a variety of health-relevant labels.[21] On the front of the can, the label provides a name for the food, the name of the food's manufacturer or brand, and likely a picture as well. It also describes the quantity of food in the can, and may feature other information such as whether the food is organic or kosher and whether it contains transgenic ingredients. On the back, the label includes information about the caloric content of the food, some of the nutritional content, and the ingredients in the food. In some cases, the label will be printed in only one language; in other cases, it will be printed in multiple languages.

All these labeling decisions involve trade-offs and priority-setting decisions. For instance, the choice to include information about whether a product is organic or contains transgenic ingredients both implies the importance of this information and occupies space and attention that could have been devoted to other information. Listing the quantity of sodium on the main part of the label, while listing vitamins and other minerals elsewhere, takes the position that knowledge about sodium content is more valuable. Leaving some information, such as food miles traveled or micronutrient content, entirely off food labels means that individuals who especially value that information will have to try harder to obtain the information they are seeking.

These issues that crop up in food labeling also apply to other forms of information disclosure for health care and health promotion, such as health care provider report cards, designs for medical bills and pharmaceutical price statements, and public health disclosures such as warnings about infectious disease threats or toxic chemicals. All of these disclosures are offered in a single form to the public at large.

[18] Govind Persad, Libertarian Patriarchalism: Nudges, Procedural Roadblocks, and Reproductive Choice, 35 Women's Rts. L. Rep. 273, 277–84, 292–93 (2013).
[19] Ronald M. Epstein et al., Withholding Information from Patients – When Less is More, 362 New Eng. J. Med. 380, 380–81 (2010).
[20] See *Tucker v. SmithKline Beecham Corp.*, 596 F. Supp. 2d 1225, 1230, 1230 n.5 (S.D. Ind. 2008).
[21] Carrie Griffin Basas, "V" is for Vegetarian: FDA-Mandated Vegetarian Food Labeling, 4 Utah L. Rev. 1275, 1285–86 (2011).

IV. DISTRIBUTING TRANSPARENCY FAIRLY

If transparency decisions involved no trade-offs among the interests of different individuals, they would involve no issue of distributive justice. The proper framework to think about transparency would instead be (solely) a framework of civil rights and freedoms, where – at most – the interest of sellers in not being regulated, or in speaking freely, would be compared to the interest of the public in obtaining information. Transparency itself would not be the distribution of a good among individuals, but rather the fulfillment of consumers' rights.

However, the fact that transparency decisions inevitably involve setting priorities makes them a proper subject for analysis through a lens of distributive fairness. Problems of distributive fairness in health are familiar in other contexts, such as priority setting for global health funding or determining who should receive specific scarce resources such as organs or vaccines in a pandemic. In these contexts, some have suggested that these priorities be set using a single principle for distribution, such as the principle of maximizing population health or the principle of treating people identically.[22] The former principle has been operationalized in approaches that aim to maximize the quality-adjusted life-years (QALYs) achieved by providing a given intervention, while the latter has been operationalized in approaches that use random selection to choose between individuals. In other work, I have argued for using a multiprinciple approach that combines several different principles of distributive justice to decide what to do. Still others, most prominently Norman Daniels, have eschewed principles altogether in favor of relying on whatever judgments are produced by bodies deliberating under certain procedural rules.[23]

This subpart pursues the positive aim of developing and applying a multiprinciple distributive framework to the problem of fairly distributing the benefits of transparency. In doing so, it first examines how several different distributive frameworks for health – including welfare maximization, autonomy maximization, and priority to the least advantaged – might be applied to the case of transparency. It then argues for a multiprinciple approach that combines these values.

WELFARE MAXIMIZATION

One approach to setting priorities for transparency is simply to choose the transparency regime that maximizes overall welfare, broadly considered. However, even this

---

[22] For a review of these proposals, see Govind Persad et al., Principles for Allocation of Scarce Medical Interventions, 373 Lancet 423 (2009). A population-health-maximizing approach to allocation is defended in Peter Singer et al., Double Jeopardy and the Use of QALYs in Health Care Allocation, 21 J. Med. Ethics 144 (1995); An identical-treatment approach is defended in James F. Childress, Who Shall Live when Not All Can Live? 53 Soundings 339 (1970).

[23] See generally Norman Daniels & James Sabin, Setting Limits Fairly: Can We Learn to Share Medical Resources? (2002). But see Annette Rid, Justice and Procedure: How Does "Accountability for Reasonableness" Result in Fair Limit-Setting Decisions? 35 J. Med. Ethics 12 (2009) (critiquing this approach).

approach involves a variety of choices. The primary choice involves deciding how to define welfare. Some law and economics scholars have suggested understanding welfare as a matter of wealth maximization.[24] However, this is implausible because individuals value goods other than wealth – for instance, individuals typically are willing to trade some wealth for health improvements or for a more fulfilling career. More common definitions of welfare focus on the improvement of human capabilities, on individuals' subjective experiences, on the satisfaction of preferences, or on individuals obtaining some set of objective goods.[25] Which definition is selected will in turn affect which approach to transparency is chosen.

Many legal frameworks for evaluating regulatory transparency use – or claim to use – a welfare-maximization approach, namely, cost–benefit analysis.[26] Health care frameworks that use cost-effectiveness analysis also regard welfare maximization as their ultimate goal. Welfare maximization has the appeal – at least superficially – of being neutral. It also represents a principled and easily operationalizable alternative to ad hoc decisions about labeling. However, it also faces well-known problems.[27] We typically care about more than welfare maximization – in particular, we often care about the well-being of specific individuals or of the least advantaged. We also care about other values, such as autonomy.

Some might respond that the right way to incorporate other values, such as the well-being of the least advantaged or autonomy, is to regard the transparency process simply as a vehicle for welfare maximization, and then to use some other mechanism – such as taxation – to promote values other than welfare maximization, such as the well-being of the least advantaged.[28] This approach is frequently favored by economists. But it faces several problems. First, transparency regulations might empirically prove to be a more effective way of promoting nonwelfare values than a later redistributive process would be.[29] Second, some of the nonwelfare values at issue – such as autonomy – have a closer conceptual connection to transparency, such that a welfare-maximizing approach to transparency might not be able to later redistribute in order to promote autonomy.[30]

---

[24] E.g., Richard A. Posner, Wealth Maximization Revisited, 2 Notre Dame J.L. Ethics & Pub. Pol'y 85 (1985).
[25] See, e.g., Simon Keller, Welfarism, 4 Phil. Compass 82 (2009).
[26] Matthew D. Adler, QALYs and Policy Evaluation: A New Perspective, 6 Yale J. Health Pol'y, L., & Ethics 1, 58–61 (2006) (discussing FDA's use of cost–benefit analysis to analyze a disclosure rule).
[27] Alexander Volokh, Rationality or Rationalism? The Positive and Normative Flaws of Cost–Benefit Analysis, 48 Hous. L. Rev. 79, 82 (2011); Douglas A. Kysar, Politics by Other Meanings: A Comment on "Retaking Rationality Two Years Later," 48 Hous. L. Rev. 43, 76–77 (2011).
[28] See generally Louis Kaplow & Steven Shavell, Fairness versus Welfare (2002).
[29] Zachary Liscow, Note, Reducing Inequality on the Cheap: When Legal Rule Design Should Incorporate Equity as Well as Efficiency, 123 Yale L.J. 2478, 2482–85 (2014) (arguing that equity-informed legal rules are better equipped than taxes for reducing income inequality).
[30] Cf. S. Andrew Schroeder, Consequentializing and Its Consequences, 174 Phil. Stud. 1475, 1483–84 (2017).

Accordingly, I conclude that while considering the welfare implications of transparency is important, fairly distributing benefit/burden transparency requires doing more than maximizing welfare.

AUTONOMY MAXIMIZATION

Transparency is often regarded as a way of promoting individual autonomy, rather than individual well-being. Accordingly, another way of approaching the problem of priority setting would be to focus on transparency's informational role and instead aim to maximize the extent to which the choices in question are autonomous. This requires providing some definition of autonomy; possibilities include the extent to which the decision reflects the considered judgments of the decision maker, or the extent to which the decision reflects the decision maker's true or deep values.[31]

As with welfare maximization, autonomy maximization faces the problem that we care about more than autonomy. One might reply that even if we care about other values, the point of transparency is to promote autonomy. But this is incorrect. Many defenses of transparency identify values other than autonomy – such as population welfare or improvement of individual health and capability – as part of the case for promoting transparency.

PRIORITY TO THE LEAST ADVANTAGED

Another way of approaching the problem of how to set priorities for transparency is to design transparency in such a way that it protects and assists the least advantaged. While the value of assisting the least advantaged is widely identified as important, the question of who counts as the least advantaged is contested – for instance, should transparency focus on the interests of those who are least advantaged overall, or least advantaged with respect to health alone?[32] Even with respect to health, there are complicated issues in determining who is worst off with respect to health. Some see being worst off as being sickest right now, while others see it as having the worst health over one's lifetime.

There are also questions about whether to focus on the immediate effects of transparency (whether transparency promotes access to some form of health care and reduces unintended harm) or, also, to consider the more remote effects of informational transparency. For instance, transparency requirements could raise the price of certain health care interventions, making it more difficult to access

---

[31] Sarah Buss, Personal Autonomy, The Stanford Encyclopedia of Philosophy (2013), https://plato.stanford.edu/archives/win2016/entries/personal-autonomy/, archived at https://perma.cc/RM7Q-V5JC.

[32] Daniel Sharp & Joseph Millum, Prioritarianism for Global Health Investments: Identifying the Worst Off, 34 J. Applied Phil. (2015), doi: 10.1111/japp.12142, sections 6 and 7.

them even while making the interventions themselves more valuable to their recipients.[33]

MULTIPRINCIPLE APPROACHES

In work on the allocation of scarce, lifesaving medical resources, I have defended a multiprinciple approach that considers four principles of distributive justice – treating people equally, maximizing utility, assisting the worst off, and promoting and rewarding usefulness.[34] Allocating time and space for benefit/burden transparency efforts – most of which involve medical interventions that are not immediately lifesaving – is a different problem with less immediate stakes, and calls for different principles. What is appropriate where scarce, lifesaving resources are concerned may not be appropriate elsewhere. People who receive less useful information are in a quite different position from people who lose out in priority setting for scarce organs or vaccines. This difference makes the principle of treating people equally (through first-come, first-served or lottery procedures) less important, because the downside of losing out and the upside of gaining an intervention are both much smaller, and there is no obvious way to use queuing or lotteries to design labeling.[35] Principles of promoting and rewarding usefulness are similarly less important. In contrast, principles of maximizing utility and priority to the least advantaged remain important. Additionally, the close relationship of information to autonomy makes autonomy an especially important consideration in the labeling context.

Accordingly, I defend a multiprinciple strategy that combines principles of welfare promotion; respect for and promotion of autonomy; and protection and assistance to the worst off. Even though none of these principles are sufficient on their own to settle questions of how transparency should be provided, none of them are flawed principles that undermine the merit of a multiprinciple approach that includes them.[36]

Consider the application of this multiprinciple approach to the case of food labeling. In deciding which pieces of information should receive priority, we should consider the overall benefits to the population as a while, but should also look at

[33] On higher prices as an effect of food labeling, see Elise Golan et al., Economics of Food Labeling, 24 J. Consumer Pol'y 117 (2001); on price transparency, see Margaret K. Kyle & David B. Ridley, Would Greater Transparency and Uniformity of Health Care Prices Benefit Poor Patients?, 26 Health Aff. 1384 (2007).
[34] Persad et al., supra note 22, at 423–26; Govind Persad et al., Standing by Our Principles: Meaningful Guidance, Moral Foundations, and Multi-Principle Methodology in Medical Scarcity, 10 Am. J. Bioethics 46, 47 (2010); Govind Persad, Public Preferences About Fairness and the Allocation of Scarce Medical Interventions, in Interdisciplinary Perspectives on Fairness, Equity, and Justice 53–56 (Meng Li & David Tracer eds., 2017).
[35] That is, the "fair chances/best outcomes" problem identified by Norman Daniels is less urgent where transparency is concerned. See Norman Daniels, Rationing Fairly: Programmatic Considerations, 7 Bioethics 224 (1993).
[36] On this distinction, see Persad et al., supra note 22, at 423.

whether the information is important to making an autonomous decision about the product in question and to maintaining one's autonomy in the future. We should also consider how the information bears on the welfare and autonomy of those who are most disadvantaged with respect to either welfare or autonomy. As an example of how this would work, we might consider whether information about a given nutrient is especially valuable to people in general or to the least advantaged; whether this information is important to making an autonomous decision in light of what we know about people's values; and how ways of presenting this information would bear on autonomy.

This section concludes with a brief comment on the alternative strategy of eschewing principles altogether in favor of procedural rules. The same concerns about using this approach to allocate scarce medical resources apply in the transparency context as well. Even after procedural rules are optimized, those engaged in a fair decision-making process must still have some recourse to substantive principles in order to reach decisions within that process.[37] Fair procedures, while important, are not an alternative to substantive principles – rather, fair procedural rules should be coupled with some principles of distributive justice. The principles suggested here are offered as potential guides on which decision makers may rely.

V. LEGAL IMPLICATIONS

What are the legal implications of recognizing trade-offs within transparency, and designing those trade-offs in light of a multiprinciple approach to distributive justice?

Matthew Adler has recently discussed the use of cost–benefit information in creating labeling requirements.[38] Once we recognize the importance of multiple principles, this might motivate moving away from a simple cost–benefit or cost-effectiveness analysis toward some type of analysis that incorporates a greater plurality of values. Some of these approaches include extended cost-effectiveness analysis (ECEA) and social-welfare function approaches that include values other than welfare.[39]

Another implication of using a multiprinciple system of transparency is that information presentation might properly vary not just by the type of good at issue, but by the likely consumers of the good and by the interests that the good promotes or threatens. Right now, caviar and chicken nuggets are labeled in the same way.

---

[37] Dan Brock, Ethical Issues in the Use of Cost Effectiveness Analysis for the Prioritization of Health Care Resources, in WHO Guide to Cost-Effectiveness Analysis 289, 291 (T. Tan-Torres Edejer et al. eds., 2003) ("[M]uch important work remains to be done on the substantive issues of equity in health care, and that work should inform the deliberations of those taking part in ... fair procedures.").

[38] See Adler, supra note 26.

[39] Matthew Adler, Social Welfare Functions, in Global Health Priority-Setting: Beyond Cost-Effectiveness (Ole Norheim et al. eds., forthcoming 2018); Stephane Verguet et al., Extended Cost-Effectiveness Analysis, in the same volume.

But – if we are concerned with autonomy promotion and with the interests of the least advantaged – it might well make sense to allow greater variation in caviar labeling, given that caviar consumption is less closely tied to autonomy or to the interests of the least advantaged. The same might be true for transparency regarding different types of medical services – a physician report card for an emergency room physician or rural family medicine provider might contain different information from that of an ophthalmologist or orthodontist. In contrast, the labeling of goods frequently purchased by the least advantaged or by individuals who experience challenges in autonomous decision making might need to be tailored to protect these individuals, just as consent processes sometimes need to vary when specific vulnerable populations are being enrolled in medical research.[40] This would support an approach to benefit/burden transparency that focuses on the individuals and interests affected by transparency, rather than on specific physical categories of goods and services such as foods or medicines.

Another implication of conceiving of benefit/burden transparency as a good is the strengthened case for judicial caution. For issues that are purely matters of individual civil rights and liberties, courts are frequently well placed to make decisions. In contrast, there is good reason for courts to be much more cautious when intervening in systems of health care priority setting that involve inevitable trade-offs.[41] Concerns about the judicialization of health care provision have been raised in countries that recognize an individual, justiciable right to health.[42] In the United States, similar worries have been raised about lawsuits that challenge allocation procedures for scarce medical resources such as organs and vaccines, and more generally about individually justiciable legal claims that bypass an allocation system.[43]

As such, courts should be more willing to intervene in issues of procedural and personal transparency than in disputes regarding benefit/burden transparency. Benefit/burden transparency, which involves the distribution of a scarce resource – informational space – is a topic better considered by agencies and legislatures. However, the importance of affording some sort of appeals process for questions of distributive justice means that judicial systems will likely need to maintain some involvement in evaluating benefit/burden transparency proposals.

---

[40] Rebecca L. Sudore et al., Use of a Modified Informed Consent Process Among Vulnerable Patients: A Descriptive Study, 21 J. Gen. Internal Med. 867, 871 (2006); see also Suzanne V. Arnold et al., Converting the Informed Consent from a Perfunctory Process to an Evidence-Based Foundation for Patient Decision Making, 1 Circulation 21, 27 (2008).

[41] Alex Voorhoeve et al., Three Case Studies in Making Fair Choices on the Path to Universal Health Coverage, 18 Health and Hum. Rts. 11, 18–20 (2016). But see Keith Syrett, Courts, Expertise and Resource Allocation: Is there a Judicial 'Legitimacy Problem'?, 7 Pub. Health Ethics 112, 120 (2014).

[42] See generally Alicia Ely Yamin & Siri Gloppen, Litigating Health Rights: Can Courts Bring More Justice to Health? (2011).

[43] See, e.g., Scott D. Halpern, Turning Wrong into Right: The 2013 Lung Allocation Controversy, 159 Annals Internal Med. 358, 358 (2013).

A final aspect of conceiving of benefit/burden transparency as a distributive justice issue is that distributive justice frequently involves inquiries that are highly empirical and quantitative. Comparatively few empirical inquiries are required when granting or protecting a civil right, because the interest at stake is an individual one. Granting a civil right immediately confers on an individual the legal ability to perform a given action without sanctions or penalties. In contrast, improving benefit/burden transparency is more akin to setting tax or allocation policy, where selecting the best tax or resource allocation regime involves empirical examination of the effects of different policies. Even though benefit/burden transparency implicates autonomy in addition to well-being, assessing the effect of certain interventions on individual autonomy should also be possible.

VI. CONCLUSION

This chapter has argued that transparency should be approached as a problem of distributive justice. The challenge of trade-offs in transparency reflects the fact that transparency involves offering a one-size-fits-all regime to people whose interests differ over time, and across different people who may have different interests. It is therefore interesting to consider whether advances in personalized medicine will reduce the trade-offs involved in transparency.[44] If each intervention could be targeted to a specific person, labeling and information as well as physiological efficacy could be tailored to person and context. These individualized interventions would present fewer interpersonal trade-offs.[45]

However, many types of goods, such as staple foods and public health interventions that affect populations rather than discrete individuals, are unlikely to become personalized. Accordingly, we will face the challenge of balancing the desire to personalize and individualize interventions with the fact that trade-offs will sometimes be inescapable. Just as this is a challenge in setting guidelines for other population-affecting rules such as formularies, drug pricing, and practice guidelines, it will also be an ongoing challenge in designing transparency.

---

[44] Cf. Jeffrey J. Goldberger & Alfred E. Buxton, Personalized Medicine vs Guideline-Based Medicine, 309 JAMA 2559 (2013).
[45] See a similar suggestion of replacing IRBs with individual risk–benefit evaluation in Meyer, supra note 12, at 299.

4

Slightly Hazy

Transparency and the Costs of Too Much Information

Oliver J. Kim*

One view of transparency is that it unites both conservatives and liberals: "conservatives ... applaud 'market facilitation' and 'bootstrapping,' and ... liberals ... favor 'empowerment' and the 'right to know.'"[1] But these rationales are worlds apart so the concept of transparency in health care begs the questions what health information are we making transparent, why are we doing so, and who really will benefit?

On its face, transparency seems simple: just provide more information for smarter decision making about care. But consider this example: a conservative lawmaker was not sure whether his son's arm was sprained or broken from a fall. Because the costs were *transparent*, he knew the difference in the cost of care in emergency and office settings. He and his wife decided to wait before taking his son to his doctor's office in lieu of going to the emergency room: "We took every precaution but decided to go in the next morning [because of] the cost difference ... If you don't have a cost difference, you'll make different decisions."[2]

That type of transparency is not going to unite conservatives and liberals. Having the costs be transparent is likely not an issue for liberals. The issue is whether the parents had the right information – not just cost information – to make the right health care decision for their son. With the future of the Affordable Care Act (ACA)[3] uncertain, transparency will likely be part of any conservative replacement.[4] And

---

* Thank you to the Petrie-Flom Center and to Tanya Harris, Lois Magner, and Davida Silverman for their comments.
[1] See David A. Hyman & William E. Kovacic, Chapter 23 (quoting William Sage, Regulating Through Information: Disclosure Laws and American Health Care, 99 Colum. L. Rev. 1701, 1825–26 (1999)).
[2] Shandra Martinez, Son's Broken Arm: Bill Huizenga Says People Must Be Responsible for Own Health Care Costs, MLive, Dec. 19, 2016, www.mlive.com/news/grand-rapids/index.ssf/2016/12/sons_broken_arm_bill_huizenga.html, archived at https://perma.cc/Q65G-SZUR.
[3] Patient Protection and Affordable Care Act, 42 U.S.C. § 18001 (2010).
[4] James Capretta & Kevin Dayaratna, Compelling Evidence Makes the Case for a Market-Drive Health Care System, The Heritage Foundation: Backgrounder, Dec. 20, 2013, www.heritage.org/health-care-reform/report/compelling-evidence-makes-the-case-market-driven-health-care-system, archived at https://perma.cc/NUL9-RJA2; Alex Azar et al., Transparency in Health Care: What Consumers Need to Know, The Heritage Foundation: Lectures, Jan. 22, 2007, www.heritage.org/health-care-reform/report/transparency-health-care-what-consumers-need-know, archived at https://perma.cc/7HC2-PVWZ.

such a use of transparency will not align liberal and conservative ideologies. In fact, it should give us pause how transparent such information should be because of how it can be used.[5]

This chapter will examine the economic, policy, and ethical issues that arise from expanding transparency. While the health care system is moving toward empowering patients and consumers to be more engaged in their own care, unfiltered information is not necessarily a panacea, and unbridled consumerism may even cause harm.

I. WHAT DO WE MEAN BY TRANSPARENCY IN HEALTH CARE?

First, what does transparency mean? Is it providing upfront the cost of a health service that consumers will be responsible for, or is it making all information available to all stakeholders in the health care system? The Government Accountability Office (GAO) advises that "information on health care prices is considered transparent when this information is available to consumers before they receive [health care] services."[6] Cost information alone is unlikely to help consumers; rather, consumers should "have access to quality of care and other information to provide context to the price information and help consumers in their decision making."[7] For example, the Agency for Healthcare Research and Quality suggested that "appropriate quality of care information for consumers may include the mortality rates for a specific procedure, the percentage of patients with surgical complications or postoperative infections, or the average length of stay, among other measures." Similarly, the GAO noted that "by combining quality and price information, some researchers argue that consumers can then use this information to choose providers with the highest quality and the lowest price – thereby obtaining the greatest value when purchasing care."[8] Thus, transparency should give consumers the appropriate information to make a health care decision that makes the most sense – both financially and for their health – in their situation.

To do so, transparency depends on *information*.[9] Such information is not only collected on behalf of the consumer but also may be collected on consumers

---

[5] Elizabeth Litten, Foreshadowing HIPAA Under the New Administration: Will Transparency Trump Privacy?, Fox Rothschild LLP, Dec. 1, 2016, https://hipaahealthlaw.foxrothschild.com/2016/12/articles/health-reform/foreshadowing-hipaa-new-administration-will-transparency-trump-privacy/, archived at https://perma.cc/9VLQ-7HCN.

[6] U.S. Gov't Accountability Office, GAO-11–791, Health Care Price Transparency: Meaningful Price Information Is Difficult for Consumers to Obtain Prior to Receiving Care 3 (2011) [hereinafter "GAO"] ("We generally refer to 'cost' as a type of price information that is reflective of what a consumer may be expected to pay for a health care service.").

[7] Id.

[8] Id.

[9] Ctrs. for Medicare & Medicaid Servs., Medicare Provider Utilization and Payment Data: Physician and Other Suppliers (2016), www.cms.gov/research-statistics-data-and-systems/statistics-trends-and-reports/medicare-provider-charge-data/, archived at https://perma.cc/7R4U-2B5E; see also Lena Sun, You Need Surgery. So How Do You Find the Right Doctor?, Wash. Post, July 20, 2015 (discussing

themselves.[10] Many stakeholders would like to have consumer information as well for a variety of research, commercial, and other reasons.[11] Thus, transparency requires someone – either a public[12] or private entity[13] – to collect health care information as well as to process it.[14] Is transparency so valuable that we need to know every detail?[15]

Both the federal government and the states are attempting to make more health care information transparent.[16] The federal Department of Health and Human Services is pursuing a number of transparency initiatives, some authorized by the ACA: greater information on both Medicare[17] and private marketplace insurance plans,[18] on geographic variation in Medicare reimbursement,[19] and on hospitals' "standard charges for items and services."[20] The additional data hopefully will help "patients, researchers, and providers ... to transform the health care delivery system" and "to understand the delivery of care and spending under the Medicare program."[21]

---

tool available to consumers on surgeons "who had performed enough surgeries to provide statistically meaningful comparisons"), http://wapo.st/1MkDifB, archived at https://perma.cc/5YNU-XMLH.

[10] Julia Hudson, Note, Have Your Cake and Eat it, Too: How States Could Leverage Data on Quality to Promote Health Care Transparency & Patient Privacy Within Consumer-Driven Health Care Initiatives, 10 Ind. Health L. Rev. 663, 685 (2013).

[11] Ed Silverman, The 'Gouge Factor': Big Companies Want Transparency in Drug Price Negotiations, STAT, Aug. 2, 2016, www.statnews.com/pharmalot/2016/08/02/drug-price-transparency-pharmacy-benefits-manager/, archived at https://perma.cc/2FX4-FHCK; see also Jon Reid, Wyden Introduces Bill to Increase Transparency of PBMs, Morning Consult, Mar. 15, 2017, https://morningconsult.com/2017/03/15/wyden-introduces-bill-increase-transparency-pbms/, archived at https://perma.cc/LBB9-9ZNB (quoting the author of legislation that "Today the public knows virtually nothing about whether pharmaceutical benefit managers are saving money for the consumer or pocketing for itself").

[12] Hudson, supra note 10, at 669–74.

[13] Id. at 674–78.

[14] Id. at 679–87.

[15] While this chapter focuses on transparency available to consumers, I will also mention areas where transparency about consumers' decisions can raise ethical, policy, and other concerns.

[16] See, e.g., Ctrs. for Medicare & Medicaid Servs., The Affordable Care Act: Increasing Transparency, Protecting Consumers, www.cms.gov/CCIIO/Resources/Fact-Sheets-and-FAQs/increasing-transparency02162012a.html, archived at https://perma.cc/5GSR-Y55M; Nat'l Conference of State Legislatures, Transparency and Disclosure of Health Costs and Provider Payments: State Actions (Mar. 2017), www.ncsl.org/research/health/transparency-and-disclosure-health-costs.aspx.

[17] Patrick Conway & Kate Goodrich, December 2016 Preview: Increased Transparency and Quality Information via New Compare Sites and Data Updates, The CMS Blog, Dec. 14, 2016, https://blog.cms.gov/2016/12/14/increased-transparency-and-quality-information-via-new-compare-sites-and-data-updates/, archived at https://perma.cc/B5X2-W8N4.

[18] GAO, supra note 6, at 3–4; see Karen Pollitz & Larry Levitt, Health Insurance Transparency under the Affordable Care Act, Henry J. Kaiser Fam. Found. (2012), http://kff.org/health-reform/perspective/health-insurance-transparency-under-the-affordable-care-act/, archived at https://perma.cc/3XHN-4DBZ.

[19] GAO, supra note 6, at 3 ("CMS's Health Care Consumer Initiatives provide information on the price Medicare pays for common health care services by various geographic areas.").

[20] Id.

[21] Ctrs. for Medicare & Medicaid Servs., New Medicare Data Available to Increase Transparency on Hospital and Physician Utilization (2015), www.cms.gov/Newsroom/MediaReleaseDatabase/Press-releases/2015-Press-releases-items/2015-06-01.html, archived at https://perma.cc/L8R3-WQ5K].

Even before the ACA, states were experimenting with price transparency.[22] They used data for price comparison tools so constituents could see the cost of common procedures and compare different practitioners by price,[23] and some states used data as a baseline for payment reform initiatives such as all-payer claims databases (APCDs).[24] However, constituents may not be aware of, or use, price comparison tools created through APCDs. For example, only one percent of New Hampshire residents used the state's health care price comparison website over a three-year period.[25]

II. TRANSPARENCY AS AN ECONOMIC PROBLEM

These efforts beg the next question: does transparency help lower costs, particularly for consumers? In theory, transparency gives consumers more information about health care so they will be more conscious about their provider or a particular service or pill.[26] Further, transparency is necessary for consumer-driven health care plans, which make consumers more "price sensitive," such as health savings accounts.[27]

But health care does not work like other economic goods because the consumer is not in the best position to make a rational decision. First, consumers are unlikely to have perfect information.[28] Most consumers do not have years of academic and clinical training to inform their decision, and relying on the Internet rather than trained professionals can lead to ineffective or even harmful results.[29] In fact, "consumerism" may discourage consumers from seeking preventative care because they feel well, do not want to spend money, or both.[30] Financial incentives such as

[22] All-Payer Claims Database Council, "Interactive State Report Map," (2017), www.apcdcouncil.org/state/map, archived at https://perma.cc/TR4Z-FWNF (finding that fifteen states had an all-payer claims database and one state had a database with voluntarily reported claims data).
[23] Nat'l Council of State Legislatures, supra note 16, at Examples of State Health Price Information Disclosure Websites.
[24] Jaime S. King & Erin C. Fuse Brown, New Health Care Symposium: States' Critical Role Overseeing Vertical Health Care Integration, Health Aff. Blog, Mar. 3, 2016, http://healthaffairs.org/blog/2016/03/03/new-health-care-symposium-states-critical-role-overseeing-vertical-health-care-integration/, archived at https://perma.cc/XH2A-2BFY.
[25] Ateev Mehrotra et al., Use Patterns of a State Health Care Price Transparency Web Site: What Do Patients Shop For?, 51 Inquiry 1, 3 (2014).
[26] Kenneth Artz, Study: Price Transparency Benefits Consumers, Heartland Inst., Jan. 16, 2015, http://news.heartland.org/newspaper-article/2015/01/16/study-price-transparency-benefits-consumers, archived at https://perma.cc/JBN3-655J.
[27] Capretta & Dayaratna, supra note 4, at 5.
[28] Sherman Folland et al., The Economics of Health and Health Care 188–93 (2001).
[29] Bradford Hesse, The Patient, the Physician, and Dr. Google, 14 Virtual Mentor 398, 398–402 (2012).
[30] Anna Sinaiko & Meredith Rosenthal, Examining a Health Care Price Transparency Tool: Who Uses It, and How They Shop for Care, 35 Health Affs. 662, 669 (2016) (finding that consumers who used Aetna's price transparency tool, "over half of these searchers did not end up receiving the service," thus suggesting that "[f]or some of these consumers, knowledge of the price of the service may contribute to a decision not to receive it"); Paul Fronstin & M. Christopher Roebuck, The Impact of an HSA-Eligible Health Plan on Health Care Services Use and Spending by Worker Income, Employee Benefit Research Institute: Issue Brief #425, 12 (2016), www.ebri.org/pdf/briefspdf/

the ACA prohibition on co-pays for high-value preventive services[31] lifts a significant barrier for consumers.[32]

Second, consumers cannot always choose when, where, and what health care services to receive.[33] The health care system includes gatekeepers; unlike purchasing a car or a television, consumers' health care choices may not be limited by financial considerations alone but also by what a physician will prescribe and what an insurer allows on its formulary. Many health care services are not affected by consumer "shopping": only about forty percent of spending on health care services and products are thought to be subject to shopping, as "[p]atients can reasonably shop only for care that is for nonemergencies and would be motivated to do so only if they stood to gain."[34]

Third, consumers may be in a position of distress, thus weakening their bargaining power, when seeking health care services.[35] Whereas one parent may feel confident in waiting to seek medical attention for his son,[36] many parents may not feel so inclined or self-assured. We do not choose to be sick or in an accident, yet if we do find ourselves or a loved one in such a situation, it can understandably be difficult to make a rational decision based on cost.[37] The choice to need health care services may not be ours to make.

Generally, consumers do not seek to purchase health care like they do a television or a car. That's why the ACA mandates insurance coverage[38] and encourages high-value preventive services[39] in hopes of encouraging consumers to actually seek out these services.[40] Thus, health care seems more like an investment rather than consumption:

EBRI_IB_425.Aug16.HSAs.pdf, archived at https://perma.cc/4DZE-DUQ6 ("The HSA-eligible health plan was associated with a reduction in various preventive services by worker income.").

[31] 42 U.S.C. § 300gg–13 (2010).
[32] Fronstin & Roebuck, supra note 30, at 12, 14, 16 (finding that generally utilization of preventive services decreased with income, and even some preventive services decreased across all income).
[33] Sinaiko & Rosenthal, supra note 30, at 663.
[34] Austin Frakt, Price Transparency is Nice. Just Don't Expect it to Cut Health Costs, N.Y. Times, Dec. 20, 2016, at A3.
[35] Folland et al., supra note 28, at 12–13; Sinaiko & Rosenthal, supra note 30, at 663 ("In many cases, health care needs are acute, and patients do not have the time or ... even the ability to shop for and choose a provider."); Mark Hall & Carl Schneider, Patients as Consumers: Courts, Contracts, and the New Medical Marketplace, Mich. L. Rev. 643, 650–53 (2008).
[36] Martinez, supra note 2.
[37] Hall & Schneider, supra note 35, at 650–51.
[38] 42 U.S.C. § 18091 (2010).
[39] 42 USC 300gg-13 (2010).
[40] Robert Berenson, The AHCA Gets It Wrong: Health Care is Different, Health Affs. Blog, Mar. 22, 2017, http://healthaffairs.org/blog/2017/03/22/the-ahca-gets-it-wrong-health-care-is-different/, archived at https://perma.cc/F9K4-6TP4] ("Empirically it turns out consumers overall display mediocre purchasing competence for preventive services and care for chronic conditions. Indeed, based on the broad experience that consumers facing high deductibles often choose not to receive effective, preventive services, high-deductible plans that link to health savings accounts are allowed under IRS rules to cover preventive services, such as vaccinations and mammograms, without cost-sharing to increase uptake.").

Health care is typically classified as a form of consumption. But if my relative spent some of his money with a back-pain specialist, who could teach him exercises that would prolong his working life by another decade, shouldn't that be considered an investment? He would be choosing to forego paying for something that he actually wants today so that he can make more money in the future.[41]

Moreover, consumers are not the ones driving pricing decisions – in most cases, it is the insurers and payers negotiating with providers, pharmaceuticals, and other stakeholders. Most Americans are covered by employer-sponsored insurance, Medicare, or Medicaid, meaning payers already have negotiated prices for health care services and products.[42] Consequently, consumers' "shopping" for health care goods and services may have little effect on the costs they pay for care.[43] Insurers can use the number of lives they cover in order to drive down providers' charges or pharmaceutical companies' prices,[44] but individuals often do not have a say in those decisions and their prices are set.[45] For some proponents of "consumer-driven health care," this point is the crux of the problem because consumers are spending other people's money.[46] However, for many consumers in the employer-based insurance system, they are sacrificing wages in exchange for benefits so such an argument about "skin in the

---

[41] Adam Davidson, What the GOP Doesn't Get About Who Pays for Health Care, New Yorker, Mar. 23, 2017, www.newyorker.com/business/adam-davidson/what-the-g-o-p-doesnt-get-about-who-pays-for-health-care.

[42] Rich Daly, Expert Warns of Flawed Price Transparency Effort, Modern Healthcare, June 17, 2013, www.modernhealthcare.com/article/20130617/NEWS/306179929, archived at https://perma.cc/7DVG-7T5R.

[43] Amanda Frost et al., Health Care Consumerism: Can the Tail Wag The Dog?, Health Affs. Blog, Mar. 2, 2016, http://healthaffairs.org/blog/2016/03/02/health-care-consumerism-can-the-tail-wag-the-dog-2/, archived at https://perma.cc/GU7T-YNDV ("Less than 7 percent of our health care spending is actually paid by consumers on shoppable services. That means that for the vast majority of health care spending, consumer-targeted activities – such as providing incentives or information in an effort to direct their spending – are unlikely to improve the value we get for our health care dollars."); see also Sinaiko & Rosenthal, supra note 33, at 668 (discussing what is a "shoppable" service).

[44] Id. ("While knowledge about price and quality is important, and is information that consumers are entitled to, we should be realistic about the ability of this information in the hands of consumers to drive changes in the market.").

[45] Jeffrey Young & Chris Kirkham, Hospital Prices No Longer Secret As New Data Reveals Bewildering System, Staggering Cost Differences, Huffington Post, May 8, 2013, www.huffingtonpost.com/2013/05/08/hospital-prices-cost-differences_n_3232678.html, archived at https://perma.cc/7QS4-5N8Q (noting that higher costs fall on the uninsured because insurance can drive down costs through negotiation); Steven Brill, Bitter Pill: Why Medical Bills Are Killing Us, Time, Apr. 4, 2013, http://time.com/198/bitter-pill-why-medical-bills-are-killing-us/ (noting "the large portion of hospital patients who have [public or] private health insurance ... get discounts off the listed chargemaster figures").

[46] Ateev Mehrotra et al., Americans Support Price Shopping For Health Care But Few Actually Seek Out Price Information, 36 Health Affs. 1392, 1392 (2017); Frakt, supra note 34, at A3 ("If patients' out-of-pocket costs are the same at both a high-cost and low-cost doctor, what's to prompt them to select the cheaper one? Insurance is paying for the difference anyway.").

game" fails to recognize this trade-off.[47] Insurers and payers are in a better position to use transparent information to determine rational prices for health care goods and services.[48]

Finally, it is worth noting that transparency tools are not widely used even when available: although insurance plans provide pricing information to enrollees,[49] very few of their enrollees utilize these tools.[50] For example, in a study of the Truven Treatment Cost Calculator,[51] only one in five employees used the calculator over two years, and the calculator did not reduce outpatient spending, even among patients with higher deductibles or who faced higher health care costs because of illness.[52] Consumers may find tools too complex and overwhelming[53] or mistakenly believe that higher costs correspond with better and higher-quality services.[54] Research has found consumers are more engaged when given a broader range of

---

[47] Young & Kirkham, supra note 45 ("The biggest irony of the U.S. health care system is that only the uninsured – often people who don't have a lot of money – are the only ones the hospital expects to pay these incredibly inflated list prices!").

[48] Cf. Sinaiko & Rosenthal, supra note 30, at 663 (noting that health plans have "access to historical claims data that can be analyzed for patterns of service use, real-time information on a consumer's health plan benefits and out-of-pocket spending to date, and proprietary information on negotiated provider rates").

[49] Health Care Incentives Improvement Inst., Report Card on State Price Transparency Laws (July 26, 2016), www.hci3.org/wp-content/uploads/2016/07/reportcard2016.pdf, archived at https://perma.cc/P854-73QD.

[50] Frakt, supra note 34, at A3 ("Health plans report that use of their price transparency tools is limited, with many enrollees unaware they exist.... only 2 percent of them look at it.").

[51] Truven Health Analytics, Truven Treatment Cost Calculator, https://truvenhealth.com/solutions/treatment-cost-calculator, archived at https://perma.cc/4HJ8-7FRH.

[52] Sunita Desai et al., Association Between Availability of a Price Transparency Tool and Outpatient Spending, 315 JAMA 1875, 1879–80 (2016); see also Christopher Whaley et al., Association Between Availability of Health Service Prices and Payments for These Services, 312 JAMA 1670, 1674–75 (2014) (finding using the price transparency tool Castlight Health did result in lower payments for lab tests, advanced imaging, and office visits but did not report on overall outpatient spending).

[53] Austin Frakt & Aaron Carroll, People Are Bad at Choosing Health Plans, Part 3, AcademyHealth: Blog, Oct. 2, 2015, www.academyhealth.org/blog/2015-10/people-are-bad-choosing-health-plans-part-3, archived at https://perma.cc/UA5R-ZLLS ("A mountain of research documents that consumers can be overwhelmed by a large number of choices, causing them to make decision errors or stick with the status quo; that market opacity can benefit firms, which exploit consumers' decision errors to increase prices and profits; and that provision of more salient and relevant comparison information can improve decisions.")

[54] Ateev Mehrotra et al., Consumers' and Providers' Responses to Public Cost Reports, and How to Raise the Likelihood of Achieving Desired Results, 31 Health Affs. 843, 843 (2012); see also S. Rep. No. 113-306, at 15–16 (2014) (discussing research on why some consumers choose brand-name drugs over generics because of "[a]ssociating the word 'generic' with something that is diminished in worth or value, or 'not as good' as brand-name drugs"). But see Kathryn Phillips et al., Most Americans Do Not Believe That There Is an Association Between Health Care Prices and Quality of Care, 35 Health Affs. 647, 649–51 (2016) (finding in a national survey that most consumers do not associate price with quality but acknowledging that a "substantial minority of respondents either believed there was an association ... or said they did not know if there was such an association").

information such as value and quality of life,[55] something many transparency tools may lack.[56]

III. TRANSPARENCY AS A POLICY PROBLEM

Transparency also raises policy concerns as lawmakers consider what information should be transparent, who should have access to and be able to process the raw data, and how the information should be presented.[57] Transparency requires having information readily available about health care costs and service utilization.[58] To do so means gathering information about patients' and consumers' utilization of health care resources as well as providers' delivery of health care services.

Some consumers may have privacy concerns with the collection of health information.[59] Indeed, states are wrestling with privacy concerns, both in collecting the data as well as how the data is released, as they develop transparency tools and APCDs.[60] State APCDs generally do collect personally identifiable information in an encrypted format and information on facility type and service providers.[61]

For those seeking care that is still stigmatized or at odds with federal policy, a fully transparent system could be disruptive to patients' access to health care services, as

---

[55] Judith Hibbard et al., An Experiment Shows That A Well-Designed Report on Costs and Quality Can Help Consumers Choose High-Value Health Care, 31 Health Affs. 560, 565–66 (2012) (finding that "using dollar signs to indicate the cost of care ... was the least effective" way of communicating transparency as "consumers worry that a low-cost provider is a sub-standard provider"); see also Phillips et al., supra note 54, at 651–52 (noting that how information is framed and communicated may contribute to confusion around whether higher prices correspond to better quality).

[56] Aparna Higgins et al., Characterizing Health Plan Price Estimator Tools: Findings From a National Survey, 22 Am. J. Managed Care 126, 130 (2016) (finding that while "two-thirds of responding plans shared provider performance data with their members, [only] half of these plans integrating such data into their price estimator tool").

[57] Hudson, supra note 10, at 671–88.

[58] Azar et al., supra note 4, at 6.

[59] Mary Madden & Lee Rainie, Americans' Attitudes About Privacy, Security and Surveillance, Pew Res. Ctr. (2015), www.pewinternet.org/2015/05/20/americans-attitudes-about-privacy-security-and-surveillance/, archived at https://perma.cc/2N2Q-W7DM (finding that 93 percent of adults want to be able to control who is collecting info and 90 percent want to be able to control what info is collected); see also Susannah Fox, The social life of health information, Pew Res. Ctr. (2014), www.pewresearch.org/fact-tank/2014/01/15/the-social-life-of-health-information/, archived at https://perma.cc/HB5A-A85A (finding "that patients and caregivers have critical health information – about themselves, about each other, about treatments – and they want to share what they know to help other people").

[60] Alyssa Harrington, Releasing APCD Data: How States Balance Privacy and Utility, All-Payer Claims Database Council (2017), www.apcdcouncil.org/publication/releasing-apcd-data-how-states-balance-privacy-and-utility.

[61] Jo Porter et al., The Basics of All-Payer Claims Databases, Robert Wood Johnson Found. (2014), http://www.rwjf.org/en/library/research/2014/01/the-basics-of-all-payer-claims--databases--a-primer-for-states.html.

patients and providers both fear potential repercussions.[62] For example, a growing number of antiabortion laws will require greater data collection on the procedure to effectuate further restrictions on abortion providers and women seeking abortions.[63] At the same time, some states are pursuing policies to make it more difficult for consumers to have accurate information about reproductive health decisions.[64] The lack of transparency here may impede women's ability to make decisions around abortion and their ability to seek out other prenatal health care services. Similarly, collecting information that may identify patients' immigration status can be a barrier to undocumented immigrants seeking health care services.[65] Despite health care facilities being seen as "sensitive locations," threats of deportation have caused individuals to forego care for fear of revealing their immigration status.[66] Last, employers and other payers may want to know if individuals are making "unhealthy" or costly decisions that result in higher costs. Critics of "workplace wellness" programs worry about the intrusion into employees' lives and the imposition of penalties on employees who do not have the capacity or the ability to participate in such programs.[67]

IV. TRANSPARENCY AS AN ETHICAL PROBLEM

Third, how we frame transparency can alter how we view insurance. Insurance relies on pooling risk across a large number of insureds in the manner of a econtract[68] but consumerism relies on individualism. What are we expecting of consumers by making more information transparent: to empower patients to make more informed decisions or to shift costs, risk, and accountability to each individual consumer?

If we believe insurance is intended to pool risk across a community, then providing transparency could make consumers more aware of how their actions can have

---

[62] See, e.g., Ike Swetlitz, Immigrants, Fearing Trump's Deportation Policies, Avoid Doctor Visits, PBS Newshour, Feb. 25, 2017, www.pbs.org/newshour/rundown/immigrants-trump-deportation-doctor/, archived at https://perma.cc/S5V9-HJV5.

[63] Brandice Canes-Wrone & Michael C. Dorf, Measuring the Chilling Effect, 90 N.Y.U. L. Rev. 1095, 1113–14 (2015); Electronic Frontier Found., Abortion Reporting (last visited Nov. 29, 2017), www.eff.org/issues/abortion-reporting, archived at https://perma.cc/LEY3-RUL7 ("While the reporting form does not include the patient's name, the demographic data is so extensive that it would not take great skill to identify the individual, particularly in a small town. Along with the facility where the procedure was performed and the name of the physician, all forms ask for the patient's age, race, ethnicity, marital status, and number of previous live births.").

[64] See, e.g., Hallie Golden, Utah's governor signs abortion-halting legislation, Associated Press, Mar. 26, 2017, https://apnews.com/ca7282c7304f4acb88of45fc7411a1be, archived at https://perma.cc/D77K-V7ZE.

[65] Karen Hacker et al., Barriers to Health Care for Undocumented Immigrants: A Literature Review, 2015 Risk Mgmt. and Healthcare Pol'y 175, 178 (2015).

[66] Swetlitz, supra note 62.

[67] Lena Sun, Employees Who Decline Genetic Testing Could Face Penalties Under Proposed Bill, Wash. Post, Mar. 11, 2017, http://wapo.st/2mULXzf, archived at https://perma.cc/RP3J-52W3.

[68] David Craig, Health Care as a Social Good, 176–80 (2014).

consequences for the whole community.[69] Transparency could be a useful tool if each individual uses such knowledge to make health care decisions that lead to lower costs, such as choosing a generic over a brand-name drug, but so could other decisions that do not necessarily rely on cost transparency, such as exercising and eating nutritious foods.[70] Designing benefits to reward healthier decisions or influence consumers' behavior could be more effective than transparency.[71]

Further, by treating health care like any other good – a car, a television, a piece of clothing – we lose the sense that health care is something special, ostensibly built on trust between patients and their health care providers.[72] One study found that consumers did not want to use performance measures to help them shop for providers, but rather want the measures to help their trusted providers "to do better."[73] Health policy is built on ensuring trust: states license health care professionals and facilities, and the FDA reviews the safety of drugs, medical devices, and other products.[74] In other words, our health care system is built on a level of trust that does not exist in other commercial sectors because we do not want a "buyer beware" attitude around health care.[75] Unlike buying other consumer goods, utilizing health care services and products is an "investment" in ourselves, our bodies, and our health.

Much of the rhetoric in support of transparency leans toward moving the risk, or shifting the burden – and the cost – of health care choices, from the risk pool and onto the individual.[76] The drive toward consumer-driven health care is as much about shifting risk and costs as it is about making individuals more aware of their decisions. Those with the best information – and sometimes the best luck – will likely do better in a health care system driven by consumerism.[77] Thus, it is critical to recognize that transparency is fundamental to the conservative view of health

---

[69] Id. at 163.
[70] Id. at 167–68.
[71] Daly, supra note 42 (noting testimony for Paul Ginsburg suggesting that "[e]ncouraging benefit designs that reward publicly and privately insured people who seek care from lower cost, higher quality providers would spur much greater savings").
[72] Paul Krugman, Patients Are Not Consumers, N.Y. Times, Apr. 22, 2011, at A23. But see Gallup, Confidence in Institutions (June 1–5, 2016), www.gallup.com/poll/1597/confidence-institutions.aspx (finding trust in the medical system at 39 percent – 17 percent believing a great deal, 22 percent believing quite a lot – which is more than the President (36 percent) or the Supreme Court (36 percent) but less than religion (41 percent)) (accessed June 29, 2017).
[73] Berenson, supra note 40 (referring to focus group studies by the Foundation for Accountability).
[74] Krugman, supra note 72.
[75] Berenson, supra note 40.
[76] Azar et al., supra note 4, at 8 ("Consumer-driven health care ... begins to encourage more cost- and value-sensitive decision-making in decentralized, individual-level decisions....").
[77] Craig, supra note 68, at 166 ("Given the cost-insensitive nature of health care for the poor, the chronically ill and the elderly, it is a mistake to project the benefits of consumer-directed health plans on the basis of people who are well positioned by decent health, health coverage, and savings to learn prudence in their discretionary health care decisions.").

care[78] and incorporated into many of the proposals that Congress considered to replace the ACA with more consumer-driven health care products.[79]

V. CONCLUSION

Perhaps these arguments suggest a dark, more paternalistic worldview where patients are incapable of understanding health information and physicians' decisions are sacrosanct, but what I really want to highlight is this: what are we actually trying to do by providing more transparency regarding health and health care? Transparent information in and of itself is not enough to drive the consumer engagement for which we are striving. Transparency should assist, not further burden, consumers in making their health care decisions. We should use transparency tools in a way that promotes shared decision making between both parties.

---

[78] Berenson, supra note 40 (arguing "the AHCA would have insurers say, 'You are on your own with your high deductible. Good luck with that.'").

[79] H.R. 1628, 115th Cong. § 215–217 (2017) (expanding the use of health savings accounts); S.A. 667 to H.R. 1628, 115th Cong. § 104 (2017) (increasing maximum contribution allowable for health savings accounts); see also Mehrotra et al., supra note 46, at 1399.

PART II

Transparency and Informed Consent

Introduction to Part II

Luke Gelinas

What is the relationship between "transparency" and "informed consent?" On its face, transparency has to do with making certain information available or accessible. It is thus natural to tie transparency to a disclosure requirement in the informed consent process, which requires the person seeking consent to use or disclose pertinent information to the person from whom consent is sought.[1] The disclosure requirement is part of what puts the "informed" in "informed consent." It ensures that the person from whom consent is sought has the opportunity to understand relevant and material information and precludes deception as a means of securing consent – both of which are needed in order for consent to do its moral and legal work of respecting personal rights.

In the context of informed consent, then, questions about transparency are most easily understood as questions about what is needed for those seeking consent to satisfy their disclosure obligations. How much information must be disclosed – what level of transparency is needed – for disclosure obligations to be satisfied? And exactly what must we be transparent about – what is the content of the disclosure requirement?

In some ways, the answers to these questions are easy: the level of transparency needed is whatever will give the person from whom consent is sought the opportunity to make a choice that coheres with his or her values and preferences. This follows from the nature of informed consent, the primary purpose of which is to enable individuals to retain control over their own personal space and affairs and decide for themselves what does, and what does not, align with their own interests and self-conception as autonomous agents. However, on closer analysis, analyzing the disclosure aspect of informed consent in terms of transparency, and gaining clarity on the appropriate level of transparency in consent and the medical arena generally, is a complex and fraught undertaking, as the chapters that follow in this volume nicely illustrate, each in its own way.

---

[1] Howard Brody, Transparency: Informed Consent in Primary Care. 19 Hastings Ctr. Rep. 5 (1989).

At the conceptual level, Craig J. Konnoth problematizes the application of "transparency" to discussions of informed consent, arguing that transparency is better suited to describe the type of informational flow characteristic of commercial transactions than what occurs, or should occur, between caregivers and patients in informed consent. He notes that "transparency" connotes a type of information disclosure that assumes stable and fully formed preferences in the person receiving the information. In addition, Konnoth points out that this model of transparency assumes a conception of autonomy that sees patients as fully independent and computationally adept agents, able to process and act on information without help from another, in ways that realize their preferences. By contrast, he argues, the disclosure of information during informed consent should not assume fixed and stable preferences in patients, but rather that patients may need help developing their preferences and applying them to the decision at hand. Information disclosure during informed consent is, or should be, crafted to enable – even provoke – dialogue about patients' preferences and what course of action they might support.

One interesting question that flows out of Konnoth's reflections is how medical caregivers should understand and operationalize the dialogical model of disclosure he endorses. Indeed, there are both requirements around, and limits on, the types and scope of patient preferences that caregivers should assume to be in play when disclosing information during informed consent. As Elizabeth Sepper's and Richard S. Saver's chapters cogently illustrate, a complex mix of normative and practical considerations impact the degree to which transparency and disclosure in informed consent should be personalized. On the one hand, there is information that caregivers have positive, and indeed at times *categorical*, ethical and legal obligations to disclose – including, as Sepper points out, their intention not to provide certain end-of-life services that conflict with their religious beliefs (or the religious mission of their institution). Such imperatives set minimum expectations on the content of disclosure during informed consent. Additionally, these minimum expectations, in the eyes of the law at least, often apply regardless of a particular patient's preferences. They can instead be seen as transparency requirements grounded in the procedural demands of justice and perhaps, more specifically, equality of opportunity – in this case, the patient's opportunity to seek care that betters the patient's own values – which transcend the dynamics of particular physician-patient relationships.

There are also appropriate limits to what caregivers should disclose, though discerning those limits is not always straightforward. For starters, caregivers do not have an obligation to disclose information that would enable a patient to act on preferences unrelated to their health. For example, medical caregivers have no duty to disclose their own sexual orientation to patients as part of informed consent, even if the caregiver knows this would cause the patient to (say) sever the physician-patient relationship. Thus, even if the information is material to the patient, it does not follow that it should be disclosed. On the other hand, caregivers may have an obligation to disclose, for example, conflicts of interest to the patient, since such conflicts have the potential to influence physician decision making and, ultimately, care of the patient. That said, as Saver suggests in his discussion of the Sunshine Act, even when information may have a bearing on health care providers' decision making or patient care, as with physician conflicts of interest, it may not always be best to disclose it. Indeed, it may be that this information *should not* be disclosed, all things considered. Perhaps the most obvious and strongest reason for this is the risk of information overload. Like everyone else, patients are only capable of processing so much information. When that limit is reached, providing more information – even if potentially relevant – will not support, but rather hinder, patient understanding. This forces caregivers to discern the capacities of patients, as well as which information will be most relevant to them. Here, Konnoth's point about attention to context and specific patient preferences shines, as these things will vary between individuals, demanding caregiver sensitivity to the patient before them.

Relatedly, as both Sepper and Saver point out, the context and manner in which information is disclosed makes a difference as to how patients are likely to process and use the information in decision making. On this point, it is worth recalling findings from behavioral economics and cognitive psychology concerning the existence of framing effects, which is the tendency for individuals to respond differently to equivalent information depending on how it is presented to them.[2] The demonstrated strength and robustness of framing effects, particularly when it comes to conveying information about risk and benefit, force deeper questions, not only about how to present information during informed consent, but about the very meaning and possibility of "transparency."[3] If, as the literature on framing effects suggests, there is no neutral way to present particular pieces of information, is genuine transparency even possible? Or are our best attempts at transparency always a disguised, perhaps unwitting, form of persuasion?

In the context of informed consent, the question is pressing, since it is generally acknowledged that certain forms of influence – including those that shade into coercion, undue influence, and manipulation – have the ability to invalidate consent. Intentional deployment of such tactics in the context of consent would of course be wrong. However, as Saver reminds us, certain types of disclosures can have *un*intended undesirable effects. The possibility that caregivers may be unintentionally influencing their patients via the manner in which they present key information, desires for transparency notwithstanding, may very well fall into this category.[4]

The relationship between transparency and informed consent, then, is far from platitudinous, but complex. While it is reasonable to locate the nub of their interaction in the disclosure requirement for valid consent, further elucidating that

---

[2] Irwin P. Levin, Sandra L. Schneider & Gary J. Gaeth, All Frames Are Not Created Equal: A Typology and Critical Analysis of Framing Effects, 76 Org. Behav. & Hum. Decision Processes 149 (1998).
[3] Barbara J. McNeil, Stephen G. Pauker, Harold C. Sox & Amos Tversky, On the Elicitation of Preferences for Alternative Treatments, 306 New Eng. J. Med. 1259 (1982).
[4] Luke Gelinas, Frames, Choice-Reversal, and Consent, 18 Ethical Theory & Moral Prac. 1049 (2015).

connection requires several things. It requires, first, close attention to the *content* of appropriate transparency: What at a minimum should be disclosed in informed consent? Conversely, what information may not, and should not, be relayed? It also requires close attention to the *manner* of presentation: How should information be disclosed, in order for the ideal of transparency, rather than persuasion, to be realized? The chapters that follow highlight the salience of these questions and make important contributions to addressing them.

5

Transparency versus Informed Consent

The Patient/Consumer Paradigms

Craig J. Konnoth

Before transparency became the buzzword in bioethics and health policy that it is today, it was somewhat parasitic on another familiar concept: that of informed consent. In 1989, Howard Brody offered what has come to be known as the "transparency model" of informed consent.[1] In his elaboration of the model, Brody argued that the key to informed consent was making the treatment process legible to the patient. Transparency remained part of the informed consent process in both academic and policy circles. A decade after Brody, Bill Sage observed that "disclosure obligations have been imposed by courts" in part to help vindicate "informed consent by physicians."[2] The seminal 2001 report from the Institute of Medicine, "Crossing the Quality Chasm: A New Health System for the 21st Century" similarly observed, "Transparency is necessary [to] make available to patients and their families information that enables them to make informed decisions when selecting a health plan, hospital, or clinical practice, or when choosing among alternative treatments."[3]

This chapter seeks to make three predominantly descriptive-evaluative (rather than prescriptive) points. The first claim, which I engage with in the most detail, is that informed consent and transparency – at least as the term is widely used today – are tethered to different narrative and ethical paradigms. Informed consent implicates the traditional model of the care-recipient as patient. Transparency implicates a newer model of the care-recipient as consumer. These narratives correspond to different ethical frameworks and to different contexts. The former better corresponds to a vision of autonomy where the individual is rendered autonomous through the relationship she builds with others. Transparency, by contrast, is more consonant with an absolutist, Kantian sense of autonomy, which takes the individual as

---

[1] Howard Brody, Transparency: Informed Consent in Primary Care, 19 Hastings Ctr. Rep. 5 (1989). See Heather Gert, Avoiding Surprises: A Model for Informing Patients, 32 Hastings Ctr. Rep. 23 (2002).
[2] William Sage, Regulating Through Information: Disclosure Laws And American Healthcare, 99 Colum. L. Rev. 1701 (1999).
[3] Inst. of Med., Crossing the Quality Chasm: A New Health System for the 21st Century (2001).

a developed decision maker that merely needs data in order to compute the correct outcome.

Second, the paradigms separate the contexts that constitute the health care system. Health care involves various contexts and social roles. These include traditional clinical contexts in which patients interact with their doctors. But they also include interactions that do not traditionally fall within this category such as shopping for elective procedures, medical supplements, or insurance. Informed consent can be understood as a ritual that tells the actors within the health system which social role they are occupying. Maintaining some degree of separation between our understanding of the practices helps maintain sickness and medical care as contextually distinct areas of human interaction. This separation serves important social functions by determining, for example, when individuals are entitled to care and social support, and when they are not.

Finally, the discourse someone deploys – transparency or informed consent – demonstrates their own normative priors as to whether a particular activity should be considered consumerist or medical in nature. My own take is that transparency is the appropriate framework, for example, when an individual is choosing a primary care doctor for a routine checkup. Informed consent is appropriate when the patient is choosing a treatment plan. But those who advocate transparency versus informed consent with respect to certain activities are essentially arguing about what paradigm is appropriate and where the boundary between medicine and nonmedicine should be drawn.

I. PATIENTS AND CONSUMERS

A. *The Roles of Patient and Consumer*

Informed consent first involves passing on certain information; second, it involves the act of consenting. For some, transparency is merely a part of informed consent. Brody, for example, treats transparency as involving passing information on to the patient. "[F]irst, [the doctor] has to share her thinking with the patient; secondly, she has to encourage and answer questions; and third, she has to discover how participatory he wishes to be and facilitate that level of participation."[4] But suggesting that transparency and informed consent are always linked is misleading. The word "transparency" appears not once in Ruth Faden and Tom Beauchamp's 1986 magnum opus on informed consent. Similarly, doctor or hospital report cards are usually promoted as tools for transparency, without any reference to informed consent.[5]

Transparency's life independent of informed consent came into being with increased consumerization of health care discourse. Although consumer regulation

---

[4] Brody, supra note 5.
[5] Ruth Faden & Tom Beauchamp, A History and Theory of Informed Consent (1986).

has always played a role in health care to some degree,[6] a range of forces in the 1980s sped the process. Rising health care costs and a loss of faith in government, particularly with respect to controlling health care costs, made marketplace solutions attractive.[7] Those using health care became rebranded as consumers, who would shop for the best deal.

With the vision of consumers who shop on the market for best services at the lowest price, came that of transparency. One very rough assessment using the PubMed database shows that relative to "informed consent," the terms "transparency" (used in conjunction with health care, health, or medicine) and "consumer" increased dramatically since 1988 (the first year the use reached double digits in the database). The count has been adjusted to enable comparison.[8] Although not shown below, the use of "transparency" with "quality" increased at about the same rate. Its use with "price" or "pricing" increased at a faster rate than other terms.

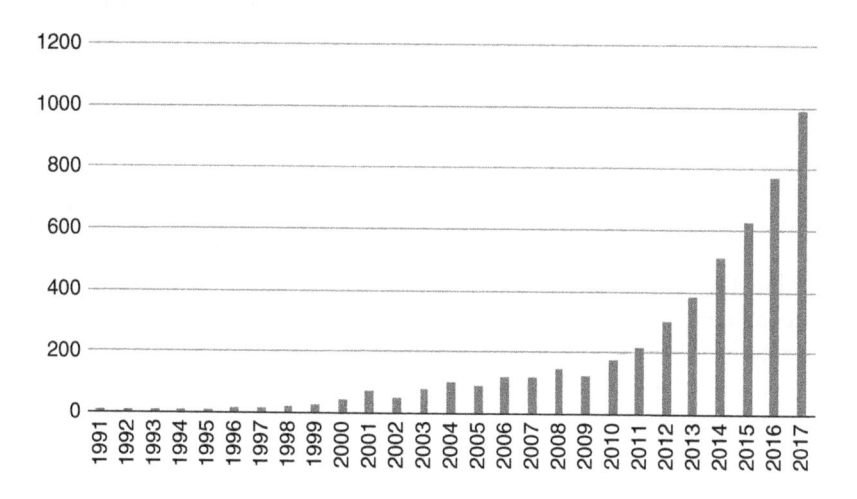

This push for increased transparency in health care has corresponded with a similar push in other areas with a simultaneous decrease in reliance on government regulation.[9] As long as the consumer has information, she can navigate the market herself.

The consumerization narrative has led to debate. As Paul Krugman asks, "How did it become normal, or for that matter even acceptable, to refer to medical patients as 'consumers'?"[10] Many critics note that the consumer narrative does not fit well

[6] Sage, supra note 6, at footnote 34.
[7] Id.
[8] For example, "informed consent" today is used at approximately four times the rate of "transparency" in conjunction with health, health care, and medicine in absolute terms. Graphing its usage in absolute terms would obscure the increase in the usage of "transparency." I accordingly scale the numbers to the frequency with which the term "transparency" is used: if they each appeared one hundred times in PubMed today, the graph shows the rate at which their use reached that number over time.
[9] Sage, supra note 6.
[10] Krugman, Patients are Not Consumers, N.Y. Times, Apr. 21, 2011.

with situations such as those involving emergency care.[11] Some fear that it would lead to medicine following "the model of the used car sale," rather than that of a public good.[12] Doctors might lose their sense of fiduciary and broader societal obligation, becoming a shill for their consumer patient.[13]

Yet, the relationship between doctor and patient has always been fraught. In 1951, Talcott Parsons identified the sharply delimited roles doctors and patients occupy. The patient is characterized by "helplessness and need of help, technical incompetence, and emotional involvement."[14] Implicit in this relationship is a hierarchy, where the patient must place herself in the hands of a doctor in order to get better. This hierarchy was reinforced by paternalistic behavior on the part of the physician – concealment of information for the patient's own good, even if the patient is subjected to treatment.[15]

In theory, informed consent was introduced as one mechanism among others that sought to equalize the power relationship.[16] Informing the patient of her options gave the patient rather than the physician the final choice. Patients are now "grown up."[17]

Or so the story goes. Reality appears to be quite different. Study upon study has shown that patients will defer to their doctors in most situations.[18] "[B]oth parties to the consultation constitute and enact asymmetry throughout their interaction [to] handl[e] the interactional difficulties of the doctor-patient encounter."[19] A recent study, for example, shows that a majority of patients prefer to use the title of "doctor" even while they are addressed by their first name to maintain the hierarchy throughout the interaction.[20]

The studies attribute this to "an asymmetry of topic, in that it is the patient's condition, rather than the doctor's, that is under review [and] a related asymmetry of task, in that the doctor's work of diagnosis or management necessarily involves

[11] Beth Kutscher, Consumers Demand Price Transparency, but at What Cost?, Modern Healthcare, June 23, 2015.
[12] Chris Robertson, Should Patient Responsibility for Costs Change the Doctor–Patient Relationship?, 50 Wake Forest L. Rev. 363, 368 (2015).
[13] Leana Wen, Should You Be a "Patient" or "Healthcare Consumer"?, Psychol. Today, May 9, 2013.
[14] Talcott Parsons, The Social System 298 (1951).
[15] Eva Kittay, The Liberal Autonomous Subject and the Question of Health Inequalities, in Understanding Health Inequalities and Justice 121 (Buchbinder et al eds., 2016) (describing "consultations focused on physicians and their agendas, to the apparent exclusion of patient concerns"). For a review of recent research, see Alison Pilnick & Robert Dingwall, On the Remarkable Persistence of Asymmetry in Doctor/Patient Interaction: A Critical Review, 72 Soc. Sci. & Med. 1374, 1375 (2011).
[16] Brody, supra note 5.
[17] Angela Coulter, Patients Have Grown Up – and There's No Going Back, 319 BMJ 719 (1999).
[18] For a recent example, see Doherty et al., The Consent Process: Enabling or Disabling Patients' Active Participation?, 21 Health 205 (2017).
[19] Pilnick & Dingwall, supra note 19, at 1376.
[20] Dror Limon et al., Perspectives of Patients, Caregivers, and the Medical Staff on Greeting in Oncology Practice: A Prospective Survey, J. Oncology Prac. (2015); see also Dror Limon & Salomon M. Stemmer, In Response to "The Title "Doctor" is an Anachronism that Disrespects Patients," 351 BMJ h6240 (2015).

questioning, investigating and decision making, in order to establish the possible courses of action." As a result, patients defer because they share a goal with the physician: "accurate diagnosis, and successful or appropriate treatment" and also because some deference is "the most efficient strategy for achieving this," given the doctor's expertise.[21] These reasons are remarkably similar to those Parsons offered over a half-century ago. The studies show that an individual undergoing medical care is often not fully capable of making the best medical decisions and is dependent on those around her. Traditional informed consent paradigms that assume a competent and autonomous medical decision maker therefore seem inapposite.

B. Informed Consent and Transparency in Operation

Proponents of traditional approaches to informed consent see themselves as presenting competent patients with information and letting them choose, thus respecting their autonomy and dignity and precluding coercion.[22] Although I cannot detail the debate here, that perception has come under attack.[23] Many ethicists argue that the process effectively results in "shared decision-making" between the doctor and patient.[24] Thus, a recent step-by-step guide for doctors noted that "[i]f all responsibility for decision making is transferred to patients they may feel 'abandoned.' Some patients initially decline a decisional responsibility role, and are wary about participating."[25] The model envisages that the provider and the patient will come together and engage in a discussion. The provider gives answers and elicits further questions, and guides the patient through his decision-making process. Her influence over the process, however, renders it "shared." The literature and practice are replete with tools ranging from videos to interactive computer programs, cartoons, and the like, that address not just what information the patient gets, but how that information is structured.[26]

---

[21] Pilnick & Dingwall, supra note 19, at 1376.
[22] For a good overview, see Nir Eyal, Informed Consent, Stan. Encyclopedia of Phil. (Edward Zalta, ed. 2012).
[23] Id.
[24] See, e.g., Erica S. Spatz, Harlan M. Krumholz & Benjamin W. Moulton, The New Era of Informed Consent: Getting to a Reasonable-Patient Standard Through Shared Decision Making, 315 JAMA 2063 (2016); President's Comm'n for the Study of Ethical Probs. in Med. and Biomedical and Behav. Res., Making Health Care Decisions: A Report on the Ethical and Legal Implications of Informed Consent in the Patient-Practitioner Relationship (1982). Some articles distinguish between informed consent and shared decision making, see, e.g., Whitney et al., A Typology of Shared Decision Making, Informed Consent, and Simple Consent, 140 Annals Internal Med. 54 (2004), but in my view, which I cannot more elaborate more fully here, the distinction is chimerical.
[25] Glyn Elwyn et al., Shared Decision Making: A Model for Clinical Practice, 27 J. Gen. Internal Med. 1361 (2012).
[26] See, e.g., Whitney et al., supra note 28.

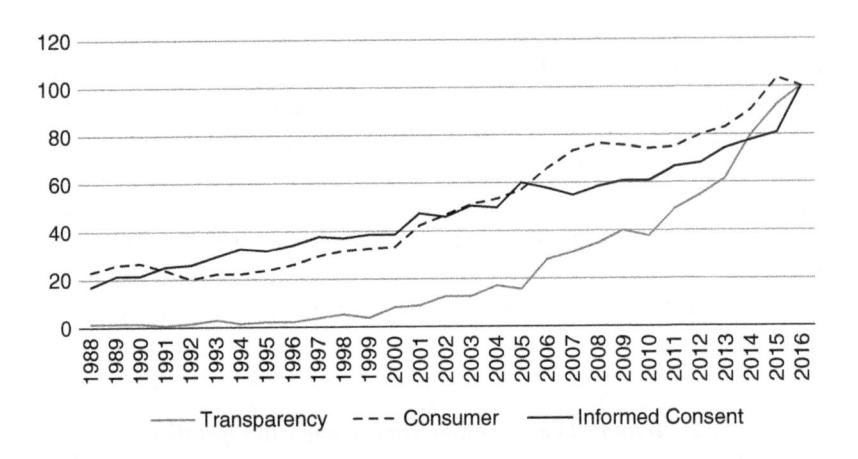

```
120
100
 80
 60
 40
 20
  0
     1988 1989 1990 1991 1992 1993 1994 1995 1996 1997 1998 1999 2000 2001 2002 2003 2004 2005 2006 2007 2008 2009 2010 2011 2012 2013 2014 2015 2016

——— Transparency     - - - Consumer     ——— Informed Consent
```

The interactive ideal indeed assumes a shift of some kind. The guide envisages "initial preferences" (such as they are) transforming into "informed preferences."[27] This tracks decision aids such as optiongrid.org that ask what a patient's initial preferences are. The doctor (or artificial intelligence tool) acts on the patient to produce an understanding that renders them informed. Thus, some ethicists argue (not without controversy) that the shared process can (and should) nudge patients toward correct decisions per the medical professional.[28] As one proponent explains: "the doctor can prevent the very formation of an unhealthy preference – never through breaching the requirements of proper disclosure, only through choosing its modes."[29]

Transparency models do not make a similar distinction between initial and subsequent preferences. Consumer preferences are taken as given – thus, depending on the situation, we assume, for example, that people prefer lower prices and higher quality. Transparency's goal is simply to help effectuate those preferences by providing the right data in a comprehensible format. Once you have the right kind of ranking, score, or report card, the consumer can pick accordingly.

Because of that, transparency does not need much information from the consumer in a particular interaction. To be sure, before a transparency tool is constructed, we might consider the kind of information people want to know (their preferences) and how they will engage with the data. We also consider what data best represent the concept we wish to convey – price, quality, and the like – and the best way to ensure it is accurate. But once we construct the tool, it is generally one size fits all.

With informed consent (at least in the clinical, as opposed to the research context), however, we engage in customized one-on-one interactions with patients

---

[27] Elwyn et al., supra note 29.
[28] See Shlomo Cohen, Nudging and Informed Consent, 13 Am. J. Bioethics 3 (2013) and the responses in the same volume.
[29] Id.

where we first elicit information from them. We seek their preferences, their cultural background, and that of their relatives.[30] Doctors then determine how to present information and shape their presentation in a way that is both respectful and helpful (concepts that are fleshed out below).

In practice, the distinctions might sometimes blur, but analytically, they are distinct. With transparency, the right measures or report card render various aspects of medical care and the system in which it is situated see-through, passively yielding their essence to a consumer able to exercise her discretion at will. With informed consent, a passive patient is first interrogated and then given the information that the doctor thinks is best. She then engages with the doctor. The rest of the process remains a black box, with the doctor as translator and mediator.

II. ETHICAL OBJECTIONS TO THE NARRATIVE DISTINCTION

Defenders of traditional models of informed consent (to whom I cannot fully do justice here) would argue that the vision that I present accepts a certain degree of manipulation and thereby fails to respect patient autonomy. However, informed consent inevitably aims for a certain degree of (appropriate or, some might say, inappropriate) manipulation by shaping perception and opinion.[31] Transparency avoids such manipulation. Each approach ultimately rests on two different visions of autonomy. I first describe the elements of autonomy and then explain how informed consent and transparency interact with those elements.

A. Key Terms

Autonomy can be conceptualized in two ways: descriptive and normative. I claim that either kind of autonomy has two sets of components: resource or capabilities, and status or respect. I first lay out these two key distinctions.

"Descriptive autonomy"[32] sees autonomy as "substantially an empirical question with the answer depending on criteria that can be satisfied to varying degree."[33] A person with more money or resources, or even social standing, is more autonomous than someone with less. Resources or constraints can be internal or external. An enslaved person suffers from external constraints; someone with an intellectual

---

[30] The Joint Comm'n, Div. of Health Care Improvement, Informed Consent: More than Getting a Signature, Quick Safety, Feb. 21, 2016.

[31] Cf. Thomas Ploug & Søren Holm, Doctors, Patients, and Nudging in the Clinical Context – Four Views on Nudging and Informed Consent, 15 Am. J. Bioethics 28 (2015) (arguing that doctors should aim for rational reasoning even if they do not achieve it). My response follows but also departs in important ways from the critiques of traditional understandings of informed consent in the literature. See, e.g., Cohen, supra note 32 and responses.

[32] Richard H. Fallon, Jr., Two Senses of Autonomy, 46 Stan. L. Rev. 875 (1994) uses this term. My analysis beyond this point differs significantly from Fallon's and better tracks Feinberg's analysis.

[33] Id.

abnormality might suffer internal constraints. Descriptive autonomy is necessarily relative – there is no binary distinction between an autonomous and nonautonomous individual.

The second approach is what I shall call normative.[34] A person is autonomous if the descriptive autonomy she possesses passes a certain threshold and has certain characteristics. In the medical context, most bioethicists agree that an individual must be conscious, uninfluenced by drugs or substances, and free of coercion (though all of those terms admit of degree). Others have their own pet lists. Joel Feinberg, for example, requires self-possession, authenticity, self-determination, and individuality, among other abilities. The key is identifying the normative standard that determines how much of these various characteristics the individual should possess to be considered autonomous.

On this account, both descriptive and normative autonomy are highly relational.[35] They depend heavily on the resources that society gives to or retains from the individuals, what is permitted and supported by the network of relationships in which the individual is enmeshed, and how the individual's own capabilities interact with her social environment. Someone who would have made an excellent computer programmer and made millions in modern-day America may not have done very well in medieval India if she lacked the skills relevant to and valued by that period. In other words, social environment is key to developing, and even constituting, the relevant capabilities and freedoms that determine the individual's autonomy.[36] This relational position rejects decontextualized Kantian visions of autonomy that dominate bioethics scholarship, and draws on a more richly textured literature.[37]

As Feinberg's list suggests, the enumeration of possible freedoms that could go into a definition of autonomy could be endless. A taxonomy seems appropriate. Nancy Fraser, among others, argues that social justice inheres in two separate interests.[38] First, there is status, a "dimension of recognition." This is a symbolic interest in appropriate social standing, which in turn is determined by "institutionalized meanings," cultural cues, roles, and by expressive behavior that mark status.[39]

The second is the resource approach, a "dimension of distribution, which involves the allocation of ... resources to social actors." Fraser appears to consider only "economic" resources, but I see no reason for such a limitation. Resource autonomy

[34] This is most closely analogous to what Joel Feinberg terms autonomy as "a condition." Joel Feinberg, Harm To Self 27–97 (1986).
[35] For useful statements on "relational autonomy," see Jennifer Nedelsky, Reconceiving Autonomy: Sources, Thoughts and Possibilities, 1 Yale J.L. & Feminism 7 (1989).
[36] For a similar point, see Konnoth, Health Information Equity, 165 U. Pa. L. Rev. 1317 (2017).
[37] See Ploug & Holm, supra note 35 (calling those visions traditional).
[38] See, e.g., Nancy Fraser, Rethinking Recognition, 3 New Left Rev. 107 (2000). I will elsewhere flesh out the relationship between justice, liberty, and autonomy.
[39] See Konnoth, An Expressive Theory of Privacy Intrusions, 102 Iowa L. Rev. 1533 (2017).

can include those of a mental and intellectual nature. An individual who is competent and in control of her faculties has a certain level of autonomy. But providing an individual with an education, with coaching, with money, with health care, will all enhance this autonomy by increasing her options and capabilities.

As Fraser observes, the dimensions are interlinked, and can cause "vicious circles of subordination." Being perceived as having low status may disqualify you, as far as society is concerned, as a worthy recipient of certain resources. At the same time, being denied certain capabilities helps mark individuals as having low status, as I have explained elsewhere in detail.[40]

Respect for autonomy requires ensuring that an individual achieves the normative threshold of autonomy. This means supplying both status/recognition and resources. Occupying sufficiently low social status (slavery) brings autonomy below this level. Lacking basic mental or material resources – say, basic mental competency or access to basic necessities – also harms autonomy.

B. Informed Consent, Transparency, and Respect for Autonomy

Informed consent and transparency conceive of autonomy in different ways. In the clinical context where informed consent holds sway, respecting autonomy requires providing the resources and status that comprise autonomy, that is, ensuring that an individual has a certain level of mental (and some may argue, material) resources, such as basic faculties and understanding, and enjoys certain indicia of respect. Consumer contexts that implicate transparency assume that the individual already has analytical resources; autonomy only requires providing the consumer with information and respecting her decisions.

In the informed consent context, providing resources to educate a patient and inform her preferences may very well be the result of nudging.[41] In other contexts – education for example – nudging is generally inevitable and even celebrated. The job is, in fact, to shape young minds. Even presenting a list of cases in a torts class and one's interpretation of them is likely to insert some of the instructor's point of view. Providing advice that promotes the patient's understanding to the best of the doctor's ability effectively involves nudging in certain ways.

To be sure, nudging cannot involve coercion or deceit. Such behavior would negate the second component of autonomy by disrespecting or diminishing the status of the patient.[42] Ultimately, even while educating the patient, the doctor must

---

[40] Id.
[41] Nudging involves taking advantage of, altering, or educating people's cognitive biases or predilections so that they make choices that improve well-being for themselves and others. This approach accepts the necessity of some degree of paternalism. See Richard H. Thaler & Cass R. Sunstein, Nudge (2008).
[42] Unlike other authors who defend nudging, I do not claim that this is an exhaustive list of unacceptable behavior – and, moreover, do not believe that the list can ever be exhaustively defined. See Cohen, supra note 32.

treat her as a "full partner ... in social interaction"[43] through the conventions of interaction that are culturally relevant. A doctor might treat a gay man in his thirties differently than she would treat a straight sixty-year-old iron welder, or internal medicine professor; the doctor's behavior might depend on who she is as well. And yet the different behavior might seek to communicate the same level of respect, and even affection, in all cases.

Where informed consent requires building up the patient's resources so that he or she can function appropriately in a medical context, as well as respecting the patient, transparency tools address an already-autonomous consumer with fully formed preferences. Thus, the transparency approach, at least as a general matter, can be distinguished because enhancing the consumer's capabilities – the first component of autonomy – is less important.

Some might argue that the consumer narrative of transparency is somewhat naïve or even deceptive. Consumer narratives might carry out a kind of nudging because of the way they present data and the kind of data they present. I think it is fair to say, though, that given the lack of one-on-one interaction and the more passive hands-off approach that transparency takes, that the information providing, resource building, and nudging, is – relative to informed consent, at least – a less important component.[44]

III. DRAWING THE LINE

Not only are informed consent and transparency associated with two different narratives of autonomy, they also help mark contexts as medical and nonmedical. With informed consent, the patient and the doctor are playing certain social roles. Deviating from those roles, by say, framing the relationship as one involving transparency and consumerism, would upset not just the doctor–patient relationship, but the place of medicine in society and our understanding of sickness.

As Talcott Parsons's work suggests, medicine is charged with managing who gets the special marker of being sick – with its benefits and its obligations. Maintaining the border is practically important. Today, unwell individuals can lay claim to certain social resources, and in turn, have the obligation to take steps to get well. The border, Parsons argues, ensures productivity and, relatedly, prevents malingerers from reaping the benefits of being unwell.[45] Further, insulating the medical context from broader social norms of interaction allows doctors and patients to interact in ways that would be considered improper in society more generally.

[43] Fraser, supra note 42.
[44] Further, targeted "nudging" in the consumer context is rarely, to my knowledge, defined as a form of transparency, but rather is acknowledged as nudging. Its desirability in that context is beyond the scope of this chapter.
[45] See Parsons, supra note 18, at 304 ("The privileges and exemptions of the sick role may become objects of a 'secondary gain' which the patient is positively motivated, usually unconsciously, to secure or to retain.").

The breach of normal etiquette with respect to nudity or physical contact is often unique to the medical and sexual contexts.[46] Finally, patients are often helpless in medical contexts; insulating them from the profit-seeking motives that characterize business as usual is vital. The doctor's role is vocational, focused on patient welfare. "Perhaps only the clergy," says Parsons, excludes the "profit motive" to a greater degree.[47]

The different ethical narratives undergirding informed consent and transparency reflect these practical functions of medical and nonmedical role separation. The implications and processes involved in medical procedures and treatments are hard to understand. A patient's preferences regarding them may be ill-formed, so it is perfectly appropriate to treat their preferences as in flux, as "initial," and to seek to educate her.[48] But transparency putatively engages with matters that are familiar to an individual's everyday life. Thus, it is fair to treat her preferences as given.

But the border between medical and nonmedical is more than just practical – it also maintains cultural and identity-generating norms. Medicine defined homosexuality as a sickness at the time Parsons was writing. Such a determination, if anything, was *im*practical, creating inefficiencies. Yet, this norm maintained sexual and cultural hierarchies (as problematic as those seem to modern eyes). Many in the deaf and intersex communities would argue that defining their respective conditions as illnesses that deserve treatment today perform similar functions.[49] On the flip side, some groups fight for medical recognition. Determining whether certain treatments such as gender reassignment or abortion merit medical coverage engages the boundary creation function of medicine. While some of these norms might be problematic and should be addressed, the overall separation (between what is medicine and what is not) is inevitable however problematic it may be. Equally important, as I have argued here, is that the distinction has social uses and social value.

Transparency and informed consent are best seen as rituals or practices that help perform the work of demarcating these contexts. Rituals and practices have expressive effect that determine social context and invoke certain social roles. A playground and courtroom can both be contexts of dispute resolution – but the rituals of both help define and differentiate the two contexts.[50] The practices of consent are one such ritual that tell the participants what social role they are operating in. A practice of consent that recognizes the vulnerability of the recipient of care and focuses on building autonomy tells observers and participants that she is

---

[46] Id. at 304, 307–08.
[47] Id. at 293.
[48] See Elwyn et al., supra note 29.
[49] See, e.g., Robert Sparrow, Defending Deaf Culture: The Case of Cochlear Implants, 13 J. Pol. Phil. 135 (2005); Charlotte Greenfield, Should We 'Fix' Intersex Children?, The Atlantic, July 8, 2014, www.theatlantic.com/health/archive/2014/07/should-we-fix-intersex-children/373536/.
[50] Cf. Erving Goffman, The Nature of Deference and Demeanor, 58 Am. Anthropologist 473 (1956).

a patient. A practice that takes autonomy more for granted signals she is a consumer. Maintaining some degree of separation between our understanding of the practices helps maintain sickness and medical care as contextually distinct areas of human interaction.

CONCLUSION

We will continue to rely on both transparency and informed consent concepts in describing the processes of transmitting information to patients. The key claim of this chapter is to argue that doing so actually brings into play conceptually different narrative and ethical frameworks. There is no magic in the expressions "informed consent" and "transparency" when viewed in the abstract, but their cultural, economic, and legal pedigree or provenance carry and convey substantial differences. Informed consent relates to concepts of individual relationships and fiduciary responsibility. Transparency sounds in contract and consumerism. These different frameworks, in turn, play a role in the socially important task of separating medical and nonmedical contexts.

Thus separating out the frameworks renders certain bioethical problems more clear. To be sure, in some cases, the applicable framework is somewhat straightforward. A decision regarding which surgical option to pursue is a medical one, and deserves the full support of informed consent. A decision taken while well, before any doctor–patient relationship is established as to who should be one's primary care provider, is likely a consumer decision and merits only transparent data.

But in other cases, recognizing the distinctiveness of the frameworks presents problems. Should the process of deciding which surgeon to consult to determine whether to undergo surgery be considered a question of transparency or of informed consent? How about conflict of interest disclosures? For some (including me) deciding whether to take Viagra seems to be a consumer decision; deciding whether to purchase contraception or abortifacients a medical one.

The answer will determine whether to use informed consent tools that provide support, that even nudge patients appropriately, that explicitly see their task as guiding patients in making a decision – or a transparency tool that merely seeks to present data in an easy-to-read fashion.

A better approach might be to think of the two paradigms I offer as the poles of a spectrum. Some forms of informed consent, some conversations between doctor and patient, are more moderated, and veer closer to a transparency model. Transparency and consent tools can be adjusted accordingly depending on a contextual analysis of where in the spectrum a decision falls.[51]

[51] Some might also argue that the consumer, caveat emptor paradigm of consumerism I present is itself faulty, and that we should adjust consumer discourse to provide similar support. I am sympathetic to that argument but it lies beyond the scope of this chapter.

This chapter merely offers a framework within which to situate these debates. Resolving the debates in a particular situation under any of these approaches (where possible) will largely depend on context. A middle-aged man deciding to purchase Viagra is differently situated from someone experiencing impotence due to depression or as a side effect of other medication. Suffice it to say that informed consent and transparency are vital concepts that represent the breadth of the health care system. The system spans vast areas of our lives – we engage with the system in contexts where we are both capable and vulnerable, both self-assured and deferential, both consumers and patients. Recognizing the separate spaces each concept occupies makes clearer the normative and narrative commitments underpinning the claims of the stakeholders that advocate for their deployment.

6

Transparency and Financial Conflicts

The Uncertain Case for Sunshine

Richard S. Saver[*]

INTRODUCTION

The health care system has entered a new era of sunshine about financial conflicts. The Physician Payments Sunshine Act,[1] enacted in 2010, is the first comprehensive federal legislation mandating public reporting of payments between drug companies, device manufacturers, and medicine. But is the new era of sunshine making any difference? This chapter examines the Sunshine Act's uneven record and how it reflects the uncertain case for transparency regulation in health care.

As a threshold matter, this chapter uses the terms "financial conflicts" and "conflicts of interest" as defined by the Institute of Medicine. A health care provider's primary interests include rendering professional care, engaging in research, and supporting medical education. A "conflict of interest" involves "circumstances that create a risk that professional judgment or actions regarding a primary interest will be unduly influenced by a secondary interest,"[2] such as financial gain.

What to do about financial conflicts is a question ever pressing and elusive. Drug companies and device manufacturers now pay a staggering amount, about $7 billion each year, to physicians and teaching hospitals for consulting, speaking fees, research support, and other services.[3] Industry's interaction with medicine offers numerous benefits such as accelerating development of novel therapies and educating frontline clinicians about complex medical products. However, the resulting financial ties correlate with a wide range of problematic behaviors, including harming patient care, increasing costs, limiting choice, eroding trust, and threatening the integrity of medical research.[4]

---

[*] Special thanks to MacKenzie Dickerman and Kerry Dutra for excellent research assistance.
[1] 42 U.S.C. § 1320a-7h (2012).
[2] Inst. of Med. of the Nat'l Acads., Conflict of Interest in Medical Research, Education, And Practice 6 (Bernard Lo & Marilyn J. Field eds., 2009) [hereinafter IOM Conflict of Interest Report].
[3] The Facts About Open Payments Data: 2015 & 2016 Totals, Ctrs. for Medicare & Medicaid Servs., https://openpaymentsdata.cms.gov/summary.
[4] IOM Conflict of Interest Report, supra note 2, at 23, 27.

Unfortunately, significant uncertainties complicate and potentially undermine financial conflicts regulation. Whether certain harms, in particular negative clinical outcomes, directly result from industry's extensive financial influence remains subject to intense debate.[5] While various studies demonstrate correlation,[6] definitive causal links have not been established by rigorous evidence and may be impossible to prove. Further difficulties arise in correctly identifying problematic financial ties and developing management strategies when the evidence base for many interventions remains limited.

Amid such uncertainty, mandated disclosure has considerable promise. Transparency regulation offers many theoretical benefits for the health care system, including facilitating efficient market operations, strengthening fiduciary relationships, and enhancing evaluation of financing and delivery.[7]

But, as this chapter details, the Sunshine Act suggests that enthusiasm for transparency needs tempering. Part I reviews the key components of the legislation. Part II analyzes the considerable implementation challenges. Part III considers how the law suffers from poor design as to primary audiences. Nonetheless, as Part IV discusses, the Sunshine Act has generated valuable data about the nature and scope of industry–medicine financial ties, which can better inform evidence-based regulation. This part further traces the downstream effects of transparency, exploring how information intermediaries are already starting to make productive use of Sunshine Act data.

I. SUNSHINE ACT BASICS

Enacted as part of the Patient Protection and Affordable Care Act, the Sunshine Act's lofty goals include deterring inappropriate financial relationships and improving medical decision making. It requires that drug and device manufacturers of products covered by Medicare, Medicaid, or the Children's Health Insurance Program report annually to the Centers for Medicare and Medicaid Services (CMS) their physician investors.[8] In addition, manufacturers must report payments to physicians and teaching hospitals.[9] CMS releases most of the data on a publicly available, searchable website, known as the Open Payments Database.[10]

---

[5] See Lisa Rosenbaum, Understanding Bias – The Case for Careful Study, 372 New Eng. J. Med. 1959, 1959–60 (2015).

[6] See, e.g., Stanford Taylor et al., Physician-Industry Interactions and Anti-Vascular Growth Factor Use Among US Ophthalmologists, 134 JAMA Ophthalmology 897, 901–02 (2016).

[7] William M. Sage, Regulating Through Information: Disclosure Laws and American Health Care, 99 Colum. L. Rev. 1701, 1704–07, 1710–11 (1999); Kristin Madison, Regulating Health Care Quality in an Information Age, 40 U.C. Davis L. Rev. 1577, 1589–92 (2007).

[8] 42 U.S.C. § 1320a-7h(a)(2).

[9] 42 U.S.C. § 1320a-7h(a)(1).

[10] See Open Payments Database, Ctrs. for Medicare & Medicaid Servs., https://openpaymentsdata.cms.gov/

As of August 2017, industry–medicine financial transactions posted to the Open Payments Database cover the latter part of 2013 and all of 2014–2016.

Any transfers of value to physicians and teaching hospitals of greater than $10 per instance or $100 per year must be disclosed.[11] Manufacturer reports must characterize each transfer as a research payment or general payment, and place each general payment in a limited number of categories, such as consulting fees, travel and lodging, royalty and license fees, and education.[12] Manufacturers who violate the reporting requirements risk civil fines up to $10,000 for each violation, capped annually at $150,000. Knowing violations are subject to civil fines of up to $100,000 for each incident, capped annually at $1 million.[13]

The Sunshine Act builds upon and amplifies trends already favoring increased transparency of industry–medicine financial relationships, such as medical journal rules for authors' conflict disclosures.[14] A handful of states, such as Massachusetts and Vermont, had previously enacted their own sunshine laws, but the material terms vary.[15] Also, the Department of Justice has negotiated fraud and abuse settlements with several pharmaceutical companies, such as Eli Lilly, requiring public disclosure of their payments to physicians.[16] The Sunshine Act goes far beyond these previous disclosure programs because of the very low dollar threshold and the extensive range of financial relationships covered.

II. IMPLEMENTATION CHALLENGES

The Sunshine Act's bumpy, troubled roll-out offers a cautionary lesson. Meaningful transparency cannot be accomplished simply by legislative command. It requires keen attention to pragmatic implementation, as inherent challenges arise in data selection and communication.

A. Capturing All Relevant Information

For any transparency program, the output can only be as good as the input. But the Sunshine Act does not account for all important recipients of industry payments. It excludes reporting about medical residents and ancillary nonphysician personnel, such as nurse practitioners and physician assistants. Wary of public reporting, manufacturers may reallocate more industry spending toward these prescribers.

---

[11] 42 U.S.C. § 1320a-7h(e)(10)(B).
[12] 42 U.S.C. § 1320a-7h(a)(1)(A)(v), (vi); 42 C.F.R. § 403.904(e)(2).
[13] 42 U.S.C. § 1320a-7h(b)(1)-(2).
[14] See, e.g., Form for Disclosure of Potential Conflicts of Interest, Int'l Committee Med. J. Editors, www.icmje.org/downloads/coi_disclosure.pdf
[15] See, e.g., Mass. Gen. Laws ch. 111N, § 6 (2012); Minn. Stat. § 151.47(f) (2011); Vt. Stat. tit. 18, § 4632.
[16] Press Release, Dep't of Just., Eli Lilly and Company Agrees to Pay $1.415 Billion to Resolve Allegations of Off-Label Promotion of Zyprexa (Jan. 15, 2009), www.justice.gov/archive/opa/pr/2009/January/09-civ-038.html.

In addition, many physicians view the Sunshine Act as unfair because it does not include reporting about these other prescribers.[17] Such perceived disparities contribute to physician distrust and cynicism about the law, making it more difficult to enforce.

The Sunshine Act is also underinclusive as to the other side of the transaction: the entities making payments. The legislation imposes reporting obligations only on manufacturers.[18] An independent wholesaler or distributor of a drug or device need not report its payments, even though these entities also have a direct economic interest in encouraging greater provider utilization of the product. Thus, potentially significant financial influences from downstream entities in the production and distribution chain remain undisclosed.

Another set of problems arises from standardizing complex transactional practices into a uniform reporting system. Inevitably data glitches develop and important information gets lost, left out, or remains obscure. The Open Payments Database contains multiple instances of affiliated companies making payments connected to the same product.[19] Relatedly, analysts found instances where the same drug or device is mentioned in the Open Payments Database under different names for different payment reports.[20]

B. Presenting the Information Optimally, with Context and Comparatives

Studies of physician financial incentives in several contexts indicate that a financial incentive's actual risk of creating bias and undue influence in the recipient depends on a number of important variables, including: the amount of money at stake; how this compares relative to the physician's other sources of income; the nature of the physician's services involved in the transaction; how long the financial relationship will continue; the length of any measurement periods to earn compensation; whether explicit quality of care measurements also impact the physician's receipt of compensation; the number of patients affected; whether many other physicians enjoy the same financial relationship; the historical relations between the transacting parties; the recipient physician's ability to direct referral and prescription decisions for the company's products; and the physician's interest in maintaining relations with the company in other settings.[21]

---

[17] Susan Chimonas et al., Bringing Transparency to Medicine: Exploring Physicians' Views and Experiences of the Sunshine Act, 17 Am. J. Bioethics 4, 10 (2017).

[18] See Medicare, Medicaid, Children's Health Insurance Programs; Transparency Reports and Reporting of Physician Ownership or Investment interests, 78 Fed. Reg. 9458, 9461–62 (Feb. 8, 2013).

[19] See Charles Ornstein et al., Data on Payments from Drugmakers to Doctors is Marred by Error, N.Y. Times, Jan. 22, 2015.

[20] See Charles Ornstein, 5 Things We Learned From New Database of Payments to Doctors, NPR, Oct. 1, 2014, www.npr.org/sections/health-shots/2014/10/01/352978027/5-things-we-learned-from-new-database-of-payments-to-doctors.

[21] See, e.g., Richard S. Saver, Squandering the Gain: Gainsharing and the Continuing Dilemma of Physician Financial Incentives, 98 Nw. U. L. Rev. 145, 207–10 (2003); Brian Armour et al., The Effect

How is a transparency program supposed to disclose all this, and yet still be easily comprehensible and readily accessible to the public? The architects of the Open Payments Database have opted to keep the disclosure deceptively simple, omitting much important contextual information. A payment report displays the company and physician/teaching hospital in the transaction, the dollar value conveyed, and one of the applicable payment categories (consulting, travel/lodging, speaker fees, and so forth). End users do not necessarily understand, from just the associated category descriptor, the fuller context. As behavioral economist George Loewenstein has noted, "[i]t's very difficult to distinguish real consulting and research money from gifts – putting it nicely – that are really bribes."[22]

The Open Payments Database clearly shows, for each transaction, the amount of money associated. However, the focus on payment amount may mislead. The scholarly literature on financial conflicts urges increased attention to restricting even small gifts and de minimis payments. Even low-dollar financial relationships can create indebtedness, unconscious gratitude, and reciprocity obligations for the physician recipients, pressures that exert potential bias in subtle but powerful ways.[23]

Further, the limited contextual information may skew patient responses. A study, modeled on the Sunshine Act reports, found that the category a payment was placed in had the strongest influence on patient perceptions.[24] Patients generally viewed physicians who received consulting payments as experts with more knowledge about medical advances, but physicians paid for travel were perceived as less trustworthy.[25] Importantly, these responses do not necessarily correspond to the payment's actual risk of bias and undue influence. For example, despite the perception that industry selects physicians as consultants because of their expertise, fraud and abuse investigations have revealed use of consulting payments as schemes to secure physician loyalty.[26]

A well-functioning disclosure program would be able to provide "relative transparency," where the information is packaged to facilitate meaningful comparisons.[27] How a physician's industry ties compare to other physicians is presumably very material information. Unfortunately, the Open Payments Database lacks important comparative benchmarks. Only in 2017 did CMS add comparative information in response to ordinary searches, but this shows how a physician's payments compare to

of Explicit Financial Incentives on Physician Behavior, 161 Archives Internal Med. 1261, 1265–66 (2001).
[22] Sara Reardon, Disclosing Conflicts of Interest Has Unintended Effects, Nature (Oct. 3, 2014).
[23] See generally Jason Dana, How Psychological Research Can Inform Policies for Dealing with Conflicts of Interest in Medicine, in IOM Conflict of Interest Report, supra note 2, app. D at 358–74.
[24] Joshua E. Perry et al., Trust and Transparency: Patient Perceptions of Physicians' Financial Relationships with Pharmaceutical Companies, 42 J.L. Med. & Ethics 475, 484–85 (2014).
[25] Id. at 487.
[26] See, e.g., Plea Agreement at ¶ 6, United States v. Reinstein, No. 15-CR-044, 2015 WL 6167410 (N.D. Ill. Feb. 13, 2015).
[27] Nathan Cortez, Regulation by Database, 89 U. Colo. L. Rev. 1 (2018).

national and specialty peers, not regional, and does not address which general payment categories are involved.

Missing contextual and comparative information is a recurring implementation problem for transparency programs generally, but including such data adds costs and complexity. Achieving transparency that is simultaneously accurate, revealing, efficient, accessible, and useable frequently requires working at cross-purposes.

III. DISCLOSURE'S DOWNSIDES AND PRIMARY AUDIENCE

A. Disclosure's Downsides

Prominent critics Omri Ben-Shahar and Carl Schneider argue that mandated disclosure frequently fails and should be presumptively barred.[28] First, as they warn, many disclosure programs generate information too complex for end users to process successfully. As previously discussed, the Open Payments Database may mislead users with informational noise, skew patient responses, and obscure instances of actual undue influence and bias. Second, transparency regulation may be too attractive because of apparent low cost and political acceptability. Disclosure's broad appeal can trap policymakers into a cycle of reworking flawed disclosure programs. Indeed, the Sunshine Act has arguably crowded out consideration of additional financial conflicts regulation.

Third, transparency's apparent low cost may be misleading. CMS estimates $180 million in annual compliance costs arising from companies making the payment reports, physicians and hospitals verifying the reported information, and other recordkeeping.[29] Meanwhile, deterring problematic industry–medicine financial ties through public disclosure may help lower health care costs overall. But economic theory predicts that other financial relationships, particularly those of strategic importance to manufacturers, will be continued, with higher payments offered to the physicians to offset the reputational costs incurred for transacting with industry.[30] In short, required disclosure can have complex and uncertain impacts on overall health care costs.

Fourth, transparency runs the risk of, ironically, distorting public perceptions. The Sunshine Act can fuel and magnify overly negative reactions about industry–medicine collaborations. The media have not helped in this regard. News reports about Sunshine Act disclosures have identified, often alarmingly, which physicians in a community were top-dollar recipients of industry money

---

[28] Omri Ben-Shahar & Carl E. Schneider, More Than You Wanted to Know: The Failure of Mandated Disclosure 3 (2014).
[29] See Medicare, Medicaid, Children's Health Insurance Programs; Transparency Reports and Reporting of Physician Ownership or Investment interests, 78 Fed. Reg. 9458, 9466–67 (Feb. 8, 2013).
[30] Daniel L. Chen at al., Mandatory Disclosure: Theory and Evidence from Industry-Physician Relationships (2017), http://users.nber.org/~dlchen/papers/Mandatory_Disclosure.pdf.

without sufficient explanation as to the types of payments and whether the underlying financial relationships lacked legitimacy.[31] The end result is that public attention around Sunshine Act disclosures has sullied often valuable industry–medicine collaborations, such as physicians with needed expertise consulting with device companies about possible treatment innovations.[32]

B. The Audience

Effective transparency programs account for the end users expressly in questions of format, translation, framing, and operability to ensure useful engagement with the information.[33] The Sunshine Act lacks this fine-tuned design.

1. Patients

If, as may be self-evident, patients are part of the Sunshine Act's primary audience, one must question whether they have the inclination, resources, and capabilities to use the disclosed information productively. A recent focus group survey indicates that patients have a strong preference not to learn of financial conflicts via searchable websites, and instead desire live discussion of the conflict with their physicians.[34] Financial conflict searches may not be worth the effort to patients due to informational fatigue.

Indeed, the early Sunshine Act data indicates that patients are engaging with the information in only modest numbers. From September 30, 2014, to August 1, 2015, the Open Payments Database received 1.1 million unique page views from visitors and data within the Open Payments Database was searched over 6.5 million times.[35] This is a relatively small number when one considers that there are over 57 million Medicare patients,[36] and the Open Payments Database covers financial relationships related to products covered not only by Medicare but also Medicaid and the Children's Health Insurance Program.

The relatively low rate of patient engagement is particularly distressing because patients likely lack accurate understanding of industry–medicine financial ties.

---

[31] See, e.g., Victor Fiorillo, These 10 Philly Docs Received $12.8 Million From Medical Device and Pharmaceutical Companies Last Year, Phila. Mag., July 9, 2015, www.phillymag.com/news/2015/07/09/dollars-for-docs-propublica/.

[32] Lisa Rosenbaum, Beyond Moral Outrage- Weighing the Trade-Offs of COI Regulation, 372 New Eng. J. Med. 2064, 2066, 2068 (2015).

[33] Cortez, supra note 27.

[34] Michael Oaks et al., How Should Doctors Disclose Conflicts of Interest to Patients; A Focus Group Investigation, Minn. Med. 38, 40–41 (2015).

[35] Annual Report to Congress on the Open Payments Program 20, Ctrs. for Medicare & Medicaid Servs. (2016).

[36] Medicare Enrollment Dashboard, Ctrs. for Medicare & Medicaid Servs. (April 2017), www.cms.gov/Research-Statistics-Data-and-Systems/Statistics-Trends-and-Reports/Dashboard/Medicare-Enrollment/Enrollment%20Dashboard.html.

A recent survey of a national patient sample group indicated that 45 percent of the patients were generally aware of industry payments to physicians, but only 12 percent knew that this information was publicly available through programs like the Sunshine Act.[37] Moreover, only 5 percent of the patients reported knowing whether their own physician had received industry payments. Even worse, among patients who believed that their physician did not receive an industry payment, a review of the Open Payments Database revealed that 41 percent were incorrect.[38]

Other research suggests that disclosure can have unintended consequences. Behavioral theorists posit that learning of a financial conflict may create new pressures, or "insinuation anxiety," for a patient to follow the physician's recommendation, as to not follow it would send an implied message that the patient believes the physician is dishonest, something the patient prefers to avoid.[39] Also, rather than evaluating the physician's recommendations more critically, the patient may become more trustworthy of the physician simply because of the act of disclosure. Or, if inclined to discount the physician's recommendation, the patient may not know how to do so and to what degree.[40]

Moreover, a growing body of research suggests that financial ties disclosures have limited sway over patient and research subject decision making. Previous investigations and surveys indicates that while a majority of patients and subjects say they wish to know about financial ties, only smaller numbers (less than a majority and, in several studies, no more than one-third) indicate that this information would affect their decision making about type of clinical care or whether to participate in research.[41]

2. Physicians

Physicians seem another likely primary audience. Faced with public disclosure, they may decline certain transactions and reevaluate their own prescribing patterns. But it remains to be seen whether increased transparency really impacts physician behavior in this manner. A 2017 focus group study found that many of the participating physicians had only limited interactions with the Open Payments Database, reflecting in part their distrust and skepticism about the utility of Sunshine Act disclosures.[42] Further, in the 2013–2016 data

---

[37] Genevieve Pham-Kanter et al., Public Awareness of and Contact with Physicians Who Receive Industry Payments: A National Survey, J. Gen. Internal Med., Mar. 6, 2017.
[38] Id.
[39] George Loewenstein et al., The Unintended Consequences of Conflict of Interest Disclosure, 307 JAMA 669, 670 (2012).
[40] George Loewenstein et al., The Limits of Transparency: Pitfalls and Potential of Disclosing Conflicts of Interest, 101 Am. Econ. Rev. 423, 424 (2011).
[41] See, e.g., Adam Licures et al., The Impact of Disclosing Financial Ties in Research and Clinical Care: A Systematic Review, 170 Archives Internal Med. 675 (2010). C.f. Mark W. Camp et al., Patients' Views on Surgeons Financial Conflicts of Interest, 95 J. Bone & Joint Surgery e9(1), e9(6) (2013).
[42] Chimonas, supra note 17, at 6–7.

in the Open Payments Database, there is no indication of major changes year to year in terms of number of physicians reported or overall general payments spending,[43] suggesting that any such blanket deterrence more likely had stronger impact in the run-up to the Sunshine Act data going public than afterward.

Also, the experience with the few state sunshine laws casts doubts whether financial conflicts disclosure programs strongly influence physician behavior. A study of Maine's and West Virginia's sunshine laws looked at physician prescribing rates of brand name statins and selective serotonin reuptake inhibitors (SSRIs), two classes of drugs where industry's financial influence has raised concerns. But the investigation found almost no difference in physician prescribing rates before and after each state's disclosure law went into effect.[44] One caveat is that it is not clear how generalizable the West Virginia and Maine disclosure programs are to the Sunshine Act as the reporting information was not made as easily accessible to the public at large.[45]

Additionally, behavioral research suggests that, similar to patients, disclosure can have unintended, counterproductive effects on physicians. Psychological studies of advisors and their advisees, analogous to the doctor–patient relationship, indicate that when advisors have to reveal their financial conflicts they tend to offer more biased guidance than if the financial ties remain undisclosed. This may be due to strategic exaggeration, where advisors offer more extreme advice to offset the anticipated discounting of their recommendations.[46] Another possible explanation is moral licensing, where advisors may feel more emboldened to give biased advice because their advisees have been warned about the underlying financial conflict.[47]

IV. WHAT'S BEING LEARNED AND PRELIMINARY DOWNSTREAM EFFECTS

Despite the Sunshine Act's many challenges, the information disclosed offers the most comprehensive accounting to date of the financial ties between industry and medicine. This emerging epidemiology of financial relationships is crucial for evidence-based regulation.

---

[43] See The Facts About Open Payments Data, Summary Data for 2013, 2014, 2015, and 2016, Ctrs. for Medicare & Medicaid Servs., https://openpaymentsdata.cms.gov/summary.

[44] Genevieve Pham-Kanter, Effect of Physician Payment Disclosure Laws on Prescribing, 172 Archives Internal Med. 819 (2012).

[45] Meredith B. Rosenthal & Michelle M. Mello, Sunlight as Disinfectant-New Rules on Disclosure of Industry Payments to Physicians, 368 New Eng. J. Med. 2052, 2053 (2013).

[46] Sunita Sah, Conflicts of Interest and Your Physician: Psychological Processes That Cause Unexpected Changes in Behavior, 40 J.L. Med. & Ethics 482, 485 (2012).

[47] Id.

A. Pervasiveness and Variation by Physician Specialty

The Sunshine Act has confirmed that financial relationships with industry pervade medicine. About 48 percent of all physicians received some industry payment in 2015, according to Open Payments Database reports.[48]

Financial ties also vary considerably by clinical specialty. For example, in 2015 a large number of cardiologists (75 percent) and gastroenterologists (72 percent) received some form of industry general payment.[49] This contrasts with family medicine physicians (48 percent), pediatricians (40 percent), anesthesiologists (38 percent), and radiologists (29 percent).[50]

Tremendous variation also can be found in how much money flows within each financial relationship. According to reported transactions in the last five months of 2013, the mean value of general payments per surgeon ($2,383) was more than twice as much as reported for physicians in general medical specialties ($976).[51] Orthopedic surgeons were at the top in terms of lucrative financial ties, with a mean value of general payments per orthopedic surgeon of $7,114, driven largely by the high value of royalty and license payments.[52]

The fact that financial relationships have not proceeded in lockstep indicates different incentives and perceived acceptance within each medical field to engage with industry. This further suggests that the actual risks, facilitating conditions, and optimal responses to financial conflicts likely vary across specialties as well. At the very least, this raises doubt about generalized regulatory rules. Monolithic approaches, such as transactional bans based on certain dollar thresholds or requiring second medical opinions from nonconflicted peers within the same clinical field, may be ill fitting within particular specialties.

B. Variation by Physician Gender

Gender matters. According to the 2015 Open Payments Database reports, with all specialties combined, 50.8 percent of male physicians but only 42.6 percent of female physicians had a reportable general payment from industry.[53] Female physicians nationally also had a lower mean value of general payments per physician than their male peers ($1,390 compared to $5,031).[54] Of the 300 doctors who received

---

[48] Kathryn R. Tringale et al., Types and Distributions of Payments from Industry to Physicians in 2015, 317 JAMA 1774, 1780 (2017).
[49] Id. at 1779.
[50] Id.
[51] Deborah C. Marshall et al., Disclosure of Industry Payments to Physicians: An Epidemiologic Analysis of Early Data from the Open Payments Program, 91 Mayo Clinic Proc. 84, 88 (2016).
[52] Id.
[53] Tringale et al., supra note 48, at 1779.
[54] Id.

the most money for speaking and consulting payments in the 2013 reports, 90 percent were male.[55]

Because gender is a predictor, among other factors, for potential financial conflicts, this suggests regulators might recalibrate enforcement priorities under the health care fraud and abuse laws. For example, Medicare contractors' selective fraud audits of billing records, as well as compliance advising, could skew more heavily toward male physicians in certain fields. Moreover, the reasons that female physicians have less financial entanglement with industry warrant further study for informing future regulation.

C. Skewed Distribution

Sunshine Act data further indicates that within many medical specialties large dollar amounts flow to a few top earners. For example, within obstetrics-gynecology, the top 10 percent of practitioners receiving the most industry payments in 2014 attracted 92 percent of the total value of general payments to all physicians within the specialty.[56]

The skewed payment distribution patterns can be interpreted in different ways. A more benign explanation is that industry reaches out to the few respected opinion leaders, hoping to tap their expertise and standing in the field in a variety of legitimate collaborations. Likewise, it may be that only a few physicians are able to earn hefty royalty and license fees as successful innovators because of the arduous process for a product to earn regulatory approval and enter into common clinical use. But a more troubling explanation is that industry heavily leverages a few select physicians, relying upon these targets to influence their peers' prescribing and referral choices. In any event, the skewed payment distribution patterns suggest a need for more fine-tuned regulatory responses, such as concentrated audits of the top-dollar physicians' prescribing.

D. Use of the Data by Secondary Audiences and Promising Applications

The Sunshine Act's real value rests on what it may accomplish in the longer term, as the information disseminates. Health care disclosure laws often work best by enlisting the power of intermediaries to identify the relevant data among disclosed information, translate it, and use it for further regulation and advocacy on behalf of primary audiences.[57] There are signs that such promising applications are already occurring.

---

[55] Charles Ornstein, Men Dominate List of Doctors Receiving Largest Payments from Drug Companies, N.Y. Times, Oct. 9, 2014.
[56] Nicole Tierney et al., Industry Payments to Obstetrician-Gynecologists, 127 Obstetrics & Gynecology 376 (2016).
[57] See, e.g., Sage, supra note 7, at 1736–37.

1. Building Up the Evidence Base and Enforcement

One advantageous application is linking Open Payments Database information to databases detailing the Medicare-reimbursable services provided by individual physicians[58] and the prescription drugs ordered by individual physicians as part of the Medicare Part D prescription drug program.[59] Such analysis allows for comparing industry spending directed at an individual physician and that physician's prescribing and referral decisions. A first wave of such studies has recently been published. One noteworthy investigation looked at prescribing of angiotensin receptor blockers, cardioselective-B-blockers, and SSRIs. Researchers found a strong correlation between a physician receiving a single meal and higher rates of prescribing costlier brand name medications.[60] Studies such as this, made possible by the Sunshine Act, can better inform evidence-based regulation of industry's promotional activities. More immediately, Sunshine Act data helps regulators enforce the existing health care fraud and abuse laws by revealing unknown financial ties or outliers that warrant further scrutiny.

A dramatic example of the Sunshine Act buttressing fraud and abuse enforcement in this manner is the ongoing saga of Insys Therapeutics. Insys, an Arizona pharmaceutical company, markets Subsys, a schedule II opioid painkiller. Subsys, intended for cancer patients already taking other painkillers but still in distressing pain, has significant risks of addiction. Indiscriminate prescribing of Subsys for a much wider range of patients raised serious concerns. Attention eventually turned toward Insys's aggressive marketing. Various regulatory investigations gathered steam and widened considerably after release of the first batch of Sunshine Act data. The Open Payments Database revealed that Insys had been paying speaker fees, travel, and meals, and making other payments to the nation's top prescribers of Subsys, including several physicians disciplined by state medical boards for problematic conduct.[61] The ever-expanding enforcement actions include Insys's $1.1 million settlement of charges by the Oregon Attorney General regarding improper financial incentives to physician-prescribers;[62] a guilty plea by Dr. Gavin Awerbuch, a top prescriber of

---

[58] Medicare Provider and Utilization and Payment Data: Physician and Other Supplier, Ctrs. For Medicare & Medicaid Servs., www.cms.gov/Research-Statistics-Data-and-Systems/Statistics-Trends-and-Reports/Medicare-Provider-Charge-Data/Physician-and-Other-Supplier.html (last modified June 15, 2017).

[59] Medicare Provider and Utilization and Payment Data: Part D Prescriber, Ctrs. For Medicare & Medicaid Servs., www.cms.gov/Research-Statistics-Data-and-Systems/Statistics-Trends-and-Reports/Medicare-Provider-Charge-Data/Part-D-Prescriber.html (last modified May 25, 2017).

[60] Colette Dejong et al., Pharmaceutical Industry-Sponsored Meals and Physician Prescribing Patterns for Medicare Beneficiaries, 176 JAMA Internal Med. 1114 (2016).

[61] Katie Thomas, Using Doctors with a Troubled Past to Market a Painkiller, N.Y. Times, Nov. 27, 2014; Roddy Boyd, The Black World of Insys Therapeutics, Southern Investigative Reporting Found. (July 14, 2015), http://sirf-online.org/2015/07/14/the-darkening-world-of-insys-therapeutics/.

[62] Press Release, Or. Dep't of Just., AG Rosenblum Settles with Pharmaceutical Company Insys Over Unlawful Promotion of the Powerful Opioid Subsys (Aug. 5, 2015), www.doj.state.or.us/media-home/news-media-releases/ag-rosenblum-settles-with-pharmaceutical-company-insys-over-unlawful-promotion-of-the-powerful-opioid-subsys/.

Subsys with extensive financial ties to Insys, for Medicare fraud;[63] and the filing of racketeering charges against former Insys executives.[64]

2. Litigation

As the Insys saga demonstrates, savvy lawyers are recognizing that Open Payments Database information provides powerful evidence in civil litigation. Much of this litigation is still pending. Nonetheless, it is useful to trace the downstream effects of transparency even in the initial pleadings and how it affects litigation strategy. Counsel have mined the Open Payments Database to support allegations of improper industry influence. These lawsuits are likely the first wave of multiple actions that will subject disclosed financial ties to exacting litigation scrutiny, increasing pressures on manufacturers and providers to defend certain transactions.

The Insys saga has spilled over into private litigation. In 2014, investors filed a class action alleging that the company violated federal securities laws in making misleading statements about and failing to disclose its marketing practices for Subsys and the risk of regulatory scrutiny. The complaint expressly referenced Open Payments Database information.[65] The action resulted in a settlement of over $6 million.[66]

Sunshine Act data seems particularly ripe for use in personal injury litigation. Industry–medicine financial relationships, presented with the inference of misleading promotion or biased decision making, can be explosive evidence in support of malpractice and products liability claims. For example, a 2016 tort suit against Bristol-Myers Squibb Co. alleged strict liability, negligence, and related claims in connection with the development and marketing of Abilify, a psychiatric drug.[67] The plaintiffs assert that Bristol-Myers Squibb failed to warn sufficiently of the risk of gambling and other compulsive behaviors associated with use of Abilify. To further buttress allegations of Bristol-Myers's improper promotion of the drug while downplaying its risks, the complaint references Open Payments Database records showing over $10 million in payments related to Abilify that the company made to over 21,000 physicians.[68] In October 2016, the suit was consolidated with over twenty other

---

[63] Jennifer Chambers, Oakland Co. Doc With Rare Coin Collection Pleads Guilty, Detroit News, Nov. 17, 2016, www.detroitnews.com/story/news/local/oakland-county/2016/11/07/doc-coin-collection/93446828/.

[64] Katie Thomas, Former Insys Officials Charged in Scheme to Push its Painkiller, N.Y. Times, Dec. 8, 2016.

[65] See Amended Complaint at ¶¶ 58–59, Larson v. Insys Therapeutics, Inc., No 2:14-cv-01043-GMS (D. Ariz. Oct. 27, 2014).

[66] Claims Administrator Angeion Group Announces Proposed Settlement in Insys Therapeutics Class Action, PR Newswire, July 8, 2015, www.prnewswire.com/news-releases/claims-administrator-angeion-group-announces-proposed-settlement-in-insys-therapeutics-class-action-300110081.html.

[67] Sears v. Bristol-Myers Squibb Co., No. 1:16-cv-00065-CJO-BAM (E.D. Cal. Jan. 15, 2016).

[68] Complaint at ¶ 76, Sears v. Bristol-Myers Squibb Co., No. 1:16-cv-00065-CJO-BAM (E.D. Cal. Jan. 15, 2016). This information comes from ProPublica's Dollars for Docs database, which utilizes information from the Open Payments Database.

similar actions against Bristol-Myers Squibb into a pending multidistrict proceeding.[69]

Open Payments Database records also seem ripe for application to False Claims Act and related health care fraud litigation. These lawsuits often involve allegations that manufacturers encouraged ordering of drugs and devices for unapproved uses. Sunshine Act data calls into question how manufacturers in fact promoted the products and for which uses. Indeed, pending complaints, relying upon Open Payments Database information, suggest that manufacturers used financial ties with physicians for improper promotion of spinal devices not approved for clinical use by the FDA[70] and testosterone replacement therapy drugs for off-label uses.[71]

3. Professional Self-Regulation

Finally, Sunshine Act data is also furthering professional self-regulation. Many professional societies, journals, and institutions have adopted their own conflict of interest policies. These rules frequently rely upon the physician to declare financial relationships. The Sunshine Act offers a more robust mechanism for vetting speakers and guideline panelists. For example, researchers scrutinizing the Open Payments Database found that among clinical practice guideline authors for the National Comprehensive Cancer Network (NCCN), 6 percent had financial relationships in excess of NCCN's own conflict of interest policies.[72]

V. CONCLUSION

The new era of sunshine about financial conflicts has not been entirely radiant. Financial conflicts data is especially challenging for transparency regulation because of the complicated transactions involved, the apparent low concern about financial conflicts among patients, the lack of a firm empirical basis for understanding the effects of industry–medicine interaction, and the necessary importance of contextual and comparative information to assess risk of bias and undue influence.

Nonetheless, even when disclosure on the ground inevitably becomes a mess, transparency still can offer value over the longer term. In some respects, the experience with financial conflicts transparency mirrors what has been observed with hospital report cards and other provider quality reporting. Although patients are

---

[69] In re Abilify (Aripiprazole) Prod. Liab. Litig., No. MDL 2734, 2016 WL 5846032 (U.S. Jud. Pan. Mult. Lit. Oct. 3, 2016).
[70] First Amended Complaint at ¶ 136, *United States v. Medtronic*, No. 2:15-cv-01212 (C.D. Cal. 2015).
[71] Third Amended Complaint at ¶¶ 747, 999, 1036, *Medical Mutual of Ohio v. AbbVie Inc.*, No. 1;14CV08857 (N.D. Ill. 2014) (relying upon both Dollars for Docs and Open Payments Database information).
[72] Aaron P. Mitchell et al., Financial Relationships with Industry Among National Comprehensive Cancer Network Guideline Authors, 2 JAMA Oncology 1628 (2016).

not directly using quality reporting in large numbers, providers, regulators, payers, and other stakeholders are starting to engage with the information more productively, such as facilitating quality-based reimbursement and internal provider quality control, which may benefit patients down the line.[73] Likewise, the Sunshine Act is yielding significant insights into the epidemiology of industry–medical financial relationships, with important implications for financial conflicts regulation. Moreover, secondary audiences beyond patients are starting to mine the Open Payments Database in productive and creative ways.

Looking forward, the oversight system critically needs more evidentiary support in several key areas, including the actual causal impact of financial conflicts, the comparative effectiveness of different regulatory approaches, the optimal way to disclose conflicts, and what fully informed patients really think about industry–medicine financial relationships. Unfortunately, important questions persist even in the new era of sunshine.

---

[73] See, e.g., Kristin Madison, Health Care Quality Reporting: A Failed Form of Mandated Disclosure?, 13 Ind. Health L. Rev. 310, 330–33 (2016).

7

Making Religion Transparent

The Substance, Process, and Efficacy of Disclosing Religious Restrictions on Care

Elizabeth Sepper

Religion may drive medical practice in ways that are obscured from public view. In a survey of 2,000 physicians in the United States, 55 percent reported that their religious beliefs influence their practice of medicine.[1] In another survey, most physicians expressed the belief that "when faced with a controversial request, they are not obligated to provide services to which they have moral or religious objections."[2] It is well known that some physicians refuse to provide abortions or contraceptives due to religious belief. Physicians often selectively turn away patients seeking assisted reproductive technology for moral reasons.[3] Others report maintaining or declining to withdraw life support from patients to comply with their own religious or moral values.[4] Faced with nondiscrimination duties under the Affordable Care Act, other doctors have asserted religious objections to providing health care to transgender people.[5]

Health care facilities affiliated with Seventh Day Adventist, Baptist, Latter Day Saint, Orthodox Jewish, and Catholic faiths likewise limit care for religious reasons. The predominant religious affiliation, Catholic health care also has the most wide-ranging restrictions – prohibiting a range of assisted reproductive technologies and infertility treatments, abortion, contraception, and sterilization and limiting the use of terminal sedation and the withholding of artificial nutrition and hydration in

---

[1] Farr A. Curlin et al., Religious Characteristics of U.S. Physicians: A National Survey, 20 J. Gen. Internal Med. 629, 629 (2005).
[2] Ryan E. Lawrence & Farr A. Curlin, Physicians' Beliefs About Conscience in Medicine: A National Survey, 84 Acad. Med. 1276, 1278 (2009).
[3] Ryan E. Lawrence et al., Obstetrician–Gynecologists' Beliefs About Assisted Reproductive Technologies, 116 Obstetrics & Gynecology 127 (2010) (finding 14 percent of ob-gyns would refuse assisted reproduction to a patient with a female partner and 12.7 percent would not help her find an alternative provider).
[4] Clive Seale, The Role of Doctors' Religious Faith and Ethnicity in Taking Ethically Controversial Decisions During End-of-Life Care, 36 J. Med. Ethics 677, 681 (2010) (reporting from nationwide survey of physicians in the U.K. that those who reported being very or extremely religious were less likely to endorse certain end-of-life decisions and were less likely to discuss such options with patients).
[5] *Franciscan All., Inc. v. Burwell*, 227 F. Supp. 3d 660 (N.D. Tex. 2016).

certain circumstances.[6] Across the country, women have found Catholic hospitals unwilling to authorize their ob-gyns to perform tubal ligations following labor and delivery – requiring them to undergo two surgeries or to travel to another hospital. Other women have suffered injuries when hospitals denied them abortions and ectopic pregnancy treatment.[7] Yet, one national survey has shown that most women either do not realize that Catholic hospitals limit care or do not recognize the extent of restrictions.[8]

Other institutions similarly impose religious barriers about which patients may be ignorant. Individual pharmacists and pharmacies sometimes refuse to stock or fill prescriptions for emergency contraception. Crisis pregnancy centers (CPCs) frequently deceive women into believing that they provide medical care and/or abortions.

Transparency – a favored measure of market and regulation enthusiasts alike – has gained currency as a way to address situations where a provider denies care to patients or restricts procedures available in a community for religious, rather than medical, reasons. Scholars, legislators, and regulators increasingly propose disclosure as striking an appropriate balance between patient and provider interests. In order to understand these proposals, we must – as Frederick Schauer argues – "specify ... who must make what available to whom."[9] Even more fundamentally, we must know *why* information should be disclosed.[10]

Part I of this chapter evaluates the substance – what must be disclosed? – and process – how, when, and by whom are relevant populations made aware of religious identity or restrictions. The remainder of the chapter surfaces and analyzes the aims of religion-based transparency. Part II reviews transparency as efficiency. In some contexts, disclosure of religious restrictions can foster access to market alternatives. Part III turns to transparency as democracy. Given its largely private market nature, health care delivery might seem an odd candidate for democratic engagement. In mergers and acquisitions of hospitals, however, transparency permits community knowledge of, and involvement in, negotiating over

---

[6] See generally United States Conference of Catholic Bishops, Ethical and Religious Directives for Catholic Health Care Services (6th ed. 2018), www.usccb.org/about/doctrine/ethical-and-religious-directives/upload/ethical-religious-directives-catholic-health-service-sixth-edition-2016-06.pdf [hereinafter ERDs].

[7] Nat'l Health L. Program, Health Care Refusals: Undermining Quality Care for Women 15, 40, 57 (2010), www.healthlaw.org/issues/reproductive-health/health-care-refusals/health-care-refusals-undermining-care-for-women#.W6rK0WhKhPa; Angel M. Foster et al., Do Religious Restrictions Influence Ectopic Pregnancy Management? A National Qualitative Study, 21 Women's Health Issues 104, 106 (2011).

[8] Belden, Russonello & Stewart, Religion, Reproductive Health and Access to Services: A National Survey of Women (Apr. 2000), www.catholicsforchoice.org/wp-content/uploads/2014/01/2000religionreproductivehealthandaccesstoservices.pdf.

[9] Frederick Schauer, Transparency in Three Dimensions, 2011 U. Ill. L. Rev. 1339, 1346 (2011).

[10] Id. at 1351.

the availability of care in the face of religious constraints. Part IV evaluates transparency in informed consent. Various bioethicists and law scholars have proposed informing patients of religion-based restrictions within the consent process at the point of medical service. The aims of transparency in this area, however, are rarely made explicit and may run counter to the ideals of informed consent.

I. THE SUBSTANCE AND PROCESS OF TRANSPARENCY OF RELIGION IN HEALTH CARE

Legislators and regulators occasionally have implemented transparency measures to address situations where a health care institution or provider denies care to patients or restricts procedures available in a community for religious or conscientious, rather than medical, reasons. Such mandates are commonplace for end-of-life care.[11] A health care institution may only decline to comply with a health care decision that runs contrary to a conscience-based policy of the institution if it has been timely communicated to the patient.[12] Other recently enacted state measures – now subject to litigation – call for providers who object to abortion or birth control to make clear they do not offer these services. Health insurance also has inspired measures for transparency of religious perspectives, due to similar concerns about consumer deception or lack of competitive marketplaces.[13] In crafting a religious accommodation to the Affordable Care Act's contraceptive mandate, for example, the Department of Health and Human Services required notice from employers to both their insurers and employees.

Most commonly, scholars argue that religious restrictions should be surfaced through the informed consent process.[14] A number of bioethicists supportive of conscientious refusals have endorsed a duty to disclose religion-

---

[11] See, e.g., Cal. Prob. Code § 4734.

[12] Thirty-two states provide protections for refusals related to end-of-life decision making. See, e.g., Cal. Prob. Code § 4734 ("A health care institution may decline to comply with an individual health care instruction or health care decision if the instruction or decision is contrary to a policy of the institution that is expressly based on reasons of conscience and if the policy was timely communicated to the patient or to a person then authorized to make health care decisions for the patient.").

[13] Robert E. Moffit et al., Patients' Freedom of Conscience: The Case for Values-Driven Health Plans, Heritage Found. (2006), www.heritage.org/health-care-reform/report/patients-freedom-conscience-the-case-values-driven-healthplans http://www.heritage.org/research/reports/2006/05/patients-freedom-of-conscience-the-case-forvaluesdriven-health-plans (arguing for patients' "freedom to choose health plans and physician networks that respect and support their ethical, moral, and religious values").

[14] See, e.g., Maxine M. Harrington, The Ever-Expanding Health Care Conscience Clause: The Quest for Immunity in the Struggle Between Professional Duties and Moral Beliefs, 34 Fla. St. U. L. Rev. 779, 813–14 (2007); Sylvia A. Law, Silent No More: Physicians' Legal and Ethical Obligations to Patients Seeking Abortions, 21 N.Y.U. Rev. L. & Soc. Change 304 (1994).

or conscience-based objections.[15] I too have suggested that providers – both institutions and individuals – should reveal to patients the limits on services they provide.[16]

Across these contexts, proposed or enacted transparency measures are fairly consistent as to what should be disclosed: procedures, tests, or services restricted for religious or moral reasons. For example, a number of municipalities and the state of California require crisis pregnancy centers to disclose whether they have a licensed medical provider on staff and whether they provide, or provide referrals for, abortion, emergency contraception, and prenatal care.[17] Illinois also recently enacted a law requiring doctors to make clear any objections to performing abortions.[18] With a few exceptions, these transparency measures anticipate disclosure of information to a current or prospective patient.

Disagreement arises as to the specifics – must only the procedure restricted be disclosed? A physician then could state, "I don't prescribe emergency contraception." Or must she make clear the religious motive for refusal? John Davis, for example, contends that failure to explain why the service is not offered may cause patients to "mistakenly conclude that there are medical reasons for the refusal."[19] Should providers be transparent about their religious values more generally – making clear that the hospital is Catholic or the doctor Buddhist? Some scholars suggest discussing religious values with an eye toward matching patients and providers according to their moral positions.[20]

Timing and location also are key. Disclosure of the relevant information might occur when the treatment relationship begins. The Patient Self Determination Act (PSDA), for example, requires that providers and institutions discuss their policies on advance directives when a patient is admitted to a medical facility or comes into a hospice or nursing home. More broadly, Edmund Pellegrino has argued, "physicians have an obligation to make their religious or other beliefs overt and clear at the

---

[15] See, e.g., Armand H. Matheny Antommaria, Conscientious Objection in Clinical Practice: Notice, Informed Consent, Referral, and Emergency Treatment, 9 Ave Maria L. Rev. 81, 92–93 (2010); Edmund D. Pellegrino, Commentary: Value Neutrality, Moral Integrity, and the Physician, 28 J.L. Med. & Ethics 78, 78 (2000).

[16] Elizabeth Sepper, Not Only the Doctor's Dilemma: The Complexity of Conscience in Medicine, 4 Faulkner L. Rev. 385 (2013).

[17] N.Y.C. Local Law 17; California Reproductive Freedom, Accountability, Comprehensive Care, and Transparency (FACT) Act.

[18] Lisa Schencker, Pregnancy Centers Win Early Victory against Illinois Abortion Info Law, Chi. Trib., Dec. 21, 2016, www.chicagotribune.com/business/ct-illinois-abortion-lawsuit-1222-biz-20161221-story.html.

[19] John K. Davis, Conscientious Refusal and a Doctor's Right to Quit, 29 J. Med. & Phil. 75, 86 (2004); see also T.A. Cavanaugh, Professional Conscientious Objection in Medicine with Attention to Referral, 9 Ave Maria L. Rev. 189, 191 (2010) (proposing refusing providers disclose restricted treatment, but only explain their reasoning to patients who further inquire).

[20] Holly Fernandez Lynch, Conflicts of Conscience in Healthcare: An Institutional Compromise 101 (2008); Farr A. Curlin, A Case for Studying the Relationship Between Religion and the Practice of Medicine, 83 Acad. Med. 1118 (2008).

beginning of the medical relationship," whether through conversation or disclosure forms.[21] Alternatively, the key moment for disclosure may come when "the service becomes relevant for the patient's condition" – requiring the provider to iterate or reiterate objections to care.[22] At either of these points in time, we might choose between imposing mandates on health care institutions, as with the PSDA, or on individual physicians, as with regard to informed consent.

II. TRANSPARENCY AS EFFICIENCY

Transparency in health care most commonly aims to serve as a tool of market efficiency. In this sense, informational asymmetries between patients and providers and obscured inputs into clinical decision making can be resolved by informing patients. Armed with information, consumers/patients can choose providers, treatments, and insurers to match their needs.

Regarding religion, scholars frequently portray transparency as efficiency, remedying informational failures and reducing transaction costs. Institutional-level obligations of disclosure are particularly likely to be defended on efficiency grounds. For example, Robert Vischer argues that pharmacies should be required to publicize their positions on controversial drugs so that patients may participate in the market effectively.[23] In the absence of such mandates, patients may experience delays in accessing care, an inability to obtain procedures, and health- and life-threatening complications due to religious refusals of services. Transparency, it is claimed, instead can lead to access, ultimately avoiding physical or dignitary harm from refusal.[24]

While efficiency continues to hold appeal, disclosure in health care often proves imperfect as a mechanism for achieving access due to the particularities of health care.[25] As regards religion in particular, the ability of transparency to achieve market values depends crucially on the procedure at issue and the setting of refusal. Notice of the scope of services provided by CPCs, for example, seems likely to reduce women's search costs, whether for an abortion procedure or full-service maternity care, and to avoid deception about procedures available at CPCs. Sometimes religiously restricted services may be more available on the market than other medical care. With the move to over-the-counter sales, emergency contraception

---

[21] Pellegrino, supra note 15, at 79.
[22] Dan W. Brock, Conscientious Refusal by Physicians and Pharmacists: Who is Obligated to do What, and Why?, 29 Theoretical Med. & Bioethics 187, 195 (2008).
[23] Robert K. Vischer, Conscience in Context: Pharmacist Rights and the Eroding Moral Marketplace, 17 Stan. L. & Pol'y Rev. 83, 112 (2006).
[24] Nadia N. Sawicki, Mandating Disclosure of Conscience-Based Limitations on Medical Practice, 42 Am. J. L. & Med. 85, 103 (2016); Seale, supra note 4, at 681 (noting the suggestion that "religious doctors disclose their moral objections to certain procedures to patients so that patients can choose other doctors if they wish").
[25] See Barry R. Furrow, Chapter 1 (discussing limited capacity of consumers in health care); and Wendy Netter Epstein, Chapter 10 (discussing lack of price information in contracts for medical service).

may be one such example. Similarly, assisted reproductive technology is readily available to those who can afford it. Market efficiency proves illusory, however, for access to abortion where few providers exist or compliance with advance directives where the institution has the patient under its control.

Hospitals (and possibly other institutions) also must be distinguished from private practices. Given hospital market consolidation, patients in most places have few alternative hospitals, whereas individual willing providers may be available. Market efficiency, moreover, is stymied in emergent and urgent situations. As I have previously argued, "[i]n a hospital, it seems implausible to expect patients to take action based on disclosure posted on the hospital wall. Even if notice were distributed as part of the intake process, patients and their families are unlikely to register their import. By contrast, notice might be an important tool for individual doctors or practice groups. For instance, disclosure at the point of first contact (before the patient schedules an appointment or comes to the office) could inform a patient's choice."[26]

Being informed of refusal alone, however, is less likely to produce access than is disclosure combined with referral. Consequently, with regard to end-of-life care, legislation combines duties to disclose refusal and to "immediately make all reasonable efforts to assist in the transfer of the patient" to a willing provider or institution and to comply with the treatment request during the search.[27] Similarly, a 2016 Illinois law requires medical facilities and physicians who object to involvement in abortions to provide women seeking abortions with a list of providers "they reasonably believe may offer" them. Such passive referral responds to religious concerns about active referral that requires the provider to ensure the patient actually connects with a willing provider. Requiring information and referral also reflects professional ethical obligations[28] and, in practice, should impose minimal burdens on conscientious refusers, the vast majority of whom refer for and counsel about procedures they find morally objectionable.[29]

Counterintuitively, transparency around religious refusals could undermine health care access for two reasons. First, for individual providers who do not object to particular treatments, obscurity may facilitate their ability to work around institutional religious restrictions. For example, in Catholic health care facilities that

[26] Elizabeth Sepper, Taking Conscience Seriously, 98 Va. L. Rev. 1501, 1567 (2012).
[27] Thaddeus Mason Pope, Medical Futility Statutes: No Safe Harbor to Unilaterally Refuse Life-Sustaining Treatment, 75 Tenn. L. Rev. 1, 58–60 (2007). That said, in cases in which the treatment is judged futile by the medical provider, a willing provider rarely is found. Pope hypothesizes that this pattern is proof not of the physician's moral values prevailing over the patient's, but rather of consensus among providers of the medical inappropriateness of the requested intervention. Id. at 62.
[28] Am. Med. Ass'n Council on Ethical & Jud. Aff., Report 6-a-07, Physician Objection to Treatment and Individual Patient Discrimination (2007), www.ama-assn.org/sites/default/files/media-browser/public/about-ama/councils/Council%20Reports/council-on-ethics-and-judicial-affairs/a07-ceja-physician-objection-treatment.pdf.
[29] Lawrence & Curlin, supra note 2, at 1278.

restrict provision of information or referrals for prohibited care, reports suggest that doctors – who commonly do not share the institutional values – routinely violate policy. They meet patients in parking lots to dispense emergency contraception, surreptitiously offer referrals for abortion, or indicate false diagnoses in patient charts in order to perform sterilizations or prescribe contraceptives.[30] Second, a lack of transparency may permit institutional flexibility. In the past, religiously affiliated health care has evolved in response to, and in conversation with, shifting societal and legal norms. As I previously have noted, "[I]n states that have mandated emergency contraception for rape victims or condoms as part of HIV counseling, Catholic facilities have agreed to compromises: either directly delivering the services, allowing independent counselors to do so, or advising and referring to another facility."[31] If, by contrast, they had to commit to clear disclosures of refusal, Catholic health care entities might, for example, ban all tubal ligations, rather than grant patients access on a case-by-case basis. Over time, they might become more rigid and less willing to adapt.

III. TRANSPARENCY AS DEMOCRACY

Transparency may also foster democratic engagement.[32] As William Sage has pointed out, in healthcare, "disclosure can increase public awareness and political accountability regarding scarce resources and the rights and obligations of citizens."[33] While most health care institutions and providers are private rather than governmental, they receive substantial public funding and, often, tax benefits. In the aggregate, they affect what the public sees as a public good. Although health care initiatives typically emphasize transparency as efficiency, democratic transparency inheres in others, such as the ACA's mandate that nonprofit hospitals perform and disclose a community needs assessment.

Mergers and acquisitions with religious health care entities provide just such an opportunity for transparency to advance democracy. Such transactions involve public-facing decisions about the allocation of health care and call for consideration of societal questions like what kind of community do we want to be? When consolidation risks the loss of reproductive or end-of-life care due to religious restrictions, transparency enables such care to become part of discussions, on par to issues like the institutions' willingness to engage in collective bargaining and their commitments to provide other community benefits. Such open and informed deliberation and discourse may themselves be valuable. Of course, the ability of

---

[30] Sepper, supra note 26, at 1572 (compiling examples).
[31] Id. at 1571.
[32] Cass R. Sunstein, Informing America: Risk, Disclosure, and the First Amendment, 20 Fla. St. U. L. Rev. 653 (1993).
[33] William M. Sage, Regulating Through Information: Disclosure Laws and American Health Care, 99 Colum. L. Rev. 1701, 1711 (1999).

disclosure to achieve democratic goals depends critically on the community – or state attorneys general – to act as engaged partners in negotiating the terms of agreements. In practice, states show substantial variation in the degree to which attorneys general oversee health care consolidation and conversion of nonprofits to for-profits.

Transparency sometimes has empowered communities. Local populations have defeated mergers where purchasing entities were not adequately responsive to community needs. In other cases, transparency allowed creative solutions that preserved reproductive health care access and respected religious identity.[34] On occasion, public review of proposed religious restrictions has instantiated constitutional constraints. For example, Kentucky's attorney general rejected an agreement between Catholic and public facilities in part due to concerns that a public institution's compliance with religious doctrine violated the Establishment Clause.[35]

Other transparency efforts similarly might encourage engagement of affected communities. For example, hospitals' community needs assessments could surface unmet reproductive health care needs. Greater transparency on restricted care – particularly at the institutional level – would enhance the ability to evaluate health care delivery in local contexts. Mandated disclosure of religious restrictions on, for example, tubal ligations or miscarriage management also might prevent hospitals from marketing themselves as premier and comprehensive labor and delivery providers. Such transparency, of course, might come at a cost – enhancing stigma or sending the message that the majority can veto individual women's health care decisions.

IV. TRANSPARENCY AS INFORMED CONSENT

Among legal scholars, Nadia Sawicki has advanced the most detailed proposal for incorporating religious refusal into the informed consent process. Consistent with Howard Brody's approach to informed consent as transparency,[36] she argues that "[w]hen a physician's religious or conscientious beliefs impact her practice and treatment recommendations, being transparent about those influences on medical judgment would be consistent with the principles of informed consent."[37] She

---

[34] Sepper, supra note 26, at 1571.
[35] Proposed Consolidation of Jewish Hospital Healthcare Services, Inc., CHI Kentucky, Inc., Catholic Health Initiatives, University Medical Center, Inc., Jewish Hospital & St. Mary's Healthcare, Inc., Flaget Healthcare, Inc., Saint Joseph Health System, Inc., and JH Properties, Inc., Report of the Kentucky Attorney General 10, 13 (Dec. 29, 2011), www.modernhealthcare.com/Assets/pdf/CH769761230.PDF.
[36] Howard Brody, Transparency: Informed Consent in Primary Care, 19 Hastings Ctr. Rep. 5 (Sept.–Oct. 1989) (arguing for a model of informed consent where "the physician's basic thinking has been rendered transparent to the patient").
[37] Nadia N. Sawicki, A Common Law Duty to Disclose Conscience-Based Limitations on Medical Practice 187, 197, in Law, Religion & Health in the United States (Holly Fernandez Lynch, I. Glenn Cohen & Elizabeth Sepper, eds. 2017).

proposes mandated religious disclosure for "providers from whom a reasonable patient might expect specific services or information."[38] Sawicki further advocates informed consent at the institutional level, such that health care facilities would "notify patients of any conscience-based limitations on either the clinical care that is provided or the information that is shared with patients by individual providers within the facility or by the facility itself."[39] While inclusion of religion in informed consent partly aims at efficiency, it has heterogeneous aims – including ensuring agency and presuming consent, which this Part unpacks.

According to the *agency rationale*, sharing information with patients reduces agency costs and ensures patients find skilled and loyal agents.[40] At the patient level, disclosure should foster therapeutic goals of medicine by creating trust. On a system-wide basis, disclosure should encourage physicians to consider conflicts of interest and avoid "situations that compromise their skills or loyalties."[41] Scholars disagree, however, over whether conflict-of-interest disclosures bolster or undermine trust. Marc A. Rodwin, for example, expresses concerns that disclosure puts patients and providers in an adversarial posture and reduces open, trusting communication. As Richard S. Saver shows in this volume, "disclosure can have unintended consequences" – potentially distorting public perceptions and creating new pressures on patients to comply with physician's recommendations.

The agency rationale underlies much of the ethical and legal argument for transparency about religious restrictions. Physician qualifications or financial conflicts of interest are employed by analogy. Sawicki, for example, argues that as with financial conflicts of interest, physicians conflicted by their faith must so disclose. The informational asymmetry between patient and physician supports a duty of informed consent here as elsewhere, she says, because only the physician knows her own religious prohibitions and can easily disclose them.[42] Sawicki rejects the notion that a physician's conscience-based disclosure highlights "conflict with his patient's self-defined interests" to the detriment of trust.[43]

While refusing providers might resist the characterization of their religious beliefs as a conflict of interest with patients, the analogy proves apt with regard to medical providers who work under religious restrictions but do not share the religious perspective of their institutions. The physician's contractual duties toward the institution are potentially in conflict with the patient's best interests. Like doctors with financial incentives or contracts to withhold care or information, these doctors would make evident the practice restrictions that they work under. Anecdotally, in

---

[38] Nadia N. Sawicki, Mandating Disclosure of Conscience-Based Limitations on Medical Practice, 42 Am. J. L. & Med. 85, 105 (2016).
[39] Id. at 86.
[40] Sage, supra note 33, at 1764.
[41] Id. at 1770.
[42] Nadia N. Sawicki, Modernizing Informed Consent: Expanding the Boundaries of Materiality, 2016 U. Ill. L. Rev. 821, 860 (2016).
[43] Sawicki, supra note 38, at 115.

Catholic health care systems, doctors often already do so – telling patients that they will get around restrictions by prescribing contraceptives for a noncontraceptive purpose. In this context, disclosure seems conducive to trust in the physician, who has declared herself a loyal agent to the patient. Even then, patients may have lower levels of trust in the health care system, having been made aware of potential deficits of care.

With regard to providers who themselves hold religious beliefs against accepted medical practices, I am dubious that transparency builds confidence in physicians as agents. A patient told her physician will not prescribe birth control because of his religion might take it as a declaration of prioritizing his interests above hers. To put it starkly, consider Tamesha Means, a pregnant woman who was repeatedly denied miscarriage management and was not told why she was being mistreated (or, better, transferred to a willing facility) due to the hospital's religious mandates. She undoubtedly lost faith in the medical establishment, but it seems unlikely that disclosure that religious reasons motivated refusal of care would have led her to trust future health care providers to act as her skilled and loyal agents.[44]

Transparency as part of informed consent sometimes takes on the meaning of *presumed consent*. Once the religious identity of an institution or the religious limitation on a provider is known, patients (or the community) may be taken to have consented to limits on care. In this sense, a lack of alternative access seems to result in assumption of risk: If we tell you that we have religious reasons to allow harm to you and you fail to act on that information, you assume the risk of injury.

On its own terms, presuming consent through disclosure raises a central question: consent to what? In some of her writing, Nadia Sawicki advocates for permitting physicians to refuse information to patients provided that the patient is notified, perhaps at the beginning of the treatment relationship, of the objection to delivering information about the particular procedure.[45] This view comes perilously close to skirting informed consent altogether. For example, an ob-gyn could inform all patients about his refusal to provide information on miscarriage management and, seemingly, could then withhold information about miscarriage management when faced with a patient who is undergoing pregnancy loss (legally, if Sawicki's proposal were adopted). If, at an initial well-patient visit, a doctor tells a patient that he won't discuss any stem cell-based treatments for religious reasons, such information may be meaningless to a patient who has no known need for such treatments. Such transparency departs significantly from the ideal of informed consent, which aspires to patient autonomy over medical decision making and to alignment of health care

---

[44] Tamesha Means, Catholic Hospitals Shouldn't Deny Care to Miscarrying Mothers Like Me, Guardian, Feb. 23, 2016, www.theguardian.com/commentisfree/2016/feb/23/catholic-hospitals-abortion-womens-health-care-miscarrying-mothers.

[45] Sawicki, supra note 38, at 102–06. Cf. Thomas May & Mark P. Aulisio, Personal Morality and Professional Obligations: Rights of Conscience and Informed Consent, 52 Persps. Biology & Med. 30, 32 (2009).

with patient values. A patient might reasonably take disclosure of religious restrictions as a statement by the physician that "when your values and mine conflict, mine will prevail." Given, most states authorize providers to refuse to deliver certain reproductive health care services (most commonly, abortion and sterilization) and to comply with patients' end-of-life decisions. But – and this is important – the vast majority do not authorize physicians to withhold information about treatment options and diagnosis or to refuse referrals for continued care. Providers cannot escape liability by telling patients that they won't provide information for religious reasons. Reformed to ensure religious disclosure, the law of informed consent might shift the culture of medical practice, which right now, despite a significant number of dissenters, supports disclosure of information about treatments, not just religious restrictions, and requires referral.[46]

Even assuming a patient could validly consent to future refusals, it may be nearly impossible to provide a religious disclosure statement that is clear, complete, and meaningful. For instance, Catholic policies limit dispensing emergency contraception to rape victims to cases where conception has not occurred (despite the absence of any such medical test). Does a Catholic hospital disclose that it won't provide EC? Only to rape victims? Only to rape victims who can establish conception hasn't occurred? Religious objectors similarly often object selectively to IVF or contraception, differentiating between types of patients or uses. Even with regard to abortion, objecting providers may claim to take an anti-abortion stance, but differ significantly on the moral status of an ectopic pregnancy, which involves a pregnancy outside the uterus that cannot come to term, or on abortions necessary for a woman's health or life. The ambiguity of religious doctrine would plague meaningful consent. Moreover, given the lack of expertise of physicians (even religious physicians) in theology, transparency as informed consent would seem to require a significant shift toward institutional obligations of informed consent to which the law has long been resistant.[47]

Requirements to disclose may mitigate harm for some patients and for some categories of procedures. For others, disclosure may inform, but will not empower. These patients will suffer harm – dignitary and physical – with full transparency as to the motive behind their injuries. More broadly, disclosure may replace minimum quality standards. Insurance gag clauses – preventing physicians from informing patients of treatments not covered by a plan – are the closest analogy to prohibitions on informing patients of religiously objectionable treatment. But gag clauses were banned, rather than disclosed, due to concerns about patient harm.

---

[46] Joan H. Krause, Can Health Law Truly Become Patient Centered? 45 Wake Forest L. Rev. 1489, 1491 (2010) (noting the way that informed consent doctrine "corresponded with, and in turn reinforced, a cultural shift in our attitudes toward the patient's role in medical care").

[47] See generally Robert Gatter, The Mysterious Survival of the Policy Against Informed Consent Liability for Hospitals, 81 Notre Dame L. Rev. 1203 (2006).

Transparency can be stigmatizing as well. In many contexts, religious accommodation is authorized because refusal is seamless; if one nurse refuses to assist in IVF, another nurse can step in, and the accommodation is invisible to the patient and her fellow citizens. Transparency may send the message to the wider public that a particular kind of health care is objectionable or not health care at all: "Before I accept you as a patient, I have to tell you that this hospital won't perform tubal ligations." If physicians have to inform patients of the institutional refusal policies, they might signal their agreement to the religious beliefs – notwithstanding their individual positions. The result might be that the public overestimates commitment to a particular religious position.

CONCLUSION

Evaluation of the wisdom and effectiveness of making religion in health care transparent requires identifying the aims of transparency measures with precision. Suggestions for surfacing religious commitments and objections – including my own – have frequently mixed transparency as efficiency, democracy, and informed consent. This chapter aimed to disentangle these aims in the context of religious objections to health care.

With regard to religion in health care, transparency as efficiency is constrained by conscience laws that authorize the withholding of religiously contested reproductive and end-of-life care by both individual physicians and entire institutions. Against this background, transparency becomes a limited solution to problems of access. Where entire institutions may withhold care, access becomes more difficult to obtain. Nonetheless, with regard to treatments or drugs in a competitive market and in nonurgent situations, individual disclosure may work to achieve efficiency.

Health care transparency initiatives focused on democratic decision making similarly have some promise. Religious hospital mergers have spurred community and political engagement in the allotment of the public good of health care. Religious transparency has generated compromises in disputes thought intractable.

Transparency of religious objections, however, fits uneasily into an informed consent ideal. Instead of facilitating patient values and autonomy, it seems merely to administer information. In this sense, as with HIPAA privacy policies, a receptionist seems a more appropriate person to disclose that a gynecologist does not prescribe contraceptives than does a doctor. Fundamentally, while transparency as to contested procedures, treatments, and drugs might permit a trusting and informed relationship for some patient–provider pairs, disclosure of objections to providing information flies in the face of professional ethics and renders informed consent the assumption of risk.

PART III

Transparency and Economics: Health Care Costs and Billing

Introduction to Part III

Kristin M. Madison

Health care markets have long been murky. Patients regularly buy health care goods and services with little idea of their ultimate price or quality. Price-setting mechanisms are mysterious, with prices often varying over time and across payers. This lack of transparency in health-related markets is problematic. Patients are not able to exercise their autonomy as consumers; without information about price or quality, they cannot identify the goods or services that best suit their needs. A lack of information hobbles competition, weakening forces that might otherwise lead to lower-cost goods and services and a more efficient marketplace. Information gaps can also impede regulation that might otherwise address marketplace shortcomings.

Each of the four chapters in this section highlights a potential path by which greater transparency could benefit the health care system. At the same time, each chapter reveals limits to the transparency strategy it sets forth. Collectively, the chapters demonstrate that achieving transparency is hard. Realizing transparency's full potential as a transformative tool is even harder.

The chapter by Wendy Netter Epstein, "Price Transparency: A Contracts Solution," contemplates a court confronted with a contract dispute between patient and provider. What should the court do when the parties have failed to discuss price? Epstein suggests that under some circumstances, courts should turn to a penalty default rule: they should recognize a price of zero. This may seem a harsh outcome for the provider, but it would push providers to disclose their prices before delivering their services, increasing transparency and ultimately rendering application of the rule unnecessary.

Epstein's key insight is that provider–patient interactions bear a close resemblance to a contracting situation that has long interested contracts scholars: a situation in which one party withholds information that the other party needs for efficient contracting. In such circumstances, a penalty default rule can elicit information from a party not otherwise inclined to share it. Applying the penalty default rule to the health care marketplace is a creative and potentially workable solution that could help improve transparency in settings in which contract formation is possible.

And yet it is a solution with limits. First, as Epstein explains, penalty default rules are only appropriate under a limited set of conditions. Second, even when these conditions hold, it is not clear how often courts would be willing to make the leap from current law to a penalty default. Under current law, if a court views a provider–patient relationship as quasi-contractual, rather than contractual, it would generally apply the principle of quantum meruit, so that the patient's payment would be based on the reasonable value of services provided. Alternatively, if a court determines that a bargain is sufficiently well defined to constitute a contract, despite a missing price term, the Restatement (Second) of Contracts suggests that the court should supply "a term which is reasonable in the circumstances."[1] The patient would therefore pay a "reasonable" amount. Epstein highlights a third possibility: a court might not view a price term as missing at all, but instead as being contained within a hospital chargemaster. Any of these approaches would yield a price greater than zero. Thus, a critical question is whether courts would be willing to abandon rules generating positive prices in favor of a price-of-zero penalty default that would dramatically transform providers' interactions with patients. The existing academic literature on penalty default rules provides little guidance on this question. The literature devotes significant attention to which traditional common law rules might be classified as penalty defaults, or not, but much less attention to the real-life evolution of rules from traditional defaults to penalty defaults. The question of courts' willingness to embrace penalty default rules merits further exploration in future work.

In "Solving Surprise Medical Bills," Mark A. Hall considers a variation on the problem at the heart of Epstein's chapter. What happens when an insured patient discovers, after receiving care, that a provider responsible for some aspect of that care is not actually part of the insurer's network, substantially increasing the patient's out-of-pocket costs? Hall contributes to the conversation around transparency by recognizing that it is a tool that could help solve this problem: in some situations, providers could disclose their non-network status to patients before delivering care. Patients could respond by turning to another provider.

Hall's systematic analysis also makes clear, though, that transparency is at best only part of the solution. As Epstein also recognizes, in emergency situations, disclosure may not be useful, because the patient may be unable to take action in response. Further, even in nonemergency situations, the complex relationships among different types of providers may leave a patient unable to assemble a fully in-network provider team. In such cases, the charges might be problematic even if not a surprise – the bill might just be very high, for no reason other than the presence of a non-network provider. Hall suggests several approaches that would rein in non-network providers' price-setting practices, such as a requirement for arbitration between plans and providers.

---

[1] Restatement (Second) of Contracts § 204.

While Epstein and Hall examine legal mechanisms that can help achieve greater transparency, in the chapter "Is Pharmaceutical Price Transparency an Effective Means to Reduce High Prices and Wide Price Variations?" Mark A. Rodwin studies a market in which transparency has already increased: the retail market for prescription drugs. He explains that past studies have shown considerable variation in retail drug prices, and that previous authors have pointed to a lack of transparency as an explanation. Rodwin's thorough empirical analysis shows convincingly that even in an era in which prices are available online and apps facilitate comparison, price variation persists. His findings demonstrate that the impact of increased transparency is limited. It does not always yield perfect competition.

Rodwin's work raises several interesting questions. First, the study shows that online prices and mobile apps are not market panaceas. But what would the market for retail pharmaceuticals look like today, if these transparency tools did not exist? Were these tools completely ineffective? Or did they help, at least to some extent? Did the tools matter for some drugs more than others, and, if so, why? Second, to what extent is the persistence in price variation due to limits in the currently available tools, as opposed to characteristics of the health care marketplace? Rodwin provides a thoughtful discussion of potential reasons for continued price variation, but further studies in this area are warranted. Might the perfect app be around the corner? Or will retailers always have the ability to respond in ways that undermine the salutary effects of transparency?

The chapter by Ameet Sarpatwari, Jerry Avorn, and Aaron S. Kesselheim, "Transparency on Prescription Drug Research Expenditures: A Lever for Restraining Pricing," shares with the other chapters in this section a hypothesis that greater transparency might benefit patients. The mechanism it focuses on, however, is different: the chapter explores ways in which greater transparency might improve the regulatory process.

The authors first consider the potential impact of laws requiring disclosure of pharmaceutical companies' research and development costs. These laws are motivated by the idea that the disclosures will facilitate an assessment of whether drug prices are too high. After explaining why these laws might not work as anticipated, the authors discuss alternative disclosure requirements that might produce better results. Specifically, they focus on disclosure requirements that facilitate regulators' work by illuminating the complex workings of current pharmaceutical markets.

When it comes to transparency, the shift in focus from patients to regulators is an important move. There has been plenty of academic criticism of disclosure as a regulatory strategy,[2] and while there are circumstances in which greater disclosure may be beneficial,[3] Epstein's, Hall's, and Rodwin's chapters all indicate that there

---

[2] See generally Omri Ben-Shahar & Carl E. Schneider, More Than You Wanted to Know: The Failure of Mandated Disclosure (2014).
[3] See generally Kristin Madison, Health Care Quality Reporting: A Failed Form of Mandated Disclosure?, 13 Ind. Health L. Rev. 310 (2016).

are limits to the benefits of transparency directed toward patients. But regulators have the capacity to understand information that patients cannot begin to comprehend, and regulators can put this information to use in ways that consumers cannot. With more information about the way that the world actually works, regulators could potentially craft regulations that respond to market shortcomings.[4] But just as there are limits to the usefulness of transparency in the consumer context, there are limits to the usefulness of transparency in the regulatory context. Creating an effective reporting regime is challenging. What information, exactly, must be reported, and when? What kinds of reporting burdens are acceptable? Will required reporting influence regulated entities' behavior in unexpected, or unwanted, ways? Once informed, will regulators really be able to put that information to good use, or will regulatory solutions remain elusive? Sarpatwari, Avorn, and Kesselheim point us to specific areas in which these questions ought to be more fully explored.

Taken together, these four chapters make significant contributions to the growing literature on transparency in health care by illustrating both the promise of transparency in the health marketplace and transparency's limits as a tool for achieving policy goals. In doing so, they provide considerable insight into how legal tools might be used to improve the health care system.

---

[4] See, e.g., Kristin Madison, Harald Schmidt & Kevin G. Volpp, Using Reporting Requirements to Improve Employer Wellness Incentives and Their Regulation, 39 J. Health Pol. Pol'y & L. 1013 (2014) (discussing disclosure requirements in the regulatory context).

8

Transparency on Prescription Drug Research Expenditures

A Lever for Restraining Pricing?

Ameet Sarpatwari, Jerry Avorn, and Aaron S. Kesselheim[*]

I. INTRODUCTION

U.S. spending on prescription drugs has risen sharply over the past three years. This growth has been driven by the introduction of costly new agents, routine markups of existing brand-name products, and exorbitant price increases of a small number of generic drugs.[1] In the absence of meaningful steps by the federal government to reduce rising drug prices, some states have recently experimented with novel solutions. The most notable and politically successful of these have been based on the principle of transparency or disclosure. Legislators in several states have proposed bills that would require pharmaceutical companies to reveal research and development costs for high-priced drugs, enabling assessment of the claim that such prices are justified by the expense of bringing the products to market.[2]

In this chapter, we review these bills and evaluate the ethical, legal, and practical considerations they raise. After describing the impact of rising prescription drug prices on payers, patients, and the health care system, we highlight the provisions and status of pharmaceutical research cost transparency bills proposed in 2016. We argue that while states may have the legal power to compel the disclosures sought, challenges exist in obtaining accurate cost estimates and in translating the provided information into effective drug pricing policy. Finally, we discuss the type of transparency that could be most effective in facilitating better policymaking, concluding that greater knowledge of markups at each stage of the supply chain and incentives for high-cost medication use (for example, drug coupons) would best help

---

[*] This work is based in part on the following article: Ameet Sarpatwari, Jerry Avorn & Aaron S. Kesselheim, State Initiatives to Control Medication Costs – Can Transparency Legislation Help?, 374 New Eng. J. Med. 2301 (2016). Used with permission.
[1] See generally Aaron S. Kesselheim, et al., The High Cost of Prescription Drugs in the United States: Origins and Prospects for Reform, 316 JAMA 858 (2016).
[2] Rebecca Robbins, With Tens of Millions on Hand, Drug Makers Fight State Efforts to Force Down Prices, STAT News, June 9, 2016, www.statnews.com/2016/06/09/drug-companies-fight-back/.

states develop and prioritize pragmatic solutions to the growing unaffordability of prescription drugs.

II. RISING DRUG PRICES AND THEIR CONSEQUENCES

Between 2013 and 2015, net U.S. spending on prescription drugs increased approximately 20 percent,[3] outpacing all other health care costs.[4] This growth was primarily fueled by rising launch prices and markups on existing brand-name drugs. In 2014, for example, the average annual retail price for a new oral cancer medication was $135,900, $50,000 (inflation adjusted) higher than in 2011.[5] In 2013 alone, the average retail price of brand-name drugs most commonly used by the elderly rose 13 percent.[6] Prices of select generic drugs have also increased, in some cases sharply. Although the average price of a fixed basket of 1,441 generic drugs decreased 14 percent from 2010 to 2015, prices of 315 (22 percent) products more than doubled.[7] These products included treatments for relatively uncommon conditions such as toxoplasmosis (pyrimethamine [Daraprim]) and parasitic infections (albendazole [Albenza]).[8] They also encompassed generic drugs coupled to patented delivery systems. Between 2009 and 2016, for example, the price of epinephrine autoinjector (EpiPen) increased 486 percent.[9] Similarly, since 2014, the price of one formulation of the opioid reversal agent naloxone (Evzio) has risen 550 percent.[10]

Such trends have strained budgets, particularly those of government payers. Net spending on retail prescription drugs in Medicaid – the federal- and state-sponsored health insurer for low-income Americans – increased 25 percent in 2014 and 14

[3] Medicines Use and Spending in the U.S.: A Review of 2015 and Outlook to 2020, IMS Inst. for Healthcare Informatics (Apr. 2016), https://morningconsult.com/wp-content/uploads/2016/04/IMS-Institute-US-Drug-Spending-2015.pdf.
[4] Anne B. Martin, et al., National Health Spending: Faster Growth in 2015 as Coverage Expands and Utilization Increases, 36 Health Aff. 166, 170 (2017).
[5] Stacle B. Dusetzina, Drug Pricing Trends for Orally Administered Anticancer Medications Reimbursed by Commercial Health Plans, 2000–2014, 2 JAMA Oncology 960, 960 (2016).
[6] Stephen W. Schondelmeyer & Leigh Purvis, Trends in Retail Prices of Prescription Drugs Widely Used by Older Americans, 2006 to 2013, AARP Pub. Pol'y Inst. (Feb. 2016), www.aarp.org/content/dam/aarp/ppi/2016–02/RX-Price-Watch-Trends-in-Retail-Prices-Prescription-Drugs-Widely-Used-by-Older-Americans.pdf.
[7] U.S. Gov't Accountability Off., GAO-16–706, Generic Drugs Under Medicare: Part D Generic Drug Prices Declined Overall, but Some Had Extraordinary Price Increase (Aug. 2016), http://www.gao.gov/assets/680/679022.pdf.
[8] Jing Luo, et al., Regulatory Solutions to the Problem of High Generic Drug Costs, 2 Open F. Infectious Diseases 1, 1 (2015).
[9] Shefali Luthra, Massive Price Hike for Lifesaving Opioid Overdose Antidote, Scientific American, Feb. 2, 2017, www.scientificamerican.com/article/massive-price-hike-for-lifesaving-opioid-overdose-antidote1/.
[10] Matt Miller, There's Absolutely No Reason Why an EpiPen Should Cost $300, Slate, July 8, 2016, www.slate.com/articles/health_and_science/moneybox/2016/07/epipen_costs_have_soared_450_per cent_in_the_past_12_years_for_no_good_reason.html.

percent in 2015.[11] Between 2013 and 2016, per beneficiary expenditures in Medicare Part D – the government drug benefit program for Americans sixty-five years and older – rose on average 4.4 percent annually.[12] Private employers have not been immune. Retail medication costs now account for 19 percent of expenditures in employer health insurance plans.[13]

When possible, payers have shifted more of this burden directly onto patients. Almost all Medicare Part D plans now require coinsurance (that is, a percentage payment as opposed to a flat amount) for more than one tier of covered drugs.[14] As a result, some seniors have been forced to pay up to $12,000 annually in out-of-pocket costs for certain medications.[15] Coinsurance tiers and higher deductibles have also impacted recipients of employer-sponsored health insurance. The percentage of people in large employer health plans who paid more than $1,000 in out-of-pocket costs on prescription drugs almost tripled from 2004 to 2014.[16]

The consequence of this shift has been predictable, but nonetheless tragic. Among 648 respondents to a 2015 Kaiser Family Foundation survey, 25 percent reported that they or another family member did not fill a prescription drug in the past year because of cost; 19 percent reported cutting their pills in half or skipping doses.[17] Many Americans can no longer afford all of their medications.

III. PHARMACEUTICAL RESEARCH COST TRANSPARENCY BILLS

With little relief coming from Congress despite ongoing efforts by federal legislators, states have started experimenting with novel approaches to the problem of high drug prices. One tactic has been to tighten eligibility requirements for some high-cost products. In the case of the hepatitis C treatment sofosbuvir (Sovaldi), for example, most state Medicaid programs limit coverage to patients who already have moderate

---

[11] Medicaid Payment for Outpatient Prescription Drugs, MACPAC. 1–1 (Mar. 2017), www.macpac.gov/wp-content/uploads/2015/09/Medicaid-Payment-for-Outpatient-Prescription-Drugs.pdf.
[12] The Medicare Part D Prescription Drug Benefit, The Henry J. Kaiser Fam. Found. (Oct. 2017), http://files.kff.org/attachment/Fact-Sheet-The-Medicare-Part-D-Prescription-Drug-Benefit.
[13] Drew Altman, Prescription Drugs' Sizeable Share of Health Spending, Washington Post, Dec. 13, 2015, http://blogs.wsj.com/washwire/2015/12/13/prescription-drugs-sizable-share-of-health-spending/.
[14] Dan Mangan, New Drug Cost Picture for Seniors in Medicare Part D, CNBC, Mar. 10, 2016, www.cnbc.com/2016/03/10/new-drug-cost-picture-for-seniors-in-medicare-part-d.html.
[15] Although a Small Share of Medicare Part D Enrollees Take Specialty Drugs, A New Analysis Finds Those Who Do Can Face Thousands of Dollars in Out-of-Pocket Costs Despite Plan Limits on Catastrophic Expenses, The Henry J. Kaiser Fam. Found. (Dec., 2015), http://files.kff.org/attachment/Fact-Sheet-The-Medicare-Part-D-Prescription-Drug-Benefit.
[16] New Analysis Finds Out-of-Pocket Prescription Drug Spending Decreasing on Average, But More People Spending in Excess of $1,000 a Year, The Henry J. Kaiser Fam. Found. (Sept. 2016), http://kff.org/health-costs/press-release/new-analysis-finds-out-of-pocket-prescription-drug-spending-decreasing-on-average-but-more-people-spending-in-excess-of-1000-a-year/.
[17] 2015 Employer Health Benefits Survey, The Henry J. Kaiser Fam. Found. (Sept. 2015), http://kff.org/report-section/ehbs-2015-summary-of-findings.

liver damage, as measured by their fibrosis scores.[18] Several states additionally required patients to abstain from drug and alcohol use.[19] Such coverage restrictions have been criticized for being non-evidence-based and discriminatory, and also for limiting access to highly effective drugs treating a communicable disease.[20] For example, in May 2016, a federal district court judge granted a preliminary injunction requiring Washington's Medicaid program to provide sofosbuvir and other newer therapies to adult Medicaid recipients with hepatitis C regardless of fibrosis score.[21]

Another strategy has been to contract with nonprofit academic detailing organizations to assess the most current evidence about medications and educate prescribers about the relative effectiveness, safety, and cost-effectiveness of their therapeutic choices.[22] Between 2013 and 2015, for example, Pennsylvania's Pharmaceutical Assistance Contract with the Elderly (PACE) program partnered with the nonprofit Alosa Health to provide nine academic detailing modules for primary care physicians caring for PACE beneficiaries.[23]

Yet many policymakers argue that still more is needed. To evaluate the controversial argument that high drug prices are a fair and necessary reflection of the costs incurred in bringing a product to market, numerous states introduced bills requiring pharmaceutical companies to disclose such costs in 2016 (Table 1). Many of the proposed laws would have applied to drugs with wholesale acquisition costs (WAC) of at least $10,000 annually or per course of treatment, and most would have required companies to report on the extent to which public funding supported their research and development. Bills introduced in Massachusetts and Tennessee in 2016 would have further compelled reporting of prices charged in other countries as well as those paid by other purchasers in the state, including pharmacy benefits managers (PBMs), entities that manage prescription drug insurance plans and often receive substantial rebates from manufacturers as part of the formulary determination process that are kept secret as proprietary information.

[18] Hepatitis C: The State of Medicaid Access, National Virus Hepatitis Roundtable & Ctr. for Health Law & Pol'y Innovation (Nov. 14, 2016), www.chlpi.org/wp-content/uploads/2013/12/HCV-Report-Card-National-Summary_FINAL.pdf.
[19] Mangan, supra note 18.
[20] Felice J. Freyer, Hepatitis C Drug Costs Leave Many Without Care, Boston Globe, Apr. 9, 2016, www.bostonglobe.com/metro/2016/04/09/for-hepatitis-patients-cure-for-high-drug-prices/j2X4aVi7BEpU5BSL0YVovN/story.html.
[21] JoNel Aleccia, Judge Orders Washington Medicaid to Provide Lifesaving Hepatitis C Drugs for All, Seattle Times, updated May 30, 2016, www.seattletimes.com/seattle-news/health/judge-orders-apple-health-to-cover-hepatitis-c-drugs-for-all/.
[22] Michael A. Fischer & Jerry Avorn, Academic Detailing Can Play a Key Role in Assessing and Implementing Comparative Effectiveness Research Findings, 31 Health Aff. 2206, 2207 (2012).
[23] Annual Report to the Pennsylvania General Assembly, Pharmaceutical Assistance Contract for the Elderly (Jan. 2015), www.aging.pa.gov/publications/annual-reports/Documents/2014%20PACE%20Annual%20Report.pdf.

TABLE 1 *Representative Pharmaceutical Research Cost Transparency Bills in 2016*

State	Applicable Drugs	Reporting Requirements
California	– New drugs with ≥$10,000 WAC per patient per year or per course of treatment – Brand-name drugs for which WAC has increased >$10,000 or 10% in the past year – Generic drugs with ≥$100 WAC per month's supply for which WAC has increased > 25% in the past year	Cost – Research and development – By company, predecessors, and others (e.g., state) – Clinical trials – Company, predecessors – Acquisition or licensing – Manufacturing – Marketing and advertising – Consumers, physicians – Patient assistance programs Price – WAC and AWP increases
Colorado	≥$50,000 WAC annually or per course	
New York	≥$10,000 WAC annually or per course	
Oregon	≥$10,000 WAC annually or per course	
Pennsylvania	All drugs delivered for treatment in the state	
Massachusetts Tennessee	Critical drugs identified on the basis of cost to public programs, cost in the state, utilization in the state, and impact of the drug on state health care cost growth	Costs – Production – Research and development – Total, with public funds, after tax, and by others Price – In select countries – Paid by purchasers within state – Paid by prescription benefits managers (post-rebate)
North Carolina	Brand-name antidepressants; biologics; injectables; oral cancer therapies; oral analgesics; oral medications for asthma, allergies, or other respiratory conditions; and statins	Cost – Research and development – Production – Administration, marketing, and advertising – Direct-to-consumer coupons – Financial assistance programs Price – WAC and AWP increases Profit
Vermont	Up to 15 drugs for which the state spends a substantial amount and for which WAC has increased by 50% or more over the past 5 years or by 15% or more in the past year	Justification for the price increase in a format the state attorney general determines to be understandable and appropriate, which may include an explanation and percent of contribution for each factor

TABLE 1 *(continued)*

State	Applicable Drugs	Reporting Requirements
Virginia	≥$10,000 WAC per course of treatment	Cost – Research and development, including clinical trials – By company and others (e.g., state) – Manufacturing – Acquisition or licensing Price – WAC and AWP increases

WAC = wholesale acquisition cost; AWP = average wholesale price.

The bills were unsurprisingly met with strenuous opposition from the pharmaceutical industry,[24] and only Vermont's passed.[25] Vermont's law requires the state's Green Mountain Care Board to compile an annual list of fifteen different-class drugs for which the state spends a substantial amount and for which the WAC increased 50 percent or more over the past five years or 15 percent or more over the past twelve months.[26] Manufacturers of the drugs must provide a justification for the price increase to the state attorney general, who will then issue a public report on the price increases stripped of identifiers.[27] Some 2016 bills have since been reintroduced in the 2017 state legislative sessions, but only one – in California – has passed.[28]

A. Possible Merits of Research Cost Transparency

Pharmaceutical research cost transparency bills are motivated by the notion that the price of a drug should reflect not only an assessment of its clinical benefit – represented by its cost-effectiveness or economic value – but also the effort and resources expended in its creation. Proponents of these bills argue that payers have a right to know how a drug's current price relates to such factors as its development, manufacturing, and marketing costs. In theory, this information would assist policymakers in determining when a price is reasonable, and in pushing back when it is

---

[24] Adrianne Appel, PhRMA Wins Most Battles Against States' Price Transparency Laws, Bloomberg BNA, July 25, 2016, www.bna.com/phrma-wins-battles-n73014445219/.
[25] Ed Silverman, Vermont Becomes First State to Require Drug Makers to Justify Price Hikes, STAT News, June 6, 2016, www.statnews.com/pharmalot/2016/06/06/vermont-drug-prices-transparency/.
[26] Vt. Stat. Ann. tit. 18, § 4635.
[27] Id.
[28] Tracey Seipel, California Drug Pricing Transparency Bill Heads to Gov. Brown, Mercury News, Sept. 13, 2017, www.mercurynews.com/2017/09/13/california-drug-pricing-transparency-bill-heads-to-gov-brown/.

not. For example, according to this perspective, knowledge that drug development was heavily subsidized by the public through funding by the National Institutes of Health or a public–private partnership program, such as the Biomedical Research and Development Authority, would make a proposed steep price increase less reasonable and provide additional ammunition to states to resist it.

Such transparency could prove particularly useful when manufacturers have explicitly invoked investment in research and development to justify their high launch prices or price increases. Last year, for example, Mylan claimed that it had invested about $1 billion to improve its epinephrine autoinjector since 2007.[29] However, the company failed to offer specifics to back up its assertion. Compulsory disclosure of research costs could shine light on whether such assertions were true and, in this manner, indirectly encourage manufacturers to invest more heavily in drug development. Prior research has found that large pharmaceutical companies allocate on average only 15 percent of their revenues to basic and translational research – about half as much as they spend on marketing.[30] Knowing that their proposed launch prices and price increases would be evaluated in light of their spending priorities, manufacturers could be incentivized to dedicate more resources to such activities in order to justify their prices.

More widespread knowledge of the cost of drug development could also encourage policies to promote innovation in areas of high public health importance, such as prizes for the creation of novel antibiotics. Currently preferred policy levers to spur drug development – exclusivity provisions and priority review vouchers – are frequently associated with windfall profits.[31] More narrowly tailored incentives, developed based on information gleaned from pharmaceutical research cost transparency laws, could help save scarce public health resources while still providing adequate motivation for companies to enter the field.

Finally, greater clarity on drug development costs could facilitate exercise of government patent use rights. Under federal law, the government may use a patented invention without permission provided it pays "reasonable and entire compensation for such use and manufacture."[32] Louisiana is actively exploring petitioning the Department of Health and Human Services to exercise this right for sofosbuvir and other new high-priced hepatitis C treatments.[33] However, determining what constitutes reasonable and entire compensation has proven difficult.

---

[29] Robert King, Mylan CEO Believes EpiPen Price "Fair", Wash. Examiner, Sept. 21, 2016, www.washingtonexaminer.com/mylan-ceo-believes-epipen-price-fair.
[30] Ben-Shahar and Schneider, supra note 2.
[31] See generally Aaron S. Kesselheim, et al., Experience With the Priority Review Voucher Program for Drug Development, 314 JAMA 1687 (2015); Jennifer S. Li et al., Economic Return of Clinical Trials Performed Under the Pediatric Exclusivity Program, 297 JAMA 480 (2007).
[32] 42 U.S.C. § 1498.
[33] Sarah Jane Tribble, Louisiana Proposes Tapping a Federal Law to Slash Hepatitis C Drug Prices, Kaiser Health News, May 5, 2017, http://khn.org/news/louisiana-proposes-tapping-a-federal-law-to-slash-hepatitis-c-drug-prices/.

Industry-backed economists have hypothesized that it now costs on average $2.6 billion to bring a drug to market,[34] but this estimate has been highly criticized – in part based on a lack of transparency as to the data used to derive it.[35] Pharmaceutical research cost transparency bills could help provide a more objective, evidence-based figure.

B. Drawbacks of Research Cost Transparency

Opponents of the pharmaceutical research cost transparency bills have raised several counterarguments, some of which carry more weight than others. One of the most common criticisms is that the information that states would receive would not account for expenditures on failed products or unsuccessful research programs,[36] which constitute a large component of the development costs of the minority of drugs that reach the market. But nothing would prevent drug companies from supplying the cost of failures or states from demanding such information in addition to the cost of successfully marketed drugs. In fact, the edited version of California's failed 2015 bill demanded that applicable companies supply the "total costs of drugs or research projects that failed to succeed through the process to market approval."[37]

Determining which "sunk costs" should count, though, is challenging. Would companies be allowed to recoup the costs of a failed drug for Alzheimer's disease by raising the price of a new drug for diabetes? Should states or private-sector payers have the right to make such resource-allocation decisions? Insufficient attention has been given to such fundamental questions, which will have to be worked out if pharmaceutical research cost transparency legislation is to be equitable and effective.

Critics of pharmaceutical research cost transparency also argue that it is unclear whether cost is the appropriate metric for a fair assessment of selling price. If a company had a tortuous and inefficient process for developing yet another statin, and it was no more safe or effective than existing statins, would that justify a higher price? The economics literature would suggest that the price of a product should be aligned with the actual value (that is, the clinical utility) it provides, an assessment traditionally based on a drug's cost-effectiveness, rather than how much it cost to develop.[38] In the case of generic drugs, for which value-based pricing would not

---

[34] Joseph A. DiMasi, et al., Innovation in the Pharmaceutical Industry: New Estimates of R&D Costs, 47 J Health Econ. 20, 20 (2016).
[35] Jerry Avorn, The $2.6 Billion Pill–Methodologic and Policy Considerations, 372(20) New Eng. J. Med. 1877, 1877–78 (2015).
[36] Rachel King & Doug Doerfler, Md. Drug Pricing Transparency Bill Misunderstands U.S. Medicine Market, Baltimore Sun, February 22, 2017, www.baltimoresun.com/news/opinion/oped/bs-ed-drug-pricing-con-20170222-story.html.
[37] AB-463, Reg. Sess. (Ca. 2016).
[38] Peter J. Neumann & Joshua T. Cohen, Measuring the Value of Prescription Drugs, 373 New Eng. J. Med. 2595, 2595 (2015); see also Adrian Towse et al., The Oxford Handbook of the Economics of the Biopharmaceutical Industry 398 (Patricia M. Danzon & Sean Nicholson eds., 2012).

be optimal, robust competition would lead to prices close to the marginal cost of production.

Equally important, without increased flexibility to determine eligibility for inclusion in public payer program formularies – a hard sell politically that has not yet found much traction – defining development costs will not actually provide states much of an ability to push back. Federal law, for example, mandates that state Medicaid programs cover nearly all drugs approved by the Food and Drug Administration (FDA),[39] a requirement that undercuts states' abilities to extract price concessions. Medicare must likewise cover all FDA-approved drugs for six therapeutic classes, including cancer,[40] and the Centers for Medicare and Medicaid is barred from negotiating prices on behalf of Part D programs[41] even though it uses its purchasing power to negotiate reimbursement for nearly all other medical goods and services. Thus, the actual leverage that states have to use the information secured through greater transparency is limited. If identifiable information were kept confidential to respect claimed trade secrets, as with Vermont's statute, private insurers would likewise be unable to benefit directly.

IV. MORE BENEFICIAL TRANSPARENCY

Such challenges suggest that focusing on research cost disclosure is misguided. Greater benefits are instead possible from illuminating price markups by middlemen and incentives for expensive medication use. This alternate approach would yield information needed for states to develop and prioritize policy solutions regarding rising pharmaceutical costs that are within their power to implement.

First, transparency could help policymakers better understand the attempts by drug companies and PBMs to blame each other for rising drug prices, in turn empowering legislation effective at addressing spiraling medication costs. Brand-name drug makers contend that while list prices are rising rapidly, net prices are not.[42] They allege that PBMs are extracting ever-steeper discounts on products, which are not being passed to patients.[43] These artificially inflated rebates reflect a perverse incentive of PBMs, many of which are paid in part based on this spread.[44] PBMs counter that drug companies are merely attempting to deflect attention from rising net drug prices, that negotiated discounts are largely passed

[39] 42 U.S.C. § 1396r-8.
[40] 42 U.S.C. § 1395w-104(b)(3)(G).
[41] 42 U.S.C. § 1395w-111(i).
[42] Carolyn Humer, Pharma Pushes Back in Drug Price Debate, Medpage Today, Jan. 18, 2016, www.medpagetoday.com/publichealthpolicy/healthpolicy/55707.
[43] Meg Tirrell, In the Debate Over Rising Drug Prices, Both Drugmakers and PBMs Claim Innocence, CNBC, Apr. 19, 2017, www.cnbc.com/2017/04/19/in-the-debate-over-rising-drug-prices-both-drug makers-and-pbms-claim-innocence.html.
[44] King and Doerfler, supra note 40.

onto patients, and that insurers are free to set their own terms.[45] While the feud has escalated – the principal brand-name pharmaceutical trade association recently launched a "Share the Savings" advertising campaign[46]– the uncertainty in the parties driving rising pharmaceutical prices contributes to legislative inertia on the matter of high drug prices.

States could help address this uncertainty, as Massachusetts attempted, by demanding net prices for drugs paid for by PBMs operating within the state. Obtaining this information from drug companies rather than the PBMs may avoid potential preemption issues under the Employment Retirement Income Security Act.

Similar concerns over savings pass-through have been raised about so-called 340(b)-covered entities – designated hospitals and clinics that receive substantial discounts on outpatient drugs by virtue of caring for many low-income patients. The number of 340(b) organizations increased sharply, from 8,605 in 2001 to 16,572 in 2011,[47] and the populations served by the newer entities have been more affluent.[48] This finding prompted speculation that a growing percentage of 340(b) drugs were going to insured patients who paid full price. To evaluate this hypothesis, states could require all 340(b)-covered entities operating within their jurisdiction to report the margins for each 340(b)-covered drug dispensed.

Transparency could additionally help policymakers evaluate and address problems posed by prescription drug coupons. By reducing out-of-pocket but not insurer costs, coupons make expensive therapies attractive to physicians and patients when clinically comparable, lower-cost therapies are available. As with 340(b)-covered entities, the number of prescription drug coupon programs has grown, increasing 612 percent from 2009 to 2012.[49] A recent investigation estimated that coupons for brand-name drugs first facing generic entry between 2007 and 2010 resulted in $700 million in forgone savings from the underutilization of bioequivalent generics.[50] In addition to distorting insurance incentives, prescription drug coupons have raised privacy concerns over drug company ownership of

---

[45] Jared S. Hopkins & Zachary Tracer, Blame Game Over High Drug Prices Escalate with New Ad, Bloomberg, Apr. 6, 2017, www.bloomberg.com/news/articles/2017-04-06/blame-game-over-high-drug-prices-gets-worse-with-lobby-s-new-ad.

[46] AB-463, Reg. Sess. (Ca. 2016).

[47] U.S. Gov't Accountability Off., GAO-11-836, Drug Pricing: Manufacturer Discounts in the 340B Program Offer Benefits, but Federal Oversight Needs Improvement (Sept. 2011), www.gao.gov/assets/330/323702.pdf.

[48] Rena M. Conti & Peter B. Bach, The 340B Drug Discount Program: Hospitals Generate Profits by Expanding to Reach More Affluent Communities, 33 Health Aff. 1786, 1788 (2014).

[49] Dep't of Health and Hum. Servs., Office of Inspector General, Manufacturer Safeguards May Not Prevent Copayment Coupons Use for Part D Drugs (Sept. 2014), https://oig.hhs.gov/oei/reports/oei-05-12-00540.pdf.

[50] Leemore Dafny et al., When Discounts Raise Costs: The Effect of Copay Coupons on Generic Utilization, NBER Working Paper No. 22745 (Oct. 4, 2016), www.nber.org/papers/w22745.

protected health information. These programs are also often population- and time-limited,[51] which can pose a problem for chronically ill patients who need affordable access to medication for the foreseeable future. To provide a more comprehensive perspective, states could require manufacturers to disclose details of prescription drug coupon programs they directly or indirectly sponsor, including their terms and the number of prescriptions dispensed to state residents for which they were used.

V. CONCLUSION

While pharmaceutical research cost transparency laws could help provide information in a historically opaque area of the marketplace, methodologic complexities and political realities hamper the ability of state policymakers to translate this information to policies that would effectively lower drug prices. Using transparency to secure data that would help assess the extent to which markups by middlemen have increased drug prices and the harm caused by prescription drug coupon programs would be a better use of limited political capital.

---

[51] Joseph S. Ross & Aaron S. Kesselheim, Prescription-Drug Couponsv– No Such Thing As a Free Lunch, 396 New Eng. J. Med. 1188, 1188–89 (2013).

9

Is Pharmaceutical Price Transparency an Effective Means to Reduce High Prices and Wide Variations?

Marc A. Rodwin[*]

Recent literature has noted that prescription drugs are expensive in the United States compared to other countries, and that retail prices vary widely. Many observers suggest this occurs because prices are not transparent. To shed light on these issues, we sought to identify the extent of retail price variations, to explore why such variations occur, and to examine the relationship to price transparency.

Our survey of six national pharmacies reveals large price variations both among and within pharmacies for consumers purchasing drugs without insurance even while price information was available online. Pharmacies sold identical medications at up to six different prices based on various discounts available through phone apps. At five of the six pharmacies, the difference between the lowest and highest price for an individual drug ranged between $233 and $719 for a thirty-day prescription. Moreover, medications sold on pet websites were sometimes much less expensive than the lowest discounted pharmacy price. We also found that insured consumers sometimes pay more out of pocket to purchase medicines due to high co-payments than if they purchased them without insurance.

Our analysis suggests that differences in prices and out-of-pocket consumer spending are due to marketing practices that employ price discrimination, the high cost of interpreting price information, and high co-payments, rather than the lack of publicly available price information. Policymakers seeking to reduce disparities in the amounts that consumers pay need to consider strategies other than price transparency, including regulating pharmaceutical marketing practices and prices, and changing the co-payment structure of insurance policies.

OVERVIEW AND METHODS

We conducted three related surveys to identify variations in consumer out-of-pocket costs for prescription medications: (1) prices of drugs purchased at pharmacies

---

[*] Thanks are due to Samantha Cannon, Jana Lewis, David M. Narkunas, Jose Perez-Carbonell, and Ashley Berger for research assistance. Thanks also to Dr. Elene Fingerman for insights into choices physicians and patients face.

without insurance; (2) co-payments for insured patients; and (3) prices for human drugs sold on pet websites.

DRUGS PURCHASED AT PHARMACIES WITHOUT INSURANCE

We surveyed the prices of twenty-one branded drugs and their generic equivalents when consumers paid without insurance in Boston pharmacies in January through March 2017. We surveyed CVS, Rite Aid, Walgreens, Costco, Walmart, and Health Warehouse, a mail order pharmacy. We obtained list prices and discount prices from pharmacy membership plans and from discount coupons available using four different phone apps: Good Rx, WellRx, Rx Price Quotes, and Easy Drug. We selected drugs from a list of generic medications that substantially increased in price over the last few years.

Many retailers market selected low-cost generics to uninsured patients, including the medications listed on what they refer to as the "four-dollar" or "ten-dollar" list because they charge approximately four or ten dollars for a thirty-day or ninety-day supply respectively. The number of medications on retailer lists varies as follows: Costco (84); CVS (72); Rite Aid (140); Walmart (104); Walgreens (212). Retailers often sell more than one dose or form of administration.

All other medications have a list price, which is the starting point in negotiating reimbursement from insurers and pharmaceutical benefit managers (PBMs). People without insurance pay the list price unless they obtain some discount.[1]

Some pharmacies have membership discount plans. Some plans are free while others charge fifteen or twenty-five dollars a year. Costco's $110 annual membership includes all Costco products. Consumers can also obtain discounts through pharmacy discount networks (PDNs) that help manufacturers and PBMs market drugs. They make pharmacy discounts available through phone apps and online Web pages. We identified discounts available with four phone apps: GoodRx, Well Rx, Rxpricequotes.com, and Easydrugcard.com. Pharmacies offered different discounts depending on which app was used to check prices. We found seven additional phone apps but did not examine their discounts.[2]

The phone apps are marketing tools. Each app reports discounts from manufacturers, PBM, and pharmacies that participate in their program. They do not list all discounts and are not designed to identify the best available price.

---

[1] Differential pricing is a characteristic of pharmaceutical sales. See Richard G. Frank, Prescription Drug Prices: Why Do Some Pay More than Others Do?, 20 Health Affairs 116, 115–127 (2001).
[2] Other phone apps to obtain discounts include Blink health, LowestMed, Prescription saver, WeRx, Mobile Rx Card, Express Scrips, and Help Rx.

CO-PAYMENTS FOR DRUGS PURCHASED WITH INSURANCE

Consumers using insurance pay out of pocket until they reach a deductible and thereafter pay a co-payment. Co-payments vary in three ways: (1) with the drug type and drug cost; (2) with the type of policy purchased; and (3) among distinct insurance markets – employer-sponsored insurance, insurance sold through exchanges, and the Medicare drug market.

Insurers establish multiple co-payment tiers. They charge consumers higher co-payments for expensive medications as an incentive to choose lower-cost medications. Most policies set three to five tiers. We obtained co-payment information for thirty-two health plans: twenty employer-sponsored policies, twelve Mass Connector-exchange policies, and three Medicare drug policies. We compared co-payments for twenty-one drugs to the lowest price available when purchasing without insurance.

PET WEBSITE PRICES

Consumers can purchase many medications through websites that market human drugs for pets. Pet websites process prescriptions written by veterinarians and physicians. Some physicians inform patients they can cut medication costs by purchasing from pet websites.

Several medications in our pharmacy survey were not sold by pet websites. Therefore, we surveyed prices of eighteen additional human medications sold on three pet websites (1–800 PetMed, 1–800-PetSupplies.com, and Petsupplies4less.com) and compared these prices to prices at the six retail pharmacies we surveyed.

RESULTS

Drugs Purchased without Insurance

Prices Among Pharmacies

Table 1 reports highest, lowest, and second-lowest price with retailer name, the mean price charged, and the dollar difference between the lowest and second lowest price. No retailer consistently sold these twenty-one medications at the lowest or highest price. Health Warehouse and Costco offered low prices, but with few special discounts, although they did not always offer the lowest price. Health Warehouse had the lowest prices for seven medications but also the highest price for two others. Costco had six of the lowest prices and one of the highest prices. The retailer who sold the greatest number of highest-price medicines was Rite Aid, which had seven, followed by CVS, which had six.

TABLE 1 *Summary of Retail Price Variation for 21 Drugs: Highest Price, Lowest Price, 2nd-Lowest Price, Price Difference between Lowest and 2nd-Lowest Price, and Mean Price*

Prescription Drug	Highest Firm	Lowest Firm	2nd Lowest Firm	Price Difference	Mean Price
Abilify (Aripiprazole)	Walgreens: $944	Costco: $90	CVS: $159	$68	$522
Advair (Fluticasone)	Rite Aid: $330	Costco: $150	Walmart: $153	$3	$233
Albenza (Albendazole)	CVS: $5,512	Costco: $5006	Walmart $5,254	$248	$5,380
Capoten (Captopril)	CVS: $81	Costco/Walmart: $9	Rite Aid: $10	$1	$26
Anafranil (Clomipramine)	H Warehouse: $333	Walgreens: $10	CVS: $106	$91	$197
Cymbalta (Duloxetine)	Walgreens: $232	H Warehouse: $16	Walmart: $26	$10	$109
Lanoxin (Digoxin)	Walmart/Costco: $69	Walgreens: $5	Rite Aid: $10	$5	$34
Monodox (Doxycycline Monohydrate)	Walmart: $125	H Warehouse: $15	Walgreens: $15	$0.02	$56
Hyclate: Vibramycin (Doxycycline)	CVS: $183	Rite Aid: $10	Walgreens: $15	$5	$70
Erythrocin (Erythromycin)	H Warehouse: $661	Costco: $61	CVS: $183	$122	$432
Lipitor	Rite Aid: $150	H Warehouse: $6	Costco: $10	$4	$64

(continued)

TABLE 1 *(continued)*

Prescription Drug	Highest Firm	Lowest Firm	2nd Lowest Firm	Price Difference	Mean Price
(Atorvastatin)					
Glucophage (Metformin)	Walmart: $29	Walmart: $4	Walgreens/ H Warehouse: $5	$1	$10
Neptazane (Methazolamide)	CVS: $186	CVS: $31	Walgreens: $47	$16	$96
Plavix (Clopidogrel)	Rite Aid: $153	H Warehouse: $8	Walmart: $18	$11	$74
Actos (Pioglitazone)	Rite Aid: $348	H Warehouse: $7	Costco: $15	$8	$132
Feldene (Piroxicam)	Rite Aid: $123	Walmart: $48	CVS: $51	$3	$72
Pravachol (Pravastatin)	CVS: $65	Walgreens: $5	Rite Aid: $10	$5	$24
Ranexa (Ranolazine)	Walgreens: $508	Costco: $154	Walmart: $154	$0.05	$280
Risperdal (Risperidone)	Rite Aid: $120	Costco: $9	Walgreens: $15	$6	$53
Singulair (Montelukast)	Rite Aid: $170	H Warehouse: $8	Costco: $11	$3	$67
Zyprexa (Olanzapine)	CVS: $437	H Warehouse: $12	Costco: $12	$0.55	$189

TABLE 2 *Range of Prices Offered within a Single Pharmacy: Lowest Price Difference between Highest and Lowest Price, Highest Price Difference between Highest and Lowest Price, and Mean Savings by Purchasing Drug at Lowest Price*

Pharmacy	Lowest $ amount between highest and lowest price for a single medication	Highest $ amount between highest and lowest price for a single medication	$ amount between lowest and highest price difference	Mean savings when purchasing at lowest price*
Health Warehouse	$0 (Aripiprazole Digoxin, Erythromycin, Piroxicam, Risperidone. No price difference	$14 (Doxycycline)	$14	$3
Costco	$2 (Metformin)	$590 (Aripiprazole)	$588	$151
CVS	$12 (Metformin)	$731 (Aripiprazole)	$719	$172
Rite Aid	$6 (Metformin)	$507 (Aripiprazole)	$501	$145
Walgreens	$10 (Metformin)	$675 (Aripiprazole)	$665	$150
Walmart	$11 (Methazolamide)	$233 (Olanzapine)	$222	$92

* The number is obtained by calculating the difference between the highest and lowest price for each medication in each pharmacy, adding these numbers, and dividing by the number of drugs.

The average price difference between the lowest and second-lowest firm ranged between a low of $0.05 (Ranolazine) to a high of $248.26 (Albendazole). There were six drugs with a difference between the lowest and second-lowest price greater than $10 and four greater than $68.

Prices within Pharmacies

Retailers typically sold each medicine at multiple prices based on whether consumers paid list price or obtained discounts through a pharmacy membership program or used one of six phone apps. Discounts offered through pharmacy membership programs were generally smaller than with phone app coupons. We do not know the number of purchasers at each price point.

Table 2 displays the range in prices that consumers could pay when purchasing within a single pharmacy. It displays the drugs with the lowest and the highest difference between its high and low price and the dollar amounts. It also displays the dollar amount difference between the lowest and highest prices, and the mean savings available when purchasing the drug at the lowest price.

The smallest variation between a firm's highest and lowest price was $14.12 at Health Warehouse. In contrast to most retailers, Health Warehouse had few price differences because it offers no discounts through Well Rx, RX Price Quotes, or Easy Drug, nor does it offer a membership plan. It sells its drugs at comparatively low prices with some discounts through GoodRx.

Except for Health Warehouse, most retailers sold drugs at a wide range of prices. The difference between the lowest and highest prices ranged from a low of $232.70 for Olanzapine at Walmart to a high of $731.18 for Aripiprazole at CVS. The mean savings when purchasing at the lowest price ranged from $3.47 at Health Warehouse to $172 at CVS.

The highest mean savings between the highest and lowest prices was $172.18 at CVS followed by $150.98 at Costco. The lowest mean savings between the highest and lowest prices was $3.47 at Health Warehouse. The second lowest was $91.58 at Walmart.

Table 3 displays the price variations for CVS drugs. Appendices 1 and 2 have price variations for Rite Aid and Walgreens.

Drugs Purchased with Insurance

Insurance Co-payments

Policyholders pay varying amounts out of pocket depending on which co-payment tier their medication is assigned. Employer-sponsored polices have wide co-payment variations. For example, Harvard Pilgrim has co-payments of $5 (Tier 1), $25 (Tier 2), and $40 or $50 (Tier 3) for many of its health plans. Co-payments for Tier 4 range from $60 to $110. Tier 5 drugs have co-payments of 20 percent of the pharmacy price capped at $250 per prescription.

In contrast, the co-payments for Mass Connector plans offered by Tufts, Harvard Pilgrim, and Blue Cross were identical for Bronze, Silver, Gold, and Platinum type plans and were generally larger than those for employer-sponsored policies. Co-payments were as follow: Bronze policies – generics $25, preferred brands $75, nonpreferred brands and specialty drugs $100; Silver plans – generics $20, preferred brands $60, nonpreferred brands and specialty drugs $90; Gold plans – generics $20, preferred brands $30, nonpreferred brands and specialty drugs $50; and Platinum plans: generics $15, preferred brands $30, nonpreferred brands and specialty drugs $50. Deductibles and maximum out-of-pocket costs varied with each policy type.

CO-PAYMENTS COMPARED TO PHARMACY PRICES WITHOUT INSURANCE

Insurers use their purchasing power to secure price concessions but do not necessarily pass on these savings to policyholders. Insured individuals often pay a higher co-

TABLE 3 *CVS Generic Drug Pricing*

Pharmacy/Plan Name	Dose	Listed Price	Generic GoodRx	Well Rx	Rx Price Quotes	Easy Drug	Care-mark generic	Care-mark Brand-by Mail	Price Diff -High to Low	Mean All generic
Abilify (Aripiprazole)	2mg	$890	$159	$682	$845	$584	$299	$296	$731	$522
Advair	100/50mcg	N.A.	N.A.	N.A.	N.A.	N.A.	N.A.	N.A.	N.A.	N.A.
Albenza (Albendazole)	400mg	N.A.	N.A.	N.A.	N.A.	N.A	N.A.	N.A.	N.A	N.A.
Capoten (Captopril)	12.5mg	$27	$20	$27	$27	$35	**$81**	$73	$70	$26
Anafranil capsules (Clomipramine)	50mg	$267	$106	$244	$121	$209	$281	N.A.	$175	$197
Cymbalta DR capsule (Duloxetine)	20mg	**$196**	$42	$96	$190	$132	$72	$63	$154	$109
Lanoxin (Digoxin)	125mg	**$40**	$11	$33	$12	$48	$49	$29	$38	$34
Monodox (Doxycycline)	100mg	$57	$33	$73	$44	**$95**	$37	$28	$67	$56
Doryx (Doxycycline Hyclate)	100mg	$90	$46	$77	$46	$106	**$182**	$81	$137	$70
Ery-Tab (Erythromycin)	500mg	N.A.	$290	**$498**	$183	$444	$327	$440	$315	$432
Lipitor (Atorvastatin)	20mg	**$135**	$19	$70	$90	$110	$61	$52	$91	$64
Glucophage (Metformin)	500mg	$12	$13	$11	$13	**$19**	$17	$7	$12	$10
Neptazane (Methazolamide)	25mg	$106	**$49	$88	$31	$75	**$186**	$180	$154	$96
Plavix (Clopidogrel)	75mg	**$142**	$85	$80	$112	$132	$73	$64	$78	$74

(continued)

TABLE 3 (continued)

Pharmacy/Plan Name	Dose	Listed Price	Generic GoodRx	Well Rx	Rx Price Quotes	Easy Drug	Care-mark generic	Care-mark Brand-by Mail	Price Diff -High to Low	Mean All generic
Actos (Pioglitazone)	45 mg	$306	$26	$251	$183	$216	$115	$107	$280	$132
Feldene (Piroxicam)	20mg	$80	$51	$51	$54	$87	$75	$66	$36	$72
Pravachol (Pravastatin)	20mg	$34	$23	$26	$37	$65	$37	$28	$43	$24
Ranexa (Ranolazine)	500mg	$425	$365	$360	$188	$156	N.A.	N.A.	$60	$280
Risperdal (Risperidone)	1mg	$94	$19	$49	$77	$88	$80	$71	$74	$53
Singulair (Montelukast)	10mg	$129	$22	$68	$95	$108	$70	$61	$107	$67
Zyprexa (Olanzapine)	10mg	$437	$27	$96	$309	$365	$190	$184	$410	$189

payment than the price charged to consumers without insurance for the 70 to 140 generics on most pharmacies' low-cost list.

Paying for drugs without using insurance was often less expensive than purchasing the same drug under Medicare prescription drug policies. Of the twenty-one drugs that we surveyed, only two were always more expensive to purchase without insurance (Clomipramine at $106.06 and Erythromycin at $313.53).

With employer-sponsored policies, the potential benefit from purchasing drugs without insurance varied by insurer. In the Harvard Pilgrim plan, of the twenty-one drugs surveyed, only Metformin, at $3, was less expensive than the $5 co-payment. However, for the Tufts and Blue Cross plans, more cost savings were possible by purchasing without insurance. The co-payments were higher than the lowest discount price for six drugs for Blue Cross and Tufts plans.

Current insurance company business practices result in some individuals paying too much for medications. According to *Bloomberg News* and *Consumer Reports*, when an insured individual fills a prescription and the co-payment is higher than the price charged to patients without insurance, contracts between the insurer and pharmacy require pharmacies to charge the patient the co-payment.[3] The consumer pays the lower price only if she explicitly inquires whether it is possible to obtain the medication at lower cost without insurance.

PET WEBSITE PRICES COMPARED TO PHARMACY PRICES

Of the eighteen drugs on pet websites, five generic versions were priced lower than at standard pharmacies. Cefpodoxime proxetil, sold at 1–800-Petsuppplies.com for $40.20, cost $48.15 less than the lowest pharmacy price (Walgreens with Easy Rx discount for $88.35) and $99 less than the mean pharmacy price. The four other medications cost $5 or less than the lowest discount price available at pharmacies. Table 4 compares generic prices on pet sites to pharmacies.

Fewer pet sites offered branded versions of the eighteen drugs. Pet sites offered a low price for two of the branded drugs: Lanoxin sold at PetcareRx for $78.72 while the lowest price at a standard pharmacy was at Walmart, with Easydrug, for $237. Salix, Lasix was sold at PetCareRx for $5.76 while Health Warehouse, the pharmacy with the lowest price, sold it for $20.70. Table 5 compares brand drug prices on pet websites to pharmacies.

[3] Jared S. Hopkins, You're Overpaying for Drugs and Your Pharmacist Can't Tell You, Bloomberg, Feb. 24, 2017), www.bloomberg.com/news/articles/2017-02-24/sworn-to-secrecy-drugstores-stay-silent-as-customers-overpay; Aaron Smith, "Deceptive" CVS Overcharged for Drugs: Lawsuit, CNN (July 31, 2015), http://money.cnn.com/2015/07/31/news/companies/cvs-drugs-overcharge/; Teresa Carr, Can I Really Get Cheaper Meds if I Don't Use My Insurance? Consumer Reports (Apr. 30, 2013), www.consumerreports.org/cro/news/2013/04/can-i-really-get-cheaper-meds-if-i-don-t-use-my-insurance/index.htm?loginMethod=auto.

TABLE 4 *Pet Website Pricing Compared to Pharmacies*

Drugs	Firm w/Highest Price	Highest Price	Pet Firm w/Lowest Price	Lowest Pet Price	Non-Pet Firm w/Lowest Price	Non-Pet Lowest Price
Elavil (Amitriptyline)	Walmart	$12.00	petsupplies4less	$5.40	Walmart	$4.00
Vantin (Cefpodoxime Proxetil)	H Warehouse	$225.80	1800petsupplies	$40.20	Walgreens	$88.35
Lanoxin (Digoxin)	Costco/Walmart	$69.15	PetcareRx	$48.48	CVS	$10.97
Vibramycin; Adoxa (Doxycycline Hyclate)	Costco	$137.61	1800petsupplies	$21.99	Costco	$15.24
Vasotec	CVS	$41.49	**petsupplies4less**	**$5.70**	Costco	$10.76
Enalapril						
Prozac (Fluoxetine)	CVS	$151.60	1800petsupplies	$4.95	Walmart	$4.00
Salix, Lasix (Furosemide)	CVS	$14.22	PetcareRx	$3.60	Walmart	$4.00
Vistaril, Hyzine (Hydroxyzine)	1800 PetMeds	$24.30	petsupplies4less	$5.70	H Warehouse	$5.00
Cephulac, Chronulac, Constulose (Lactulose Solution)	Walmart	$30.55	petsupplies4less	$14.99	Walmart	$8.02
Synthroid, Levoxyl, Levothroid (Levothyroxine)	H Warehouse	$23.40	**1800 PetMeds**	**$3.30**	Walmart	$4.00
Tapazole	RiteAid	$25.99	**petsupplies4less**	**$8.70**	Costco	$12.03

Drug					
(Methimazole)					
Robaxin (Methocarbamol)	CVS	$15.70	PetcareRx	$9.84	H Warehouse	$5.00
Flagyl (Metronidazole)	Costco	$36.12	1800petsupplies	$10.20	H Warehouse	$10.08
Feldene (Piroxicam)	RiteAid	$123.34	PetcareRx	$77.76	Walmart	$48.04
Prednisone (Deltasone, Sterapred)	petsupplies4less	$14.70	1800petsupplies	$6.60	H Warehouse	$5.00
Aldactone, CaroSpir (Spironolactone)	RiteAid	$14.85	1800petsupplies	$12.82	Wallmart	$4.00
Theo-24, Theo-Dur, Theochron, Quibron-T/SR (Theophylline)	RiteAid	$41.69	1800 PetMeds	$24.00	H. Warehouse	$21.00
Ultram, Ultram ER (Tramadol)	CVS	$21.58	1800 PetMeds	$62.99	Wallmart	$4.90

* The items in bold font indicate drugs where pet med websites had the lowest price available.

TABLE 5 Pet Website Pricing Compared to Pharmacies for Branded Drugs

Drugs	Highest Firm	Price Highest	Lowest Firm Pet	Price Pet	Lowest Firm Non-pet	Price Non-pet
Elavil (Amitriptyline)	CVS	$654	N.A.	N.A.	Walmart	$634
Vantin (Cefpodoxmine, Proxetil)	N.A.	N.A.	N.A.	N.A.	N.A.	N.A.
Lanoxin (Digoxin)	CVS	$347	**PetCareRx**	$79	CVS	$236
Vibramycin; Adoxa (Doxycycline Hyclate)	RiteAid	$44	petsupplies4less.com	$54	CVS	$35
Vasotec (Enalapril)	Health Warehouse	$607	N.A.	N.A.	Costco	$533
Prozac (Fluoxetine)	RiteAid/Wal-greens	$417	N.A.	N.A.	Walmart	$351
Salix, Lasix (Furosemide)	RiteAid	$28	**PetCareRx**	$6	Health Warehouse	$21
Vistaril, Hyzine (Hydroxyzine)	CVS	$87	N.A.	N.A.	Walmart	$78
Cephulac, Chronulac, Constulose (Lactulose Solution)	RiteAid	$232	N.A.	N.A.	Walmart	$213
Synthroid, Levoxyl, Levothroid (Levothyroxine)	RiteAid	$43	N.A.	N.A.	Walmart	$37
Tapazole (Methimazole)	CVS	$104	PetCareRx	$84	Costco	$78

Robaxin (Methocarbamol)	CVS	$58	N.A.	Walmart $50
Flagyl (Metronidazole)	RiteAid	$429	N.A.	Walmart $321
Feldene (Piroxicam)	RiteAid/Walgreens	$366	N.A.	Walmart $277
Prednisone (Deltasone, Sterapred)	RiteAid/Walgreens	$2,490	N.A.	Costco $2,276
Aldactone (Spironolactone)	RiteAid/Walgreens	$75	N.A.	Costco $57
Elixophyllin (Theophylline)	RiteAid/Walgreens	$349	N.A.	Walmart $338
Ultram (Tramadol)	RiteAid/Walgreens	$102	N.A.	Costco $85

* The items in bold font indicate drugs where pet med websites had the lowest price available.

DISCUSSION

History of Price Transparency and Variation

Since the 1960s, scholars have documented prescription drug price variations and attributed them to lack of transparency or price discrimination. Writing in *The New England Journal of Medicine* in 1967, Glen Hastings summarized studies that found "prices ... may vary widely among pharmacies and within the same pharmacy at different times."[4] In 1973 Albert Wertheimer found that "[i]dentical prescription medicine is available at differing prices in neighboring pharmacies as well as a single pharmacy at different times."[5] In 1975 John Cady and Alan Andreasen reported that prescription prices were not readily available, that many states prohibited advertising prices, and that this prohibition facilitated price discrimination.[6] Their survey found variations ranging between 146 and 251 percent. Half of the time, the same pharmacy charged various individuals different prices. In 1977 Richard, Berki, and Weeks found price variations of 200 percent for the fifteen most frequently dispensed medications. No pharmacy consistently offered the highest or lowest prices.[7] The authors suggested that the absence of price information caused variations. In 1986, Bernard Bloom and colleagues found wide pharmaceutical price variations and that generics were not always cheaper than branded versions.[8]

In 2002, Attorneys General surveys in Arizona and Michigan found wide pharmaceutical price variations.[9] A 2004 survey in the five New York boroughs found that prices varied as much as $80 per prescription and sometimes were twice as costly in one pharmacy as another.[10] Consumer Reports published guides between 2013 and 2018 to help consumers shop for medication.[11] Several states

[4] Glen E. Hastings & Richard Kunnes, Predicting Prescription Prices, 277 New Eng. J. Med. 625, 625–628 (1967).
[5] Albert I. Wertheimer, Pricing Pharmaceutical Service—Art, Science or Whim, 13 J. Am. Pharmaceutical Ass'n 11, 11 (1973).
[6] See generally John F. Cady & Alan R. Andreasen, Price Levels, Price Practices and Price Discrimination in a Retail Market for Prescription Drugs, 9 J. Consumer Affairs 33–48. (1975).
[7] S. E. Berki, J.W. Richard, & H. A. Weeks, The Mysteries of Prescription Pricing in Retail Pharmacies, 15 Med. Care 241, 247, 241–250 (1977).
[8] Bernard S. Bloom, David J. Wierz, & Mark V. Pauly, Cost and Price of Comparable Branded and Generic Pharmaceuticals, 256 J. Am. Med. Ass'n 2523, 2523–2530 (1986). This study, which found generics were not always less expensive than branded drugs, was funded by a grant from Ayerst Labs.
[9] Andrew Caffrey & Russell Gold, States Find Variations in Drug Prices Among Pharmacies in the Same Area, Wall St. J., Mar. 6, 2002, www.wsj.com/articles/SB1015383422479968120
[10] Council of the City of New York, Prescription Drug Prices: All Over the Map (Feb. 2004), www.nyc.gov/html/records/pdf/govpub/859prescdrugs.pdf. The difference in cost of purchasing medicines for an individual needing drugs for arthritis, high cholesterol, hypertension, and gastric acid disorders could vary by as much as $2,600 annually.
[11] See Consumer Reports, How to Pay Less for Your Meds (April 05, 2018), www.consumerreports.org/drugs/6-tips-for-finding-the-best-prescription-drug-prices/; see also Consumer Reports, Pharmacy Buying Guide (May 2016), www.consumerreports.org/cro/pharmacies/buying-guide; Consumer Reports, Lower Your Drug Costs With These 6 Hacks (June 1, 2018), https://www.consumerreports.org/drug-prices/lower-your-drug-costs/; Carr, supra note 3.

enacted legislation to promote pharmaceutical price transparency as a means to control costs.[12]

Price disparities have persisted while obstacles to transparency have been chipped away. In the 1970s, courts held that state prohibitions on pharmacist price advertising violated the First Amendment.[13] The rise of a computer and Internet economy has facilitated rapid access to price information. Today pharmacies can advertise prices and typically post price information online. Consumers can use phone apps and websites to search for pharmacies that sell a medication along with its price by zip code. Moreover, the phone apps offer discount coupons to obtain price reductions at certain pharmacies. Continued disparities today, despite these changes, suggest that price variations are not due to lack of transparency alone.

Too Much Information

Our survey reveals wide price variations within and among pharmacies, but this trend is not new. Our survey also reveals that firms market drugs by using phone apps and websites that make selective price information and discounts available to consumers. The problem consumers face is not the absence of price information. Indeed, proponents of competition acknowledge "[c]onsumers have never had more opportunities to obtain information about drugs" from Internet searches and public and private sector programs.[14] Rather, the key problems for consumers are high search and transaction costs due to volume of price information, extreme price variability, and the difficulty in evaluating price options in light of differences in the time spent traveling to various pharmacies or purchasing medications through the mail. In some ways, the overload of information serves to undermine transparency by making it difficult for consumers to evaluate price options.

The Bureau of Economic Research states that the wide price differences should induce comparison shopping but estimates that only five to ten percent of consumers do so for a typical prescription.[15] Why do so few consumers compare pharmaceutical prices? Despite information technology, comparing prices imposes high information costs. To identify the lowest price, consumers need to consult multiple phone apps. Insured consumers also need to identify each medication's co-payment. In addition, most insured consumers incorrectly believe that they are always better off using insurance to purchase medications. Furthermore, consumers also often have difficulty purchasing from the lowest-cost provider. They often purchase

---

[12] Ameet Sarpatwari, Jerry Avorn, & Aaron S. Kesselheim, State Initiatives to Control Medication Costs — Can Transparency Legislation Help?, 74 New Eng. J. Med. 2301, 2301–2304 (2016).
[13] *Terry v. California State Board of Pharmacy*, 395 F. Supp. 94 (N.D. Cal. 1975); *State Board of Pharmacy v. Virginia Citizens Consumer Council, Inc*, 425 U.S. 786 (1976).
[14] Devon M. Herrick, Shopping for Drugs: 2007, Nat'l Center for Pol'y Analysis (2006). (Report No. 293)
[15] Alan T. Sorenson, An Empirical Model of Heterogeneous Consumer Search for Retail Prescription Drugs, National Bureau of Economic Research Working Paper No. 8548 (Sept. 14, 2001), www.nber.org/papers/w8548.

medications when they are ill or lack the time, ability, or willingness to travel or wait. In short, consumers lack the time or ability to adequately search for price information and to evaluate the options.

Our survey shows that pharmaceutical firms engage in price discrimination and sell identical drugs within a single pharmacy at multiple prices. Simply providing more information while still imposing high transaction costs to comparison shopping is unlikely to eliminate such discrimination. Recall that airlines and hotels sell their services at different prices based on how close to the time of use consumers make their purchase and which sales agent or website consumers use to make the purchase even while these price differences are public. Similarly, pharmaceutical firms also sell identical products at different prices depending on the county where they make the sale, the insurer or hospital that purchases the product, and which of various marketing strategies they employ.[16]

To counteract the information overload that undermines the goals of price transparency, public policy could ensure that consumers have comprehensive prescription price information. It could require firms to disclose all prices and discounts and display this information through one source. But in order to promote price competition and restrict price discrimination, the law would need to require that all manufacturers, PBMs, and retailers offer all consumers the same prices and discounts. Pharmaceutical manufacturers, PBMs, and pharmacies will oppose this kind of regulation. Moreover, firms could sometimes offer discounts to all consumers with the expectation that many consumers would not use the discounts, in which case various consumers would still pay different prices. If policymakers seek to eliminate wide variations in retail pharmaceutical prices, they need to consider developing policies that regulate prices.

Our survey also shows that insurance contributes to differences in the amount that individuals pay for medications. Individuals with high co-payment plans (for example, exchange and Medicare plans) pay more than persons with better coverage. Furthermore, insurers typically charge full co-payments even if they are greater than the cost of purchasing medicine without insurance. Ending disparities in the amount consumers pay for drugs also requires addressing these problems.

CONCLUDING OBSERVATIONS

Price transparency is a necessary condition to ensure effective market competition. However, it is not a sufficient condition. There are other market imperfections besides lack of transparency, including high transaction costs. These other market imperfections can be present even when price information is available online, as it currently is today. Even more importantly, firms often engage in price discrimination as a competitive strategy, so price disparities can persist even with market competition.

---

[16] Frank, supra note 1.

APPENDIX 1 WALGREENS GENERIC DRUG PRICING

Bold font indicates highest price; italic font indicates lowest price.

Pharmacy/Plan Name	Dose	Listed Price	Generic Good Rx Coupon Price	Well Rx	Rx Price Quotes	Easy Drug	Member-Ship Price (Generic)	High Phone App Price	Low Phone App Price	Price Difference (High to Low)	Mean All Generics
Abilify (Aripiprazole)	2mg	**$944**	$317	$269	$844	$397	N.A.	$944	$269	$675	$522
Advair	100/50mcg	N.A	N.A.	N.A.	N.A.	N.A.	N.A.	N.A.	N.A.	N.A	N.A.
Albenza (Albendazole)	400mg	N.A	N.A.	N.A.	N.A.	N.A.	N.A.	N.A.	N.A.	N.A	N.A.
Capoten (Captopril)	12.5mg	$30	$15	$29	$13	$25	$10	$30	$10	$20	$26
Anafranil capsules (Clomipramine)	50mg	**$260**	$32	$234	$33	$143	$15	$260	$147	$112	$197
Cymbalta DR capsule (Duloxetine)	20mg	$232	$76	$75	$189	$92	N.A.	$232	$75	$157	$109
Lanoxin (Digoxin)	.125mg	$43	$16	$31	$15	$34	$5	$43	$5	$38	$34
Monodox (Doxycycline)	100mg	$59	$33	$57	$51	**$66**	$15	$66	$15	$51	$56
Doryx (Doxycycline Hyclate)	100mg	**$96**	$52	$51	$58	$74	$15	$96	$15	$81	$70
Ery-Tab (Erythromycin)	500mg	**$532**	N.A.	$514	$505	$443	N.A.	$532	$443	$88	$432
Lipitor (Atorvastatin)	20mg	$135	$58	$37	**$138**	$77	N.A.	**$138**	$37	$102	$64
Glucophage (Metformin)	500mg	$5	$5	$7	$10	$15	$5	**$15**	$5	$10	$10
Neptazane (Methazolamide)	25mg	N.A	$58	**$104**	$47	$53	N.A.	$104	$47	$57	$96
Plavix (Clopidogrel)	75mg	$145	$76	$39	$149	$91	N.A.	**$149**	$39	$110	$74
Actos (Pioglitazone)	45 mg	**$311**	$77	$80	$15	$148	N.A.	$311	$15	$296	$132
Feldene (Piroxicam)	20mg	**$94**	$52	$61	$92	$61	N.A.	$94	$52	$42	$72

(continued)

APPENDIX 1 *(continued)*

Pharmacy/Plan Name	Dose	Listed Price	Generic Good Rx Coupon Price	Well Rx	Rx Price Quotes	Easy Drug	Member-Ship Price (Generic)	High Phone App Price	Low Phone App Price	Price Difference (High to Low)	Mean All Generics
Pravachol (Pravastatin)	20mg	$10	$10	$17	$28	$46	$5	$46	$5	$41	$24
Ranexa (Ranolazine)	500mg	$508	$366	$361	$188	$156	N.A.	$508	$156	$352	$280
Risperdal (Risperidone)	1mg	$105	$34	$30	$35	$62	$15	$105	$15	$90	$53
Singulair (Montelukast)	10mg	$133	$63	$32	$142	$75	N.A.	$142	$32	$110	$67
Zyprexa (Olanzapine)	10mg	$325	$90	$120	$424	$248	N.A.	$424	$90	$334	$189

APPENDIX 2 RITE AID GENERIC PRICES

Bold font indicates highest price; italic font indicates lowest price.

Pharmacy/Plan Name	Dose	Listed Price	Generic Good Rx Coupon Price	Well Rx	Rx Price Quotes	Easy Drug	Membership Price (Generic)	High Phone App Price	Low Phone App Price	Difference (High to Low)	Mean All Generics
Abilify (Aripiprazole)	2mg	$900	$944	$437	$844	$440	N.A.	$944	$437	$507	$522
Advair	100/50mcg	N.A.	N.A.	N.A.	N.A.	N.A.	N.A.	N.A.	N.A.	N.A.	N.A.
Albenza (Albendazole)	400mg	N.A.	N.A.	N.A.	N.A.	N.A.	N.A.	N.A.	N.A.	N.A.	N.A.
Capoten (Captopril)	12.5mg	$45	$10	$25	$28	$28	$10	$45	$10	$35	$26
Anafranil capsules (Clomipramine)	50mg	$309	$142	$156	$300	$158	N.A.	$309	$142	$167	$197
Cymbalta DR capsule (Duloxetine)	20mg	$200	$91	$98	$189	$101	N.A.	$200	$91	$109	$109
Lanoxin (Digoxin)	.125mg	$10	$10	$35	$57	$38	$10	$57	$10	$47	$34
Monodox (Doxycycline)	100mg	$100	$81	$70	$46	$73	N.A.	$100	$46	$54	$56
Doryx (Doxycycline Hyclate)	100mg	$110	$81	$79	$41	$81	$10	$110	$10	$100	$70
Ery-Tab (Erythromycin)	500mg	N.A.	$237	$517	$505	$440	N.A.	$517	$237	$280	$432
Lipitor (Atorvastatin)	20mg	$150	$36	$82	$112	$84	N.A.	$150	$36	$114	$64
Glucophage (Metformin)	500mg	$10	$10	$14	$10	*$16*	$10	$16	$10	$6	$10

(continued)

APPENDIX 2 *(continued)*

Pharmacy/Plan Name	Dose	Listed Price	Generic Good Rx Coupon Price	Well Rx	Rx Price Quotes	Easy Drug	Membership Price (Generic)	High Phone App Price	Low Phone App Price	Difference (High to Low)	Mean All Generics
Neptazane (Methazolamide)	25mg	$115	$130	$56	$83	$58	N.A.	$130	$56	$74	$96
Plavix (Clopidogrel)	75mg	$153	$21	$98	$92	$100	N.A.	$153	$91	$62	$74
Actos (Pioglitazone)	45 mg	$348	$147	$156	$21	$163	N.A.	$348	$21	$327	$132
Feldene (Piroxicam)	20mg	$86	$61	$65	$123	$67	N.A.	$123	$61	$62	$72
Pravachol (Pravastatin)	20mg	$10	$10	$48	$21	$51	$30	$51	$10	$41	$24
Ranexa (Ranolazine)	500mg	$440	$358	$364	$188	$155	N.A.	$440	$155	$285	$280
Risperdal (Risperidone)	1mg	$120	$62	$65	$26	$68	N.A.	$120	$26	$94	$53
Singulair (Montelukast)	10mg	$170	$75	$80	$40	$83	N.A.	$170	$40	$130	$67
Zyprexa (Olanzapine)	10mg	$307	$246	$273	$19	$275	N.A.	$307	$19	$287	$189

10

Price Transparency

A Contracts Solution

Wendy Netter Epstein[*]

In the current health reform landscape, free market solutions dominate plans to improve the quality of health care and reduce its cost. Many of these solutions aim to address the well-documented moral hazard problem in health care. If purchasing insurance entitles patients to obtain unlimited care at a very low cost, they will purchase inefficiently more care than they would at market prices. In a system where patients pay monthly premiums and then have low out-of-pocket costs for incremental care, patients have little incentive to turn down care. Unsurprisingly, moral hazard creates an overutilization problem in the United States where too much high-cost but low-value care is being consumed.[1]

A popular solution has been to give patients more skin in the game. This theory predicts that increasing out-of-pocket costs through the addition of co-pays, coinsurance, and higher deductibles will make patients more cost sensitive, turning down unnecessary or expensive care to avoid the personal expense.

There are many reasons to be concerned about whether health care patients can (or should) be made to act like purchasers of consumable goods,[2] but at least one thing is clear – if patients do not know how much care costs before they agree to it, then cost is less likely to impact their decision making in the ways policymakers hope.[3] A patient who does not know that the potentially unnecessary PET scan she is about to consent to will cost her $7,000 out of pocket is not likely to reconsider the choice to undergo the scan based on cost.[4] And the patient who does not know that

---

[*] This book chapter is adapted from Wendy Netter Epstein, Price Transparency and Incomplete Contracts in Health Care, 67 Emory L. J. 1 (2017).
[1] See, e.g., Aaron L. Schwartz et al., Measuring Low-Value Care in Medicare, 174 JAMA 1067 (2014) (discussing a study of Medicare claims data that found that in a single year, 42 percent of Medicare beneficiaries had received care known to provide minimal clinical benefit).
[2] Not the least of which is concern that comparative quality information is not readily available.
[3] Some might argue, and many have, that cost should never impact health care decision making. A particularly valid concern, for instance, is that it will force low-income patients to turn down *necessary*, not just unnecessary, care.
[4] See Peter Ubel, Are High Out-Of-Pocket Costs Forcing Patients To Settle For Substandard Care?, Forbes, May 13, 2016, www.forbes.com/sites/peterubel/2016/05/13/are-high-out-of-pocket-costs-forcing-

his $68,000 angioplasty would cost $11,000 at another hospital is not likely to comparison shop effectively.

Indeed, evidence is abundant that patients do not know the cost of care before they consent to treatment. Authors have written articles with provocative titles like: "How much will surgery cost? Good luck finding out"[5] and "The Doctor Will Charge You Now – But You Don't Know How Much."[6] A recent study found that "63 percent of those who had received medical care during the last two years did not know the cost of the treatment until the bill arrived."[7]

To fix the price transparency problem, attention has focused on legislative solutions, but they are highly imperfect.[8] Most state statutes require the disclosure of pricing information, but not in a user-friendly or patient-specific way.[9] For instance, states may list average prices, or even less helpfully, hospital chargemaster rates.[10] No state requires the disclosure of the price that an insured patient will actually be required to pay out of pocket. Industry pushback on requirements to release pricing information because it is confidential or protected as a trade secret[11] has made it difficult to improve these solutions. The federal government has also made efforts to address the price transparency problem, but its efforts suffer the same problems as the state efforts in that strong enforcement has been lacking.[12]

---

patients-to-settle-for-substandard-care/#49325c30713a (discussing a patient's choice between a more accurate but more costly PET scan and a less costly and probably good enough full body CT).

[5] Steve James, How Much Will Surgery Cost? Good Luck Finding Out, NBC News.com, Feb. 11, 2013, www.nbcnews.com/id/50748682/#.V6fwmldEdiM; see also Lisa Aliferis, How Much for A Hip Replacement? Good Luck Trying to Finding Out, Kqed News, Feb. 11, 2013, ww2.kqed.org/stateof health/2013/02/11/how-much-for-a-hip-replacement-good-luck-trying-to-find-out/; Martha Bebinger & Sacha Pfeiffer, Trying To Find the Cost of a Medical Procedure? Good Luck, WBUR, Aug. 2, 2012, http://legacy.wbur.org/2012/08/02/health-care-shopping.

[6] Cody Fenwick, The Doctor Will Charge You Now – But You Don't Know How Much, Patch, May 23, 2016, https://patch.com/us/across-america/doctor-will-charge-you-now-you-dont-know-how-much-0.

[7] Devon M. Herrick & John C. Goodman, The Market for Medical Care: Why You Don't Know the Price; Why You Don't Know about Quality; And What Can Be Done about It., Nat'l Ctr. For Pol'y Analysis 1, Mar. 12, 2007, www.ncpathinktank.org/pub/st296?pg=9; Bianca DiJulio et al., Few Consumers are Using Quality, Price Information to Make Health Decisions, Kaiser Fam. Found., Apr. 21, 2015, http://khn.org/news/few-consumers-are-using-quality-price-information-to-make-health-care-decisions/.

[8] See, e.g., Ariz. Rev. Stat. Ann. § 36–125.05 (2016); Ark. Code Ann. §§ 20–7-301–307 (2016); Cal. Health & Safety Code §§ 1339.55, .056, .58, .585 (2016).

[9] See generally Report Card on State Price Transparency Laws, Health Incentives Improvement Inst. 8–16, Mar. 25, 2014,: https://www.catalyze.org/product/2017-price-transparency-physician-quality-report-card/ (indicating all but seven states receive a failing grade on price transparency laws).

[10] See, e.g., Cal. Health & Safety Code § 1339.55 (2016); see also Hospital Chargemasters, Cal. Office Statewide Health Planning & Dev., www.oshpd.ca.gov/Chargemaster/ (last accessed Oct. 1, 2018).

[11] See, e.g., 2015 Report Card on State Price Transparency Laws, Appendix I: An Analysis of Popular Legal Arguments Against Price Transparency, Health Incentives Improvement Inst. 3 (2015), www.hci3.org/wp-content/uploads/files/files/2015_Report_PriceTransLaws_06.pdf.

[12] See, e.g., Richard Daly, Expert Warns of Flawed Price Transparency Effort, Modern Healthcare, June 17, 2013, www.modernhealthcare.com/article/20130617/NEWS/306179929.

There have also been private efforts. Insurance companies have started to offer tools on their websites for their insureds to estimate the prices of procedures. Unfortunately, these tools require that the patient understand the codes for which the physician will ultimately bill. And the calculators are not binding and are often inaccurate.[13]

Contract law offers a yet unexplored solution to the price transparency problem. At its core, the problem stems from courts enforcing incomplete contracts – patient–provider contracts that lack a price term. Courts encourage providers' failures to give patients pricing by finding contracts that lack a price term to nonetheless be enforceable. Contract theory can help courts discern when contractual incompleteness is desirable and when it is undesirable.[14] Applied to health care, contractual incompleteness, including leaving out the price, is generally undesirable. Fixing contract law just might go a long way toward fixing the price transparency problem.

I. COURTS INCENTIVIZE INCOMPLETE CONTRACTS IN HEALTH CARE

Patients become obligated to pay for their health care by entering into contracts.[15] If a patient is uninsured, the patient signs a contract accepting full financial responsibility for the cost of treatment, whatever it ends up being.[16] If a patient is insured, the patient contracts with an insurance company; the insurance company contracts with providers (who become "in-network"); and the patient also contracts directly with the provider.

In a hospital setting, these patient–provider contracts almost always contain language binding the patient to pay whatever the cost of treatment ends up being. Most patient–provider contracts use language like: "The undersigned agrees ... that in consideration of the services to be rendered to the Patient, he/she hereby individually obligates himself/herself to pay the account of the Hospital *in accordance with the regular rates and terms of the Hospital*."[17] The "regular rates" of a hospital are listed in the hospital chargemaster, which is a file listing by code everything a hospital might charge for and the standard price for that item.[18]

---

[13] Elana Gordon, Patients Want to Price-Shop for Care, But Online Tools Unreliable, NPR, Nov. 30, 2015, www.npr.org/sections/health-shots/2015/11/30/453087857/patients-want-to-price-shop-for-care-but-online-tools-unreliable.

[14] Wendy Netter Epstein, Public-Private Contracting and the Reciprocity Norm, 64 Am. Univ. L. Rev. 1, 10, 28 (2014); Ronald J. Gilson et al., Contracting for Innovation: Vertical Disintegration and Interfirm Collaboration, 109 Colum. L. Rev. 431, 451 (2009).

[15] In an emergency, it may be that a quasi-contract is formed, but for the most part, patients contract for health care.

[16] Although, practically, there may be posttreatment negotiation for uninsured patients.

[17] Conditions of Admission, Cedars-Sinai Med. Ctr., www.cedars-sinai.edu/Patients/Programs-and-Services/Pain-Center/Documents/PainCenterConditionsofAdmission-75446.pdf (last accessed Aug. 13, 2016) (emphasis added).

[18] See Erin C. Fuse Brown, Irrational Hospital Pricing, 14 Hous. J. Health L. & Pol'y 11, 14 (2014); Carrie Pallardy, Deconstructing the Enigmatic Hospital Chargemaster, Becker's Hospital CFO,

While a "typical hospital bill might contain between ten to fifty items, the chargemaster contains an average of 25,000 [different] items."[19] Items are not listed by procedure name, diagnosis, or any other descriptor that would be recognizable to a patient.[20] Hospitals are permitted to change their chargemaster rates at any time without notice.[21] And the chargemaster does not reflect the rates negotiated by insurance companies.[22]

Although the law in general has struggled with when to enforce contracts that do not contain a price term and when to deem them unenforceable,[23] the law concerning open price term patient–provider contracts is remarkably well settled. Even where contracts fail to specify a price for the services to be provided, courts find them enforceable.[24]

Courts provide two primary reasons. First, many opinions state that patient–provider agreements are not really open price term agreements at all because they incorporate the chargemaster by reference.[25] In reality, these agreements are ones to simply let the provider set the price later. Patients usually cannot reference the chargemaster.[26] And even if they are able to obtain a copy, they cannot make sense of it and it is subject to change. It would be impossible for an insured patient to know the negotiated rate he or she will be charged by referencing the chargemaster. A hospital essentially reserves the right to later charge whatever it wants as long as it puts the charge into its chargemaster.[27]

Second, courts have tended to rely on the justification that it would be impossible for providers to commit to a price before the procedure because of medical uncertainty. Before treatment, "nobody yet knows just what condition the patient has, and

---

Sept. 4, 2015, www.beckershospitalreview.com/finance/deconstructing-the-enigmatic-hospital-chargemaster.html.

[19] Gerard F. Anderson, From 'Soak The Rich' To 'Soak The Poor': Recent Trends in Hospital Pricing, 26 Health Aff. 780, 786 (2007).

[20] Id.; Erin C. Fuse Brown, Resurrecting Health Care Rate Regulation, 67 Hastings L.J. 85, 105 (2016).

[21] Erin C. Fuse Brown, Irrational Hospital Pricing, 14 Hous. J. Health L. & Pol'Y 11, 14 (2014).

[22] Further, Erin C. Fuse Brown notes that "[h]ospitals readily concede that chargemaster prices do not represent the costs of providing the service, or the price anyone else pays, referring to them instead as starting points for negotiation." Erin C. Fuse Brown, Fair Hospital Prices are Not Charity: Decoupling Hospital Pricing and Collection Rules From Tax Status, 53 U. Louisville L. Rev. 509, 517–18 (2016).

[23] See Epstein, supra note *.

[24] See, e.g., Mark A. Hall & Carl E. Schneider, Patients as Consumers: Courts, Contracts, and the New Medical Marketplace, 106 Mich. L. Rev. 643, 646, 674 (2008) (noting that "courts have generally tolerated low levels of specificity in medical contracts").

[25] Id.

[26] Doe v. HCA Health Servs. Of Tenn., 46 S.W.3d 191, 194 (Tenn. 2001); see also Uwe E. Reinhardt, The Pricing Of U.S. Hospital Services: Chaos Behind A Veil Of Secrecy, 25 Health Aff. 57, 59 (2016), http://content.healthaffairs.org/content/25/1/57.full.pdf+html ("With the exception of California ... hospitals are not required to post their chargemasters for public view.").

[27] In the case of insured patients, the provider's price must be subject to the provider's negotiated rates with the insurance company.

what treatments will be necessary to remedy what ails him or her."[28] This reasoning is pervasive in court opinions.[29]

But while certain aspects of medical care may indeed be uncertain, the traditional concerns are overstated as to modern medicine. Today, providers usually know in advance what code will be used to charge the patient (for example, for an office visit, an x-ray, a flu shot, and so forth).[30] And whether the patient is insured or not, that is enough information for the provider to determine the price.[31]

A degree of complexity is potentially introduced depending on the treatment. For instance, it might be more difficult to provide a price for the oncology surgery where the surgeon really will not know the extent to which the cancer has spread until she opens up the patient[32] than for a routine flu shot. But it would be wrong to assume that all or even the majority of health care falls into the category of being highly complex and difficult to predict. Emergency room care accounts for as little as 2 percent of expenditures by some measures.[33] While some surgeries are unpredictable and uncertain, many have become more routinized over time and will only continue to be more so. Between the flu shot and the cancer surgery lies a broad spectrum of medical care. For most of it, providers should be able to determine a price, or at least a small range for the price, prior to the patient undergoing the treatment.[34]

---

[28] DiCarlo v. St. Mary's Hosp., No. CIV.A.05–1665(DRD-SD, 2006 WL 2038498, at *4 (D.N.J. July 19, 2006).

[29] See, e.g., Shelton v. Duke Univ. Health Sys. Inc., 633 S.E.2d 113, 114 (N.C. Ct. App. 2006).

[30] Indeed, trade associations, medical device companies, and others spend much time educating physicians on what coding choices will maximize their compensation. See, e.g., American Association of Neurological Surgeons, Coding Tips: Managing Coding & Reimbursement Challenges in Neurosurgery 2018, www.aans.org/Education%20and%20Meetings/Live%20CME%20Courses/Coding%20Tips%20-%20Managing%20Coding%20and%20Reimbursement%20Challenges%20in%20Neurosurgery%20Courses.aspx; Medtronic, Directory of [Reimbursement] Resources, www.medtronic.com/us-en/healthcare-professionals/reimbursement.html.

[31] Kevin R. Riggs & Peter A. Ubel, Overcoming Barriers to Discussing Out-of-Pocket Costs With Patients, 174 JAMA Intern Med. 849, 850 (2014), www.ncbi.nlm.nih.gov/pmc/articles/PMC4467553/pdf/nihms697298.pdf. Although if the patient is insured, to determine the price the patient must actually pay requires interfacing with the insurer.

[32] This is not to say that it could not be priced. It would require a complex flow chart of potential complications, but there are only so many complications that are really a possibility, and those are already detailed in the informed consent documents.

[33] Medical Expenditure Panel Survey, Dep't Health & Human Servs., Agency for Healthcare Res. & Quality (2008), http://tinyurl.com/489fa06 (citing emergency room costs at 2 percent of national spending); Michael H. Lee et al., Owning the Cost of Emergency Medicine: Beyond 2 Percent, 62 Annals of Emergency Med. 498, 501 (2013) (describing emergency room costs between 5 percent and 6 percent, but as high as 10 percent).

[34] Medicare Provider Utilization and Payment Data, Ctr. Medicare & Medicaid Srvs., www.cms.gov/Research-Statistics-Data-and-Systems/Statistics-Trends-and-Reports/Medicare-Provider-Charge-Data/index.html (last modified June 23, 2016); Peter Ubel, If Costs Are Unknown, Can Doctors Still Talk About Them?, Forbes, June 17, 2014, www.forbes.com/sites/peterubel/2014/06/17/if-costs-are-unknown-can-doctors-still-talk-about-them/#13a751ff329f.

II. SOMETIMES INCOMPLETE CONTRACTS ARE EFFICIENT AND SOMETIMES THEY ARE INEFFICIENT: HOW DO WE TELL?

Open price term contracts are one type of a larger category of "incomplete contracts."[35] Incomplete contracts, which range from those that are missing material terms like price to those that do not address possible future states of the world[36] have been the focus of intense scholarly inquiry.[37] Because the law gives incentives to parties in their drafting choices, the difficult task of distinguishing "good" incompleteness from "bad" incompleteness is particularly important to legal doctrine.

There are many variables that affect the efficiency and general desirability of contractual incompleteness. In the law and economics account, whether it is efficient to bear the cost of detailed drafting can be determined by a cost–benefit analysis.[38] Where the cost of detailed drafting is less than expected gains – including likelihood that litigation will result because parties take advantage of contractual vagueness – detailed drafting is the efficient choice.[39] In most situations, complete contracts are preferred.[40] There may be times where it is costly to detail the contract because the deal is complicated, future states of the world are uncertain, or reputational sanctions[41] or operating within a network[42] make litigation and opportunism unlikely. Then, it may be more efficient to draft a more incomplete contract.

On the other hand, the behavioral science literature focuses on the effect of drafting choices on party behavior and motivation. While there is solid evidence suggesting that detailed drafting can prompt compliance,[43] there is also evidence that specification causes agents to focus on what is enumerated in the contract, sacrificing the larger goals of the endeavor. Also, detail can sometimes motivate, but it can signal distrust, hamper cooperation and collaboration, and dampen an agent's

[35] See generally Robert E. Scott, A Theory of Self-Enforcing Indefinite Agreements, 103 Colum. L. Rev. 1641, 1643–45 (2003).
[36] Id. at 1641.
[37] See, e.g., Ian Ayres & Robert Gertner, Filling Gaps in Incomplete Contracts: An Economic Theory of Default Rules, 99 Yale L.J. 87, 92–94 (1989).
[38] Id. at 92; Judge Richard Posner is the most prominent supporter of this view. See Richard A. Posner, Economic Analysis of Law 1–2, 13–15 (4th ed. 1992); The Economics of Contract Law 1–7 (Anthony T. Kronman & Richard A. Posner eds., 1979); see also Adam B. Badawi, Interpretive Preferences and the Limits of the New Formalism, 6 Berkeley Bus. L.J. 1, 23 (2009).
[39] See, e.g., Keith J. Crocker & Kenneth J. Reynolds, The Efficiency of Incomplete Contracts: An Empirical Analysis of Air Force Engine Procurement, 24 Rand J. Econ. 126, 135 (1993).
[40] Louis Kaplow & Steven Shavell, Fairness Versus Welfare, 114 Harv. L. Rev. 961, 1135 (2001). For two parties to reach an optimally efficient agreement, information asymmetries may need to be mitigated. See, e.g., Eric H. Franklin, Mandating Precontractual Disclosure, 67 U. Miami L. Rev. 553, 563 (2013).
[41] Claire A. Hill, Bargaining in the Shadow of the Lawsuit: A Social Norms Theory of Incomplete Contracts, 34 Del. J. Corp. L. 191, 212–16 (2009).
[42] See Lisa Bernstein, Beyond Relational Contracts: Social Capital and Network Governance in Procurement Contracts, 7 J. Legal Analysis 561 (2015).
[43] See, e.g., Erik A. Mooi & Mrinal Ghosh, Contract Specificity and its Performance Implications, 74 J. Mktg. 105, 106 (2010); Kenneth H. Wathne & Jan B. Heide, Opportunism in Interfirm Relationships: Forms, Outcomes, and Solutions, 64 J. Mktg. 36, 36 (2000).

intrinsic desire to perform well.[44] In particular, task specification has been shown to decrease motivation where the task is complex.[45] Therefore, whereas the law and economics literature tends to favor completeness in drafting,[46] much of the behavioral literature touts the virtues of incompleteness.[47]

In synthesizing these literatures, an analytical framework emerges to help courts determine if, in any particular set of circumstances, more complete or less complete contracting is desirable.

The first factor concerns transaction costs. Where a party would incur only low transaction costs to detail a contract, a court should tend to require a detailed contract. Transaction costs will tend to be highest where the subject matter is particularly complex and/or where the future is highly uncertain. For instance, a simple sales transaction would not be costly to detail while a multiyear contract for innovation where the product to be built does not yet exist would be much costlier to detail. All else being equal, where transaction costs for detailing a contract are high, contractual completeness becomes less desirable.

The second factor requires an assessment of information asymmetry. Where one party has ready access to information that the other party does not have, often a more efficient contract can be designed when the information is disclosed. But, in general, where the more sophisticated party is a repeat player and has access to better information than the less sophisticated party, a more efficient contract will result when that information is disclosed through more complete drafting.[48] High degrees of information asymmetry counsel in favor of more detailed contracts being desirable.

The third factor concerns the extent to which a deal requires trust and cooperation to develop between the parties. Less complete contracts have been shown to build relational capital. But context matters. For instance, for some contracts, the main goal is compliance. Consider again the simple sales transaction. The parties expect that each will simply comply with the terms – for the seller to sell the item to the buyer at the agreed upon date and time for the agreed upon price. There is little need

[44] Ernst Fehr & Simon Gächter, Fairness and Retaliation: The Economics of Reciprocity, 14 J. Econ. Persp. 159, 170 (2000); see also Ernst Fehr et al., Reciprocity as a Contract Enforcement Device: Experimental Evidence, 65 Econometrica 833, 833 (1997).
[45] See Nicholas Argyres et al., Complementarity and Evolution of Contractual Provisions: An Empirical Study of IT Services Contracts, 18 Org. Sci. 3, 15 (2007).
[46] Notably, however, prominent law and economics scholars have started to accept that different contexts might merit different doctrinal treatment. See, e.g., Gilson, Sabel, and Scott, Text and Context: Contract Interpretation as Contract Design, 100 Cornell L. Rev. 23 (2014); Lawrence A. Cunningham, Contextualism in Contract Interpretation: Doctrine, Debate, and Beyond, 85 Geo. Wash. L. Rev. (2017) (compiling work).
[47] Indeed, this author has written before about circumstances where relative incompleteness is likely to engender better results than more complete drafting. See Wendy Netter Epstein, Facilitating Incomplete Contracts, 65 Case W. Res. L. Rev. 297 (2015).
[48] Ian Ayres & Robert Gertner, Majoritarian vs. Minoritarian Defaults, 51 Stan. L. Rev. 1591, 1593 (1999); Shmuel I. Becher, Asymmetric Information in Consumer Contracts: The Challenge that is Yet to be Met, 45 Am. Bus. L.J. 723, 733 (2008).

for trust to develop or for the parties to learn to collaborate. On the other hand, there are some contracting situations where developing trust and collaboration is essential. Where the development of relational capital is, relatively speaking, important and relative contractual incompleteness is likely to foster that development, courts should tolerate incompleteness. But where simple compliance is the goal, courts should prompt more complete drafting.

III. MOST HEALTH CARE CONTRACTS SHOULD CONTAIN A PRICE TERM

Applying this framework to the typical patient–provider contract suggests that in *most* cases, courts should encourage complete contracts that contain price terms. Although it is not a costless endeavor for providers to fill in the price term, for most medical treatments, the transaction costs incurred in providing a fee before treatment are relatively low. If the patient presents the provider with insurance information, the provider should have ready access to the insurer-negotiated rate. Even if some providers will not easily be able to access the pricing database, the possible technological hurdles are not insurmountable.

Certainly in some contexts, transaction costs will be higher than in others. Depending on the complexity and uncertainty in treatment, transaction costs could be quite high. Smaller providers may also bear higher costs than larger, more sophisticated ones. But for the majority of medical care, providers should be able to include a price in the patient's contract without incurring much cost to do so.

The second factor to consider is the extent of information asymmetry. Here, the provider clearly has better access to pricing information than the patient. Providers know the relevant codes and are the ones that have either set the rates (uninsured patients), negotiated the rates (privately insured patients), or been informed of the rates (publicly insured patients). While patients do have some options – for instance, they can call their insurance companies and get a sense of cost for various procedures – providers are undoubtedly better situated to obtain the information.[49]

As to the last factor, in most instances, there seems to be limited potential that leaving out a price term will serve to build positive relational capital between the provider and the patient. A provider's refusal to state a price for an x-ray is not going to make the patient trust the provider more or facilitate better collaboration on the patient's care the way that less task specification signals trust and a desire to collaborate in other settings. There is an argument to be made that keeping discussions of cost out of patient–provider communications builds relational capital, particularly when it comes to long-term relationships involving chronic disease. On the other hand, one could imagine that a doctor–patient relationship built on

---

[49] Douglas C. Berry et al., Open Price Agreements: Good Faith Pricing in the Franchise Relationship, 27 Franchise L.J. 45, 46 (2007).

trust could suffer if patients feel they are not being given critical information to make decisions about treatment – like cost.

This framework may yield different results depending on the circumstances of any individual case. But some clear guidance to the parties will emerge. For instance, it should be clear that providing a price for an x-ray is required. The transaction costs a provider would have to bear to provide the fee should be low. Information asymmetry is high. And the goal is simply to take the image – in other words, compliance with the task rather than relationship building. On the other hand, one could imagine a complex and unpredictable procedure that would be hard to price, where information asymmetry may still be high, but there is a significant need to develop a strong, long-term collaboration between the parties. There, a court could find that a level of incompleteness – including leaving price out of the contract – is the efficient course.

IV. A SOLUTION: AN INFORMATION-FORCING PENALTY DEFAULT

Theory suggests that *in most cases* it would be more efficient for patients and providers to enter into contracts that include the price. But courts enforce contracts lacking a price term. This mismatch between theory and doctrine could be fixed in a way that would prompt meaningful price transparency, by implementing a penalty default. Specifically, where providers fail to include a price, and it would have been reasonable to do so, courts should fill the gap with a price of $0.

A. What Is a Penalty Default?

Robert Gertner and Ian Ayres were the first to describe the concept of a penalty default.[50] They observed that sometimes contracts are incomplete because one party strategically withholds information from the other party, which reduces the efficiency of the deal. They suggested that lawmakers should reduce this rent-seeking, strategic behavior by "sometimes choos[ing] penalty defaults that induce knowledgeable parties to reveal information by contracting around the default penalty."[51]

Penalty defaults "operate on pre-contractual behavior" because it is the potential contractors' aversion to the penalty default that causes them to change their contractual offers.[52] An example is the rule that an agreement include a quantity term to be enforceable.[53] If the parties do not specify a quantity, the court will not fill the gap with a reasonable quantity. Instead, the court will find the contract to be invalid. The zero-quantity rule sends a message to contracting parties: specify a quantity term or

[50] Ayres & Gertner, supra note 37, at 94.
[51] Id.
[52] Ian Ayres, Ya-Huh: There Are and Should Be Penalty Defaults, 33 Fla. St. U. L. Rev. 589, 595 (2006).
[53] U.C.C § 2–201 (Am. Law Inst. & Unif. Law Comm'n 1977) ("[T]he contract is not enforceable under this paragraph beyond the quantity of goods shown in [the] writing.").

you have no contract. The effect of the penalty default is that parties are forced to contract around the default of zero quantity and instead include a quantity term.[54]

B. How Would a Penalty Default Work to Ensure Price Transparency?

In addressing the mismatch between theory and doctrine as to patient–provider contracts, courts should require that at least for low-complexity, relatively predictable health care services, providers must include the price the patient must pay. If providers leave a contractual gap as to price, courts should fill the gap with a price of $0. If a provider fails to include a price term, and the patient subsequently does not pay, the provider will not be able to recover its rate by bringing a cause of action for breach of contract. Courts could implement this penalty default simply with a change to the common law.[55] If the penalty default works, providers will respond by including pricing in their contracts where it is reasonable to do so to avoid the possibility of later being able to recover nothing.

Courts, however, would only employ the penalty default where the analytical framework set out above suggests that more complete contracting is desirable, so the emergency room patient whose care is highly uncertain would be exempted from the penalty default.[56] It is not a costless endeavor to ask courts to engage in this exercise – to determine where to employ the penalty and where not to – but neither is it particularly complicated. A regulatory framework could further simplify the task. But even without it, if litigation sends appropriate signals, the market should respond with price disclosure.

Consider the case of a patient who seeks medical attention after an injury. His doctor strongly suspects a gastrocnemius muscle tear but informs the patient that only an MRI can definitively confirm the diagnosis. With a penalty default rule, the hospital performing the MRI would likely choose to include the *out-of-pocket* cost of the test to the patient[57] in the patient–provider contract. This requires that the hospital's systems communicate with those of the insurer, but it is in the hospital's best interests to provide the lower patient-specific cost that the insured patient will actually be asked to pay if it wants the patient to consent.[58] With this information, the patient could then make an informed decision about whether to incur the cost of the expensive MRI.

---

[54] Ayres, supra note 52, at 609.
[55] See Mark A. Hall, The Legal and Historical Foundations of Patients As Medical Consumers, 96 Geo. L.J. 583, 596 (2008) (suggesting that the law could be more demanding in requiring price terms but that it would conflict with long-standing practices).
[56] Principles of quasi-contract typically apply to emergency room scenarios anyway.
[57] This will require interaction between the hospital and the insurer, for example, to ascertain how much of the deductible the insured has already satisfied, how much coinsurance would cover, how much the patient will owe, and so forth.
[58] This could also be mandated by regulation if necessary.

One concern is that providers will pass any extra cost of putting in place the pricing administrative apparatus onto patients.[59] However, while it may be true that there is some additional cost to provide pricing, the magnitude is probably not very high for most procedures. And all that is necessary for the regime to be efficient is for the savings from patients having access to cost information to be higher than the additional cost to providers of predicting cost at contract execution.

Another possibility is that instead of raising prices, providers may respond to the new regime by providing worse treatment. If providers must commit to a price in advance of a procedure, but it later turns out that the provider estimated low, the provider may do less for the patient. Negligence law would presumably address some of these concerns. But also, this is how normal markets work, and there is no reason to think that medicine is more problematic than say, building a house. Nor have we seen these effects in other priced markets, such as the market for cosmetic surgery.[60]

There are also some practical concerns. For instance, if a patient is first presented with the price right before she is taken in for the procedure (when patients typically sign consent forms), it would likely be too late for the patient to engage in the cost–benefit analysis that consumerism predicts. A better scenario would be if the patient is presented with pricing information before scheduling the procedure. Once the market reacts to the doctrinal change, market forces should dictate that cost information be produced in patient-accessible forms at the salient time.

Another concern would be that consumers will not read the contract and, therefore, will not change their behavior because of price. Or it very well might be the case that even informed patients, for any number of reasons, do not price shop or turn down unnecessary care.[61] But of course these are problems with any regime that depends on consumerism.

Finally, the purpose of a penalty default rule is to target pre-contractual behavior – to give the right incentives to the parties at the drafting stage. Where the penalty default is actually applied in litigation, however, the result seems harsh – not providing payment for services already rendered. Courts may be tempted to order payment on equitable grounds. Perhaps that would be appropriate for close-call cases. But for the penalty default to function properly, and to send the right signals, some harsh results in one-off cases are necessary.

Despite these open questions, however, the penalty default solution holds much promise. It addresses the reasons that legislation is ineffective because it requires a price specific to the individual patient, but does not run afoul of gag clauses between insurers and providers. And it allows for more nuance, only requiring price where

---

[59] See, e.g., Michelle Boardman, Penalty Default Rules in Insurance Law, 40 Fla. St. U. L. Rev. 305, 330 (2013).
[60] Herrick & Goodman, supra note 7.
[61] Patients who cannot afford care but nonetheless need it will still consent to that care under this regime. This is unavoidable in the current system.

the analytical framework suggests it should be included, so emergencies and highly uncertain procedures may be exempted. The contract solution simply takes information that was going to be provided to patients anyway and discloses it earlier in the process. Policymakers and advocates would be well advised to consider the promise of contract law in addressing the urgent price transparency problem.

11

Solving Surprise Medical Bills

Mark A. Hall*

The problem of surprise medical bills for out-of-network care is receiving increasing attention by lawmakers, media, and the public policy community. In various situations – such as emergencies and with consulting specialists – patients are billed by providers that do not participate in their health plan's contracted network, even though patients did everything they reasonably could to remain in-network. As a result, patients incur much higher charges, which sometimes are exorbitant and can lead to financial distress. There is broad bipartisan agreement that this problem exists, is increasing, and needs to be addressed.[1] Important differences exist, however, over how the problem should be solved. This paper aims to identify a satisfactory solution to surprise medical billing, beginning by describing the nature and extent of the problem, then analyzing the competing merits of the different approaches that governments have taken and others have proposed, and finally adopting key recommendations for successful reform.

THE NATURE AND EXTENT OF SURPRISE MEDICAL BILLING

Surprise medical bills result from providers (physicians, hospitals, outpatient facilities, laboratories, and so forth) that patients reasonably assumed would be in-network, but actually are out-of-network, or when patients have no real choice over the network status of their provider. The most obvious situation is when patients seek emergency care, in which case they have no time to determine which hospital is in-network, or they have no choice. In many locations, even the ambulance ride to the emergency room itself, unbeknownst to patients, can be out-of-network.[2] Another common situation that gives rise to surprise billing is the use of ancillary specialists, especially in the hospital setting. Even when a hospital is in-network,

---

* This chapter is a revision of a paper that was previously published by the Brookings Institution, as part of The Schaeffer Initiative for Innovation in Health Policy. I am grateful for their contributions and support. See Mark A. Hall, et al., Solving Surprise Medical Bills, Brookings Institution (2016).
[1] Id.
[2] Michelle Andrews, Out-Of-Network Ambulance Rides Can Bring Out-Of-Pocket Expenses, Kaiser Health News, June 14, 2011; Elisabeth Rosenthal, Think the E.R. Is Expensive? Look at How Much It Costs to Get There, N.Y. Times, Dec. 4, 2013.

patients unavoidably, and unknowingly, can receive out-of-network care when physicians at the hospital are not in-network. Many patients simply are not aware that network status can, and often does, differ between hospital facilities and the physicians who practice there. Even if patients might be aware (or made aware) that network status can differ between hospitals and various doctors, patients often have no choice over which providers care for them in hospitals. Lastly, surprise billing can occur in the outpatient setting as well. Patients obviously have more opportunity to determine network status in outpatient settings, but even there, unavoidable surprises arise. For instance, primary care and other "ambulatory" physicians usually choose which laboratories to send samples to for testing, without advising patients. Additionally, physicians that are in-network might practice at one or more facilities that are out-of-network with a particular health plan. A patient might choose an in-network surgeon with clinical privileges at several hospitals or ambulatory surgery centers, some of which are not in the network for that patient's health plan.

The Financial Consequence of Surprise Bills

Patients can suffer substantial financial harm due to surprise medical bills. Not only do patients and their health plans lose the advantage of the substantially lower rates negotiated with participating providers, out-of-network care is not covered at all by certain types of health plans. Even when plans do have such coverage, patients generally have to pay much higher cost sharing out-of-network. Moreover, insurance with out-of-network coverage typically leaves patients exposed to an additional portion of the bill that the insurer does not pay.

Insurers will only pay bills they think reflect reasonable market rates. Insurers view rates as "allowable" only if they are "usual, customary, and reasonable" – abbreviated "UCR." Substantial controversy surrounds how insurers determine when nondiscounted rates are allowable. Insurers claim widespread price gouging by providers.[3] Providers note that they often have good reason to charge patients more when they are out-of-network, and complain that insurers use inaccurate information when they calculate UCR.[4] When insurers and providers disagree on reasonable rates, the financial consequences for patients can be serious, or even ruinous. Out-of-network providers usually bill patients not only higher cost-sharing amounts, but also for the balance that exceeds what insurers consider allowable. This is especially true for the lower-income people who have acquired insurance recently under the Affordable Care Act, but surprise bills can be a financial burden for higher-income people as well.

[3] Am.'s Health Ins. Plans, Charges Billed by Out-of-Network Providers: Implications for Affordability (2015).
[4] Carol K. Lucas & Michelle A. Williams, The Rights of Nonparticipating Providers in a Managed Care World: Navigating the Minefields of Balance Billing and Reasonable and Customary Payments, 132 J. Health & Life Sci. L. (2009).

Sample Balance Billing Scenarios

	HMO In-Network	HMO Out-of-Network	PPO In-Network	PPO Out-of-Network
Provider Charge	$10,000	$10,000	$10,000	$10,000
Plan Contracted Rate	$4,000	N/A	$4,000	N/A
Plan's Allowed Amount for Out-of-Network Care	N/A	$0	N/A	$6,000
Cost Sharing	$30 co-payment plus any remaining deductible	100%	20% coinsurance (after deductible is met)	30% coinsurance (after deductible is met)
Deductible	$1,200	NA	$1,200	$2,400
What the Plan Pays	$3,970 if deductible was previously met, otherwise at least $2,770 ($3,970 − $1,200).	$0	$3,200 ($4,000 x 80%), if deductible was previously met, otherwise $2,240 [80% x ($4,000 − $1,200)].	$4,200 ($6,000 x 70%) if deductible was previously met, otherwise $2,520 ($3,600 X 70%).
What Patient Owes	$30 if deductible was previously met, otherwise up to $1,230.	$10,000	$800 ($4,000 x 20%), if deductible was previously met, otherwise $1,760 ($4,000 minus the $2,240 paid by the plan).	$5,800 if deductible was previously met, otherwise $7,480 ($10,000 minus what the plan pays).

Consider the sample surprise billing scenarios in the accompanying table. These scenarios are based on a hypothetical medical service that, in-network, is billed at a contracted rate of $4,000. If a patient otherwise satisfies the deductible sometime during the year, that service would likely be free or subject to only a moderate co-payment. Out-of-network, however, the provider is able to charge whatever she wants or feels the "market can bear." Not uncommonly, that is two or three times more, and sometimes is tenfold more than the discounted rates negotiated by insurers with network providers. The health plan might refuse to pay some part of that extra charge, either viewing it as price gouging – beyond "usual, customary, and reasonable" rates – or simply because the bill exceeds what the health plan has agreed to pay in its contract with an employer. If so, the patient is left holding the balance of the bill. Or, the health plan might be one that covers no out-of-network care at all, leaving the patient to pay the entire nondiscounted bill. Even with full coverage, the health plan will charge the patient a deductible that usually is at least twice as high as the deductible for in-network care.[5] And even if that deductible is met, health plans also usually require patients to pay a substantial coinsurance percentage out-of-network – anywhere from 10 to 40 percent of the allowable charge (plus 100 percent of the amount above the allowable charge).

A 2010 study of larger out-of-network bills submitted under New York health plans found that, on average, patients who received these larger bills were charged for about half of the cost of emergency care delivered out-of-network, which amounted to patient charges of $3,778 per case.[6] The same study reported that larger balance bills from out-of-network assistant surgeons averaged $12,120. Often a patient's financial exposure might be tens of thousands of dollars or more. The *New York Times*,[7] for instance, reported that a nonparticipating surgeon who only assisted with a neck surgery billed $117,000, almost *twenty times* more than what the lead surgeon, who was in-network, received from the patient's health plan.

Frequency of Surprise Billing

There is no serious dispute among observers or stakeholders that surprise medical billing happens to a significant extent. There are numerous case reports both in academic literature and in widespread media accounts and other credible sources.[8] In addition, a number of research studies systematically document the dimensions of this problem.[9] For instance, a nationally representative survey in 2016[10] reported

---

[5] Michelle Andrews, Out-Of-Network Care Is Expensive But a Couple of New Options Help, Kaiser Health News, Apr. 16, 2012; Stephanie Armour, Surprise Bills for Many Under Health Law, Wall St. J., June 11, 2015.

[6] These were bills greater than $2,500 that were also more than 200 percent of the Medicare payment rate; thus, they do not represent an overall average, but instead a reflection of the higher end of billing. N.Y. State Dep't of Fin. Servs., An Unwelcome Surprise: How New Yorkers Are Getting Stuck with Unexpected Medical Bills from Out-of-Network Providers (2012).

[7] Elisabeth Rosenthal, After Surgery, Surprise $117,000 Medical Bill From Doctor He Didn't Know, N.Y. Times, Sept. 20, 2014.

[8] See, e.g., id.; N.Y. State Dep't of Fin. Servs., supra note 6; Pub. Citizen, Out of Control: Patients Are Unwittingly Subjected to Enormous, Unfair, Out-of-Network "Balance Bills" (2014); Elisabeth Rosenthal, Costs Can Go Up Fast When E.R. Is in Network but the Doctors Are Not, N.Y. Times, Sept. 28, 2014; Kelly A. Kyanko et al., Patient Experiences with Involuntary Out-of-Network Charges, 48 Health Serv. Res. 1704 (2013); Karen Pollitz et al., Medical Debt Among People with Health Insurance, Kaiser Fam. Found. (2014).

[9] See Liz Hamel, et al., The Burden of Medical Debt: Results from the Kaiser Family Foundation/New York Times Medical Bills Survey, Kaiser Fam. Found. (2016); Kelly A. Kyanko et al., Out-of-Network Physicians: How Prevalent are Involuntary Use and Cost Transparency?, 48 Health Serv. Res. 1154 (2013).

[10] Munira Z. Gunja et al., The Commonwealth Fund, Americans' Experiences with ACA Marketplace Coverage: Affordability and Provider Network Satisfaction (2016).

that 21 percent of nonelderly adults have received care at a hospital they thought was in-network but were billed by a noncovered physician.

Not only is surprise medical billing fairly widespread, it is a problem that is likely to continue growing. First, the parties involved are not likely to solve the problem themselves, under existing market structures and rules. The surprise element means, almost by definition, that this is not something consumers are likely to focus on when selecting insurance; thus, health plans have diminished market incentives to pay providers more in order to avoid the problem. Also, the ability of health plans and hospitals to negotiate reasonable rates with nonparticipating physicians is especially hampered for emergency services by the legal requirements that hospitals must provide such services, and plans must cover them, regardless of network participation.

Second, under existing market forces, provider networks are becoming narrower, creating more situations where patients encounter a mix of network and non-network providers. This is particularly the case in the nongroup (individual) market, where narrow networks are especially pronounced,[11] though network narrowing is also seen to some extent in the group market.[12] In some instances, narrower networks are due not just to health plan strategies, but also to specialist physicians consolidating into larger groups wielding enough market power to refuse payment terms that health plans offer. For instance, some hospitals have no anesthesiologists or emergency physicians in-network because the only relevant physician groups in the area have not reached an agreement with area health plans.[13] The trend towards narrower networks only increases the chances of consumers facing surprise billing.

SOLUTIONS TO SURPRISE MEDICAL BILLING

The obvious unfairness to patients of the prototypical surprise billing situations, coupled with the increasingly severe financial consequences, has produced widespread recognition of a need for policy action. In Congress, one of the Republican bills introduced to rework the Affordable Care Act (H.R. 5284, titled the "World's Greatest Healthcare Plan Act of 2016") limits how much hospitals and physicians can charge patients for non-network emergency services. At the state level, support for some type of reform is even more clearly bipartisan. More than a dozen states have enacted various protective measures.[14] Notably, these reform leaders are a mix

---

[11] Christina Cousart, Answering the Thousand-Dollar Debt Question: An Update on State Legislative Activity to Address Surprise Balance Billing, Nat'l Acad. for State Health Pol'y (2016); Noam Bauman et al., McKinsey & Co., Hospital Networks: Evolution of the Configurations on the 2015 Exchanges (2015); Dan Polsky & Janet Weiner, Leonard Davis Inst. for Health Econ., Univ. of Pa., The Skinny on Narrow Networks in Health Insurance Marketplace Plans (2015).
[12] Mark A. Hall & Paul Fronstin, Emp. Benefit Res. Inst., Narrow Provider Networks for Employer Plans (2016).
[13] Pollitz, supra note 8; Rosenthal, supra note 8.
[14] Jack Hoadley, Kevin Lucia & Sonya Schwartz, Cal. HealthCare Found., Unexpected Charges: What States Are Doing About Balance Billing (2009); Pub. Citizen, supra note 8.

of "red" states (such as Texas, West Virginia, and Utah); "blue" states (such as California, New York, Illinois, and Maryland); and "purple" states (such as Colorado, Minnesota, and Florida).

The consensus for meaningful reform is reflected by the absence of any serious opposition to taking some well-considered action. None of the major relevant interest groups or stakeholders appear to dispute that surprise medical bills are an important problem. Yet, despite this consensus, there are divisions about what action lawmakers should take. Moreover, even where public policy has coalesced around a course of action, it inevitably has failed to address some important dimensions of the problem, in part because a federal law – the Employee Retirement Income Security Act of 1974 (ERISA) – limits the applicability of state measures to fewer than one half of the privately insured. While ERISA prevents state solutions from having a broad reach, federal lawmakers so far have not undertaken a comprehensive solution.

To advance public policy deliberations and contribute to the existing literature, this chapter shifts its focus away from the details of previous legislation and considers more systematically what might or should be done (or not done), either at a state or federal level, considering all of the major dimensions of surprise medical billing.[15]

Transparency and Consent

Patients who knowingly agree to incur extra costs cannot complain of mere surprise. They might, however, complain of coercion or undue pressure. Surprise billing situations do not typically arise in the calm atmosphere of selecting a primary physician; instead, they arise when patients are sick – looking mainly to the physician or hospital they chose, but then confronted with the news that a secondary, non-network, provider is required. Ideally, the principal provider would present in-network options alongside any recommendation for a nonparticipating provider. But sometimes, no in-network provider is available (such as in an in-network hospital that lacks any participating anesthesiologists). Even when in-network options exist, referring physicians often do not know who is and is not in-network. And patients in vulnerable situations will be hard-pressed to go against their principal provider's recommendation in the midst of treatment.

There have been some attempts to provide consumers with greater notice and opportunities to consent. Perhaps the most straightforward way to mitigate surprise billing is to attempt to eliminate the element of surprise, by informing patients in a meaningful way when providers are out-of-network. At a minimum, directories of participating providers should be accurate, up to date, and reasonably accessible.

[15] See, e.g., Jack Hoadley, Sandy Ahn & Kevin Lucia, Ctr. on Health Ins. Reforms, Balance Billing: How are States Protecting Consumers from Unexpected Charges? (2015); Karen Pollitz, Surprise Medical Bills, Kaiser Fam. Found. (2016); Kelly A. Kyanko & Susan H. Busch, The Out-of-Network Benefit: Problems and Policy Solutions, 49 Inquiry 352 (2013); Pub. Citizen, supra note 8.

State and federal regulators are doing more to bring that about.[16] However, accurate directories do not resolve the surprise element when a patient does not have reason, or opportunity, to investigate a provider's network status, or where no network provider is available.

Going further, therefore, some states, and the NAIC's model act,[17] require health plans and/or hospitals to be more active in notifying patients that providers might not be in-network. It is unrealistic, however, to think that posted or form notification will be sufficient. Some patients may notice these, but many may not, and those who do not will still be genuinely surprised. Moreover, even if "warnings" are noticed, concerns remain over what patients reasonably can and should do if they are aware of the potential for surprise situations.

Beyond notice of the mere possibility that some providers might be out-of-network, institutions might give patients much more specific information about which providers are out-of-network, and how much their charges will be. Obviously, nothing can or should be expected of patients in emergency situations. But in nonemergency situations, it might be feasible to give patients the information they need to consider whether to agree to incurring any extra out-of-network charges or instead to pursue other options. However, in many of the situations previously described, patients may not have a meaningful choice, which limits the efficacy of this remedy.

Coercive aspects are difficult to avoid once a course of treatment has begun. Taking that fact, and other inherent limitations, into account greatly reduces the potential scope of situations where notice and consent might realistically be a satisfactory primary solution to surprise billing. Nevertheless, notice and consent might be a useful adjunct to a more aggressive regulatory approach. If regulators, for instance, were to ban balance billing in some circumstances, they might consider, as Medicare does, lifting that ban in prescribed situations where it seems appropriate to allow physicians to ask their patients to consider paying more than what others usually pay. Alternatively, regulators might withhold stronger remedies if patients are given adequate notice of providers' network status *and* rates. When mere notice or specific consent is insufficient to avoid unfair out-of-network billing, patients should be held harmless. Holding patients harmless means either that the health plan should pay the difference, that the provider should absorb the difference, or that some compromise should be struck between these two options. The following sections explore each of those possibilities for where the onus should lie.

Require the Health Plan to Pay

There is emerging agreement that, in emergency situations, health plans should pay as needed to hold patients harmless for going out-of-network. Emergencies are

---

[16] Am.'s Health Ins. Plans, Provider Directory Initiative Key Findings (2017).
[17] Health Benefit Plan Network Access and Adequacy Model Act (Nat'l Ass'n of Ins. Comm'rs 2015) [hereinafter "NAIC's Model Act"].

where patients have the least choice, and where the need for patient protection is most compelling. Providers also have less choice in true emergencies. Their professional ethics, backed by federal and state law, compel providers to treat patients in serious emergencies, regardless of how much they will be paid. Because, ultimately, someone must pay for such treatment, we naturally tend to look to insurers to foot the bill for emergency care.

The Affordable Care Act (ACA) forbids health plans (including employer self-funded plans) from treating emergency care as out-of-network.[18] This builds on similar laws previously adopted by most states, but this federal law applies to both self-insured employer plans as well as insured plans. Treating emergency care as in-network means only that health plans cannot deny coverage, or impose higher deductibles or coinsurance, simply because a provider is out-of-network. Federal law, however, still allows the providers themselves to charge patients what they want. Although the ACA requires health plans to reimburse nonparticipating emergency providers at normal out-of-network UCR rates, this does not fully solve surprise billing issues because the ACA allows health plans to adopt their own methodology for determining "usual and customary." Health plans are becoming increasingly stringent about the market benchmarks used to determine allowable payment. If health plans pay less than providers' full charges, the ACA leaves providers free to bill patients for the balance.[19]

One obvious solution is to require health plans to hold patients fully harmless by paying emergency providers' *full* charges (perhaps subject to an outside limit). However, doing that would tie the hands of insurers attempting to negotiate network participation with emergency facilities and physicians and likely would lead to even higher charges. Some critics claim that emergency physicians sometimes refuse to negotiate at all with health plans (or refuse reasonable discounts), realizing that patient protections in emergency settings allow them to pressure health plans to pay much higher rates out-of-network.[20] Lawmakers should be reluctant to further tilt market forces as it invites price gouging.

Require Participating Hospitals to Protect Patients from Surprise

Instead of requiring health plans to pay non-network physicians more, a different approach is to look to hospitals to use their leverage over, or relationship with, physicians to keep patients from receiving care from any nonparticipating physicians at network facilities. Insurers often include provisions in contracts with participating

---

[18] 45 C.F.R. § 147.138 (defining "emergency" from the perspective of a "prudent layperson").

[19] U.S. Dept. of Labor, Affordable Care Act Implementation FAQs Part I (Sept. 20, 2010), www.dol.gov/sites/default/files/ebsa/about-ebsa/our-activities/resource-center/faqs/aca-part-i.pdf.

[20] Lucas & Williams, supra note 4; Jeff Goldsmith, Nathan Kaufman & Lawton Burns, The Tangled Hospital–Physician Relationship. Health Affairs: Health Affairs Blog, May 9, 2016, www.healthaffairs.org/action/showDoPubSecure?doi=10.1377%2Fhblog20160509.054793&format=full.

hospitals that require hospitals to use their best efforts to obtain network participation by hospital-based ancillary physicians on the medical staff, and sometimes insurers insist that hospitals obtain physician participation.[21]

Looking to all hospitals to exert this much leverage through medical staff privileges or contracting, however, is unrealistic. In competitive hospital markets where physicians can choose among hospitals, the hospitals that do this more aggressively might find themselves with inadequate staffing. In many situations, hospitals may need to pay specialists extra to convince them to join networks; paying physicians directly is what hospitals often do currently in order for consulting specialists to agree to be on call for emergency patients.[22] But, if additional hospital payment became commonplace across a broader range of patients and specialists, hospitals would have to add much of those extra costs into the rates they seek from health plans. Moreover, if pressure intensified for designated specialists to join networks, these physicians might legitimately question whether forcing network participation is fair to them.

On balance, public policy should encourage hospitals to do what they reasonably can to ensure participation by key specialists in hospitals' primary insurance networks. However, a firm requirement that hospitals do so is too fraught with a risk of untoward market effects. Thus, it may be difficult to avoid biting the bullet of adopting some public mechanism to determine how much insurers must pay nonparticipating providers in surprise situations. The following sections examine two general approaches to such a mechanism.

Limit what Providers Can Charge Patients in Surprise Scenarios

Viewed from a Goldilocks perspective, we could hold patients harmless in surprise billing situations by placing the onus on health plans, but that could lead to provider payments that are too "hot." Placing the onus on providers, though, could lead to payments that are too "cold." Some policy analysts believe the "just right" middle approach is to regulate the rates that nonparticipating providers may charge, and that health plans must pay, in surprise billing situations.[23]

A limited form of rate regulation could take the form either of a prescribed fee schedule that must be paid or a cap on rates that leaves market forces to operate below the cap. Maryland, for instance, requires HMOs to pay out-of-network providers at least 125 percent of their average in-network rates or 140 percent of Medicare rates, depending on the circumstances. California requires health plans to

---

[21] N.Y. State Dep't of Fin. Servs., supra note 6.
[22] Ann S. O'Malley, Debra A. Draper & Laurie E. Felland, Ctr. for Studying Health System Change, Issue Brief No. 115, Hospital Emergency On-Call Coverage: Is There a Doctor in the House? (2007).
[23] Robert Murray, Hospital Charges and the Need for a Maximum Price Obligation Rule for Emergency Department & Out-Of-Network Care, Health Affairs: Health Affairs Blog, May 16, 2013, www.healthaffairs.org/do/10.1377/hblog20130516.031255/full/.

pay the greater of their average contracted rates or 125 percent of Medicare. Others propose to cap out-of-network billing in surprise situations at 200 percent of Medicare rates.[24]

In theory, an approach like this is workable. The difficulties are in determining the appropriate benchmarks for payment rates, and in the political and policy willingness to undertake any form of regulating provider payment rates under private insurance. Many stakeholders view provider rate regulation as anathema, and so would resist it in any form, even in surprise or emergency settings, fearing a slippery slope that leads to regulating all forms of balance billing (as Medicare does). Or, if limited rate regulation were considered, views would differ strongly on whether Medicare is a legitimate benchmark for payment rates and what multiple of Medicare might be reasonable or excessive. Starting with a generous multiple could give way to ever-tightening limits (as Medicare imposed in a series of steps that limited physician balance billing twenty-five years ago). Lawmakers' reluctance to take on these lightning-rod issues has more often led them to instead require health plans and providers to settle between themselves, on a case-by-case basis, how much to pay for surprise out-of-network care.

Require Health Plans and Providers to Settle Surprise Balance Bills Between Themselves

Balance bill payment resolution can occur in several different ways. The most straightforward approach (used in Colorado, for instance) is simply to prohibit balance billing patients beyond their normal cost sharing, but leave providers free to balance bill the health plan. The health plan can then challenge particular bills for being excessive, and those challenges can be resolved like any other billing dispute – through negotiation and settlement, or in court – under governing principles of contract law.

Resorting to courts routinely, however, is expensive and uncertain. An alternative approach is to create some more efficient means of nonjudicial dispute resolution. Rather than leaving providers and plans to their own legal devices, several states (notably Florida, Illinois, New York, and Texas) and the NAIC's model act either allow or require parties to use mediation, arbitration, or independent administrative review to determine appropriate payment amounts for out-of-network care. Some states provide nonbinding processes (such as mediation in Texas). Others are binding, but voluntary (the parties decide whether they want to use the process in California and Florida). When participation is optional, these processes are seldom used, reportedly because providers feel they are not likely to receive favorable decisions.[25] Accordingly, at least one state (Illinois) calls for mandatory arbitration,

---

[24] Pub. Citizen, supra note 8.
[25] Hoadley et al., supra note 14; Hoadley et al., supra note 15.

but full formal arbitration can be complex and expensive. Overall, we lack much comparative experience with the different dispute resolution approaches taken by various states, except to know that in those with voluntary approaches (such as California and Florida), such approaches are seldom used.

New York has enacted a streamlined form of mandatory and binding dispute resolution for surprise medical bills. In the New York approach – which is referred to as "baseball style" or "final offer" arbitration – the provider and the insurer both submit a best and final offer, and a state-contracted independent reviewer must select which side best approximates UCR rates, with no compromise. This approach is considered more streamlined for two reasons.[26] First, when cases are decided, it may be more efficient for the reviewer to make a choice between one of two predetermined figures rather than needing to determine the precisely correct number. Second, the distinct possibility that either side can lose outright creates a strong incentive for both sides to negotiate and settle without having to submit to "coin-toss" arbitration. Moreover, if arbitration decisions are made public, this process has the added advantage of developing a set of precedents that make future outcomes more predictable, which further increases the prospects that the two sides will reach agreement independently.

It is also possible, however, to combine the rate regulation and dispute resolution approaches. A payment rate could be established as a default ceiling or floor that, absent unusual circumstances, applies if a provider and health plan fail to reach agreement, or that limits what a dispute reviewer may impose. For instance, providers might be limited to no more than twice what Medicare pays, or health plans could be required to pay at least 50 percent above Medicare rates – unless one of the parties establishes that this figure is out of sync with reasonable market rates.[27] The intent of such an approach would be to leave the parties able to seek payments that are below a ceiling or above a floor.

RECOMMENDATIONS

Unfortunately, there is no single, simple solution to surprise medical billing. Instead, the complexity of the United States health care system requires a multifaceted approach – one that leaves room for ongoing adjustment and further

---

[26] Jason B. Shorter, Final-Offer Arbitration for Health Care Billing Disputes: Analyzing One State's Proposed Dispute Resolution Process, 9 Appalachian J. L. 191 (2009); Jeff Monhait, Baseball Arbitration: An ADR Success, 4 Harv. J. Sports & Ent. L. 105 (2013).

[27] For instance, the NAIC's Model Act (2015), supra note 17, establishes a "benchmark" payment rate that is "presumed to be reasonable" if it is a specified percentage of Medicare's payment rate or of some other "public, independent, database of [prevailing] charges." California recently enacted a similar approach for surprise billing (AB-72) that requires plans to pay the greater of 125 percent of Medicare rates or the health plan's average contracted rates for the services in question. However, if providers are not satisfied with this amount, they may seek independent review to determine if the amount is "appropriate" based "on all relevant information" (which is a standard taken from California case law regarding reasonable charges or value for medical services).

development. Based on experience to date, the following are major recommendations.

1) Take a Comprehensive Approach

The need for protection is most compelling in emergency situations, but patients clearly deserve protection from surprise bills in other common hospital scenarios. Solutions should target all out-of-network billing at in-network facilities, along with all care resulting from emergency screening and patient transfers (including ambulance transport) at out-of-network facilities.

2) Take Federal Action to Protect More Patients

State enactment provides the greatest room for adapting to local market conditions and experimentation. However, federal action may be necessary to address the half of the privately insured market that is in self-funded employer plans. A federal remedy could be extended from the ACA's existing patient protections for emergency treatment. Or federal legislation could give the states flexibility to tailor alternative measures that are at least as protective as those provided by a federal default solution.

3) Recognize that Improved Information Is Necessary but not Sufficient

Patients need good access to current, accurate information about network membership, but this alone will not solve most surprise billing situations. Notifying patients sometimes makes it feasible to freely consent to out-of-network billing. However, for notice to be adequate, it should include a case-specific estimate of the extra costs and information about feasible in-network alternatives. These options should be presented to avoid pressure on the patient to capitulate.

4) Hold Patients Harmless when Unfair Surprise Cannot Be Avoided

Although the best remedies for surprise billing can be controversial, the controversy should not deter lawmakers from crafting a solution that holds patients financially harmless when they take reasonable steps, or have no reasonable opportunity, to avoid out-of-network billing.

5) Resolve How Much Health Plans Should Pay Nonparticipating Providers in Surprise Situations

Lawmakers have two basic options for determining how much health plans should pay nonparticipating providers, keeping in mind the need for administrative feasibility and to avoid unduly distorting market dynamics:

- regulate provider rates in surprise situations; or
- mandate a form of dispute resolution.

Rates can be regulated as a multiple of rates either that Medicare pays or that health plans negotiate in their networks.[28] The advantage of health plan-negotiated rates is that they are market determined. Medicare rates, however, are easier to determine and often they are used as the basis for private market negotiations.[29]

An acceptable alternative to rate regulation is mandatory dispute resolution of surprise medical bills. The most efficient method appears to be "baseball style" arbitration, which requires the reviewer to choose one of the two parties' final offers. Arbitration can also be used to resolve disputes over fair payment terms in contracts that health plans negotiate with hospital-based specialists in order to reduce situations where these specialists are out-of-network.

A hybrid method could be considered that combines rate regulation with mandatory dispute resolution. In this approach, a payment rate is established as a default ceiling or floor that applies if the provider and health plan fail to reach agreement or that limits what a dispute reviewer may impose.

---

[28] A third approach is to limit rates to a percentile of UCR, as defined by a credible source. Connecticut, for instance, requires insurers to pay up to the 80th percentile of the range of undiscounted charges from similar providers, as determined by FAIR Health, an independent nonprofit firm that maintains a database of provider charges. Although this database reflects what billing practices are actually "usual and customary," prevailing charges are not necessarily "reasonable," especially for specialties where consumers do not choose the physician and so normal market forces are absent.

[29] Jeffrey Clemens & Joshua D. Gottlieb, In the Shadow of a Giant: Medicare's Influence on Private Physician Payments (Nat'l Bureau of Econ. Res., Working Paper No. 19503, 2015).

PART IV

Transparency and Innovation

Introduction to Part IV

Holly Fernandez Lynch

Can transparency itself be an innovation? In the world of pharmaceutical product development, the generation of data and regulatory processes have traditionally been so secretive that even modest steps toward greater transparency can be reasonably depicted as paradigm shifts, with substantial potential to promote scientific advancement. The chapters in this section each argue in favor of such shifts, with regard to information about Food and Drug Administration (FDA) communications with sponsors, sharing of individual-level clinical trial data, and disclosure of information held by the European Medicines Agency (EMA), while grappling with some of the difficulties that have prevented greater transparency until now.

In each of these contexts, the primary drivers of nontransparency have been commercial considerations and desires to protect "confidential commercial information," or otherwise avoid sharing any valuable information that could provide an advantage to a potential competitor. With their business interests in mind, companies do not want others to know that they are in conversations with regulators, let alone how those meetings are progressing, lest their competitors find ways to capitalize on that information. This concern is understandable in an industry in which reducing time to market by even a few weeks or months can have massive financial ramifications. In an effort to promote innovation, or at least avoid disincentives for it, regulatory agencies have often been willing (or even legally required) to provide secrecy about a range of activities. The motivating concern, of course, is that if commercial information that is expensive to produce is shared without restraint, entities will no longer produce it.

This raises an important empirical question: how much nontransparency is necessary to maintain adequate incentives, or put another way, how much transparency can be tolerated in the system? These questions are testable. In fact, we are now seeing some important "natural experiments" because the norms around sharing clinical trial data are changing, as are the legal requirements around sharing information submitted in marketing applications to the EMA. The impetus for these changes is recognition that, in fact, we do want to allow some learning from what has been done before, rather than demand constant reinvention of the wheel by each separate party. As Rachel E. Sachs and Thomas J. Hwang note in their chapter, "[o]ther pharmaceutical companies would benefit from the disclosure of both positive and negative pieces of information about a competitor's progress through the drug pipeline...", such as the FDA's willingness to accept certain trial designs or concerns about other products in development using similar biological mechanisms. Barbara E. Bierer, Mark Barnes, and Rebecca Li similarly note that sharing individual participant-level data can permit verification of original trial results, in addition to facilitating evaluation of adverse event rates, identifying surrogate endpoints, preventing duplicative trials, and promoting public trust more generally. Stefano Marino and Spyridon Drosos add to this list more foundational considerations related to legitimacy, accountability, and respect.

A transparent approach is better for patients and consumers, as the hope is that transparency will speed access to important regulated products, and this approach is more respectful of those who contribute to the generation of knowledge as research participants, maximizing the utility of their contributions. But, of course, it does require some "sacrifice" on the part of first movers, as those who come later will be able to engage in a level of free riding. The key question, then, centers on how to maximize innovation across parties: what is the sweet spot of required disclosure that will not kill the innovation to be built upon, but that will allow others to innovate upon it? Moving forward, evidence-based policy should be the goal as it will be important to collect data to assess the impact of changing requirements trending toward greater transparency, and to design studies that test different approaches.

Another helpful approach will be to assess alternative mechanisms of incentivizing knowledge production, even when the end goal is for that knowledge to be shared with others. This is the topic of a lively discussion in the context of clinical trial data sharing, where academic researchers who conduct the trials have expressed concern that, by sharing data with others (sometimes unaffectionately called "research parasites"), they will be undercutting their own ability to analyze and publish journal articles, to their professional detriment.[1] To address this concern, there has been discussion of finding ways for original data generators to be "credited" – through citations and academic recognitions relevant to promotion – whenever their data are utilized by others.[2]

This may be more complicated for commercial entities who care not about publications and academic advancement, but about profit. Existing approaches to incentivizing the production of knowledge about pharmaceutical products are aligned to that desire by offering additional periods of marketing exclusivity or other ways to keep competitors off the market for a period of time. The problem with encouraging transparency and disclosure through such mechanisms is that they may reduce the value of the disclosures in question; even if the disclosures facilitate

[1] Dan N. Longo & Jeffrey M. Drazen, Data Sharing, 374 New Eng. J. Med. 276 (2016).
[2] Barbara E. Bierer, Mercè Crosas, & Heather H. Pierce. Data Authorship as an Incentive to Data Sharing. 376 New Eng. J. Med. 1684 (2017).

innovation by other entities, the fruits of that innovation would be artificially withheld from the public for some period of time. This sort of trade-off is typical of innovation policy, however. The trick is to "split the difference" by providing sufficient exclusive rights for initial innovators to motivate their socially valuable behaviors, but for those exclusive rights to be shorter than the time it would otherwise have taken for competitors to have innovated on their own, without the benefit of greater transparency regarding the activities of first movers. Of course, these are not simple policy calculations.

In addition to commercial considerations, there are issues around protecting the individuals about whom information may be shared in the interest of promoting innovation, the topic at the heart of both the Bierer, Barnes, and Li contribution and the chapter by Marino and Drosos. This is particularly relevant in the context of sharing individual-level clinical trial data with others beyond those to whom research participants gave their informed consent. There are a number of protections that can be implemented, however, such as adding information to the consent process explaining how data may be used beyond a particular study, as will now be required following recent changes to the regulations governing most federally funded research in the United States; requiring confidentiality agreements from those with whom data will be shared; and removing individual identifiers whenever their inclusion is not essential. Thus, privacy considerations cannot be ignored, but they are manageable.

Moreover, while study sponsors and investigators are certainly adding their valuable labor to participant data to render it meaningful for clinical innovation, this should not be taken to suggest that the data sources – trial participants – have no interest in how the data is used once they render it. To the contrary, participants often add their own valuable labor to the clinical innovation enterprise precisely through the time and effort they contribute to research participation.[3] Thus, they have an interest in transparency around the progress of regulatory discussions, as well as maximizing the value of their data by having it shared widely among all who may innovate from it. In this sense, it is important not to view research participants as passive sources of data that can be ignored in the transparency debate. That said, given the social value of this data, we must be careful about providing participants with inordinate control. They should not be permitted to block important uses of the anonymized data derived from their participation, so long as their privacy interests are appropriately protected, as Bierer, Barnes, and Li note.

Another theme articulated by the chapters in this section is that of regulatory transparency. As government agencies whose decisions have profound impacts on the public, there is an increasing recognition of the need for agencies responsible for medical product approval to make their decisions in a manner that lends itself to

---

[3] Holly Fernandez Lynch, Human Research Subjects and Human Research Workers, 14 Yale J. Health Pol'y L. & Ethics 122 (2014).

accountability to the public. In Europe, this has resulted in new legal requirements for greater transparency of information held by the EMA as part of applications for marketing approval, as described by Marino and Drosos in their chapter. The United States has been slower to promote transparency at the FDA, as Sachs and Hwang note, although they discuss baby steps toward an approach that could facilitate greater disclosure while protecting sponsor interests. It will be interesting and important to carefully assess the impact of the different approaches on innovation behaviors and outcomes by both sponsors and others.

Ultimately, what these chapters demonstrate is that transparency is not an on/off switch, but a variable with many different formulations, including to whom, about what, and how much transparency is provided, as well as whether transparency is provided freely or only upon request. These formulations may be tweaked to balance and accommodate different goals and potentially competing interests in the name of promoting innovation, as discussed by each of the authors in this section. The key is not to stifle innovation of some in the name of promoting innovation by others, which has been the fear behind the secrecy that has pervaded much of medical product development to date. But what seems clear is that the winds of change are blowing, such that nontransparency is now requiring more substantial justification and a default approach in favor of transparency unless there is a strong reason to behave otherwise is taking its place. This seems to be the right trajectory in a field to which patients simultaneously contribute as research participants and depend on for medical advancement.

12

Increasing the Transparency of FDA Review to Enhance the Innovation Process

Rachel E. Sachs and Thomas J. Hwang

Recent controversies around the approval of new medicines by the Food and Drug Administration (FDA) have highlighted the need for greater transparency in the drug development process.[1] For example, relatively little information was provided to the public or the patient community when serious safety issues were identified during clinical trials for investigational therapies, such as the patient deaths that occurred during trials for Juno's experimental cancer immunotherapy product, JCAR-015.[2] In our view, more systematic public disclosure of communications between the FDA and sponsors at specific, key points within the clinical trial process would benefit both patients and the innovation process.

This chapter proceeds as follows. Part I provides an overview of the FDA's current information disclosure practices, in which the legal framework around the FDA approval process results in little information about communications between the FDA and drug sponsors being disclosed to the public. Part II details some of the harms this lack of disclosure causes, not only to patients and physicians but also to innovators and investors in new biopharmaceutical ventures. Part III introduces a proposal for reform, arguing that an intermediate system of limited disclosure of particular events in the context of a drug's approval process can be valuable to other innovators and can be accomplished under current law.

I. THE FDA'S CURRENT INFORMATION DISCLOSURE PRACTICES

As pharmaceutical companies complete the clinical trials necessary to win FDA approval for their products, enormous amounts of information about the clinical trial results as well as the drug's biochemical properties and manufacturing flow between the drug sponsor and the agency. This information is often developed in concert with the FDA; sponsors typically meet with the agency at various points

---

[1] Aaron S. Kesselheim & Jerry Avorn, Approving a Problematic Muscular Dystrophy Drug: Implications for FDA Policy, 316 JAMA 2357 (2016).

[2] Rob Waters, Father of patient in Juno immunotherapy trial speaks out: "He died for greed", STAT News, Dec. 12, 2016, www.statnews.com/2016/12/12/juno-patient-death-cancer-immunotherapy.

during the development process to discuss important aspects of clinical trial design, manufacturing and quality controls, and risk evaluation and mitigation strategies.[3]

At present, the FDA publicly discloses very little information about its communications with drug sponsors. By its own regulations, the FDA will not publicly disclose the *existence* of an investigational new drug application unless the sponsoring company has already done so.[4] This secrecy is largely due to federal statutes involving trade secret protections, but informal agency norms contribute to this practice as well.

The FDA's current practice of nondisclosure is largely driven by concerns that the agency will inadvertently disclose trade secrets. Such disclosure would be prohibited by law under two different statutes governing the agency. First, the Federal Trade Secrets Act prohibits federal employees generally from "publish[ing], divulg[ing], disclos[ing], or mak[ing] known" any information that qualifies as a trade secret.[5] Second, the Federal Food, Drug, and Cosmetic Act specifically targets the FDA and, with limited exceptions, prohibits the agency from publicly revealing trade secrets. Such exceptions include disclosures to Congress or disclosures made in the course of judicial proceedings.[6]

But what counts as a trade secret, exactly? As defined generally under the Uniform Trade Secrets Act, a trade secret is any piece of information that "derives independent economic value ... from not being generally known" and which is the "subject of efforts ... to maintain its secrecy."[7] It is easy to see how a company's manufacturing process might qualify as a trade secret. If other companies knew the process by which an innovator pharmaceutical company manufactures its blockbuster drug, they could free ride on that effort (assuming all relevant patents have expired) and avoid expending the time and costs to engineer the process themselves.[8] But it is not so obvious that the mere existence of an FDA application itself ought to qualify.[9] In practice, it appears that the FDA has chosen to err on the side of caution rather than face legal action and potential monetary damages for disclosing trade secrets.[10]

---

[3] Food & Drug Admin., Formal Meetings Between the FDA and Sponsors or Applicants of PDUFA Products: Guidance for Industry (Dec. 2017), www.fda.gov/downloads/Drugs/GuidanceComplianceRegulatoryInformation/Guidances/UCM590547.pdf.
[4] 21 C.F.R. § 314.430(b) (2012).
[5] 18 U.S.C. § 1905 (2012).
[6] 21 U.S.C. § 331(j) (2012).
[7] Uniform Trade Secrets Act § 1(4) (Unif. Law Comm'n 1985).
[8] This is particularly valuable in the context of biologics, where the manufacturing process is much more difficult to reverse engineer than is the process to produce a small-molecule drug. W. Nicholson Price & Arti K. Rai, Manufacturing Barriers to Biologics Competition and Innovation, 101 Iowa L. Rev. 1023, 1028 (2016).
[9] Cf. Annemarie Bridy, Trade Secret Prices and High-Tech Devices: How Medical Device Manufacturers Are Seeking to Sustain Profits by Propertizing Prices, 17 Tex. Intell. Prop. L.J. 187, 189 (2009).
[10] 18 U.S.C. § 1905 (2012); FDA Transparency Task Force, FDA Transparency Initiative: Draft Proposals for Public Comment Regarding Disclosure Policies of the U.S. Food and Drug Administration 13 (May 2010).

Despite the FDA's caution, companies typically report positive events to their investors, such as the successful completion of a new clinical trial, the grant of an orphan drug designation, or the inclusion of their drug in an expedited approval pathway. Publicly traded companies may be required by law to disclose the existence of negative events about their drug applications. The FDA and the Securities and Exchange Commission (SEC) have a long-standing relationship to identify instances of securities fraud among companies regulated by the FDA.[11] And in certain cases, the SEC has taken enforcement action against companies who fail to disclose information to their shareholders, including the existence of clinical holds (which are issued where a serious safety issue appears during the clinical trial process), or who mislead their shareholders about what the FDA has requested of them moving forward.[12]

Further, sometimes the FDA itself is required to disclose information. Some drugs submitted to the FDA for approval are reviewed by an advisory committee, made up of non-FDA experts in the field in question.[13] Federal law requires that materials submitted for review to the advisory committee (which include the results of clinical trials) be made available to the public as well.[14] Advisory committee meetings are also open to the public.[15] The Orphan Drug Act provides another example. The Act requires the FDA to notify the public when a drug has been awarded an orphan designation.[16]

But in general, meaningful information about a drug and its progress through the approval pipeline is difficult to obtain, and relying on regulators or the courts to uncover instances of nondisclosure or inaccurate disclosure after the fact is costly and time consuming. The FDA will typically decline to disclose information at all stages of the review process as well as procedural and substantive dimensions within each stage. If the FDA issues a "complete response letter" informing a drug company that its product will not be approved, the FDA will not disclose either the contents *or the existence* of that letter. Similarly, the existence of a clinical hold is generally not disclosed by the FDA. More substantively, the contents of a meeting between the agency and a sponsor or the content of the FDA's recommendations on clinical trial design are closely held.

The FDA is aware of some of the problems its secrecy can create, acknowledging that transparency both enables the "public to better understand the Agency's decisions, increasing credibility and promoting accountability"[17] and can be useful to

[11] Liora Sukhatme, Deterring Fraud: Mandatory Disclosure and the FDA Drug Approval Process, 82 N.Y.U. L. Rev. 1210, 1234 (2007).
[12] Id. at 1231, 1233.
[13] Food & Drug Admin., Advisory Committees: Critical to the FDA's Product Review Process (May 2016), www.fda.gov/Drugs/ResourcesForYou/Consumers/ucm143538.htm.
[14] Federal Advisory Committee Act § 10(b), 5 U.S.C.A. App. 2.
[15] Food & Drug Admin., Guidance for the Public, FDA Advisory Committee Members, and FDA Staff: The Open Public Hearing at FDA Advisory Committee Meetings (May 2013).
[16] 21 U.S.C. § 360bb(c) (2012).
[17] FDA Transparency Task Force, supra note 13, at 2.

the regulated industry in "foster[ing] a more efficient and cost-effective regulatory process."[18] As a result, the agency has previously taken steps to become more transparent. In 2009, the agency announced a transparency initiative, opening for public comment a series of proposals for greater disclosure.[19] However, to date, most of these proposals have not been developed further.

In light of moves toward transparency taken by other pharmaceutical regulators around the world,[20] experts have once again returned to the question of FDA transparency, with a number of scholars and former agency officials releasing a 2017 "Blueprint for Transparency."[21] We agree with the recommendations of these scholars and write here both to provide greater detail on the particular harms suffered by different institutional actors and to provide more detail on how some of these disclosures may be accomplished legally in practice.

II. THE HARMS OF NONDISCLOSURE

The overwhelming secrecy about drugs and their progress through the approval pipeline poses real harms to a number of actors within the system. The harms to each actor may be different (patients are harmed in a different way than rival pharmaceutical companies are harmed), but each harm is important to detail separately. Policymakers must appreciate the harms suffered by different actors before they can decide which, if any, are significant enough to redress and which reforms would be most usefully targeted at that particular population. In general, there are two different categories of harms: those experienced by users of the products, chiefly patients and physicians; and those experienced by producers of the products, chiefly investors and competitor pharmaceutical firms.

In prior work,[22] we have focused on this first category of harms: those that affect patient groups and physicians in terms of the integral role they play in the clinical trial process, their expectations about products, and the translation of research into clinical care. Particularly in the case of something like a clinical hold, the research subjects in that trial and any patient community supporting that effort may justifiably feel entitled to that information. Physicians may similarly need access to more information than is currently published by the FDA to make an informed decision

---

[18] FDA Transparency Task Force, supra note 13, at 3.
[19] See generally FDA Transparency Task Force, supra note 13. We discuss some of these proposals in more detail in Part III, infra.
[20] Anna L. Davis & James Dabney Miller, The European Medicines Agency and Publication of Clinical Study Reports: A Challenge for the US FDA, 317 JAMA 905 (2017).
[21] FDA Transparency Working Group, Blueprint for Transparency at the U.S. Food and Drug Administration: Recommendations to Advance the Development of Safe and Effective Medical Products (Mar. 2017); see also Joshua M. Sharfstein & Michael Stebbins, Enhancing Transparency at the US Food and Drug Administration: Moving Beyond the 21st Century Cures Act, 317 JAMA 1621 (2017); see also Part III, infra.
[22] Thomas J. Hwang et al., Transparency in the Development of New Medicines: Still a Work in Progress (unpublished manuscript) (on file with the authors).

on prescribing a new drug to their patients. For example, adverse events identified during a clinical trial could yield insights into the safety of other approved drugs in that class or in pharmacologically related classes.

Importantly, many of these harms to patients are also harmful to the FDA process. In a number of recent cases, drug sponsors released misleading information about the substance of their communications with the FDA.[23] In the controversial case of Sarepta's drug eteplirsen, approved by the FDA on the basis of a study involving twelve patients,[24] some experts contended the manufacturer misled patients and advocacy groups about the study design and kinds of information the FDA had consistently recommended.[25] Specifically, the FDA had "consistently advised" Sarepta that more than twelve patients would be needed to generate the kind of data that could support FDA approval.[26] Some time later, the FDA took the unusual step of releasing a public statement about its meetings with the manufacturer, in an effort to correct the record.[27] However, this statement was too late to address the harm created by the initial inadequate disclosure. Patients had already been enrolled, studies had already been conducted without the data the FDA had requested, and patient advocates had been led to believe that the FDA had signed off on the trials as they had been performed.

Our focus in this chapter, however, is on the second category of harms, which affect investors and competitors in the industry. As noted above, publicly traded companies are required by the securities laws to disclose some pieces of information.[28] But today, most early-stage pharmaceutical research is performed by small companies[29] that may not be publicly traded. How can investors be sure that they have complete information before choosing which companies to invest in, and how can they be sure that the companies in which they invest are being fully honest and transparent with them? Contract law likely provides some backstop, but FDA disclosure could serve as a check on corporate misconduct.[30]

More problematic is the effect of FDA secrecy on other innovative pharmaceutical companies. The clinical trial process serves multiple purposes, not only the goal of bringing a drug to market. It also serves to develop *information* about the drug in question, and specifically about its safety and efficacy.[31] Other pharmaceutical

[23] Sharfstein & Stebbins, supra note 24, at 1621.
[24] Kesselheim & Avorn, supra note 4, at 2357.
[25] Sharfstein & Stebbins, supra note 24, at 1621.
[26] Food & Drug Admin., Duchenne Muscular Dystrophy Statement (Nov. 2016), web.archive.org/web/20170324154708/https://www.fda.gov/Drugs/DrugSafety/ucm421270.htm.
[27] Id.
[28] See supra text accompanying notes 14–15.
[29] Robert Kneller, The Importance of new Companies for Drug Discovery: Origins of a Decade of New Drugs, 9 Nature Revs. Drug Discovery 867 (2010).
[30] See, e.g., Christopher Weaver, John Carreyrou & Michael Siconolfi, Theranos Is Subject of Criminal Probe by U.S., Wall St. J., Apr. 18, 2016.
[31] Rebecca S. Eisenberg, The Role of the FDA in Innovation Policy, 13 Mich. Telecomm. Tech. L. Rev. 345, 347 (2007).

companies would benefit from the disclosure of both positive and negative pieces of information about a competitor's progress through the drug pipeline – did a serious side effect arise in clinical trials, why was a drug rejected, and so forth. Failures in drug development are exceedingly common, but it is unclear if the innovation system adequately learns from its failures. One study estimated that 54 percent of new drugs entering late-stage development fail, with most failures attributed to inadequate efficacy or to safety concerns.[32] Companies seeking to develop drugs that rely on similar biological pathways but who are not aware of the issuance of a clinical hold or complete response letter may not know that they should redirect their research, and so they may waste time, money, and effort on a product that another company may already know is likely to fail. Similarly, without knowledge of safety and efficacy issues that are uncovered during previous clinical trials, participants in future research studies could be exposed to futile or toxic interventions.[33]

Companies who learn about the types of trials the FDA is requesting for a particular drug application or for a class of drugs can more easily plan with certainty for their own routes through the FDA and may be able to prepare higher quality submissions for FDA review. Those studies may be published years later, or information about them released before an advisory committee meeting is scheduled, but this information about the regulatory process is beneficial to other pharmaceutical companies as well as their investors. Perhaps the most common request that pharmaceutical companies make about the FDA process is not that it be streamlined,[34] but that it be more certain and predictable. Some amount of uncertainty is inevitable, but to the extent that the FDA has already made decisions about the types of studies that will be required for a particular class or the types of end points it will accept, it is harmful to hold that information secret until a sponsor is ready to conduct those trials.

We must acknowledge that companies invoke the role of trade secrecy in precisely these cases. Pharmaceutical companies recognize that this information is both important to the innovation process and is highly valuable. Further, part of its value to the company receiving the information surely lies in its secrecy. But arguably, much of this information is not the company's to keep secret at all. Manufacturing processes, which the company has painstakingly developed, are not the same as the FDA's decision to issue a clinical hold or to decline to approve the drug. In Part III, we consider the ways in which this distinction allows for a system of limited disclosure in a way that would benefit investors and innovators going forward.

[32] Thomas J. Hwang et al., Failure of Investigational Drugs in Late-Stage Clinical Development and Publication of Trial Results, 176 JAMA Internal Med. 12 (2016).
[33] See Holly Fernandez Lynch, Chapter 22.
[34] See John LaMattina, Even if Donald Trump Changed the FDA Drug Approval Process, Patients Wouldn't Benefit, Forbes, Nov. 29, 2016, www.forbes.com/sites/johnlamattina/2016/11/29/even-if-donald-trump-changed-the-fda-drug-approval-process-patients-wouldnt-benefit/.

III. PROPOSING A SYSTEM OF LIMITED, GRADUATED DISCLOSURE

We propose a system of intermediate disclosure of information that the FDA communicates to companies. Specifically, we propose that the FDA discloses, at a minimum, (1) the existence of particular events, including the issuance of a complete response letter, the placement of a clinical hold, and a meeting between the agency and a sponsor and (2) a general categorization of their substance. Overall, this system would mitigate the harms of nondisclosure to investors and innovators while also appreciating industry's concerns about confidentiality during the drug approval process. Further, although much of the information companies disclose to the FDA may accurately be held and viewed as a trade secret, such as the manufacturing process used to make a drug or its precise product formulation,[35] in our view the information we propose to disclose is unlikely to be properly classified as such.

Procedurally, it is difficult to argue that the information the FDA gives back to the companies can be classified as a trade secret. The information is generated by the FDA, often based on the contributions of clinical trial subjects and not solely the drug sponsor, and as such it is not the sponsor's choice whether or not to keep the information secret, as the statute requires.[36] More substantively, the FDA has articulated by regulation its own view of what may count as a trade secret: "any commercially valuable plan, formula, process, or device that is used for the making, preparing, compounding, or processing of trade commodities and that can be said to be the end product of either innovation or substantial effort."[37] The FDA's own decisions, such as to place a clinical hold or reject an NDA, would appear to fall outside this definition. Even more explicitly, the FDA contemplates that data "submitted or divulged to" the agency may "fall within the definition ... of a trade secret" – but the same regulation does not contemplate that data disclosed *by* the agency may be so classified, even if that information is in part a reaction to the disclosure of the sponsor's trade secrets.[38]

Our proposal can be illustrated with the case of the complete response letter (CRL). When the FDA decides not to approve a sponsor's application to market a new drug, it issues a CRL informing the company of that fact. The letter details the FDA's reasons for declining to approve the drug and typically explains the actions the sponsor must take to obtain approval after further review. As noted above, the FDA discloses publicly neither the existence nor the contents of CRLs, which is worrisome for investors and innovators focusing on the same disease class or biological pathway.

---

[35] Food & Drug Admin., Trade Secrets (June 2010), https://web.archive.org/web/20171114200451/https://www.fda.gov/AboutFDA/Transparency/PublicDisclosure/TradeSecrets/default.htm.
[36] Uniform Trade Secrets Act § 1(4) (Unif. Law Comm'n 1985).
[37] 21 C.F.R. § 20.61(a) (2012).
[38] Id. at § 20.61(b).

Importantly, sponsors cannot be relied on to accurately disclose either the existence or contents of these letters. One study by FDA officials focused on CRLs issued between 2008 and 2013.[39] Companies never issued a press release about the existence of the letter in 18 percent of cases.[40] In another 21 percent, the companies admitted the existence of the letter, but did not explain any of the reasons the FDA had given for rejecting the application.[41] On the whole, for 78 percent of FDA's CRLs, all or almost all of the reasons for the FDA's decision were not disclosed by companies.[42] As the officials ultimately concluded, "the FDA's reasons for not approving marketing applications for new molecular entities are not being fully conveyed to the public."[43]

The potential for the FDA to disclose CRLs has been a topic of interest among various groups for several years. The 2010 FDA Transparency Task Force contained a recommendation on the subject of CRLs. The Task Force recommended not only that the agency disclose the existence of a CRL, but also that it disclose the CRL itself, as it "contains the reasons for issuing the letter."[44] More recently, the 2017 Blueprint for Transparency authors concurred, arguing that "FDA should adopt the draft proposals from the 2010 Transparency Task Force that would ... disclose FDA's communications to companies when products are not approved."[45] We support the agency officials and Blueprint authors in their call for full disclosure of CRLs (and other pieces of information they consider in their lengthy reports), as in our view that would provide the most robust benefits to patients and other innovators. However, we recognize that full disclosure of this type comes with costs. CRLs may contain trade secrets[46] and must be carefully reviewed and redacted to prevent their disclosure. The agency may face litigation over these disclosures.[47]

We suggest that, in considering a proposal for full disclosure of CRLs, the agency also consider a system of intermediate disclosure, in which the FDA discloses the existence of the CRL as well as a categorical summary of its contents. The agency might take as its starting point the characterization used by agency officials in their recent study, which includes sixty-four potential deficiencies across seven different categories.[48] These categories and particular deficiencies were based on a review of the International Conference on Harmonisation of Technical Requirements for

[39] Peter Lurie et al., Comparison of Content of FDA Letters Not Approving Applications for New Drugs and Associated Public Announcements from Sponsors: Cross Sectional Study, 350 BMJ 1 (2015).
[40] Id. at 1.
[41] Id. at 5.
[42] Id. at 6.
[43] Id.
[44] FDA Transparency Task Force, supra note 13, at 6, 46.
[45] FDA Transparency Working Group, supra note 24, at 23.
[46] FDA Transparency Working Group, supra note 24, at 26 (noting that CRLs received by generic manufacturers may contain trade secret information that would need to be redacted).
[47] See Davis & Miller, supra note 23, at 905 (noting that the EMA has faced litigation over its disclosure policies).
[48] Lurie et al., supra note 42, at 2–3.

Registration of Pharmaceuticals for Human Use E3 in conjunction with CRLs as actually issued.[49] Collectively, the categories – including "efficacy," "safety," and "chemistry, manufacturing and controls" – cover a wide range of concerns the FDA may have with a particular new product.[50] As such, we can expect these categories to be representative of the key reasons why applications are not approved.

Importantly, this system of categorization may be able to provide most of the benefits of transparency to innovators and investors while also avoiding the harms of potential disclosure of trade secrets and minimizing the risks of time-consuming litigation. Competitors who see that a drug has been rejected due to "insufficient evidence of efficacy," "general safety concerns," or similarly critical reasons may begin re-evaluating their projects on that basis. Competitors who see a rejection due to "inadequate REMS requirements or plan" or "sample size inadequate" may continue with their work but be able to plan more effectively for the FDA's requests during the approval process. And competitors who see a rejection due to more minor concerns, such as "facilities not available or ready for FDA inspection" or "revised or new labeling required," may appropriately take no negative signal about the product from the CRL.[51]

For these reasons, in public comments on the FDA's previous transparency initiative, pharmaceutical companies, insurers, and patient advocacy groups supported a system of disclosure similar to our proposal. Boehringer Ingelheim commented: "Changes in FDA's policy/practice/position on specific topics sometimes only becomes known after an application review is made public. This could be made more transparent."[52] Similarly, several patient advocacy groups, including the Prostate Cancer Foundation, the Melanoma Research Alliance, and Fight Colorectal Cancer, supported the FDA Task Force's recommendations:

> [We] support the task force's recommendations to disclose more information about the drug development process including when an application for a new drug or device has been submitted or withdrawn by the sponsor, whether there was a significant safety concern that caused a sponsor to withdraw an application, and why the agency did not approve an application. The availability of this type of information has the potential to accelerate development of new drugs.[53]

GlaxoSmithKline supported greater disclosure by the FDA, with a number of guard rails to protect sponsors:

[49] Id.
[50] Id.
[51] Id. at 6.
[52] Boehringer Ingelheim, Comment on FDA Transparency Task Force Request for Comments (Apr. 8, 2010), Docket Number 2009-N-0247.
[53] Prostate Cancer Foundation, Comment on FDA Transparency Task Force Request for Comments (July 19, 2010), Docket No. 2009-N-0247; Melanoma Research Alliance, Comment on FDA Transparency Task Force Request for Comments (July 20, 2010), Docket No. 2009-N-0247; C3 Colorectal Cancer Coalition, Comment on FDA Transparency Task Force Request for Comments (July 20, 2010), Docket No. 2009-N-0247.

GSK supports FDA disclosure of the name of the application sponsor, the date of application receipt, disclosure of the fact that an application or supplement was submitted, withdrawn or abandoned, that the drug, biological product or device is associated with a significant safety concern ... While GSK supports greater transparency in this area, this support is contingent upon continued strong protection from disclosure of discrete information when such disclosure truly would cause substantial harm to the sponsor's competitive position. To protect trade secret/ confidential commercial information, broader disclosure practice must be accompanied by reinforcement of and rededication to existing FOIA mechanisms for giving a sponsor advance notice of a proposed disclosure, and an opportunity to object. GSK believes that FDA can strike an appropriate balance that benefits the public health while maintaining an environment that protects inventions and intellectual property.[54]

The FDA could likely adopt either system of disclosure (intermediate or full) under existing statutes, through its notice-and-comment rulemaking authority. The agency has previously used this authority to propose similar actions, including a regulation proposed in 2001 to disclose clinical trial data for investigational gene therapies and a notice in 2013 for potential release of masked pooled safety and efficacy data,[55] although, to date, neither has been finalized. The notice-and-comment rulemaking process is time consuming,[56] but it would allow the agency to hear the views of investors and drug companies who might have suggestions about how the process could be optimized for meaningful disclosure, while at the same time addressing companies' interest in trade secrecy.

In our view, politics is likely to play a smaller role in moving this particular initiative forward when compared with other potential agency initiatives. The FDA Transparency Task Force was launched under President Obama and spearheaded by Commissioner Margaret Hamburg and Principal Deputy Commissioner Joshua Sharfstein. The current FDA Commissioner, Scott Gottlieb, was appointed by President Trump and has previously expressed interest in making CRLs public, with appropriate redaction.[57] The idea of encouraging FDA transparency in a way that improves the efficiency of the drug development process seems to have bipartisan support.

---

[54] GlaxoSmithKline, Comment on FDA Transparency Task Force Request for Comments (July 16, 2010), Docket Number 2009-N-0247.
[55] Notice: availability of masked and de-identified non-summary safety and efficacy data, 78 Fed. Reg. 33,421 (proposed June 4, 2013).
[56] Thomas J. Hwang, et al., Quantifying the Food and Drug Administration's Rulemaking Delays Highlights the Need for Transparency, 33 Health Aff. 2 (2014).
[57] John Carroll, Gottlieb tackles speculators, FDA transparency and the R&D gold standard in a last round of queries ahead of confirmation vote, Endpoints News, Apr. 26, 2017, https://endpts.com /gottlieb-tackles-speculators-fda-transparency-and-the-rd-gold-standard-in-a-last-round-of-queries-ahead-of-confirmation-vote/.

IV. CONCLUSION

Limits on FDA transparency at every step of the drug approval process could harm not only patients and physicians, but also other researchers seeking to develop innovative new treatments. The FDA has the ability to address the situation through a system of disclosure that balances the interests of drug sponsors in their confidential information with the provision of more procedural and substantive information to other researchers in the relevant field. This proposed reform would not solve all concerns around FDA transparency, but it would provide valuable information for innovators, patients, and researchers going forward.

13

Transparency and Clinical Trial Data Sharing

Legal and Policy Issues

Barbara E. Bierer, Mark Barnes, and Rebecca Li

Clinical trials conducted to determine the efficacy and safety of biomedical interventions generate vast amounts of individual participant-level data (IPD) and metadata. Metadata literally means "data about data," but is generally used to describe the information about data that is descriptive (for example, data such as title, author, and topic), structural (for example, organization and taxonomies of data elements and their relationship to each other), and administrative (for example, information about a data repository, access, storage, and use). These data and metadata not only inform clinical and regulatory decision making but can also be shared and made available to additional investigators for a variety of secondary research uses. The secondary research uses of clinical trial IPD and metadata permit verification of the original results, facilitate other critical secondary research (for example, evaluation of adverse event rates and identification of surrogate endpoints), prevent unnecessary and potentially risky duplicative trials, and promote public trust through transparency. To accomplish these tasks, participant-level data must be readily "Findable, Accessible, Interoperable, and Re-usable (FAIR),"[1] available for aggregation and analysis across multiple sources, thus enabling the widest range of secondary research uses. However, transparency of clinical trial IPD and metadata requires the careful balance of the privacy interests of the individual with the interests of society in promoting public health.

Data sharing is scientifically valuable, but there are important ethical complications because of various competing interests that are implicated in data sharing as a process. Most importantly, if any clinical trial data are identifiable – that is, if the data contain sufficiently detailed information to identify individual participants with a high degree of certainty – then participant consent would appear to be appropriate, even required, as a condition of sharing. Respect for persons and individual autonomy, core principles of research ethics articulated in the Belmont

---

[1] The FAIR data principles, Force11, www.force11.org/group/fairgroup/fairprinciples (last visited July 1, 2017), archived at https://perma.cc/8FUA-9WLX.

Report,[2] demand that every individual have the ability to exercise choice based on his or her values, preferences, and beliefs. Through this lens, identifiable data seem to belong to the individual such that he or she should get to decide how they will be used. If data can be sufficiently anonymized such that the individual cannot be identified, however, then autonomy interests may be diminished, such that data can be used and shared even without informed consent from the individual sources of those data.

Translation of these ethical principles into regulatory standards has been accompanied by substantial debate. Moreover, with increasing frequency, clinical trials are conducted multinationally; data aggregation – whether such data are anonymized, coded, or identifiable – depends, therefore, upon the laws and regulations of the countries in which the trials were conducted, which differ significantly across the globe. Diverse data privacy laws, regulations, and policies have important scientific implications for the use and utility of data: only a complete data set can validate the conclusions of the primary research. A data set that is incomplete – a consequence, for instance, of participants failing to consent to the reuse of their data in a country or entity in which such permission is required – will render the entire data set less valuable for secondary use and incapable of confirming the primary research findings. Challenges to the ability to reproduce the research may also undermine public trust. Further, utilization of all data, not partial or incomplete data sets, allows for science and public health to progress optimally.

This chapter will discuss the tension between the privacy interests of individuals on the one hand and public health interests demanding data transparency on the other, transparency that carries with it known and tangible, but minimal – and in some cases vanishingly small – risks of reidentifying individuals from data sources that had been previously stripped of identifying information. This chapter will also compare the U.S. and the EU regulatory frameworks as examples of differing approaches to both privacy and data transparency, the complexity illuminated by considerations of the rights of individuals, of the public, and of society. Part of the complexity in understanding country-specific regulations and policy development is differing definitions of terms, making direct comparison difficult. Here we use the definitions promulgated by the European Medicines Agency (EMA)[3] (see Table 1) and clarify where they differ from terms typically used in the United States.

[2] Office of the Secretary, Office for Human Research Protections, The Belmont Report: Ethical Principles and Guidelines for the Protection of Human Subjects of Research, The National Commission for the Protection of Human Subjects of Biomedical and Behavioral Research (Apr. 18, 1979), www.hhs.gov/ohrp/regulations-and-policy/belmont-report/index.html, archived at https://perma.cc/D6YR-CUD8.

[3] European Medicines Agency, External guidance on the implementation of the European Medicines Agency policy on the publication of clinical data for medicinal products for human use, at 7–10, EMA/90915 (2016), www.ema.europa.eu/docs/en_GB/document_library/Regulatory_and_procedural_guideline/2016/03/WC500202621.pdf, archived at https://perma.cc/KT8Z-ZKMZ.

TABLE 1 *Definitions Utilized by the European Medicines Agency (EMA)*[4]

Anonymization: "The process of rendering data into a form which does not identify individuals and where identification is not likely to take place."

Anonymized/de-identified data: "Data in a form that does not identify individuals and where identification through its combination with other data is not likely to take place." Notably, the EMA uses the terms "de-identified" and "anonymized" data as synonyms, while the United States does not define "anonymization."

Individual Patient Data (IPD): "IPD shall mean the individual data separately recorded for each participant in a clinical study."

Protected Personal Data (PPD): "Any information relating to an identified or identifiable natural person; an identifiable person is one who can be identified, directly or indirectly, in particular by reference to an identification number or to one or more factors specific to his physical, physiological, mental, economic, cultural or social identity." Identifiable data is considered personal data. PPD is not allowable under Policy 70 and must be redacted.

Pseudonymization: Pseudonymization involves "replacing one attribute (typically a unique attribute) in a record by another. The natural person is still likely to be identified indirectly. Pseudonymization reduces the linkability of a dataset with the original identity of a data subject." Utilization of a study ID is an example of pseudonymization.

In addition, we explore how these factors may be balanced in light of the evolution of big data, and how the pace of change brings greater urgency to these issues. The interplay of differing legal and ethical frameworks with scientific utility and validity will also be discussed.

U.S. REGULATIONS GOVERNING PRIVACY AND HUMAN SUBJECTS RESEARCH

In the United States, regulations under the Health Insurance Portability and Accountability Act (HIPAA) of 1996[5] outline the standards for data privacy, govern the use and disclosure of protected health information (that is, health information that can be linked to an individual, including clinical trials data) by "covered entities,"[6] and set forth standards for data de-identification. Data can be de-identified by one of two methods: (1) the removal of eighteen specific identifiers[7] or (2) documentation by an experienced statistical expert that the statistical risk of

---

[4] Id.
[5] The HIPAA Privacy Rule, 45 C.F.R. Part 160, 164(A), 164(E)(2002), www.hhs.gov/hipaa/for-professionals/privacy/index.html, archived at https://perma.cc/RPB5-GKCC.
[6] Covered entities include health care providers, health plans, and health care clearinghouses (such as billing services and community health information systems), if they engage in one or more "covered electronic transactions," such as medical claims billing. Almost all U.S.-based health care providers, plans, and clearinghouses are "covered entities" under HIPAA.
[7] The eighteen identifiers are: names, geographic data, all elements of dates, telephone numbers, fax numbers, email addresses, social security numbers, medical record numbers, health plan beneficiary

reidentification is very small. In the United States, if either of these methods is employed, de-identified clinical trial data can be shared without permission from the individual data sources. Those "de-identified" data may be either anonymized or coded – that is, a code may exist linking the de-identified data to the actual individuals, so long as the code is not available to the secondary user. The fact that both (1) coded and de-identified and (2) anonymized data may be shared without participant consent or knowledge – and are not protected by the HIPAA Privacy Rule – contrasts with the regulatory framework in the EU (as discussed in the following section).

While the HIPAA Privacy Rule provides a frame of reference for treatment of protected health information, less clear is the status of de-identified clinical trial data under the regulations governing human subjects research, codified by the U.S. Department of Health and Human Services Federal Policy for the Protection of Human Subjects and often referred to as the "Common Rule." Revisions to the Common Rule were published in January 2017 with an effective date for all relevant provisions in January 2018. The revised Common Rule includes several requirements that bear on the considerations here, notably the requirement that participants from whom identifiable data will be collected in the course of research be told whether or not identifiers will be removed and whether the de-identified information will subsequently be used, distributed, or shared without specific consent.[8] As complex as this requirement may seem, the notification is meant to increase clarity and transparency for research participants who may not otherwise understand the relevance and potential risks of identifiability. It should not be confused, however, with informed consent, because it does not give the participant a choice about such use or distribution of "their" de-identified data; should the participant not agree to such use or distribution after being notified, the only option is not to participate in the research at all. This may appear to be an unreasonable, or arguably unethical, result when a clinical trial offers the only access to an experimental treatment for a life-threatening or serious disease for which no other therapeutic options exist (an "unmet medical need").

The counterargument must, however, be understood. The privacy risk to the individual, if data are appropriately de-identified, is minimal, while the value of secondary use of the data is significant, both for replication of the clinical trial results and for further scientific discovery. The value of the data in their entirety decreases precipitously if the data set is not complete. First, the ability to replicate the findings of the clinical trial is lost, as only with a complete data set can the statistical analysis be performed. Second, after selective elimination of some data of some individuals

numbers, account numbers, certificate/license numbers, vehicle identifiers and serial numbers including license plates, device identifiers and serial numbers, Web URLs, Internet protocol addresses, biometric identifiers, full-face photos and comparable images, and any unique identifying number, characteristic, or code.

[8] 45 CFR § 46.116(b)(9) (2009).

(should they be allowed to refuse the use of even their de-identified data), the likelihood that the remaining data set is representative of a population diminishes; there is no guarantee that missing data will be randomly distributed across subpopulations, as is discussed further below.

For identifiable data, still easily linked to their human data source, the revised Common Rule retains the ability of institutional review boards (IRBs) to waive the requirement for informed consent for research classified as "minimal risk" and in which it would be "impracticable" to obtain consent. In addition, the revised Rule provides an option for researchers to obtain "broad consent" from participants if the intention is to compile identifiable data (and biospecimens accompanied by identifiable data) for research and use or share those identifiable data in the future. However, if the participant is offered broad consent to future research use and declines, his or her data can *never* be de-identified and used, nor can an IRB ever waive consent to use that data. These provisions therefore require that data of anyone who declines broad consent be "tagged" with identifiers in perpetuity in order to be excluded from future consideration, increasing the likelihood of illegal future misuse of those identifiable data. This is an unfortunate result of attempts in the revised Common Rule to increase transparency: the intent of broad consent – to respect an individual's autonomy and right to privacy – may actually result in an increased risk of identifiability, secondary to the requirement to track and link the individual's identity specifically with the individual's data. Finally, it is worth noting that given the uncertainties of research directions, whether such broad consent, which can cover unlimited future research uses of identifiable data, can ever be truly informed is questionable.

Importantly, in the United States, there is no comprehensive regulatory framework for consideration of individual privacy rights. HIPAA applies to covered entities – generally health care entities, individuals, organizations, and their business associates that electronically transmit health information. The Common Rule applies only to federally funded research involving human subjects and, similarly, the jurisdiction of the Food and Drug Administration (FDA) is also limited to drugs and devices and clinical trials that test them. Thus, there are significant data sources that can be openly shared without any regulation governing their use. While such data may be shared in the service of transparency, science, and the public good, they can also be shared for commercial, perverse, litigious, or other purposes. The absence of an overarching data protection regime in the United States is in contrast to the regulatory framework in the European Union.

EUROPEAN UNION REGULATORY FRAMEWORK FOR CLINICAL TRIALS DATA SHARING AND PRIVACY PROTECTIONS

The regulations that control clinical trial transparency for all trials submitted to the EMA have evolved over the last several years. Supporting the individual's right to access public documents and following earlier regulations on openness,[9] EU policy 0043[10] detailed the principles and procedures by which data and IPD from clinical trials that have been submitted to the EMA for marketing authorization would be made available to the public, allowing for redaction of confidential commercial information and personal data. Policy 0043 required an individual or entity to request the data, and the identity of the requester was made public. In 2014, in an effort to increase transparency and openness, the EMA released Policy 0070[11] announcing that the EMA would prospectively release documents related to clinical reports contained in Marketing Authorization Applications (MAAs) submitted after January 1, 2015. Several clarifications of the policy have since been published, including definitions of protected personal data (PPD) and confidential commercial information (CCI); methods of redaction including of personal narratives; identification of and justification for removal of CCI, including validation that the document contains no CCI; and provision of a report explaining the anonymization procedures. In October 2016, the first clinical study reports (CSRs) that include individual participant-level data (IPD) were published on the EMA website in a form that is available for view. These first two reports contained over 250,000 pages of documents summarizing over 100 clinical trials, and were heralded as a major advance for transparency in the service of public health.[12]

Given their requirement to disclose individual-level participant data, however, these regulations appear to be in some contrast to the EU data protection laws (that is, General Data Protection Regulation, or GDPR)[13] that protect not only the rights to one's own information and the privacy of that information, but also the "right to be forgotten," that is, the right of an individual to require information that was once publicly known to be removed from public view. These differences have important

[9] Regulation (EC) No 1049/2001 of the European Parliament and of the Council of 30 May 2001 regarding public access to European Parliament, Council and Commission documents, Official Journal of the European Communities, www.europarl.europa.eu/RegData/PDF/r1049_en.pdf (last visited Sept. 6, 2017), archived at https://perma.cc/T9TU-YG2T.
    European Medicines Agency, Rules for the Implementation of Regulation (EC) No 1049/2001 on Access to EMEA Documents (Dec. 19, 2006), www.ema.europa.eu/docs/en_GB/document_library/Other/2010/02/WC500070829.pdf, archived at https://perma.cc/F4MJ-RGHR.
[10] European Medicines Agency, European Medicines Agency policy on access to documents (related to medicinal products for human and veterinary use), Policy/0043 (Nov. 30, 2010), www.ema.europa.eu/docs/en_GB/document_library/Other/ 2010/11/WC500099473.pdf, archived at https://perma.cc/SC22-Q8PQ.
[11] European Medicines Agency, European Medicines Agency policy on publication of clinical data for medicinal products for human use, Policy/0070 (Oct. 2, 2014), www.ema.europa.eu/docs/en_GB/document_library/Other/2014/10/WC500174796.pdf, archived at https://perma.cc/R59E-9ZWM.
[12] European Medicines Agency Today Releases First Clinical Study Reports, (Oct. 20, 2016), http://www.alltrials.net/news/european-medicines-agency-csr-transparency-policy-0070/, archived at https://perma.cc/EP82-R86W.
[13] European Commission, Regulation of the European Parliament and of the Council on the Protection of Individuals with Regard to the Processing of Personal Data and on the Free Movement of Such Data (General Data Protection Regulation), Brussels (Jan. 25, 2012), http://ec.europa.eu/justice/data-protection/document/review2012/com_2012_11_en.pdf, archived at https://perma.cc/WSJ9-DTY3.

practical and scientific implications for transparency and data sharing: in the EU, absent any specific EU or member state legal requirement to do so, sharing personal health data of an individual will require that person's permission. Consent is required if the data are identifiable or, in contrast to the regulations in the United States, if any code links personal information to the data, even if unavailable to the individual using the data. These laws thus require all data (other than exhaustively anonymized data to which no code is retained) to be tagged indefinitely in case the individual exercises his or her right to withdraw permission for third-party access. Notably, as discussed above, data tagging itself may increase the risk of reidentification because it requires some level of identifiability to be retained. An important consequence of these regulations is that each research participant must affirmatively consent to the sharing of his or her data, raising precisely the concerns about comprehensiveness and generalizability of data sets noted above.

Other than consent of the data source(s), the GDPR – in its Articles 9(2)(j), 89(1), and 89(2) – allows for specific enactments by the EU or member states of measures to require processing of personal health data to ensure, among other things, "high standards of quality and safety of ... medicinal products or medical devices." However, such enactments must also provide for adequate protections for the "rights and freedoms of the data subject, in particular professional secrecy" by which is meant, presumably, the confidential communications inherent in the physician–patient relationship. Thus, although specific data sharing requirements could be imposed in the EU or member states without subjects' consent, each such requirement would of necessity protect subjects' welfare and respect their rights – including protecting their confidential communications to their medical providers. This takes us full circle, needing provisions to assure the protection of data subjects to be embedded in any data sharing requirements.

Reconciliation of Policy 0070 regarding clinical trial data disclosure with the EU data protection rules is complex. Table 2 compares the two regulations: EMA Policy 0070, mandated on the principle of greater openness and transparency; and the EU GDPR 2016/679, mandated on the principle of personal privacy and control over personal data. Insofar as there is any risk of reidentification of the information posted on the EMA website, either through publication of the clinical study reports or the case report forms – despite redaction – individuals may have a right to request that their data be removed, although this assumes that there is no specific legal EU or national mandate, under GDPR Article 89(2), which would act as a derogation of this personal right. Anonymization techniques, generally, are risk based and rest on statistical probabilities,[14] and none is "zero risk," particularly if the data in one data set can be triangulated with data in another domain.[15]

[14] Khaled El Emam & Luk Arbuckle, Anonymizing Health Data: Case Studies and Methods to Get You Started (2013).
[15] Rolf H. Weber & Ulrike I. Heinrich, Anonymization (SpringerBriefs in Cybersecurity) (2012); Tore Dalenius, Finding a Needle in a Haystack or Identifying Anonymous Census Records, 2 J. Official Stat. 329, 329–36 (1986).

TABLE 2 *Comparing Current Rulings in the EMA and Impact on Clinical Trials*

	Transparency	Individual Right to Privacy & Confidentiality
Policy/ Law/ Ruling/ Regulation	EMA Policy 70 mandated under article 80 of Regulation EU No. 726/2004[16] that regulates community procedures for EMA authorization and supervision of medicinal products for human and veterinary use.	EU General data protection regulation 2016/679 (GDPR).[17]
Requirement and Background	Applies to pharmaceutical companies who submit applications to the EMA.	Applies to individuals residing in the EU who can be identified.
	Motivated in part by public pressure to provide access to the data after a regulatory decision (approval or rejection).	The update was initiated to ensure that personal data should be relevant, accurate, complete and up to date. In addition, the regulation was motivated by the abiding principle that individuals ultimately have control of their own identifiable data.
	Mandates the publication of a clinical study report (CSR) (Phase 1) and individual participant-level data (IPD) (Phase 2) submitted as part of a marketing authorization application (MAA) following the conclusion of a regulatory decision.	
	The CSR and IPD reside and will be shared through the EU public database.	Provides major reforms over prior regulation EU Directive 95/46/EC including: • Right to be forgotten/ erasure (Article 18) provision • Notification of data security breaches (Articles 31–33) • Consent provisions for secondary research (termed processing) (Article 9)
	Only anonymized data as defined are allowable in the EU public database.	The Law applies to pseudonymized and identifiable data, as defined.

---

[16] Regulation (EC) No 726/2004 of the European Parliament and of the Council, Official Journal of the European Union, 136, 1–33, http://eur-lex.europa.eu/LexUriServ/LexUriServ.do?uri=OJ:L:2004:136:0001:0033:en:PDF, archived at https://perma.cc/7YZA-4CNT.

[17] EU General Data Protection Regulation (GDPR), www.eugdpr.org/ (last visited Sept. 6, 2017), archived at https://perma.cc/Z389-JS9Y.

TABLE 2 *(continued)*

	Transparency	Individual Right to Privacy & Confidentiality
Aims/ Rationale for Ruling	• Avoid needless duplication of clinical trials • Foster innovation of new drugs • Build public trust in the EMA's scientific and decision-making processes • Provide access to researchers to enable reanalysis of clinical data[18]	• Allow residents of the EU control of their data (including the right to be forgotten/erasure and export of data outside of the EU) • Clarify consent terms including the right to withdraw consent • Harmonize data protection regulation across the EU
Current status	• Phase 1 (clinical overview report, clinical study report, and appendices [study protocol, case report forms, statistical methods]) is complete and available in a downloadable pdf format for those medicines that have received EU regulatory decisions. • Phase 2 (IPD) is planned but no date has been set for publication in the EMA database.	• Published in July 2016 • In force May 25, 2018

While by law, "no personal data of trial participants shall be recorded in the EU database" (Recital 67 of Regulation (EU) 536/2014), concern regarding the risk of reidentification is more than theoretical. Patient narratives, such as those contained in adverse event reports, are often free-form dictations that frequently contain identifying information that may be difficult to discern even if checked manually. Data from ultrarare diseases are difficult to anonymize. The EMA introduced one other measure to help protect individual privacy when researchers access IPD

---

[18] European Medicines Agency, Clinical data publication (Oct. 2016), www.ema.europa.eu/ema/?curl=pages/special_topics/general/general_content_000555.jsp, archived at https://perma.cc/6B64-292Z.

submitted to EMA: prior to accessing any clinical trial data on the database, the data requester must agree to the provisions of Terms of Use (TOU) document that specifically states that the individual will not "seek to re-identify the trial subjects or other individuals from the Clinical Reports in breach of applicable privacy laws."[19]

The EU GDPR 2016/679 has yet to be implemented, but absent specific derogations of their privacy rights – which derogations, if imposed, must nevertheless be narrowly tailored and sufficiently protective of data subjects' privacy – the regulation may allow residents of the EU control of their clinical trial data (including the right to be forgotten/erasure and export of data outside of the EU). Under the original 1995 EU Privacy Directive,[20] the case of *Google Spain SL, Google Inc.* v. *Agencia Española de Protección de Datos, Mario Costeja González* (2014) was decided. The Court of Justice in the EU ruled that individuals have certain rights to have personal data deleted from search engines upon request, subject to certain exceptions for research and public health.[21] With respect to clinical trials data, those rights, if not derogated by specific enactments, would allow the right to erase data if consent is withdrawn, specifically data that have not been fully and irrevocably anonymized.

THE RIGHTS OF THE INDIVIDUAL VERSUS PUBLIC GOOD

In clinical trials, participants put themselves at risk for the benefit of generalizable knowledge. Honoring participants' voluntarism and altruism, therefore, demands using their de-identified clinical trial data optimally, including the use of "big data" methods for new discovery in the service of public health. The availability of the original complete data set, with the statistical analysis plan, permits others to reproduce the findings of the primary analysis. Finally, access to the data will prevent the unnecessary repetition of trials – and the waste and risk to individual participants – when the data already exist. These data sets are therefore valuable for a variety of purposes, and that value is maximized if the data set is complete. Academicians, industry sponsors, journal editors, and funders increasingly appreciate the value of data transparency. Further, patients and patient advocates

---

[19] European Medicines Agency, Terms of Use, Clinical Data, https://clinicaldata.ema.europa.eu/web/cdp/termsofuse, archived at https://perma.cc/B5UD-QHEV.

[20] Factsheet on the "Right to be Forgotten" Ruling (c-131/12), European Commission (2014), http://ec.europa.eu/justice/data-protection/files/factsheets/factsheet_data_protection_en.pdf, archived at https://perma.cc/JJ7S-ASPV.

[21] Mark Barnes et al., Impact of the European Union's Approved General Data Protection Regulation on Scientific Research and Secondary Uses of Personal Data, Bloomberg BNA, Medical Research Law & Policy Report (2016), www.ropesgray.com/~/media/Files/articles/2016/February/Bloomberg-BNA2-16–17.ashx, archived at https://perma.cc/YH3S-H2WL.

increasingly want their data to be shared, in the hope of propelling discovery and novel approaches to diagnosis, treatment, and prevention.[22]

Given the value derived from sharing the complete data set, how transparent must we be with participants about how their data should be shared? Both EU and U.S. regulations allow anonymized data to be shared without individual informed consent or, in the United States, IRBs may waive informed consent even when identifiers remain. That said, there are practical and important reasons to consider whether or not participants should be informed of, or asked about, future use of data.

The first argument for informing data subjects about the sharing of their data is that there is a finite, nonzero risk of reidentification, despite best efforts at anonymization, and that risk grows with the granularity, detail, and uniqueness of the data.[23] Data related to rare and ultrarare diseases are, for example, difficult if not impossible to mask without losing utility and integrity. Further, while the statistical risk of reidentification may be very small using one single data set, linking that data set with another source of identifiers or an "identification data set" will change the risk calculation. It is therefore largely impossible to guarantee that there is "no risk" to reidentification. If then, one concludes that the risk of reidentification is nonzero, is consent for future use of data a regulatory requirement? The EU GDPR regulations, absent specific EU or national derogations of those privacy rights, would appear to allow individuals to request that their individual data be removed, to the extent that a primary data set has not been completely anonymized or a link to the identifying code remains. U.S. regulations, however, allow for use of de-identified data without IRB review, and if an individual withdraws consent, or refuses "broad consent," that subject's data can be subsequently de-identified and used for future research.

A second argument in favor of transparency is one of respect for persons. If it is known that the data will be anonymized and shared, respect for persons might demand that any individual be afforded the dignity to choose, and the agency to exercise choice, as to whether data sharing is consistent with his or her preferences, beliefs, and values.

Any principle of requiring informed consent for future use of data must be balanced, however, by concerns about its significant negative impact on health

[22] Donna Zulman et al., Patient Interest in Sharing Personal Health Record Information: A Web-Based Survey, 155 Annals of Internal Med. 805, 805–10 (2011); David Grande et al., Public Preferences About Secondary Uses of Electronic Health Information, 173 Jama Internal Med. 1798, 1798–1806 (2013); Nanibaa' A. Garrison et al., A Systematic Literature Review of Individuals' Perspectives on Broad Consent and Data Sharing in the United States, 18 Genetics in Med. 663, 663–71 (2016); Saskia C. Sanderson et al., Public Attitudes Toward Consent and Data Sharing in Biobank Research: A Large Multi-site Experimental Survey in the US, 100 The Am. J. Hum. Genetics 414, 414–27 (2017).

[23] In this argument, we purposely exclude from consideration the risk of self-identification. It is relatively straightforward to self-identify from a database that for all other purposes has zero risk of reidentification. In a list of social security numbers, an individual could pick out his or her own without any other identifiers, a task that would be impossible for an unrelated viewer. In a narrative of a serious and unanticipated adverse event, a participant might recognize sufficient correlation to their own clinical course to deduce his or her own identity.

research. First, if explicit consent is required, those individuals who consent to use may be different (by, for example, age, race/ethnicity, socioeconomic class, county, and country) than those that refuse consent. In that instance, the remaining (consented) data would not be representative or generalizable, skewing future results. Second, if consent is required, at a minimum (1) human and financial resources must be expended to obtain, document, store, and provide oversight of consent, and (2) tracking infrastructure for identifying and recording consented data (and specimens) must be created and maintained to differentiate them from those data (and specimens) for which consent has been declined. The cost and complexity of the research are increased, resources are dedicated to this activity and thus diverted from potentially beneficial research, and societal benefit is thereby significantly limited. Third and importantly, maintaining a link to the data for those that decline increases the risk of privacy breaches (and the cost of maintaining the technical infrastructure). Fourth, if consent for future use is required for participation, recruitment rates will potentially decline (and time to complete enrollment increase). Finally, it is not clear that consent to unrestricted future use can ever be "informed." Research technologies and capacities change in ways that cannot now be envisioned or imagined, and the future self may or may not even remember to what it has agreed today.

On balance, therefore, there are significant drawbacks to the adoption of a consent paradigm, with potential compromise of scientific insights that would promote public health. As stated by Research Councils UK, "Publicly funded research data are a public good, produced in the public interest, which should be made openly available with as few restrictions as possible in a timely and responsible manner."[24]

ALTERNATIVES TO INFORMED CONSENT TO SUPPORT TRANSPARENCY INITIATIVES

If consent is not fully informed – because who in truth can now realize the full range of future uses of their own data? – and if the practice of consent allows "opt-outs" that thereby adulterate data sets and reduce their usefulness, then is consent even a viable basis for data sharing? In the current global digital age, personal data is collected, reused, analyzed, and shared routinely: every credit card purchase, every Google search, every FitBit step involves personal data attributed to the individual and used for commercial and other purposes. While most Internet services include a "click-through" terms of use agreement, few individuals read, and far fewer understand, the terms to which they are consenting. Nevertheless, if transparency and openness is a goal, then arguably

---

[24] RCUK Common Principles on Data Policy, Research Councils UK (July 2015), www.rcuk.ac.uk/research/datapolicy/, archived at https://perma.cc/48VK-2BB2.

individuals should be informed about how their data will be used, despite regulatory permission not to do so.

One way to be transparent with data subjects is to support education about the utility of the data and obligatory notification to subjects of any intended sharing of their data. The public and potential participants should be informed not only about the use of aggregated health data but of the value of research. Ideally, education would be a general matter, but at a minimum, individuals should be provided notice as a routine measure in health care and social service settings. Indeed, currently identifiable data is routinely used for health care and social service operations and quality improvement efforts without consent; here we argue that it would be preferable to provide notice and explanation of all uses of data, identifiable, de-identified, and anonymized.

Such notice should, in any event, be provided to prospective participants in advance of informed consent for participation in a clinical trial and should include potential risks of data sharing, including informational risks and risks to participant privacy. In the event that an individual has strong objection to the use of data, and that objection overrides and supersedes the desire to participate in the research, he or she then has the option not to participate in the research at all.

As a framework for being transparent about data sharing practices, neither informed consent nor education and notification is sufficient. Notification of data subjects further will not protect them from intentional reidentification of their anonymized data and/or misuse of those data. In the United States, there are few consequences for reidentification and/or misuse, and no privacy standards as strong as those protections provided by the EU GDPR. Like the EU, the United States should establish civil and potentially criminal penalties for unauthorized reidentification and/or misuse of data. Were such penalties established, it should nevertheless be appreciated that oversight is difficult. Once reidentification has occurred and protected personal data obtained, it is relatively easy to find alternative sources of the data (for example, work-arounds) and thus shield from view the original source. Proving that the original data source involved linking identity to de-identified data is, therefore, difficult. As with other legal sanctions, established penalties would likely act as a relative deterrent, but only to the extent that enforcement resources are also deployed to prosecute violators.

INTERNATIONAL REGULATORY HARMONIZATION OF DATA POLICIES

A significant number of clinical trials are conducted multinationally, and the collected data are pooled for analysis. Country-specific and differing regulatory and legal regimes add risk, expense, and operational inefficiencies. Further, standards of de-identification and anonymization differ among nations, as do different standards for metadata extraction. However, the informational risks – and dignity risks – of reidentification and misuse are similar across the globe. International efforts to align data sharing policies, and methods for anonymization, should commence.

Currently, the EMA is the only regulatory agency that has publicly committed to, and implemented a system for, disseminating anonymized clinical trial individual participant-level data. The availability of a publicly available database builds trust in the scientific and decision-making process at the EMA, allows derivative studies to reproduce the primary results, and has the potential to advance discovery science. While there is always the risk of a privacy breach, anonymization of the data minimizes the likelihood of an informational harm to the participant. The United States has depended upon individual informed consent to justify sharing data for secondary use; in the absence of informed consent, de-identified data may be used, largely without limitation. Yet because the risk of reidentification is nonzero, we believe that appropriate procedures should be established, and protections implemented, to minimize this risk. Those protections should include identity management of the data requester or user, communicating data through secure encrypted channels, and minimizing the data transferred to the data elements necessary for the purpose. The sensitivity of the data elements (for example, HIV status) and of the relevant population (for example, ultrarare diseases, discreet and insular communities) should factor into and dictate the extent of those protections. Finally, global regulatory harmonization will permit technical systems to be developed that optimize security while permitting cooperative data exchange, with shared expectations that investigators, organizations, and government entities will perform in ways that promote transparency in the service of public health.

14

The European Medicines Agency's Approach to Transparency

Stefano Marino and Spyridon Drosos[*]

1. INTRODUCTION

In this chapter, we examine the ways in which an agency of the European Union[1] may reconcile, in the absence of detailed legislative guidance,[2] the tensions between transparency requirements, on the one hand, and the rights to property, privacy, and protection of personal data, on the other. The notion of transparency discussed herein comprises the "reactive" aspect, which is reflected in an individual's right of access to documents held by Union institutions, and the "proactive" aspect, which concerns the obligation of the Union institutions to proactively make available to the public the documents supporting their decision-making processes.

The examined case study is that of the European Medicines Agency (EMA or Agency), which is the EU regulatory body responsible for providing scientific assessments of the quality, safety, and efficacy of medicinal products for human or veterinary use referred to it in accordance with the relevant EU legislation, as well as for the supervision and pharmacovigilance of medicinal products placed on the EU market.[3]

This chapter consists of three parts. The first part considers certain normative justifications for transparency in the field of public health. Those justifications draw on political, ethical, and scientific arguments. The second part of the chapter looks into the nuts and bolts of EMA's approach to reactive transparency. After briefly

---

[*] The views expressed in this chapter are those of the authors and do not necessarily reflect those of the European Medicines Agency or any of its committees.
[1] The terms "EU," "European Union," and "Union" are used interchangeably throughout this chapter.
[2] For the challenges faced by EU Agencies, in view of the limited legislative guidance for the implementation of Regulation (EC) No 1049/2001, see Emilia Korkea-Aho & Päivi Leino, Who Owns the Information Held by EU Agencies? Weed Killers, Commercially Sensitive Information and Transparent and Participatory Governance, 54 Common Mkt. L. Rev. 1059 (2017).
[3] For more information on EMA's remit and responsibilities, see Regulation (EC) No 726/2004 of the European Parliament and of the Council of 31 March 2004, Official Journal of the European Union [hereinafter also referred to as "EMA Founding Regulation"].

presenting the fundamentals of the right of access to documents in possession of EU institutions, this part discusses what rules EMA has developed to process requests for access to documents that may contain commercially confidential information (CCI) or personal data. The third part of the chapter examines the proactive disclosure of clinical reports, a recent development of EMA's journey toward enhanced transparency. This part discusses how EMA deals with the redaction of CCI in, and the anonymization of, proactively published clinical reports.

2. NORMATIVE JUSTIFICATIONS FOR TRANSPARENCY

There are several normative justifications advocating for the continuous enhancement of transparency in the context of the authorization, supervision, and pharmacovigilance of medicinal products.

Improving Effectiveness and Accountability in the Decision-Making Processes Concerning Medicinal Products

The first set of arguments for enhanced transparency relates to the democratic credentials of the EU.[4] The EU integration project has been subject to a longstanding critique of democratic deficit. In a nutshell, this critique posits that the EU lacks legitimacy as its institutional machinery is overly complex and therefore inaccessible to EU citizens. In addition, the fact that the chains of electoral control are lengthier and less visible in the EU, when compared against the constitutional set-ups of its Member States, has reinforced the narrative that citizens cannot easily hold the Union institutions accountable.

Transparency has been seen as the main mechanism for improving legitimacy and accountability of the Union administration and for enhancing, therefore, the democratic credentials of the Union. In the words of the Court of Justice of the European Union (CJEU), "**transparency**... seeks to ensure **greater participation** of citizens in the decision-making process and to guarantee that the administration enjoys greater **legitimacy** and is more **effective** and more **accountable** to the citizen in a democratic system" (emphasis added).[5]

In view of its mandate, EMA has in its possession an extensive number of documents related to public health. By way of example, EMA holds clinical study reports submitted by companies seeking approval of their medicinal products and EMA assessments thereof, Periodic Safety Update Reports (PSURs)[6] and EMA

---

[4] See, e.g., Adrienne Héritier, Composite Democracy in Europe: The Role of Transparency and Access to Information, 10 J. Eur. Pub. Pol'y 814 (2003).
[5] Case T-403/05, MyTravel Grp. plc v. Comm'n, 2008 E.C.R. II-2027.
[6] PSURs are reports providing an updated evaluation of the **benefit–risk balance** of a medicine, and are submitted by marketing authorization holders at defined time points following a medicine's authorization.

assessments thereof, and EMA assessments prepared during a referral procedure.[7] These documents contain critical information on the safety and efficacy of medicinal products. The possibility to make the documents in the possession of EMA publicly available facilitates scrutiny by health care professionals and patients of regulatory decisions taken by EMA and of the underlying science. This way, EMA can be held accountable for its scientific assessments. In addition, the public's ability to participate in policymaking hinges, to a large extent, on the availability of information, both technical and nontechnical, regarding the underlying policy issues.

Respecting Patients' and Health Care Professionals' Right to Have Access to Information

Another justification for transparency relates to the patients' right to have access to information regarding the safety and efficacy of the medicinal products which they take. The withholding of significant information on medicinal products from patients would make it impossible for them to understand the benefits and risks associated with a medicinal product, be it prescription only or over the counter. The unavailability of such critical information for the health and well-being of patients would undermine their autonomy.[8]

Similar ethical and legal obligations extend to health care professionals, who are called to provide informed recommendations to patients. It bears emphasizing that health care professionals have an obligation to refrain from causing any harm to patients and an obligation to contribute to their patients' welfare. In order to discharge their respective duties of care, health care professionals should have access to information related to the safety and efficacy profiles of a medicinal product, on the basis of which they are then better placed to provide informed recommendations to patients.

Transparency About Clinical Trial Data

There are also other more context-specific arguments in favor of enhanced transparency. For instance, there is an argument in favor of making publicly available the clinical reports which were submitted as part of an application for the authorization of a medicinal product. The availability of clinical reports is expected to encourage the reanalysis of data and potentially lead to optimized future study designs with regard to population selection and sample size, choice of outcomes, definition of clinically relevant differences for various end points, or identification of biomarkers

---

[7] A referral is a procedure used to resolve concerns over the safety or the benefit–risk balance of a medicine or a class of medicines. The concerns are "referred" to EMA, so that it can make a recommendation for a harmonised position across the European Union.

[8] Tom Beauchamp & James Childress, Principles of Biomedical Ethics 107 (2013).

for better disease phenotyping.[9] In turn, this optimization of study designs may improve research and development of new medicinal products. It bears noting that the European Ombudsman also emphasized the need for disclosure of clinical trial reports.[10]

3. EMA'S APPROACH TO REACTIVE TRANSPARENCY

3.1. Preliminary Considerations on the Right of Access to Documents Held by EMA

The reactive aspect of transparency is primarily reflected in the EU fundamental right of individuals to request access to documents held by EU public authorities.[11] The arrangements for the implementation of this fundamental right are laid down in Regulation (EC) No 1049/2001 ("Transparency Regulation"),[12] which imposes on certain Union institutions the obligation to disclose all documents in their possession further to a request for access to documents. The general rule laid down is that "the public is to have access to the documents of the institutions and refusal of access is the exception to that rule."[13] Those exceptions, which are exhaustively enumerated in Article 4 of the Transparency Regulation,[14] "must be interpreted and applied strictly".[15] It also bears noting that a decision denying access is valid only if it is based on one of the exceptions provided for in Article 4.[16] In addition, an institution's refusal must sufficiently substantiate how the disclosure would pose a reasonably foreseeable and not purely hypothetical risk to a protected interest.

---

[9] See Sergio Bonini et al., Transparency and the European Medicines Agency – Sharing of Clinical Trial Data, 371 New Eng. J. Med. 2452, 2454 (2014).
[10] European Ombudsman, Decision on own-initiative inquiry OI/3/2014/FOR concerning the partial refusal of the EMA to give public access to studies related to the approval of a medicinal product, ¶ 43 (2016).
[11] See Treaty on the Functioning of the EU art. 15(3), Dec. 13, 2007, 2008 O.J. C 115/47; Charter of Fundamental Rights of the EU art. 42, Dec. 12, 2007, 2010 O.J. C 83/02.
[12] See Regulation (EC) No 1049/2001 of the European Parliament and of the Council of 30 May 2001, Official Journal of the European Union. The Transparency Regulation could be likened to the U.S. Freedom of Information Act (5 U.S.C. § 552). See Amy Westergren, The Data Liberation Movement: Regulation of Clinical Trial Data Sharing in the European Union and the United States, 28 Hous. J Int'l L. 887, 900–01 (2016).
[13] See Case T-264/04, WWF European Policy Programme v. Council, 2007 E.C.R. II-931.
[14] See Regulation No 1049/2001, supra note 12, art. 4(2) (providing that: "1. The institutions shall refuse access to a document where disclosure would undermine the protection of: . . .
    (b) **privacy and the integrity of the individual, in particular in accordance with Community legislation regarding the protection of personal data.**
    2. The institutions shall refuse access to a document where disclosure would undermine the protection of:
    — commercial interests of a natural or legal person, including intellectual property, . . . unless there is an overriding public interest in disclosure . . . .") (emphasis added).
[15] See Case C-64/05 P, Kingdom of Sweden v. Comm'n, 2007 E.C.R. I-11447.
[16] Case T-211/00, Kuijer v. Council, 2002 E.C.R. II-508.

As a Union agency, the Transparency Regulation applies to documents held by EMA,[17] whether they have been drawn up by the Agency itself or by third parties.[18] Once EMA receives a request under the Transparency Regulation for access to documents in its possession, it will consider on a case-by-case basis whether the requested documents should be disclosed. If the document has been drawn up by a third party and not by the Agency, then the Agency shall consult with that third party.[19] The outcome of this consultation is not binding on EMA, but only aims at enabling EMA to ascertain whether any parts of the third-party documents fall under the exceptions listed in Article 4(1) and (2) of the Transparency Regulation and whether any redactions should therefore be applied.[20] Only the parts of the documents that come under an exception may not be disclosed.[21]

Further to Article 4(1)(b) of the Transparency Regulation, the Agency must not disclose documents in its possession when it considers that the disclosure will undermine the privacy and integrity of an individual, in particular in what regards the protection of his/her personal data.[22] Another reason for which the Agency may refuse to disclose documents is when it considers that the disclosure will undermine the protection of the "commercial interests of a natural or legal person, including intellectual property," namely the protection of commercially confidential information.[23] The exception to disclosure on grounds of an individual's privacy is a so-called mandatory exception insofar as the concerned institution may not invoke any reasons of overriding public interest to justify a decision for disclosure. By contrast, the exception on grounds of the owner's commercial interests is a so-called discretionary exception, because the concerned institution is called upon to strike a balance between the interest in keeping the documents confidential and the competing overriding public interest in disclosure. If the institution considers that there is an overriding public interest, then it shall disclose the concerned document.[24] A general reference to transparency does not suffice to establish an overriding interest in disclosure, however.[25] On the contrary, reference to specific circumstances is needed. In the context of documents held by EMA, such specific

---

[17] See Regulation No 726/2004, supra note 3, art. 73 (providing that the Transparency Regulation shall apply to documents held by EMA).

[18] Regulation No 1049/2001, supra note 12, art. 2(3) (providing that this Regulation "shall apply to all documents held by an institution, that is to say, documents drawn up or received by it and in its possession").

[19] Regulation No 1049/2001, supra note 12, art. 4(4) (providing that "[a]s regards third-party documents, the institution shall consult the third party with a view to assessing whether an exception in paragraph 1 or 2 is applicable, unless it is clear that the document shall or shall not be disclosed").

[20] Case T-380/4, *Terezakis v. Comm'n*, 2008 E.C.R. II-00011*.

[21] See Regulation No 1049/2001, supra note 12, art. 4(6).

[22] Id. at art. 4(1)(b).

[23] Id. at art. 4(2).

[24] Id.

[25] Case C-127/13 P, *Strack v. Comm'n*, 2014 EUR-Lex CELEX LEXIS 15 (Oct. 2, 2014).

circumstances could, for instance, arise when there is a safety issue related to an authorized medicinal product.

In order to better comply with its legal obligations under the Transparency Regulation, EMA has put in place a number of implementing provisions, namely the EMA Policy on access to documents,[26] the rules for the implementation of Regulation (EC) No 1049/2001 on access to EMA documents,[27] and the so-called Output Table.[28] In addition, EMA and the Heads of Medicines Agencies have developed regulatory guidance with a view to communicating to third parties what information is considered to constitute CCI.[29] Part of that publicly available regulatory guidance is the HMA/EMA Guidance,[30] which not only lays down the general principles for determining whether certain information in the application for marketing authorization could be considered as personal data or CCI, but also provides a significant number of examples that may be considered personal data or CCI.

3.2. EMA's Approach to the Redaction of Personal Data in the Context of the Transparency Regulation

In the EU, an individual's right for respect of his/her privacy and personal data is also protected at the treaty level.[31] Safeguards and obligations regarding the transfer of personal data by Union institutions, bodies, offices, and agencies are foreseen in Regulation (EC) No 45/2001 ("Personal Data Regulation"),[32] which clarifies that the term "personal data" concerns information relating to an identified or identifiable natural person.[33] The term "identifiable natural person" refers to an individual who can be identified, directly or indirectly, in particular by reference to an identification number or to one or more factors specific to his/her physical, physiological, mental, economic, cultural, or social identity.[34]

---

[26] See European Meds. Agency, European Medicines Agency Policy on Access to Documents (related to medicinal products for human and veterinary use), Policy/0043 (Nov. 30, 2010).
[27] See European Meds. Agency, Rules for the Implementation of Regulation (EC) No 1049/2001 on access to EMEA documents, MB/203359 (Dec. 19, 2006).
[28] See European Meds. Agency, Output of the European Medicines Agency Policy on Access to Documents Related to Medicinal Products for Human and Veterinary Use, 127362/2006 (Nov. 30, 2010).
[29] The Heads of Medicines Agencies is a network of the Heads of the National Competent Authorities whose organizations are responsible for the regulation of medicinal products for human and veterinary use in the European Economic Area.
[30] See HMA/EMA Guidance document on the identification of commercially confidential information and personal data within the structure of the marketing authorization (MA) application – release of information after the granting of marketing authorization (Mar. 27, 2012).
[31] See Treaty on the Functioning of the EU art. 16(1), Dec. 13, 2007, 2008 O.J. C 115/47; Charter of Fundamental Rights of the EU art. 7 & 8, Dec. 12, 2007, 2010 O.J. C 83/02.
[32] See Regulation (EC) No 45/2001 of the European Parliament and of the Council of 18 December 2000, Official Journal of the European Communities.
[33] Id. art. 2(a).
[34] Id.

A request for access to documents allegedly containing personal data brings in conflict two fundamental rights, the right of access to documents and an individual's rights to privacy and protection of his/her personal data. Every such request is examined in accordance with both the Transparency and Personal Data Regulations.[35] In that respect, personal data may be transferred to a third party on the basis of the Transparency Regulation[36] only where that transfer fulfils the conditions laid down in Article 8(a) or (b) of the Personal Data Regulation and constitutes lawful processing in accordance with the requirements of Article 5 thereof. For that reason, a third party seeking to obtain access to an individual's personal data, which are in the possession of the Agency, must first establish why such disclosure is necessary by providing "any express and legitimate justification or any convincing argument."[37] Further, the disclosure of personal data by the Agency needs to abide by the requirements of the proportionality principle. For that reason, the third party must also demonstrate why the disclosure of the requested personal data would be necessary vis-à-vis other less invasive measures, why it would be the most appropriate means of attaining the applicant's objective, and how it would be proportionate to that objective.[38] Also, as the CJEU has held that "no automatic priority can be conferred on the objective of transparency over the right to protection of personal data,"[39] abstract references to the principle of transparency do not suffice for establishing the necessity of the disclosure. By way of example, and without exhausting the list of circumstances in which personal data could be disclosed,[40] the disclosure of the names of experts involved in the adoption of an act could be considered necessary if it would be argued that the concerned act would have repercussions on economic operators and if there would be concrete suspicions regarding the concerned experts' impartiality.

If the requestor of the personal data manages to establish the necessity in the disclosure, then the concerned institution has the obligation to examine whether the data subject's interests are prejudiced or not. In principle, this entails first an obligation for the concerned institution to consult with the data subject, as the subject should be informed before personal data are disclosed and should be given

---

[35] Case C-127/13 P, 2014 EUR-Lex CELEX LEXIS 9 (Oct. 2, 2014) (holding that: "where a request based on Regulation No 1049/2001 seeks to obtain access to documents including personal data, *the provisions of Regulation No 45/2001 become applicable in their entirety*") (emphasis added).

[36] Regulation No 45/2001, supra note 32, art. 8 (providing that "personal data shall only be transferred to recipients ... (b) if the recipient establishes the *necessity of having the data transferred* and if there is no reason to assume that the data subject's legitimate interests might be prejudiced") (emphasis added).

[37] Case C-28/08 P, *Comm'n v. Bavarian Lager*, 2010 E.C.R. I-6147; see also id. art. 8.

[38] Case T-82/09, *Dennekamp v. Parliament*, 2011 E.C.R. II-00418*.

[39] Case C-615/13 P, *ClientEarth and PAN Europe v. EFSA*, 2015 EUR-Lex CELEX LEXIS 7 (July 16, 2015).

[40] For additional examples, see European Data Prot. Supervisor, Public access to documents containing personal data after the *Bavarian Lager* ruling (Mar. 24 2011) https://edps.europa.eu/sites/edp/files/publication/11-03-24_bavarian_lager_en.pdf, archived at https://perma.cc/Q36X-D69R.

the opportunity to object to such disclosure.[41] Second, the concerned institution must weigh the individual's legitimate interests to have his/her privacy safeguarded against other competing interests.

Importantly, personal data related to patients included in clinical trial study reports may not be disclosed. This prohibition is in line with Article 10 of the Personal Data Regulation, which foresees that the processing of data concerning health is in principle prohibited. On the other hand, the personal data of experts or designated personnel whose responsibilities regarding the marketing authorization dossier of a medicinal product are expressly laid down in the Union legislation are disclosable. For instance, the name of the Qualified Person for Pharmacovigilance[42] is considered disclosable.

3.3. EMA's Approach to the Redaction of CCI in the Context of the Transparency Regulation

The term CCI is not defined in any piece of Union legislation. However, even though the CJEU has not yet had the opportunity to pronounce itself on the boundaries of this concept in the context of medicinal products, its case law still provides valuable guidance.

First, the CJEU has emphasized that not all information concerning a company and its business relations may be considered to be covered under the exception of commercial interests.[43] Second, in the 2017 ruling *Deza v. ECHA*,[44] the General Court rejected the argument put forward by a chemical company that the information submitted to the European Chemicals Agency (ECHA) for the evaluation, classification, and labelling of a chemical substance is allegedly covered under a general presumption of confidentiality. The General Court based its conclusion on the fact that the ECHA Founding Regulation made an unqualified cross reference to the Transparency Regulation and, as such, the documents communicated to ECHA may not be regarded as "being, in their entirety, clearly covered by the exception relating to the protection of the commercial interests of applicants for authorization."[45] Article 73 of the EMA Founding Regulation also includes an unqualified cross reference to the Transparency Regulation. It bears noting that the pharmaceutical companies have claimed, in all cases brought against EMA before the General Court and not subsequently withdrawn,[46] that such presumption

---

[41] See Regulation No 45/2001, supra note 32, art. 18.
[42] The role of the Qualified Person for Pharmacovigilance is to establish and maintain the pharmacovigilance system of a medicinal product.
[43] Case T-380/4, *Terezakis v. Comm'n*, 2008 E.C.R. II-00011*.
[44] Case T-189/14, *Deza v. ECHA*, 2017 EUR-Lex CELEX LEXIS 4 (Jan. 13, 2017).
[45] Id.
[46] For the cases brought against EMA before the General Court, and not withdrawn by the applicants, see Case T-235/15, *Pari Pharma v. EMA*; Case T-718/15, *PTC Therapeutics International v. EMA*; Case T-729/15, *MSD Animal Health Innovation and Intervet international v. EMA*, archived at https://

exists in relation to information submitted for the authorization of a medicinal product. It remains to be seen whether the CJEU will maintain its jurisprudence, as articulated in *Deza v. ECHA*, also in relation to information held by EMA.

The HMA/EMA Guidance lays down certain principles for identifying which information included in the dossier of a medicinal product should be considered as CCI. The HMA/EMA Guidance defines CCI as "any information which is not in the public domain or publicly available and where disclosure may undermine the economic interest or competitive position of the owner of the information."[47] The HMA/EMA Guidance applies this definition to different categories of information that may be associated with the dossier of a medicinal product. One category relates to information on the quality and manufacturing of medicines, namely information on composition and product development, on the active substance, and on the finished product. In principle, detailed information on quality and manufacturing will likely be considered CCI, while information couched in general terms will most likely be disclosable. The HMA/EMA Guidance illustrates this principle with a number of useful examples.[48] For instance, a general description of the types of test methods used and the appropriateness of the specification is not commercially confidential. By contrast, detailed information on the test methods used and the specification and quantitative acceptance criteria established for the active substance is in principle commercially confidential.

The HMA/EMA Guidance also clarifies that information on the nonclinical and clinical development of a medicinal product and the subsequent assessment of that information by the Agency is not per se commercially confidential. In that respect, the data included in clinical trial study reports is, in principle, not considered CCI and may therefore be disclosed. However, in the case of exceptional and duly substantiated cases, particularly where innovative study designs and/or innovative analytical methods have been used, consideration will be given to the need for redaction. Importantly, information on the outcome of inspections, namely information stating whether there were findings of compliance or noncompliance and any pending issues, is not considered as confidential.[49]

Over the period between 2014–16, EMA has received 1,942 requests for access to documents. Only six disagreements during the consultation between EMA and

perma.cc/3GEE-77S5; Case T-33/17, *Amicus Therapeutics UK and Amicus Therapeutics v. EMA*, archived at https://perma.cc/P4WZ-RBKG. By way of a postscript, it should be noted that, on 5 February 2018, and after the finalization of this chapter, the General Court delivered its Judgments in Case T-235/15, Case T-718/15, and Case T-729/15, finding in favor of EMA and rejecting the companies' actions as unfounded. Amongst else, the General Court held that there is no general presumption of confidentiality of the documents of a file submitted in the context of a marketing authorisation application for a medicinal product. The Judgments of the General Court in Case T-718/15 and Case T-729/15 have been appealed before the Court of Justice.

[47] See HMA/EMA Guidance, supra note 30, at 2.
[48] Id. at 4.
[49] Id. at 5.

marketing authorization holders (in their capacity as third parties) have led to lawsuits before the CJEU, all of which focused on the application of the exception related to the protection of commercial interests, and the majority thereof dealt with clinical reports. In those cases, the companies sought the annulment of EMA's decisions to disclose the requested documents. Two of those cases were removed from the Registry of the General Court further to the companies' withdrawal of the respective applications.[50] The low rate of legal challenges may reasonably be attributed to the wide acceptance of the HMA/EMA Guidance by pharmaceutical companies, which reflects EMA's understanding of the Transparency Regulation.

Regardless of the success of the HMA/EMA Guidance in helping identify genuine CCI in the dossiers of medicinal products, the Union pharmaceutical legislation provides enhanced guarantees to a pharmaceutical company against the risk of unfair use of its regulatory data. Those guarantees are in line with the protection afforded under Article 39.3 of the "TRIPS" Agreement.[51] By way of illustration, Article 10(1) of Directive 2001/83/EC provides that a company manufacturing a generic medicinal product may not rely on the dossier of an already authorized medicinal product for a period of eight years, and that the generic may not enter the market for a period of ten years, since the date of the marketing authorization of the referenced medicinal product.[52]

It also bears noting that the recently adopted Trade Secrets Directive established, for the first time in Union law, a definition of the notion of "trade secret," which is clearly influenced by Article 39.3 of the TRIPS Agreement.[53] However, Recital 11 of the Trade Secrets Directive clarifies that this Directive shall not affect the application of Union rules, such as the Transparency Regulation, that require the disclosure of information to the public. As the Commission stated, the Trade Secrets Directive "does not alter and does not have any impact on the regulations that foresee the right of citizens to access documents in the possession of public authorities, including documents submitted by third parties such as companies and business

[50] For the two cases which were removed from the Registry of the General Court further to the withdrawal of the application by the applicants, see Order of the President of the Fourth Chamber of the General Court in Case T-44/13, *AbbVie v. EMA*, archived at https://perma.cc/X5DP-DCDR; Order of the President of the Fourth Chamber of the General Court in Case T-73/13, *InterMune UK and Others v. EMA*, archived at https://perma.cc/UL4B-WA76.
[51] See TRIPS: Agreement on Trade-Related Aspects of Intellectual Property Rights, Apr. 15, 1994, 1867 U.N.T.S. 154.
[52] In this respect, also see European Commission, Procedures for marketing authorization, Notice to Applicants Volume 2A, Chapter 1, Revision 6, December 2016 ("During the period of data exclusivity of a medicinal product, the data contained in the preclinical and clinical file of that product and obtained through access to documents or freedom of information legislation within the EU or in third countries, cannot be relied on by other applicants or the authorities in a subsequent application to ascertain the safety and efficacy of other products.").
[53] See Directive (EU) 2016/943 of the European Parliament and of the Council of 8 June 2016 on the protection of undisclosed know-how and business information (trade secrets) against their unlawful acquisition, use and disclosure, Official Journal of the European Union, art. 2(1).

organizations."[54] An objection against the disclosure of a trade secret in the possession of a Union institution will therefore be assessed in light of the standards set forth by the Transparency Regulation.

4. EMA'S APPROACH TO PROACTIVE TRANSPARENCY

4.1. *Proactive Transparency in General and for EMA*

The proactive aspect of transparency refers to the release of information to the public in the absence of a specific request for access to that information. Neither Directive 2001/83/EC nor the EMA Founding Regulation provide a clear obligation for EMA to regularly publish all information and documents in its possession. Each time a medicinal product is granted a new marketing authorization, the Agency is bound to publish the European Public Assessment Report (EPAR), which contains – among other things – the reasons for the authorization (in lay language) and the assessment report after the redaction of the CCI. EMA had, since its inception, committed itself to publishing proactively the EPAR, before this obligation was foreseen.[55] Other initiatives across the proactive transparency axis include the publication of agendas and minutes of the EMA Scientific Committees, which aim at informing all stakeholders and interested parties about the scientific work conducted at EMA. In the same direction, Article 80 of the EMA Founding Regulation provides that, for the purpose of transparency, rules shall be adopted "to ensure the availability to the public of regulatory, scientific or technical information concerning the authorization or supervision of medicinal products which is not of a confidential nature." Based on Article 80, and relying on the consensus of twenty-eight Member States plus the European Commission, EMA introduced more recently a groundbreaking transparency measure aimed at proactively publishing clinical reports.

EMA policy on the proactive publication of clinical data ("Policy 0070")[56] entered into force on January 1, 2015, further to two rounds of public consultation,

---

[54] See European Comm'n, Trade secrets, https://ec.europa.eu/growth/industry/intellectual-property/trade secrets, archived at https://perma.cc/3UXP-JSGR. For the reaction of the European Federation of Pharmaceutical Industries and Associations, see European Parliament passes Trade Secrets Directive, The Pharma Letter, Apr. 11, 2016, in www.thepharmaletter.com/article/european-parliament-passes-trade secrets-directive, archived at https://perma.cc/T9LJ-LE6M (stating that "EFPIA welcomes the adoption of the Trade Secrets Directive ... This Directive will have absolutely no bearing on existing legislation on public access to information, on pharmaceutical companies' obligations under the new Clinical Trials Regulation, or on the European Medicines Agency's policy on the publication of clinical data. These are all outside the scope of the Directive").

[55] For more information on the evolution in the publication of the EPAR, see P. Papathanasiou, L. Brassart, P. Blake, A. Hart, L. Whitbread, R. Pembrey & J. Kieffer, Transparency in Drug Regulation: Public Assessment Reports in Europe and Australia, 21 Drug Discovery Today 1806, 1806 (2016).

[56] See European Meds. Agency, European Medicines Agency policy on publication of clinical data for medicinal products for human use, Policy/0070 (Oct. 2, 2014).

responses to some 1,500 comments received, and an impressive number of targeted stakeholders' meetings. EMA Policy 0070 is to be implemented in a stepwise fashion. Its first phase concerns clinical reports only, namely clinical overviews (module 2.5 of the application for marketing authorization), clinical summaries (module 2.7 thereof), and clinical study reports (module 5 thereof), relevant to medicinal products authorized under the centralized procedure after April 1, 2015.[57] Its second phase, which is envisaged to be implemented at "a later stage," concerns individual patient data. Over the period between 2015–16, EMA received approximately 399 requests for access to clinical reports, namely the data to be covered under the first phase of Policy 0070. This number confirms that Policy 0070 seeks to meet a genuine need for access to clinical reports.

Policy 0070 does not operate in a vacuum. Instead, it anticipates and complements the recently adopted Clinical Trials Regulation,[58] the backbone of which is the respective Clinical Trials Database on which information related to clinical trials conducted in the EU will be published. The Clinical Trials Regulation shall apply as from six months after the publication of the notice of the European Commission that it is satisfied that the EU portal and EU database have been verified as fully functional. As shown in the table below, Policy 0070, which is already operational, also covers clinical trials conducted outside the EU.[59]

	Clinical Data Publication Policy (Policy 0070)	Clinical Trials Regulation (Regulation (EU) No 536/2014)
Medicinal products covered	Centrally authorized products only	Investigational medicinal products regardless of whether they have a marketing authorization
Clinical studies covered	Clinical studies submitted to the Agency in the context of the Marketing Authorization Application (MAA), Article 58 procedure, line extension of new indication, regardless of where the study was conducted	Clinical trials conducted in the EU and pediatric trials conducted outside the EU that are part of pediatric investigation plans

---

[57] For more information on the different modules of the application for marketing authorization, see Directive 2001/83/EC of the European Parliament and of the Council of 6 November 2001 on the Community code relating to medicinal products for human use, Official Journal of the European Communities, Annex I.

[58] See Regulation (EU) No 536/2014 of the European Parliament and of the Council of 16 April 2014 on clinical trials on medicinal products for human use, and repealing Directive 2001/20/EC, Official Journal of the European Union.

[59] Website of the European Medicines Agency, https://perma.cc/PM8Q-9EJP.

(continued)

	Clinical Data Publication Policy (Policy 0070)	Clinical Trials Regulation (Regulation (EU) No 536/2014)
Documents published	Clinical data (clinical overview, clinical summaries, and clinical study reports) and the anonymization report	All clinical trial-related information generated during the life cycle of a clinical trial (for example, protocol, assessment and decision on trial conduct, summary of trial results including a lay summary, study reports, inspections, and so forth)
Publication channel	EMA clinical data publication website	Future EU portal and database
Date it applies	January 1, 2015 (MAA or Article 58 procedure) or July 1, 2015 (line extension or new indication)	Expected in 2019
Publication from	October 2016	Expected in 2019

Source: Website of the European Medicines Agency

There are two ways in which the published clinical reports are made accessible to the public under Policy 0070. On the one hand, all members of the public may view on-screen the published clinical reports, further to a simple registration process. On the other hand, the downloading of the clinical reports is available only to identified users.[60] Those two different ways of accessing the published reports are governed by different terms of use.

Prior to their publication, CCI and personal data must be removed from clinical reports. EMA has developed the so-called External Guidance[61] in order to contribute to a shared understanding of what may potentially be considered as CCI or personal data and to increase consistency in the proposed and accepted redactions.

The responsibility for the redactions lies with the applicant for MA or the marketing authorization holder (applicant/MAH), who needs to submit to EMA an appropriate redaction package. After the validation of the redaction package, EMA will begin the assessment of the justifications for the proposed CCI redactions. EMA will also scrutinize the Anonymization Report to check whether the applicant/MAH has followed and applied consistently the relevant anonymization guidance.

---

[60] Identified users need to register by obtaining an account, accepting the Terms of Use and providing EMA with elements concerning their identity (different elements are required for natural and legal persons). For more information, see Policy 0070, supra note 56, at 6.

[61] External Guidance on the implementation of the European Medicines Agency policy on the publication of clinical data for medicinal products for human use, Version 1.3, (Sept. 20, 2017).

The so-called Final Redacted Document Package will be published by the Agency on its clinical data publication website.

4.2. EMA's Approach to the Redaction of CCI in the Context of Policy 0070

During the public consultation phases which informed the drafting of Policy 0070, it became clear that all stakeholders involved had to agree on a common understanding of what constitutes commercially confidential information in the context of clinical reports. After extensive and lengthy discussions, all stakeholders (industry associations such as R&D-based entities, generic manufacturers, and small/medium enterprises; academics; and patients' and health care practitioners' representatives) consulted for this purpose welcomed a nonexhaustive, but sufficiently precise Annex 3 to Policy 0070, detailing a list of documents and information which both EMA and applicants/MAH would agree to consider CCI. If not also for its substance, Policy 0070 has been welcomed globally as a remarkable example of good administrative practice and democratic collaboration in a multilateral environment where several competing interests had to be managed in order to strike a reasonable balance, giving prevalence however to the interests of patients and of public health.

A piece of information classified as CCI under EMA's access to documents policy would be most likely considered CCI also under Policy 0070, unless changes have intervened in the status of the relevant document (for instance, a document previously classified as CCI could have entered the public domain in the meantime, due to a spontaneous publication by the marketing authorization holder). The applicant/MAH always needs to furnish relevant and appropriate justifications to explain why the concerned information should qualify as CCI.

For the reference of the applicant/MAH, the External Guidance identifies certain information that may not be considered as CCI. EMA has grouped the examples of information it will not consider as CCI into four categories: administrative information (for example, number of study sites involved in the research), quality-related information (for example, names of excipients), nonclinical-related information (for example, drug concentration measurements), and clinical-related information (for example, primary and secondary end points).[62] In that respect, the External Guidance includes a very lengthy, albeit nonexhaustive, list of information that should not be considered as CCI.

4.3. EMA's Approach to the Redaction of Personal Data in the Context of Policy 0070

When it comes to personal data, Policy 0070 seeks to strike a delicate balance between respecting the privacy of individuals and their right to respect of their

---

[62] Id. at 52–54.

personal data, on the one hand, and maintaining the data utility of the clinical reports, on the other.

In the context of the proactive publication, applicants/MAHs must submit clinical reports that have been anonymized to the requisite standard (thereby avoiding issues related to the processing of personal data in accordance with Personal Data Regulation, including the "right to be forgotten" which does not apply to anonymized data). The concept of anonymization refers to the process whereby clinical reports have been processed in such a way that it is no longer possible to identify a natural person by using all the means likely reasonably to be used. The process of anonymization is liable to lower the level of granularity, and therefore the usefulness, of the information found in the clinical report. In particular, clinical reports for orphan medicinal products are likely to be altered more extensively in view of the inherent higher risk of reidentification. The principle of maintaining the data utility of the clinical reports aims at ensuring that the anonymization of the reports does not lead to the removal or distortion of scientifically useful information. Stripping clinical reports of their scientific usefulness would undermine the need and benefits of their publication.

Generally speaking, the individuals that may be identifiable on the basis of the nonredacted clinical reports are split into two categories: trial subjects, on the one hand; and investigators, the staff of the sponsor, and the staff of the applicant/MAH, on the other.

Applicants/MAHs must exercise caution to anonymize both direct and indirect/quasi identifiers associated with individuals. Direct identifiers are elements that permit direct recognition of the respective individuals, such as the name, email, phone number, signature, or full address of individuals. In principle, and as it is may be inferred from the above examples, direct identifiers do not have data utility as they are not useful in scientific terms. As the direct identifiers lead to the immediate identification of an individual and as they are of no scientific value, their redaction is in principle always justified. One exception would be the identities of the coordinating investigator signing the clinical report. On the other hand, indirect identifiers are variables referring to an individual's background information, such as the date of birth, date of clinic visit, sex, or ethnicity of an individual. Those elements may also lead to the indirect identification of an individual. EMA requires that applicants/MAHs process the data in such a way that it can no longer be used to identify a natural person by all means likely to be used.[63] At the same time, the anonymization process is constrained by the principle of data utility, which refers to the need to maintain the scientific usefulness and information value of the data.

---

[63] Id. at 38. In its External Guidance, EMA has put forward an anonymization process for the reference of the applicants/MAHs (see pages 45–47). For a discussion of this question, see Barbara E. Bierer, Mark Barnes, and Rebecca Li, Chapter 13.

5. CONCLUSIONS

Transparency is a principle deeply embedded in the EU regulatory landscape. In the context of medicinal products, transparency is justified not only due to its contribution to a more democratic and ethical way of governance, but also due to the tangible effects it yields for public health.[64]

As part of the Union administration, EMA must uphold transparency ideals. To that end, EMA has been trying to reconcile the tensions between the principle of transparency and the right of access to documents, on one hand, and the rights to private property and the protection of privacy and personal data, on the other hand. Judging from the relatively low rate of legal challenges, the way in which EMA has been implementing the Transparency Regulation seems to have been embraced by the concerned stakeholders. In a similar vein, and on the basis of the exhaustive comments received during the relevant public consultations, the External Guidance on the proactive publication of clinical reports has also been well received, owing in particular to the extraordinary preparatory works preceding its launch.

---

[64] See Bonini, supra note 9, at 2452–55.

PART V

Transparency and Outcomes: Promoting Health and Safety

Introduction to Part V

Gregory Curfman

Before the turn of the century, the delivery of health care was often characterized by paternalism, in which health care professionals made decisions on behalf of their patients, who were usually passive participants in the care process.[1] During the past two decades, however, this traditional paradigm of provider-directed health care has entered a state of change. Increasingly, patients are becoming more personally involved in their own health care. Terms such as patient engagement, patient activation, patient-centered care, and shared decision-making are often used to characterize a new era in the physician–patient relationship, in which patients have greater access to information about their health care, are better informed, and have more opportunities to express their personal preferences about their care.

The proliferation of patient decision aids[2] is an example of how patients are becoming more involved in their health care. While some patients remain content to have their physician make treatment decisions on their behalf, there is a growing trend for patients to ask more questions about their options and to be involved in selecting the course of treatment. Patient decision aids typically present different possible options for treatment of a health condition and allow patients to engage in a dialogue with their health care providers about which course to pursue.

An important component of this growing trend toward shared decision making is transparency in personal health information. Gaining access to personal health information is both an asset and a risk to patients; in the four chapters that follow, a panel of experts will explore both the benefits and potential hazards of health information transparency. It is incumbent on all health professionals to be knowledgeable about the transparency movement, especially in the context of responsible data privacy and security practices, since it is now a fixture of our health care environment.

---

[1] Michael J. Barry & Susan Edgman-Levitan, Shared Decision Making – The Pinnacle of Patient-Centered Care, 366 New Eng. J. Med. 780 (2012).

[2] Judith J. Prochaska & Ashley Sanders-Jackson, Patient Decision Aids for Discouraging Low-Value Health Care: Procedures, Null Findings, and Lessons Learned, 176 JAMA Internal Med. 41 (2016).

In their chapter on "The Role of Transparency in Promoting Healthy Behaviors: Pros, Cons, and Perils of Information Sharing to Foster Personal Responsibility in Health Care," Anthony W. Orlando and Arnold J. Rosoff provide a fascinating examination of health information sharing in the context of employee wellness programs. Employer-sponsored health insurance is the norm for nearly 170 million Americans, in large part because employer-paid premiums for health insurance are exempt from federal income and payroll taxes and the portion of premiums paid by employees is also excluded from taxable income. Two thirds of employer-sponsored health plans are self-insured plans, which means that employers assume the financial risk for health care expenditures for their employees. Since employers are incentivized to keep their employees healthy, most employers offer some form of employee wellness program. The Affordable Care Act (ACA) allows employers to utilize financial incentives up to 30 percent of the cost of health insurance premiums to motivate employees to participate in wellness programs (and up to 50 percent of premium cost for smokers).

Employee wellness programs may offer important health benefits, such as providing discounts on gym memberships and smoking cessation programs, and more generally promoting a culture of health at the workplace.[3] However, as Orlando and Rosoff point out, these programs may also entail risks of invasion of employees' privacy when there are financial incentives for employees to participate in health risk assessments and share that information with employers. In fact, H.R. 1313, the *Preserving Employee Wellness Programs Act*, at the time of writing under consideration by the House of Representatives, would allow companies to require employees to undergo genetic testing and let employers see that genetic and other health information or risk paying a financial penalty. Furthermore, the law would permit the collection of genetic information about a disease condition in an employee's family member. Thus, employee wellness programs may raise serious concerns about data privacy in an era of transparency around personal health information. Orlando and Rosoff question whether their statutory exemptions from protections for employees' personal health information privacy may go too far and urge caution in their application.

Michelle M. Mello, David M. Studdert, Brahmajee K. Nallamothu, and Allen Kachalia in their chapter, "The Role of Transparency in Patient Safety Improvement," contribute a recognition that other attempts to improve patient safety and experiences may reinforce transparency-focused initiatives. Mello et al. draw out an important point that transparency-focused approaches exist alongside other efforts to improve patient safety. While these efforts may not be strictly transparency focused, they nevertheless have an impact on the availability of information for patients and influence the decisions that patients make. It is an important reminder that we cannot consider transparency initiatives without considering the

---

[3] Julia James, Health Affairs, Health Policy Brief: Workplace Wellness Programs (May 10, 2012).

broader health care delivery ecosystem. As Mello and her coauthors note, "success is rarely baked into an intervention itself. How the intervention is implemented, and the environment in which it is thrust, matter enormously."

In her chapter, "Personal Health Records as a Tool for Transparency in Health Care," Sharona Hoffman raises similar privacy concerns about patients' personal health records (PHRs), which are being used increasingly to promote transparency in health care information.[4] PHRs may be advantageous to patients by allowing them to store and track their own health information and gain greater access to their electronic health records (EHRs) and by promoting easier electronic communication with their physicians and other health care providers. On the other hand, as Hoffman astutely points out, PHRs also carry the risks of hacking and breaches of privacy, disruption of the doctor–patient relationship, exacerbation of health disparities, and concerns about malpractice liability. Hoffman concludes, "PHRs can contribute significantly to medical transparency, health record integrity, and patient satisfaction, but they can also do the opposite." It is likely that PHRs are here to stay, but we will need to continue to refine these technologies to optimize their benefits while minimizing their risks to both patients and providers.

In their chapters, both Jim Hawkins, Barbara J. Evans, and Harlan M. Krumholz ("Nontransparency in Electronic Health Record Systems"), and Dov Fox ("Transparency Challenges in Reproductive Health Care"), focus on a different type of risk, namely ways in which health information transparency may be subverted, placing patient safety at risk by obscuring critical aspects of health information. EHR companies and providers enter into contracts when providers purchase and install EHR systems for clinical use. Hawkins and co-authors point out that such contracts may subvert health information transparency, for example by including gag clauses that block certain types of information about unsafe EHRs from being revealed to patients. Some contracts may also be a threat to patient privacy, since clauses in some contracts may allow de-identified health data to be shared with the health care providers' business associates, without telling patients, and with the possibility that the data could later be reidentified. Thus, while EHRs may enhance information transparency by interfacing with patient portals, contractual arrangements between EHR companies and providers may undermine transparency, a fact that is not widely appreciated.

Fox discusses another area of health care that has been affected by a lack of information transparency: assisted reproductive technologies (ART). Although nearly 2 percent of babies born in the United States are conceived with ART, this field of reproductive medicine is generally unregulated and "operates largely in the shadows." Fox focuses on a lack of transparency for "never events," which he places into three categories of medical error: mishandling (contamination of embryos),

---

[4] Kenneth D. Mandl & Isaac S. Kohane, Time for a Patient-Driven Health Information Economy?, 374 New Eng. J. Med. 205 (2016).

misinformation (errors in genetic diagnosis), and misconception (inadvertent switches of sperm or embryos). Information about never events is not currently collected from ART centers. Fox proposes a system of crowdsourcing to obtain this information, which would permit patients to report such experiences in a publicly available database on a voluntary basis. Such a system would help to fill the information gap that now exists in ART, but would be an incomplete solution since it would be based on passive reporting by patients rather than required reporting by centers. Still, Fox has pointed out an important area of health care in which the breakdown of information transparency may have deleterious consequences.

The growing trend of health information transparency will continue to evolve as patients become more sophisticated about their own health care and seek greater involvement in decision making and demand greater accountability. While personal health information becomes more transparent and available in multiple electronic formats, we must also be mindful of the potential risks. Protecting the privacy of health information will become increasingly difficult as more information is shared among patients and providers and as hackers become more adept. Patients and providers will need to continue to navigate the newly transparent health care environment so that patient–provider relationships are not disrupted. Furthermore, since not all consumers have equal access to electronic health information, there is real concern that health disparities may be exacerbated, and it will be essential to develop ways of making health information technology available to all. It is also essential that regulators not allow critical health information to be hidden from patients.

We are at the dawn of a challenging new era of health information sharing. If applied judiciously and with careful attention to the potential risks, we can expect greater health information transparency to improve the processes of health care and result in better health outcomes for patients.

15

The Role of Transparency in Promoting Healthy Behaviors

Pros, Cons, and Perils of Information Sharing to Foster Personal Responsibility in Health Care

Anthony W. Orlando and Arnold J. Rosoff*

After too long a delay, the United States has made substantial progress over the past decade toward joining the world's major nations in establishing a Universal Health Care (UHC) system that assures an adequate level of care to all of its citizens. As commendable as this is, the costs of our health care system and the costs to our economy in lost productivity will be unsustainable unless more of our populace take personal responsibility for their health by routinely engaging in healthy behaviors.[1] Educating people about the implications of their lifestyle choices and motivating them to follow a healthy diet, exercise routinely, and adopt other health-supportive behaviors is a critical challenge for our nation. Even if a Republican-controlled government fulfills its pledge to "repeal and replace Obamacare" (the Affordable Care Act, or ACA) and dials back our national commitment to UHC, the issues we raise herein will remain critical because "personal responsibility" is a key pillar of conservatives' health care agenda.[2] Thus the challenge we face as individuals and as a nation – to get and stay healthier – is real, immediate, and ongoing.

We explore herein how to motivate desirable health behaviors without compromising freedom or other cherished values. Aiding this pursuit are important insights into health incentives, behavioral economics, and exciting "Electronic Age" innovations that can help individuals take better care of their health. For example, smartphone apps and wearable devices can count individuals' steps, track their calories, remind them to take their medicines, and monitor their pulses. These

---

* The authors greatly appreciate the research assistance of Elana Waldstein and George Yang, undergraduate students at the University of Pennsylvania, and Karolina Niedzwiadek, undergraduate student at the University of Southern California and a SUMR Scholar at Penn's Leonard Davis Institute of Health Economics. We also thank seminar participants at the American Society of Law, Medicine, & Ethics and the Petrie-Flom Center for Health Law Policy, Biotechnology, and Bioethics at Harvard Law School for their helpful comments.

[1] See, e.g., Rebecca J. Mitchell & Paul Bates, Measuring Health-Related Productivity Loss, 14 Population Health Mgmt. 93 (2011).

[2] See, e.g., Haeyoun Park, How Republicans Propose Changing Obamacare, N.Y. Times, Feb. 23, 2017, www.nytimes.com/interactive/2017/02/23/us/politics/republican-health-plan.html.

electronic assists also offer opportunities to create social networks in which people who share health concerns can support one another.

These health-oriented networks come, however, with their own risks, many relating to the handling of *Personal Health Information* (PHI).[3] The path to better personal and societal health requires, then, not only an appreciation of the potential of these virtual communities but also a cautious, informed regard for the risks of sharing PHI more broadly than has been done before.[4] From the Hippocratic oath to HIPAA and beyond, PHI has been recognized as sacrosanct.[5] But in today's fast-changing world, privacy, while still prized, has given up considerable ground. Greater connectivity has made safeguarding PHI more challenging. We address this challenge herein along with its related question: how should PHI be shared among insurers, vendors, and promoters of the above-mentioned electronic devices, and employers who provide employee wellness programs?

This paper explores, on one side, ways to facilitate the use of information to empower people to take better care of their health and, on the other side, knotty issues of safeguarding PHI. Transparency does not just require parties to share essential information with others; it also involves questions of what information should be shared only with appropriate safeguards. Transparency is one side of the coin, confidentiality the other; achieving the proper balance between the two is our main goal. Section I examines the magnitude and nature of the problem of unhealthy behaviors in American society. Section II describes ways information sharing is being used to improve Americans' health behaviors. Section III calls attention to ethical, legal, and practical risks that arise from broader information sharing – and offers approaches to mitigate these risks. Section IV summarizes our observations, analysis, and policy suggestions.

I. THE PROBLEM: BURDENS CAUSED BY UNHEALTHY BEHAVIORS

Unhealthy lifestyles pose serious burdens to personal well-being and social welfare in the United States. The Centers for Disease Control and Prevention (CDC) estimate that up to 40 percent of deaths from the five leading causes could be prevented with healthy behaviors if every state had the same death rate for these causes as the state with the lowest rate.[6] One in five adults smokes regularly, and four

---

[3] Or, as HIPAA defines it, "protected health information" or "individually identifiable health information." See 45 CFR 160.103.
[4] Many medical technology providers are covert about their privacy policy and how PHI is used or sold. See Future of Privacy Forum, FPF Mobile Apps Study (Aug. 2016), https://fpf.org/wp-content/uploads/2016/08/2016-FPF-Mobile-Apps-Study_final.pdf.
[5] Health Insurance Portability and Accountability Act of 1996 (HIPAA) Pub. L. 104–191, 110 Stat. 1996 (codified as amended in scattered sections of 18, 26, 29, and 42 U.S.C.); see also HIPAA Privacy Rule, 42 C.F.R. 160, 164.
[6] Ctrs. for Disease Control & Prevention, Up to 40 Percent of Annual Deaths from Each of Five Leading US Causes Are Preventable (May 1, 2014), www.cdc.gov/media/releases/2014/p0501 preventable-deaths.html.

in five do not exercise as much as the CDC recommends – with a lower percentage exercising every year.[7] Even after a heart attack, only one in twenty patients engage in three widely advocated healthy behaviors: stop smoking, eat five servings of fruits or vegetables a day, and exercise regularly.[8] Some 65 percent of U.S. adults are overweight or obese, significantly increasing their death rates *from all causes*.[9] In the last three decades, obesity has doubled among adults and tripled among children; so has the prevalence of such chronic diseases as type 2 diabetes.[10] We are not alone; obesity has doubled in over seventy countries and increased in most others.[11] As one media report recently summed up the evidence, "obesity now kills more people worldwide than car crashes, terror attacks, and Alzheimer's combined."[12]

The United States spends more on health care – both in absolute dollars and as a share of its economy – than any other nation on earth.[13] At least a third of these costs may be attributable to unhealthy behaviors. Obesity alone accounts for 10 percent of all medical costs and over a quarter of the rise in health care costs in recent decades.[14] Cigarette smoking accounts for another 9 percent[15] and excessive alcohol consumption for 13 percent.[16] (Drug addiction is a major, related problem, of course, but is different enough that it is not addressed herein.) In a study of 223,461 employees across seven industries, researchers estimated that employers would spend

[7] For smoking trends, see U.S. Dep't of Health & Human Servs., The Health Consequences of Smoking–50 Years of Progress: A Report of the Surgeon General (2014), www.surgeongeneral.gov /library/reports/50-years-of-progress/exec-summary.pdf. For exercising trends, see Ctrs. for Disease Control & Prevention, Facts About Physical Activity (May 23, 2014), www.cdc.gov/physicalactivity/ data/facts.htm.
[8] Valerie Ulene, Why Are Unhealthy People So Reluctant to Change Their Lifestyles?, L.A. Times, May 23, 2011, http://articles.latimes.com/2011/may/23/health/la-he-the-md-change-illness-20110523.
[9] Arthur H. Rubinstein, Obesity: A Modern Epidemic, 116 Transactions of the Amer. Clinical & Climatological Ass'n 103 (2005).
[10] Ryan T. Hurt, Christopher Kulisek, Laura A. Buchanan & Stephen A. McClave, The Obesity Epidemic: Challenges, Health Initiatives, and Implications for Gastroenterologists, 6 Gastroenterology & Hepatology 780 (2010).
[11] The Global Burden of Disease 2015 Obesity Collaborators, Health Effects of Overweight and Obesity in 195 Countries over 25 Years, 377 New Eng. J. Med. 13 (2017), www.nejm.org/doi/full/10.1056 /NEJMoa1614362.
[12] Julia Belluz, Obesity Now Kills More People Worldwide Than Car Crashes, Terror Attacks, and Alzheimer's Combined, Vox, Jun. 19, 2017, www.vox.com/science-and-health/2017/6/19/15819808/ obesity-global-epidemic (summarizing the findings of The Global Burden of Disease 2015 Obesity Collaborators, supra note 11).
[13] David Squires & Chloe Anderson, U.S. Health Care from a Global Perspective: Spending, Use of Services, Prices, and Health in 13 Countries, The Commonwealth Fund (Oct. 2015), www .commonwealthfund.org/publications/issue-briefs/2015/oct/us-health-care-global-perspective.
[14] Eric A. Finkelstein, Justin G. Trogdon, Joel W. Cohen & William Dietz, Annual Medical Spending Attributable to Obesity: Payer- and Service-Specific Estimates, 28 Health Aff. w822 (2009).
[15] Xin Xu, Ellen E. Bishop, Sara M. Kennedy, Sean A. Simpson & Terry F. Pechacek, Annual Healthcare Spending Attributable to Cigarette Smoking: An Update, 48 Am. J. Preventative Med. 326 (2015).
[16] Jeffrey J. Sacks, Katherine R. Gonzales, Ellen E. Bouchery, Laura E. Tomedi & Robert D. Brewer, 2010 National and State Costs of Excessive Alcohol Consumption, 49 Am. J. Preventative Med. e73 (2015).

26 percent less on health benefits if their employees engaged in healthier behaviors.[17] Clearly society would be better off if people took better care of their health through lifestyle changes.

II. THE ROLE OF PHI IN PROMOTING PERSONAL RESPONSIBILITY FOR HEALTH

How can we best get people to take better care of their health? In this section, we highlight some promising solutions, including innovative applications of health incentives, behavioral economics principles, workplace wellness programs, and social and technological assists. Each approach requires collecting and sharing PHI in new ways – with important potential consequences.

A. Lessons from Health Incentives and Behavioral Economics

Researchers have gained insights into how to design more effective health incentives, which often involve greater collection and sharing of PHI. This PHI serves three purposes: it marks a starting point, or baseline (for example, initial weight); it tracks progress toward one's goal in a measurable way (for example, pounds lost); and sharing PHI connects individuals to others who can help motivate them to achieve their goal. Research has shown that approaches that engage social connections are more effective in changing personal behavior, and sharing key metrics and personal information with others assists this dynamic.[18]

B. Employment-Based Wellness Programs

The United States is unique in its heavy reliance on employment-based health insurance. Some 80 percent of Americans who have private health insurance obtain it through their employer or that of a family member.[19] Employers thus have multiple incentives to promote healthy behaviors in their workforce: (a) familial concern for their employees' welfare, (b) higher productivity and lower absenteeism from healthy employees, and (c) potential savings on health insurance premiums. For these reasons, almost every large company (200 or more employees) offers a wellness program. Moreover, over 80 percent of these companies offer financial incentives for

---

[17] Michael P. O'Donnell, Alyssa B. Schultz & Louis Yen, The Portion of Health Care Costs Associated with Lifestyle-Related Modifiable Health Risks Based on a Sample of 223,461 Employees in Seven Industries: The UM-HMRC Study, 57 J. Occupational & Envtl. Med. 1284 (2015).
[18] See, e.g., Mitesh S. Patel et al., A Randomized Trial of Social Comparison Feedback and Financial Incentives to Increase Physical Activity, 30 Am. J. Health Promotion 416 (2016).
[19] Arnold J. Rosoff & Anthony W. Orlando, Employers and Health Insurance under the Affordable Care Act, 24 Annals Health L. 470 (2015).

employees' healthy behaviors.[20] Even some 50 percent of medium-sized firms (50 or more employees) have wellness programs – and that number is rising. Such programs are a burgeoning industry now worth $6 billion annually.[21]

C. Using Technology to Promote Healthy Behaviors

Further support for healthy behaviors can be found in new technologies. Wearable devices, such as smartwatches and fitness trackers, are worn on the body and can electronically track distance, rates, and frequency of running, walking, and biking; calories burned; and biometric data, such as heart rate and body temperature.[22] Software apps working through smartphones, tablets, and computers let users record their PHI and remind them to practice healthy behaviors.[23] These health-improvement technologies are predicted to become a $50 billion industry by 2018, although currently they reach only 2 percent of the population. Clearly the potential for private innovation is huge.

Unfortunately, at this stage not enough is known about what works, what works better, and how users can choose among alternatives to improve their health.[24] This lack of empirical evidence is concerning for more "medical" applications, such as wearable devices that monitor glucose levels or heart irregularities, or "baby cams" that watch over infants and report breathing and sleeping patterns to parents' mobile devices.[25] Over generations, the regulatory reach of the federal Food and Drug Administration (FDA) in controlling the manufacture and sale of "snake oil remedies" of questionable value, including medical devices, has grown substantially. We need to extend these protections to emerging forms of electronic equipment and social media facilitators that are being used to help improve and sustain the public's health.

---

[20] Daniel Mochon, Janet Schwartz, Josiase Maroba, Deepak Patel & Dan Ariely, Gain Without Pain: The Extended Effects of a Behavioral Health Intervention, 63 Mgmt. Sci. 58 (2017); see also Todd Rogers, Katherine L. Milkman & Kevin G. Volpp, Commitment Devices: Using Initiatives to Change Behavior, 311 JAMA 2065 (2014).

[21] See, for example, RAND Corp., Do Workplace Wellness Programs Save Employers Money? (2014), www.rand.org/content/dam/rand/pubs/research_briefs/RB9700/RB9744/RAND_RB9744.pdf; see also Mitesh S. Patel et al., Premium-Based Financial Incentives Did Not Promote Workplace Weight Loss in a 2013–15 Study, 35 Health Aff. 71 (2016).

[22] Hadi Banaee, Mobyen Uddin Ahmed, & Amy Loutfi, Data Mining for Wearable Sensors in Health Monitoring Systems: A Review of Recent Trends and Challenges, 13 Sensors 17452 (2013); see also The Economist, The Wear, Why and How, Mar. 12, 2015.

[23] See Jill Duffy, 10 Apps That Are Changing Healthcare, PC Mag., Feb. 11, 2015, www.pcmag.com/article2/0,2817,2476623,00.asp; see also Emily Schiola, Maintain Your Health and Mind with These 15 Medical Apps, Digital Trends, Jun. 27, 2016, www.digitaltrends.com/mobile/best-medical-apps/.

[24] Mitesh S. Patel, David A. Asch & Kevin G. Volpp, Wearable Devices as Facilitators, Not Drivers, of Health Behavior Change, 313 JAMA 459 (2015).

[25] Christopher P. Bonafide, David T. Jamison & Elizabeth E. Foglia, The Emerging Market of Smartphone Integrated Infant Physiologic Monitors, 317 JAMA 353 (2017).

III. PROBLEMS WITH THE SOLUTION: ETHICAL AND LEGAL CONCERNS

Whether or not smartphone apps, wearable devices, and their social network adjuncts are as positive a contribution to improving healthy behaviors as they purport to be, our health care system's entry into this brave new world of information gathering and sharing raises important issues. We are plunging ahead into adoption of these innovations without a full understanding of their risks. In this section, we examine these risks and suggest steps to address them.

A. Confidentiality Concerns

Employers who offer their employees incentives to lead healthier lifestyles may face issues on the kinds and extent of information disclosure they can request or require. For instance, an employer that offers a wellness program or a subsidy to pay for a gym membership or wearable fitness tracker might seek to know the frequency and length of gym visits, what the employee did there, and how health indicators changed. Even without employee consent, employers often can get employees' personal data from their mobile phone carriers or other consumer product companies.[26] Further, the employer might need to share such information with an affiliated health plan or insurer, or a vendor of fitness devices or equipment. Alternatively, an insurer may share PHI with the employer to justify expenditures, such as gym membership paid for by the employer. Even if this information is de-identified to protect the employee's identity, it can often be reidentified by computer algorithms.[27]

Extant laws prohibiting improper PHI use and discrimination may not be enough to cover the risks posed by new approaches and devices. For example, the Americans with Disabilities Act (ADA) protects people with disabilities from employment discrimination provided they can, with reasonable accommodation, safely and reliably perform the function(s) for which they are employed. It prohibits employers from asking about a worker's disability, but makes an exception for voluntary wellness programs.[28]

Similarly, the Genetic Information Non-Discrimination Act (GINA) bars employers and insurers from using genetic information to make employment decisions. Like the ADA, GINA limits employers' access to this information but carves out an exception for voluntary wellness programs.[29] It is questionable, however, whether such programs are truly "voluntary" if employees feel obliged to participate

---

[26] Scott R. Peppet, Regulating the Internet of Things: First Steps Toward Managing Discrimination, Privacy, Security, and Consent, 93 Tex. L. Rev. 85, 120 (2014).
[27] Id. at 128–31.
[28] Kristin M. Madison, The Risks of Using Workplace Wellness Programs to Foster a Culture of Health, 35 Health Aff. 2068 (2016).
[29] Karen Pollitz & Matthew Rae, Workplace Wellness Programs Characteristics and Requirements, Henry J. Kaiser Fam. Found. (2016), http://files.kff.org/attachment/Issue-Brief-Workplace-Wellness-Programs-Characteristics-and-Requirements.

in them.[30] Firms that offer employees incentives to take part in a wellness program may be implicitly penalizing, relative to their peers, those who do not participate. Some employers have even made nonparticipation penalties explicit. For example, in 2012 CVS Pharmacy announced a controversial policy fining employees $600 annually if they did not reveal their body fat levels, glucose levels, and weight to their insurer, yet CVS called its policy "voluntary."[31]

The Equal Employment Opportunity Commission (EEOC) has ruled that such "penalties" may not exceed 30 percent of the total cost of coverage, but this amount is far from insignificant for many families, so participation may effectively be mandatory.[32] Moreover, penalties so limited are even more unfair to employees who have a genetic predisposition for unhealthy outcomes, such as addiction or obesity, and so face a steeper challenge to avoid penalties. In a recent ruling, a key federal District Court agreed that the limit may effectively make the wellness program mandatory but let the EEOC rule stand to allow the agency opportunity to justify its position on voluntary participation in wellness programs. It remains to be seen if, when, and how the EEOC will defend or amend its rule.[33]

For many Americans, the Health Insurance Portability and Accountability Act (HIPAA) is the "face" of PHI protection; almost every traditional form of healthcare-related interaction involves some notice of HIPAA processes and protections. HIPAA protects against improper use of PHI but falls short in its protections of PHI privacy. For example, HIPAA does not regulate mobile fitness apps or wearable devices.[34]

The Employee Retirement Income Security Act (ERISA) nominally regulates group health plans, purporting to bar them from discrimination based on health. Yet ERISA exempts employers' voluntary wellness programs from some protections for PHI confidentiality and allows them to offer participation incentives of up to 30 percent of an employee's (or dependent's) insurance premium (up to 50 percent for tobacco-related incentives). As with the ADA and GINA, the "voluntariness" of such programs is questionable.

---

[30] Peppet, supra note 26; see also Adrionno McIntyre, Nicholas Bagley, Austin Frakt & Aaron Carroll, The Dubious Empirical and Legal Foundations of Wellness Programs, 27 Health Matrix 59 (2017), http://scholarlycommons.law.case.edu/healthmatrix/vol27/iss1/4/.

[31] Steve Osunsami, CVS Pharmacy Wants Workers' Health Information, or They'll Pay a Fine, ABC News, Mar. 20, 2013, http://abcnews.go.com/blogs/health/2013/03/20/cvs-pharmacy-wants-workers-health-information-or-theyll-pay-a-fine.

[32] See U.S. Equal Emp't Opportunity Comm'n, EEOC Issues Final Rules on Employer Wellness Programs (May 16, 2016), www.eeoc.gov/eeoc/newsroom/release/5-16-16.cfm.

[33] See AARP v. United States Equal Emp't Opportunity Comm'n, No. 16-2113, 2017 WL 3614430 (D.D.C. Aug. 22, 2017). See also Nicholas Bagley, A Judge Rules That EEOC's Rule on Wellness Programs Is Busted, The Incidental Economist, Aug. 23, 2017, http://theincidentaleconomist.com/wordpress/a-judge-rules-that-eeocs-rule-on-wellness-programs-is-busted/.

[34] U.S. Dep't of Health & Human Servs., Examining Oversight of the Privacy & Security of Health Data Collected by Entities Not Regulated by HIPAA (Jun. 17, 2016), www.healthit.gov/sites/default/files/non-covered_entities_report_june_17_2016.pdf; see also Peppet, supra note 26.

There is a difference between an employer having access to an employee's PHI and using that information in a discriminatory fashion; discrimination, not access to PHI, is the violation. However, since the real reasons for employers' hiring, promotion, and firing decisions may be difficult to discern, discrimination is difficult to prove. This heightened risk of discrimination underscores the need for stronger PHI safeguards. Health-related discrimination only violates federal law if it fits the narrow parameters of the laws above, for example, by relating to a disability (ADA) or genetic information (GINA). Most health-related behaviors are fair game. There is no federal law prohibiting employers from discriminating against employees who are obese or "addicted" to tobacco. Indeed, many employers have banned employees from smoking and imposed strict penalties on obese employees. Plaintiffs have generally failed to convince the courts that these health problems constitute "disabilities," so most of this discrimination has been ruled legal. Some states have adopted "lifestyle discrimination statutes" to protect employees' behaviors outside the workplace, but few explicitly address obesity and other health statuses.[35]

In sum, employment-based wellness programs, a large and growing movement, may not include the protections for PHI that they should. Moreover, current protection could erode as the Trump administration changes the regulatory environment.[36] In a world where insurers will be freer to cherry-pick their risks and where employers are freer to use PHI to exclude those who might hurt their bottom line, things do not bode well for the most vulnerable.

Exacerbating this vulnerability, financial incentives do not impact people equally across socioeconomic class lines. Poorer people are the most exposed to the effects of punitive actions; thus, overly aggressive and intrusive measures adopted to motivate healthier lifestyles may compound the growing problem of income and wealth inequality.[37] Moreover, if, as is common, low-wage workers are disproportionately racial and ethnic minorities, economic rewards and punishments that impact these demographic groups differently might violate civil rights laws.[38]

Not only should employers and insurers be required to respect PHI privacy but, similarly, manufacturers and other promoters of wearable devices and smartphone apps should have to meet reasonable requirements for PHI protection. To date, such requirements have been minimal, resting more on private contract law than

---

[35] Jessica L. Roberts, Healthism and the Law of Employment Discrimination, 99 Iowa L. Rev. 571 (2014).
[36] See, for example, Exec. Order No. 13,765, 82 Fed. Reg. 8351, 8351–52 (Jan. 20, 2017) and Exec. Order No. 13,771, 82 Fed. Reg. 9339, 9339–41 (Jan. 30, 2017).
[37] See Associated Press, Wellness Programs Grow More Popular with Employers, The Mercury News, Apr. 25, 2014, http://www.mercurynews.com/2014/04/25/wellness-programs-grow-more-popular-with-employers/. For the full story of the widening inequality gap, see Anthony W. Orlando, Letter to the One Percent (2013).
[38] See Valerie Wilson & William M. Rodgers III, Black–White Wage Gaps Expand with Rising Wage Inequality, Econ. Pol'y Inst. (Sept. 19, 2016), www.epi.org/files/pdf/101972.pdf; see also AFL-CIO, The Elusive American Dream: Lower Wages, High Unemployment and an Uncertain Retirement for Latinos, AFL-CIO Labor Day 2013 Report on Latinos (2013), www.aflcio.org/content/download/98601/2662151/file/LatinoReport.pdf.

government regulation. Regulators have mostly relied on informed consent to protect consumers, assuming users of these devices have enough information and understanding of the technologies and PHI privacy risks to make a knowledgeable decision. This assumption is tenuous at best. The relevant privacy policies are often unclear, missing important protections, and hard to find, if they are available at all. One reviewer purchased twenty different products and none came with information about privacy or data protection. A long and frustrating search yielded policies online, but they rarely addressed such basic elements as how "personal information" is defined; what data is collected; who owns it; whether it is shared, sold, and/or encrypted; or how consumers can access their data.[39]

Although there is growing need to protect PHI from naive and ill-informed actions by consumers and end users of these new technologies, the FDA seems unlikely to act aggressively. Currently, most wearable devices and apps are treated as nonmedical devices, avoiding FDA regulation.[40] Beginning under the Obama administration, the agency has struggled over how far its regulatory reach should extend in this area. Responding to Silicon Valley concerns that FDA regulation could stifle progress in this area, then-Deputy Commissioner Scott Gottlieb said in 2014 that wearable devices are not "medical devices" under the FDA's regulatory purview because they do not "help patients self-manage a health condition," even though he acknowledged "ample medical evidence to show that patients make bad decisions when they don't have adequate information about their health."[41]

Now, with Gottlieb elevated to FDA Commissioner by President Trump, the agency is exercising "enforcement discretion" to leave unregulated "medical devices" that do not, in its view, pose a sufficient risk to public health and safety. Balancing desirable advances in medical science against observed and potential risks to public health and safety has always been one of the FDA's core challenges. It seems, however, that today's FDA is considering only physical and bodily harms, such as might be caused by a defective pacemaker or defibrillator or blood glucose monitor, in assessing those risks; the risks of improper handling of PHI are not treated as a compelling concern.[42]

As explained herein, however, users of wearable fitness devices and Internet apps risk substantial harm from inadequate protection of their PHI. Many people use them as if they were medical devices, basing important decisions about their health and fitness regimens on them; and employers increasingly incorporate them into their wellness programs, making them part of the health insurance system. For all

---

[39] Peppet, supra note 26, at 139–45.
[40] See U.S. Food & Drug Admin., General Wellness: Policy for Low Risk Devices, Guidance for Industry and Food and Drug Administration Staff, (July 29, 2016), www.fda.gov/downloads/MedicalDevices/DeviceRegulationandGuidance/GuidanceDocuments/UCM429674.pdf.
[41] Scott Gottlieb & Coleen Klasmeier, Why Your Phone Isn't as Smart as It Could Be, Wall St. J., Aug. 7, 2014, www.wsj.com/articles/scott-gottlieb-and-coleen-klasmeier-why-your-phone-isnt-as-smart-as-it-could-be-1407369163.
[42] See U.S. Food & Drug Admin., supra note 40.

these reasons, we believe the FDA should reconsider and treat these technologies as "medical devices" and regulate them to protect public safety as more broadly defined.[43]

At this early stage, we take no position on what the substantive details of the regulatory regime for these innovations should be, but surely it should include requiring warning all users of these devices and apps, in simple and understandable language, that there are risks to the sharing of PHI through their product or app. It should also include links to more detailed information about the risks and how to deal with them. Ideally, that source would be the FDA itself through a well-designed, accessible, adequately updated website.

B. The Obligation to Inform

Having examined the "confidentiality" side of the transparency coin, we now turn attention to the obligation to provide or share information. To properly protect the interests of consumers and users of health-related devices, all who develop, market, and promote these behavior-influencing solutions must stay informed about known and potential risks and communicate this cautionary information to users in a timely and appropriate fashion. We cannot rely exclusively on self-interested parties to give consumers this information. Governmental and other organizations committed to safeguarding public health and safety must ensure that people know the risks and understand the options available to pursue healthy behaviors in safety.

The EEOC set a good example by requiring that employers tell employees what PHI will be collected in wellness programs, how it will be used, and with whom it will be shared. Moreover, the EEOC prohibits employers from requiring participants to agree to the sale or disclosure of their PHI in order to join a wellness program or receive a financial incentive.[44]

By contrast, although the ACA allows group plans to penalize employees for engaging in tobacco-related activities, it does not require employers, doctors, or others to inform employees when tobacco cessation services are covered health benefits. Even government programs fall short in communicating this essential information; the majority of smokers surveyed in a recent study were unaware that Medicaid covered these services.[45] Despite the seriousness of tobacco addiction, employees may find themselves penalized for a habit that they do not know they have the health care they need to break.

Wearable fitness devices can pose additional safety risks by their sharing of personal information. One in four users has a profile that potentially lets strangers

---

[43] Jay Hancock, Workplace Wellness Programs Put Employee Privacy at Risk, CNN, Oct. 2, 2015, www.cnn.com/2015/09/28/health/workplace-wellness-privacy-risk-exclusive/.

[44] U.S. Equal Emp't Opportunity Comm'n, supra note 32.

[45] Leighton Ku, Brian K. Bruen, Erika Steinmetz & Tyler Bysshe, Medicaid Tobacco Cessation: Big Gaps Remain in Efforts to Get Smokers to Quit, 35 Health Aff. 62 (2016).

observe and track their exercise routines, sometimes even revealing the person's address and when they are not at home. Further, cybersafety experts warn that even minimal hacking ability can yield PHI, such as height, weight, and age. We urge that those who promote the use of Internet devices linking people together for health-related behavior-modification should be required to provide cautionary messages to protect PHI and users' personal safety.

IV. CONCLUSION

Our goal in this chapter has been to raise awareness of a real and emerging problem facing our nation's citizens and health care system, to highlight various solutions being tried, and to explore the problems with putting those solutions into practice. We have demonstrated that, by a wide variety of measures, the U.S. population is engaged in increasingly unhealthy behaviors, behaviors that pose grave risks to the public's health and place substantial burdens on our health care system and other sectors of the U.S. economy, including employers. We have examined several "transparency" solutions that have begun to address this problem by encouraging the compiling and sharing of Personal Health Information (PHI) in ways that inform and motivate individuals to take greater personal responsibility for their own health. Then, we have called attention to a number of important risks inherent in these solutions, particularly the possibility that PHI may be shared too broadly and used to discriminate against individuals with unfavorable health characteristics or genetic predispositions. Finally, we have identified some ways in which information sharing can and should be handled more carefully and some instances where additional identification and communication of risk information should be required.

We applaud those who have focused on this problem so far and have taken steps to address it. We hope we have helped move forward the campaign toward better personal health. We will continue to try to do so, and we welcome any advice or assistance that like-minded crusaders are motivated to give.

16

The Role of Transparency in Patient Safety Improvement

Michelle M. Mello, David M. Studdert, Brahmajee K. Nallamothu, and Allen Kachalia*

INTRODUCTION

Twenty years ago, few systematic efforts to make health care safer existed. Today patient safety is a priority for patients, providers, payers, and policymakers. The Institute of Medicine's 2000 report on medical error prompted vigorous and sustained investment in safety improvement, including widespread adoption of error detection and reporting programs, movement toward "systems approaches" for addressing error, development of new clinical interventions to reduce error, and efforts to foster stronger safety cultures within health care organizations.[1] Today, although there are some indications that these activities have yielded benefits, much of health care remains too unsafe.[2]

Transparency initiatives have been at the leading edge of the movement to improve patient safety. One tributary of this river of work has sought to bring more information on provider organizations' quality and safety performance to patients and health insurers, in the hope that providers with strong performance will attract more customers and those ranking towards the bottom will perceive a stronger economic incentive to improve. A second tributary has encouraged greater candor with patients and families about unexpected outcomes of care, or "adverse events." A third has sought to promote transparency about adverse events within health care organizations by better protecting those discussions from external scrutiny.

---

* This chapter is adapted from Allen Kachalia et al., Legal and Policy Interventions to Improve Patient Safety, 133 Circulation 661 (2016), with permission of the American Heart Association, Inc. Allen Kachalia received an honorarium for a presentation on liability reform at the Medical Mutual Insurance Company of Maine. Brahmajee Nallamothu serves on the United Healthcare Cardiac Scientific Advisory Board. Michelle Mello and David Studdert receive grant funding from SUMIT Insurance Company, Ltd., a liability insurance company. The authors have no other disclosures.

[1] Linda T. Kohn et al., eds., To Err is Human: Building a Safer Health System 1, 4 (2000).

[2] C. P. Landrigan et al., Temporal Trends in Rates of Patient Harm Resulting from Medical Care, 363 New England Journal of Medicine 2124, 2124 (2010); see also Daniel R. Levinson, Adverse Events in Hospitals: National Incidence Among Medicare Beneficiaries 1, 30 (2010), https://oig.hhs.gov/oei/reports/oei-06-09-00090.pdf.

These transparency-focused approaches sit alongside several other efforts to improve safety: pay-for-performance reimbursement, new forms of regulation both inside and outside the provider community, and medical liability reform. Though separate, those streams reinforce the transparency initiatives. In this chapter, we review the leading approaches to patient safety improvement, exploring their nature, rationale, and what is known about their effectiveness.

TRANSPARENCY INITIATIVES

Health care is an opaque enterprise. Today, however, expectations are growing for providers to be more transparent with patients and the public regarding how treatment decisions are made, how much care costs, whether conflicts of interest exist, and when and why errors and unexpected outcomes of care occur.[3] These expectations are fueled, in part, by hopes that that such transparency will help boost the quality and efficiency of care. Movement toward openness and candor are particularly evident in three areas: public reporting of data, communication with patients about adverse events, and internal review of care outcomes.

Public Reporting of Performance Data

Public reporting of data on the quality and safety performance of institutions has expanded through a combination of external rules and voluntary initiatives from within health care organizations.[4] Some states have used their regulatory authority to require institutional reporting of adverse events. On the federal level, the Center for Medicare and Medicaid Services (CMS) has leveraged its purchasing power to impose public reporting mandates for a range of quality and safety metrics. A number of influential nongovernmental organizations, such as *U.S. News and World Report* and the Leapfrog Group, have also stepped up efforts to display, rank, or otherwise recognize health care organizations based on performance on various metrics.[5]

The scope and sophistication of published metrics have also expanded dramatically over the last decade.[6] Quality indicators related to cardiovascular conditions at

---

[3] Allen B. Kachalia, Improving Patient Safety Through Transparency, 369 New England Journal of Medicine 1677, 1678 (2013); see also Robert P. Kocher & Ezekiel J. Emanuel, The Transparency Imperative, 159 Annals of Internal Medicine 296, 297 (2013).

[4] Christina A. Minami et al., Public Reporting in Surgery: An Emerging Opportunity to Improve Care and Inform Patients, 261 Annals of Surgery 241 (2015); David Blumenthal & J. Michael McGinnis, Measuring Vital Signs: An IOM Report on Core Metrics for Health and Health Care Progress, 313 JAMA 1901 (2015).

[5] See Anca M. Cotet, The Impact of Noneconomic Damages Cap on Health Care Delivery in Hospitals, 14 American Law and Economics Review 192 (2012); William E. Encinosa & Fred J. Hellinger, Have State Caps on Malpractice Awards Increased The Supply Of Physicians?, Health Affairs (2005). https://www.ncbi.nlm.nih.gov/pubmed/15928256. Health Aff (Millwood). 2005 Jan-Jun; Suppl Web Exclusives:W5-250-W5-258.

[6] Blumenthal & McGinnis, supra note 4 at 1901.

both the institution and physician levels were among the first metrics published.[7] Today, indicators have expanded to cover a range of conditions and often form part of publicly accessible "ranking" systems for health care organizations.[8]

A core rationale for public reporting is that it allows patients and health plans to "vote with their feet," which in turn may press providers to compete on quality. It is well recognized, however, that various factors disrupt this aspiration. Health insurance plans often limit patients' choices about where to obtain care, and health plans may find cost control a more pressing influence on their choice of in-network providers than quality. Clinical circumstances also act as a constraint: patients in need of emergency or urgent care for conditions like chest pain are unlikely to compare performance metrics before seeking medical attention. Even for elective care, available evidence suggests that publicly reported quality data have minimal effect on the choices of patients or referring providers.[9]

But shaping consumer choices about where to obtain care is not the only way through which publicly reported performance data may drive quality improvement. The data may motivate hospitals to pursue patient safety improvement so that they may reap the reputational benefits associated with being perceived as a market leader. This is evident in voluntary moves by health care organizations to publish their performance scores. Many large hospitals now report clinical outcomes for a wide range of procedures and treatments, as well as safety culture scores, patient experience scores, and patient comments.[10] From a public-relations standpoint, this strategy signals a commitment to quality, continuous improvement, and transparency.

The pivotal question, of course, is not how or why public reporting *may* improve quality and safety, but whether it *actually* does. Hard evidence of effects on quality

[7] James G. Jollis & Patrick S. Romano, Pennsylvania's Focus on Heart Attack – Grading the Scorecard, 338 New England Journal of Medicine 983 (1998); Jesse Green & Neil Wintfeld, Report Cards on Cardiac Surgeons – Assessing New York State's Approach, 332 New England Journal of Medicine 1229 (1995).

[8] Encinosa & Hellinger, supra note 5; See also Scott B. Ransom et al., Reduced Medicolegal Risk by Compliance with Obstetric Clinical Pathways: a Case–Control Study, 101 Obstetrics & Gynecology 751 (2003).

[9] Martin N. Marshall et al., The Public Release of Performance Data: What Do We Expect to Gain? A Review of the Evidence, 283 JAMA 1866 (2000) (meta-analysis that discusses effects of public reporting on consumers); Eric C. Schneider & Arnold M. Epstein, Use of Public Performance Reports: A Survey of Patients Undergoing Cardiac Surgery, 279 JAMA 1638 (1998) (small study on patient awareness and competitive impact of reporting); Eric C. Schneider & Arnold M. Epstein, Influence of Cardiac-Surgery Performance Reports on Referral Practices and Access to Care – A Survey of Cardiovascular Specialists, 335 New England Journal of Medicine 251 (1996) (study of public reporting and its impact on physician referrals).

[10] Kathleen M. Mazor et al., Health Plan Members' Views about Disclosure of Medical Errors, 140 Annals of Internal Medicine 409 (2004); Amy B. Witman et al., How Do Patients Want Physicians To Handle Mistakes? A Survey Of Internal Medicine Patients In An Academic Setting, 156 Archives of Internal Medicine 2565 (1996); Albert W. Wu et al., Disclosing Medical Errors To Patients: It's Not What You Say, It's What They Hear, 24 Journal of General Internal Medicine 1012, 1015 (2009).

and safety remain elusive.[11] Some studies have identified improvements in performance – as measured by, for example, National Hospital Quality Measures,[12] cardiac surgery mortality,[13] and readmissions[14] – following public posting of related measures. One of the most widely cited examples is the substantial improvement in door-to-balloon times for patients undergoing primary percutaneous coronary intervention after myocardial infarction that was seen nationally after CMS began publicly reporting these times.[15] Considered as a whole, however, the evidence demonstrating a causal relationship between public reporting and performance improvement remains thin.

Another aspect of public reporting that has grown more prevalent since the publication of the Institute of Medicine report is state-mandated reporting of hospital adverse events. More than half the states have now built reporting systems to collect information about events resulting in serious harm to patients.[16] Although most states incorporate at least part of the National Quality Forum's list of twenty-eight "Serious Reportable Events," reporting requirements vary from state to state, as do levels of compliance by mandated reporters.[17] Of particular note, some states require hospitals to show they have conducted a root-cause analysis of the event and submit a corrective action plan or risk reduction strategy, while others do not.[18] The requirements are intended to support investigations and pattern analyses by state departments of health, but the resources devoted to such efforts – and thus, the results states are able to demonstrate in terms of reductions in adverse events – also vary considerably across states.[19] Finally, states have taken different approaches to the public

[11] Constance H. Fung et al., Systematic Review: The Evidence that Publishing Patient Care Performance Data Improves Quality of Care, 148 Annals of Internal Medicine 111 (2008); Nicole A. Ketelaar et al., Public Release of Performance Data in Changing the Behaviour of Health Care Consumers, Professionals or Organisations, Cochrane Database of Systemic Reviews 1, 3 (2011).
[12] Stephen P. Schmaltz et al., Hospital Performance Trends on National Quality Measures and the Association with Joint Commission Accreditation, 6 Journal of Hospital Medicine 454, 458 (2011); Peter K. Lindenauer et al., Public Reporting and Pay for Performance in Hospital Quality Improvement, 356 New England Journal of Medicine 486, 486 (2007).
[13] Mark R. Chassin, Achieving and Sustaining Improved Quality: Lessons from New York State and Cardiac Surgery, 21 Health Affairs 40, 45 (2002).
[14] Clark C. Havighurst & Lawrence R. Tancredi, Medical Adversity Insurance – A No-Fault Approach to Medical Malpractice and Quality Assurance, 51 Milbank Memorial Fund Quarterly 125 (1973).
[15] Harlan M. Krumholz et al., Improvements in Door-to-Balloon Time in the United States, 2005 to 2010, 124 Circulation 1038, 1044 (2011).
[16] National Quality Forum, The Power of Safety: State Reporting Provides Lessons in Reducing Harm, Improving Care, 1 (2010), www.qualityforum.org/Publications/2010/06/Quality_Connections__The_Power_of_Safety__State_Reporting_Provides_Lessons_in_Reducing_Harm,_Improving_Care.aspx.
[17] Id.; Lucian L. Leape, Reporting of Adverse Events, 347 New England Journal of Medicine 1633, 1634 (2002).
[18] Daniel R. Levinson, Adverse Events in Hospitals: State Reporting Systems 1, 11 (2008), https://oig.hhs.gov/oei/reports/oei-06-07-00471.pdf.
[19] See id.

availability of event reports. Most keep them confidential in the interest of encouraging reporting, while some post them online.[20]

Efforts to implement robust public reporting programs face a number of practical challenges, beginning with identification of suitable measures. To be effective, the measures must both matter and be easily comprehensible to the general public. Serious adverse events are a clearly sensible choice of safety measure, though reasonable people can disagree about whether an event is "unexpected," as the definition of such events often requires. Measures must also be technically robust, providing valid and reliable indicators of what they purport to indicate. This is a challenge in the quality domain, where faulty measures risk generating the wrong incentives. Consider, for example, a recently retired CMS measure that called for preantibiotic blood cultures for patients with pneumonia. Although the measure was well intentioned, critics questioned whether it was an appropriate indicator of high-quality care[21] and raised concerns over the unintended consequences of incentivizing unnecessary blood cultures in patients with respiratory illnesses.[22]

Another substantial challenge for public reporting is the proliferation of measures and reporting systems. Duplicative reporting requirements to multiple systems may lead to overburdened reporters being overwhelmed, resentful, and noncompliant. Confronted with a battery of metrics and no guidance about which are most important, providers and patients may be none the wiser regarding which institutions provide the best care.[23] To address these concerns, measures are sometimes "retired" once performance "tops off" – meaning, most providers are scoring near or at 100 percent – on the basis that the value in ongoing measurement will be limited.[24] For example, CMS has started retiring a number of heart failure and heart attack measures, such as prescribing of beta-blockers at discharge for patients with a myocardial infarction.[25]

A potential drawback to the implementation of public reporting of quality and safety performance is that it can create disincentives for physicians and hospitals to

[20] See id. at 13.
[21] Nima Afshar et al., Blood Cultures for Community-Acquired Pneumonia: Are They Worthy of Two Quality Measures? A Systematic Review, 4 Journal of Hospital Medicine 112, 112–113 (2009); see also Julien Dedier et al., Processes of Care, Illness Severity, and Outcomes in the Management of Community-Acquired Pneumonia at Academic Hospitals, 161 Archives of Internal Medicine 2099, 2102 (2001).
[22] Anil N. Makam et al., Blood Culture Use in the Emergency Department in Patients Hospitalized with Respiratory Symptoms Due to a Nonpneumonia Illness, 9 Journal of Hospital Medicine 521, 523–524 (2014); Robert M. Wachter et al., Public Reporting of Antibiotic Timing in Patients with Pneumonia: Lessons from a Flawed Performance Measure, 149 Annals of Internal Medicine 29, 30–31 (2008).
[23] J. Matthew Austin et al., National Hospital Ratings Systems Share Few Common Scores and May Generate Confusion Instead of Clarity, 34 Health Affairs 423 (2015).
[24] Denise Dougherty et al., Systematic Evidence-Based Quality Measurement Life-Cycle Approach to Measure Retirement in CHIPRA, 14 Academic Pediatrics S97, S102 (2014); Kirk B. Johnson et al., A Fault-Based Administrative Alternative for Resolving Medical Malpractice Claims, 42 Vanderbilt Law Review 1365, 1386–1388 (1989).
[25] Thomas H. Lee, Eulogy for a Quality Measure, 357 New England Journal of Medicine 1175 (2007).

care for the sickest patients, who are at special risk for poor outcomes. This issue was particularly highlighted when New York started posting coronary artery bypass graft (CABG) surgery outcomes. Though the evidence has been mixed, critics have been concerned the move may have resulted in lower CABG use in patients presenting emergently or with high-risk characteristics.[26] Similar worries have been noted with percutaneous coronary intervention in some states.[27] Thus, the unintended consequences of public reporting requirements need to be considered alongside their benefits when assessing the utility of this transparency-based approach to improving quality and safety.

Transparency Concerning Medical Errors

Disclosure of medical errors to patients is another form of transparency that has captured significant interest. There is now wide agreement that providers have an ethical obligation to communicate the occurrence of harmful errors and other unanticipated care outcomes to patients who experience them, and to convey what is known about why the outcome happened, including any mistakes made.[28] Survey research suggests patients and their families strongly desire this information.[29] Safety experts regard disclosure programs as an essential part of institutional efforts to improve patient safety.[30] The tide has clearly turned against the traditional risk-management strategy of saying as little as possible when an adverse event occurs; however, many errors remain undisclosed today.[31]

Two elements of disclosure practices are currently attracting considerable discussion. First, in circumstances in which patient harm was determined to be attributable to error, should an offer of compensation routinely follow the disclosure of the error? Second, do current disclosure practices adequately reflect the needs of injured patients and their families?

---

[26] Eric D. Peterson et al., The Effects of New York's Bypass Surgery Provider Profiling on Access to Care and Patient Outcomes in the Elderly, 32 Journal of the American College of Cardiology 993 (1998); Nowamagbe A. Omoigui et al., Outmigration For Coronary Bypass Surgery in an Era of Public Dissemination of Clinical Outcomes, 93 Circulation 27, 30–31 (1996).

[27] Frederic S. Resnic & Frederick G. P. Welt, The Public Health Hazards of Risk Avoidance Associated With Public Reporting of Risk-Adjusted Outcomes in Coronary Intervention, 53 Journal of the American College of Cardiology 825, 826 (2009); Karen E. Joynt et al., Association of Public Reporting for Percutaneous Coronary Intervention with Utilization and Outcomes Among Medicare Beneficiaries with Acute Myocardial Infarction, 308 JAMA 1460 (2012).

[28] Thomas H. Gallagher et al., Disclosing Harmful Medical Errors to Patients, 356 New England Journal of Medicine 2713 (2007); Medical Professionalism in the New Millennium: A Physician Charter, 136 Annals of Internal Medicine 243 (2002).

[29] Kathleen M. Mazor et al., supra note 10 at 413–415; Robert J. Blendon et al., Views of Practicing Physicians and the Public on Medical Errors, 347 New England Journal of Medicine 1933, 1938 (2002).

[30] Allen B. Kachalia & David W. Bates, Disclosing Medical Errors: The View from the USA, 12 The Surgeon 64 (2014)

[31] Gallagher et al., supra note 28 at 2713.

In most cases, error disclosures are not automatically accompanied by referral of the incident for compensation. Patients may opt to pursue a malpractice claim, but health care organizations tend to take a "wait and see" approach. Momentum is gathering, however, for an alternative approach in which error disclosures are accompanied by financial resolution of the event. A number of prominent hospitals have adopted programs – today generally referred to as "communication-and-resolution programs" (CRPs) – to provide structure for that approach.[32] Where the hospital, in collaboration with its insurer, determines that the standard of care was not met, the institution proactively offers fair compensation after explaining what happened and having the involved providers apologize. Where the care was reasonable, on the other hand, CRPs are focused on delivering transparent communication about the event, not compensation. A full explanation of what occurred is given, with an "apology of sympathy" ("I am sorry that this happened"). The institution also communicates its commitment to stand behind and defend the involved providers should a malpractice claim be filed.

Studies of CRPs suggest that they can substantially reduce the volume and cost of malpractice claims.[33] However, research also shows that not all organizations can implement CRPs successfully.[34] The best conclusion is that CRPs are effective in controlling liability costs *when they are done right*.

It is not yet clear to what extent the benefits of CRPs extend beyond liability outcomes to include real improvements to patient safety. Theory would suggest they should enhance the climate for safety improvement, and some institutions have found that adverse event reporting becomes more robust and safety-improvement interventions are frequently identified based on CRP event analyses.[35] However, a causal connection between CRPs and safety outcomes at the institutional level is difficult to establish, in part because hospitals are typically doing many things to improve safety at the same time.

Nevertheless, by facilitating open discussion of adverse events, CRPs may boost institutional awareness of errors and foster a culture that is more attuned and open to

---

[32] Michelle M. Mello et al., Communication-And-Resolution Programs: The Challenges and Lessons Learned from Six Early Adopters, 33 Health Affairs 20 (2014).

[33] Steve S. Kraman & G. Hamm, Risk Management: Extreme Honesty may be the Best Policy, 131 *Annals of Internal Medicine* 963 (1999); Allen B. Kachalia et al., Liability Claims and Costs Before and After Implementation of a Medical Error Disclosure Program, 153 *Annals of Internal Medicine* 213 (2010); Bruce L. Lambert et al., The "Seven Pillars" Response to Patient Safety Incidents: Effects on Medical Liability Processes and Outcomes, 51 Suppl 3 Health Services Research 2491 (2016). Allen Kachalia et al., Effects of a Communication-and-Resolution Program on Hospitals' Malpractice Claims and Costs, 37 Health Affairs 1836 (2018).

[34] Michelle M. Mello et al., Outcomes In Two Massachusetts Hospital Systems Give Reason For Optimism About Communication-And-Resolution Programs, 36 Health Affairs (Millwood) 1795 (2017); Michelle M. Mello et al., Challenges of Implementing a Communication-and-Resolution Program Where Multiple Organizations Must Cooperate, 51 Suppl 3 Health Services Research 2550 (2016); Michelle M. Mello et al., Case Outcomes in a Communication-and-Resolution Program in New York Hospitals, 51 Suppl 3 Health Services Research 2583 (2016).

[35] Bruce L. Lambert et al., supra note 33 at 2492; Mello et al., Outcomes in Two Massachusetts Hospitals, supra note 34 at 1799–1780.

safety and learning. In addition, best practice demands an explanation to patients of what will be done to prevent similar events in the future; in organizations that conduct rigorous investigations, propose meaningful reforms, and keep their word, substantial safety improvements may follow. Identifying whether CRPs actually realize such patient safety benefits will not be easy, but as the programs grow, so does the imperative to investigate and answer this question.

In addition to compensation, the other key issue being debated about disclosure practices today is whether they are sufficiently responsive to emerging knowledge about what patients and families need from providers in disclosure discussions. It has long been known that there are gaps between what physicians think should be conveyed in disclosure conversations and what patients want to know – for example, receiving an apology is a fundamental need, but physicians may be reticent to give an "apology of responsibility" out of fear of creating legal liability.[36]

The advent of expert guidelines for disclosure and broader use of disclosure training and just-in-time disclosure coaching in hospitals have likely led to improvement over time. However, recent research suggests that even at institutions with CRPs communications often fall short of patients' and family members' expectations.[37] Although more routine now than in the past, apologies may be conveyed woodenly and received as inauthentic. Patients frequently report a lack of communication about what the hospital will do to ensure that the event does not recur. Finally, providers may be so focused on giving patients information about what occurred that they forget to listen. Patients and family members report that "being heard" – having the opportunity to tell providers their story of the event and how it affected them – is as important or more important than receiving factual information about why the event occurred. Thus, in the disclosure context today, transparency should be a two-way street.

Strengthening Information Sharing Within Provider Organizations

Stimulating providers to engage in open conversation about safety problems can sit at odds with the objective of promoting transparency externally because it requires that providers feel safe discussing information that could give rise to liability. Regulatory interventions have sought to create a protected space for such discussions to occur. Even though these interventions remove some information from public scrutiny, they are rightly considered as among the transparency-based approaches to safety improvement.

---

[36] Thomas H. Gallagher et al., Patients' and Physicians' Attitudes Regarding the Disclosure of Medical Errors, 289 JAMA 1001, 1005 (2003); Thomas H. Gallagher et al., Choosing Your Words Carefully: How Physicians would Disclose Harmful Medical Errors to Patients, 166 Archives of Internal Medicine 1585 (2006).

[37] Jennifer Moore et al., Patients' Experiences With Communication-and-Resolution Programs After Medical Injury, 177 JAMA Internal Medicine 1595, 1602 (2017).

Professionalism dictates that physicians review harmful errors to understand why they occurred and use this knowledge to guide prevention efforts. Peer review of adverse events is often the initial step. To encourage clinicians to participate in such investigations and allay apprehension about the liability implications of statements made during the peer-review process, the federal Health Care Quality Improvement Act of 1986 provides liability (but not evidentiary) protection for statements made as part of a peer-review process.[38] This means that physicians cannot ordinarily be held liable for statements made during peer review, but that the statements may nonetheless be used as evidence in court proceedings. States have enacted their own layer of peer-review protection, and many of these laws go further, protecting statements and documents generated during peer review from any use in litigation.[39] Court decisions in a few states have subsequently weakened that additional layer of state peer-review protections[40]

Troubled by that judicial trend and eager to encourage wider generation and use of safety-related information within and among health care organizations, Congress passed the Patient Safety and Quality Improvement Act of 2005.[41] The Act allows providers to create Patient Safety Organizations (PSOs), entities that facilitate open, confidential discussion of adverse events. Adoption of PSOs has been somewhat slow, probably due in part to the slew of establishment requirements.[42] It is too soon to tell what advantages PSO status confers; the effects of PSO status in stimulating patient safety activities and reducing error have not been closely studied. Nevertheless, the legislation represents a welcome step by the federal government to create the conditions under which providers will openly discuss, analyze, learn from, and prevent adverse events.

OTHER STRATEGIES

Safety-improvement strategies centered on transparency are complemented by a number of other approaches, including pay-for-performance reimbursement, professional regulation, and liability reform. Each of these approaches has salutary effects on transparency, either by directly requiring information disclosures or by improving the environment for candor about adverse events.

Pay-for-Performance Reimbursement

Fee-for-service payment models incentivize physicians and hospitals to provide more care. These financial incentives join other forces – including liability pressure

---

[38] John K. Iglehart, Congress Moves to Bolster Peer Review: The Health Care Quality Improvement Act of 1986, 316 New England Journal of Medicine 960, 961 (1987).
[39] Alan G. Williams, Congress Saved Peer Review: Who Knew?, 149 JAMA Surgery 317 (2014).
[40] Id.
[41] Carolyn M. Clancy, New Patient Safety Organizations Lower Roadblocks to Medical Error Reporting, 23 American Journal of Medical Quality 318 (2008).
[42] Williams, supra note 39 at 318.

and physicians' natural desire to avoid clinical "misses" – to promote overuse. Overuse not only involves costly waste, but also places patients at risk of complications from unnecessary tests and procedures. Perversely, fee-for-service reimbursement may even reward some iatrogenic complications by paying providers for care and readmissions needed to treat them.

There appears to be little appetite for wholesale abandonment of fee-for-service reimbursement. Growing concerns about quality and unnecessary expenditures have instead led payers and policymakers to search for incentive-based solutions that could improve quality while simultaneously achieving cost control. One approach, pay-for-performance reimbursement, or "P4P", has assumed increasing prominence in health care over the past fifteen years. The structure of incentives in P4P schemes varies broadly and includes policies such as "no-pay" rules for preventable complications acquired during a hospital stay; payments based on performance on evidence-based process measures; payments linked to infrastructure measures; and payments based on clinical outcomes. Both private payers and CMS have experimented with these approaches; the Medicare program has been a particular focal point for such policy experiments.

Disillusionment about the potential for current P4P approaches to bring about large improvements in quality and safety is mounting alongside a growing empirical evidence base.[43] A recent analysis of sixty-nine studies from the United States and other countries concluded that results were inconsistent across studies, P4P metrics, and programs, but the best-designed studies tended to find no significant effects of P4P.[44] When positive effects were found, they tended to be small in magnitude and focused on processes of care rather than patient outcomes. Although enthusiasm for P4P within CMS appears persistently strong,[45] some experts are now calling for a fundamental rethinking of the approach,[46] while others urge more inquiry into specific design issues that may account for the disappointing results of a theoretically appealing approach.[47]

Professional Regulation

The medical profession has a long history of autonomy and self-regulation, traditionally justified by the specialized nature of medical practice and a strong code of professional ethics.[48] Self-regulation continues to play a major role in oversight of

---

[43] Austin B. Frakt & Ashish K. Jha, Face the Facts: We Need to Change the Way We Do Pay for Performance, 168 Ann Intern Med 291 (2018).
[44] Aaron Mendelson et al., The Effects of Pay-for-Performance Programs on Health, Health Care Use, and Processes of Care: A Systematic Review, 166 Annals of Internal Medicine 341, 350 (2017).
[45] Sylvia M. Burwell, Setting Value-Based Payment Goals – HHS Efforts to Improve U.S. Health Care, 372 New England Journal of Medicine 897, 898 (2015).
[46] Frakt & Jha, supra note 43 at 292.
[47] Mendelson et al., supra note 44 at 348–350.
[48] Carleton B. Chapman, Doctors and Their Autonomy: Past Events and Future Prospects, 200 Science 851 (1978); Paul Starr, The Social Transformation Of American Medicine (Basic Books, Inc. 1982); Ralph Crawshaw et al., Patient-Physician Covenant, 273 JAMA 1553 (1995); Troyen A. Brennan &

the profession, but coexists with external controls, including licensure rules, reporting requirements, and accreditation. Use of both forms of regulation to drive improvements in patient safety is growing.[49]

Medical professionalism requires physicians to maintain their clinical knowledge and skills and to help ensure colleagues do the same.[50] The rapid pace of change in clinical and scientific knowledge has led medical boards to shift from basic one-time certification requirements to maintenance of certification (MOC) requirements that seek to ensure provider competence throughout a physician's practice career.[51] MOC requirements often include periodic exams as well as other practice assessments and participation in quality-improvement projects.

The introduction of MOC requirements has been controversial.[52] Many physicians remain skeptical of the value of these requirements and troubled by the burden they impose.[53] Others see these programs as an important element of the professional duty to maintain competence and a means of warding off more burdensome, external regulation.[54] Which view will prevail is unclear,[55] particularly given the dearth of evidence on the effect of MOC programs on physician performance.

In terms of external regulation, the most salient force for physicians is the state medical board.[56] These boards control licensure and investigate reports of physician misconduct and incompetence, with the goal of protecting the public. They may impose heavy sanctions, up to and including suspension or revocation of a physician's license to practice medicine. Historically, state medical boards focused on forms of misconduct that are both egregious and relatively easy to monitor and

Donald M. Berwick, New Rules: Regulation, Markets, and the Quality of American Health Care (Jossey-Bass. 1995).

[49] John K. Iglehart & Robert B. Baron, Ensuring Physicians' Competence – Is Maintenance of Certification the Answer?, 367 New England Journal of Medicine 2543 (2012); John B. Herman, Increasing the Value of the State Medical License, 362 New England Journal of Medicine 1459, 1460 (2010); Kristyn Shaw et al., Shared Medical Regulation in a Time of Increasing Calls for Accountability and Transparency: Comparison of Recertification in the United States, Canada, and the United Kingdom, 302 JAMA 2008 (2009).

[50] Chapman, supra note 48 at 854; Starr, supra note 48; Crawshaw, supra note 48 at 1553.

[51] Iglehart & Baron, supra note 49 at 2543; James N. Thompson & Lisa A. Robin, State Medical Boards. Future Challenges for Regulation and Quality Enhancement of Medical Care, 33 Journal of Legal Medicine 93, 94 (2012).

[52] Joseph Loscalzo, Maintenance of Certification: Good Intentions Gone Awry, 25 Trends in Cardiovascular Medicine 312, 313 (2015); Paul S. Teirstein, Boarded to Death – Why Maintenance of Certification Is Bad for Doctors and Patients, 372 New England Journal of Medicine 106, 107 (2015); National Vaccine Injury Compensation Program, www.hrsa.gov/Vaccinecompensation/; Mira B. Irons & Lois M. Nora, Maintenance of Certification 2.0 – Strong Start, Continued Evolution, 372 New England Journal of Medicine 104 (2015).

[53] Paul S. Teirstein & Eric J. Topol, The Role of Maintenance of Certification Programs in Governance and Professionalism, 313 JAMA 1809, 1810 (2015).

[54] Iglehart & Baron, supra note 49 at 2548.

[55] Richard J. Baron, Professional Self-Regulation in a Changing World: Old Problems Need New Approaches, 313 JAMA 1807, 1808 (2015).

[56] Ron Paterson, The Good Doctor: What Patients Want (Auckland University Press. 2012).

prove, such as substance abuse and sexual indiscretions, and did relatively little to police physician competence.[57] With growing awareness of the outsized impact of competence problems among a small minority of practitioners on patient welfare and trust in the profession, pressure has mounted for boards to become more aggressive in the quality arena.[58] Unsurprisingly, many physicians have signalled their discomfort with the prospect of additional regulatory burdens and oversight.[59]

Finally, institutional accreditation is seen as providing an additional layer of accountability that can improve the safety of care. Technically, participation in accreditation programs is voluntary and driven by competitive forces, but U.S. hospitals see it as effectively mandatory. The Joint Commission (TJC), the best-known private accreditation organization, is particularly influential because participation in the Medicare program requires either periodic review by CMS or by an organization CMS has deemed to have the authority to review, such as TJC.[60] Further, many states have incorporated TJC's standards into their hospital licensing regimes; indeed, some even accept TJC accreditation in lieu of separate state requirements.

TJC has been seen as a national leader in the development of patient safety standards, including those relating to disclosure of adverse events.[61] To obtain accreditation, organizations must meet TJC's National Patient Safety Goals, a program established in 2002 to help hospitals address specific areas of threat to patient safety.[62] Accreditation has high face validity as a useful measure in assuring attention to safety issues. However, there remains surprisingly little evidence demonstrating its effects on patient outcomes.[63] Nevertheless, regulation from both outside and inside the medical profession will continue to form a key plank in future efforts to improve safety.

---

[57] Brennan & Berwick, supra note 48; Herman, supra note 49 at 1460; James Morrison & Peter Wickersham, Physicians Disciplined by a State Medical Board, 279 JAMA 1889, 1891–1892 (1998).

[58] Thompson & Robin, supra note 51; Lucian L. Leape & John A. Fromson, Problem Doctors: Is There a System-Level Solution?, 144 Annals of Internal Medicine 107, 114 (2006); Marie M. Bismark et al., Identification of Doctors at Risk of Recurrent Complaints: A National Study of Health Care Complaints in Australia, 22 BMJ Quality & Safety 532, 536–537 (2013).

[59] Thompson & Robin, supra note 51 at 104; Humayun J. Chaudhry et al., Maintenance of Licensure: Supporting a Physician's Commitment to Lifelong Learning, 157 Annals of Internal Medicine 287, 287–288 (2012).

[60] Lois Snyder et al., Ethics Manual: Fifth Edition, 142 *Annals of Internal Medicine* 560, 574 (2005).

[61] Michelle M. Mello et al., Fostering Rational Regulation of Patient Safety, 30 Journal of Health Politics, Policy and Law 375, 382 (2005).

[62] Medical Malpractice: Maine's Use of Practice Guidelines to Reduce Costs. GAO/HRD-94-8. 32 (1993).

[63] David Greenfield & J. Braithwaite, Health Sector Accreditation Research: a Systematic Review, 20 International Journal for Quality in Health Care 172, 174 (2008); Gerd Flodgren et al., Effectiveness of External Inspection of Compliance with Standards in Improving Health Care Organisation Behaviour, Health Care Professional Behaviour or Patient Outcomes, Cochrane Database of Systematic Reviews 1, 17–18 (2011).

Medical Liability Reform

The medical liability system is designed not only to compensate injured patients, but also to deter providers from practicing unreasonably unsafe care.[64] The economic sanctions imposed by the tort system when practitioners and health care institutions are held legally responsible for negligent injuries has long been seen as a necessary backstop for ensuring accountability. However, the performance of the medical liability system pleases no one.[65] In addition to familiar criticisms about litigation's failures as a compensation system,[66] there are real concerns about the ability of malpractice litigation to improve the safety of care. Key contributors to this problem are the relative rarity of claims compared to the incidence of negligent injury; the imprecision of the system in directing compensation to meritorious claims; and the prevalence of liability insurance coverage with little or no experience rating (meaning that an individual practitioner's insurance premiums do not go up very much after they have a claim).[67] Adding to safety concerns is a well-known, unintended consequence of malpractice liability: defensive medicine. Defensive practices are believed to be widespread, and place patients at risk from complications from unnecessary testing and treatment.

Most tort reforms – such as caps on damages – have been designed to address the fears of health care providers and their insurers about frivolous lawsuits and high, unpredictable damages awards. With rare exceptions, evaluations of the effects of these reforms have not demonstrated that they have improved the safety of care delivered.[68] Indeed, they were not designed to do so. Economic theory would suggest, to the contrary, that reduced liability should reduce incentives for safety. Because they do not appear to bolster safety, traditional reforms offer little in the way of a quid pro quo for patients. Consequently, in recent years the policy focus has been on identifying liability reforms that plausibly could also improve patient safety.[69]

A great deal of attention has focused on the potential for CRPs and the policy strategies that lawmakers could pursue to encourage their growth.[70] Those strategies include passage of apology laws that protect expressions of empathy or admissions of

---

[64] David M. Studdert et al., Medical Malpractice, 350 New England Journal of Medicine 283 (2004).
[65] Id.
[66] Id.; David M. Studdert et al., Claims, Errors, and Compensation Payments in Medical Malpractice Litigation, 354 New England Journal of Medicine 2024, 2031 (2006).
[67] Studdert et al., supra note 64 at 284–285; Troyen A. Brennan et al., Incidence of Adverse Events and Negligence in Hospitalized Patients, 324 New England Journal of Medicine 270, 274–275 (1991); Michelle M. Mello & Troyen A. Brennan, Deterrence of Medical Errors: Theory and Evidence for Malpractice Reform, 80 Texas Law Review 1595, 1616–1623 (2002).
[68] Michelle M. Mello Allen Kachalia, Medical Malpractice: Evidence on Reform Alternatives and Claims Involving Elderly Patients 1, 3–8 (MedPAC. 2016).
[69] Michelle M. Mello et al., Health Courts and Accountability for Patient Safety, 84 Milbank Quarterly 459, 470–471 (2006).
[70] William M. Sage et al., How Policy Makers Can Smooth The Way For Communication-And-Resolution Programs, 33 Health Affairs 11 (2014).

fault from being introduced into evidence at trial. Such protections may encourage greater provider dialogue with patients right after an adverse event occurs.[71] Some states have also enacted presuit notification laws that require a patient to give a provider advance notice of the intent to sue.[72] After notice is served, a waiting period for the patient to file suit follows, giving the provider a chance to resolve the matter and hopefully avert the lawsuit.

Three other liability reform proposals that have been prominent on the policy scene are enterprise liability, "safe harbors" for evidence-based practice guidelines, and administrative compensation systems.[73] Enterprise liability involves changing the rules of liability so that when a patient wishes to seek compensation, rather than filing a claim against a clinician, the patient would pursue a claim against the clinician's institution. The idea is to hold the institution that is benefiting from the clinician's actions liable for the clinician's errors as well as any broader systems failures. Focusing liability on enterprises targets the accountability signal to parties with the resources and organization to build safer systems of care.

Enterprise liability holds potential to improve safety by effecting cultural shifts. In reducing the blaming of individual clinicians, it can help build a "Just Culture," in which individuals do not feel singled out for inadvertent errors that could happen to other reasonable providers and could have been prevented by better systems of care.[74] Reducing blame and stigmatization may bolster transparency-related safety initiatives by stimulating providers to be more open about errors. On the other hand, enterprise liability removes some physician accountability. This potential decrement in individual deterrence may be outweighed by the improved incentives for safety at the institutional level, but that remains a matter of debate.

Safe harbor legislation aims to assuage physicians' fears about being sued when they have done everything right but nonetheless experience an adverse outcome.[75] States can enact legislation providing a strong defense to a malpractice claim where the provider can show that an appropriate clinical practice guideline was followed. By offering an incentive to follow evidence-based guidelines, safe harbors theoretically should improve quality and safety. Empirical data on the effect of safe harbors on safety are limited, however, as there has been minimal experimentation with the approach.[76] One simulation study found that safe harbors would not provide much legal benefit for physicians because they already tend to prevail in claims where they

---

[71] Michelle M. Mello et al., The Medical Liability Climate and Prospects for Reform, 312 JAMA 2146, 2151 (2014).
[72] Id.
[73] Id. at 2152; Allen B. Kachalia et al., Beyond Negligence: Avoidability and Medical Injury Compensation, 66 Social Science and Medicine 387, 399–401 (2008).
[74] Kachalia, supra note 3 at 1678.
[75] Mello et al., supra note 71 at 2152; Allen B. Kachalia et al., Greatest Impact of Safe Harbor Rule May be to Improve Patient Safety, Not Reduce Liability Claims Paid by Physicians, 33 Health Affairs 59, 64 (2014).
[76] Kachalia, supra note 75 at 60.

followed practice guidelines, even without a formal safe harbor.[77] The study did find that safe harbors may potentially induce physicians to provide safer care by adhering to guidelines. In at least five percent of the closed claims, reviewers judged that the injury would have been avoided had the physician followed an applicable guideline.

A third model for liability reform is to replace judicial resolution of malpractice claims with an administrative compensation system.[78] In an administrative compensation system, claims are filed with and resolved by an administrative body, with judicial appeal. The administrative body uses neutral experts, evidence-based decision guidelines, and precedent from similar cases to make determinations about the validity of claims. In most proposals, the adjudicator applies a compensation standard other than negligence in order to broaden access to compensation and avoid the stigma and adversarialism associated with negligence judgments. To control costs, administrative compensation models limit noneconomic damages and economize on overhead costs.

Proponents of administrative compensation systems point to several safety-enhancing aspects.[79] Electronically capturing detailed information about errors and contributing factors in a centralized database could power analyses of where and why errors occur across our health care system. Presently, such information resides in small, proprietary databases maintained by liability insurers. Administrative systems could also promote safety by contributing to a Just Culture. Removing the stigma associated with negligence investigations could make providers more comfortable discussing and admitting errors, in turn supporting learning.

Administrative compensation systems have operated in New Zealand and Scandinavia for decades.[80] They enjoy widespread support among physicians and the public. Their effects on patient safety have not been systematically measured, but evidence suggests that system administrators make good use of their databases to identify safety problems and that they disseminate lessons learned nationally.[81] Politically, however, the prospects for broad adoption of administrative compensation in the United States appear poor, due to the opposition of the trial bar and concern within the provider community that it could lead to higher liability insurance costs.[82]

REFLECTIONS

Although disparate, the multiple approaches to improving patient safety we have reviewed are mutually reinforcing. Of particular note, each of the nontransparency-

[77] Id. at 64.
[78] Mello et al., supra note 69 at 459–460; Kachalia et al., supra note 73 at 388.
[79] Mello et al., supra note 71 at 2153.
[80] Kachalia et al., supra note 73 at 388.
[81] Mello et al., supra note 69 at 479.
[82] Paul J. Barringer et al., Administrative Compensation of Medical Injuries: A Hardy Perennial Blooms Again, 33 Journal of Health Politics, Policy and Law 725, 747–750 (2008).

related streams of safety improvement bolsters the transparency-based approaches. P4P requires reporting of providers' performance on quality and safety metrics, such as hospital-acquired conditions rates. State board of medicine investigations contribute to the bank of publicly available information about provider competence problems. TJC accreditation requirements have spurred health care facilities to develop and adopt written policies on disclosure. Medical liability reforms that limit a provider's liability, reduce the threat of suit, or avoid stigmatizing battles over what constitutes negligence relieve the pressure that can chill physicians' willingness to engage in open conversation about errors. Apology laws encourage candid communication about adverse events with patients by reducing the risk that such communications will become evidence in a malpractice suit. Presuit notification laws create space for providers to reach out to patients to provide more information about unexpected care outcomes before the switch is thrown on the litigation roller coaster. In summary, it is striking how central transparency is to the national strategy for improving patient safety.

What is also striking in reviewing the approaches taken to date is how little we know about their effectiveness. For most, there is little or no solid evidence concerning their efficacy in improving patient outcomes (and sometimes, the evidence that is available is rather discouraging). In part, this can be explained by the short experience of most institutions with these initiatives; in part, it reflects the methodological difficulty of linking upstream interventions, like changes in culture and incentives, to patient-level outcomes. As long as the imperative to "do something" about patient safety remains, the strategy of "act now and evaluate later" is probably reasonable for interventions with a plausible mechanism for improving safety.[83] But this is not a viable long-term strategy.[84] As patient safety interventions proliferate and accumulate, priorities must be set, and the only sensible way to do that is by reference to what works best in attaining the desired outcomes.

One clear insight gained in patient safety circles is that success is rarely baked into an intervention itself. How the intervention is implemented, and the environment in which it is thrust, matter enormously. For example, moves to promote transparency will not take root in a hospital culture that is not attuned and committed to change. Public reporting may help spur performance improvement by leveraging providers' desire to be the best, but its effectiveness may be limited if there are too many measures or the measures are perceived by the medical community as invalid. Thus, realizing the potential of transparency initiatives to improve safety outcomes requires attention not just to the "what," but also to the "how."

---

[83] Lucian L. Leape et al., What Practices Will Most Improve Safety?: Evidence-Based Medicine Meets Patient Safety, 288 JAMA 501, 506–507 (2002).

[84] Kaveh G. Shojania et al., Safe but Sound: Patient Safety Meets Evidence-Based Medicine, 288 JAMA 508, 512 (2002).

17

Personal Health Records as a Tool for Transparency in Health Care

Sharona Hoffman[*]

This chapter explores the benefits and limitations of personal health records (PHRs) as a tool to promote transparency in health care. PHRs are electronic resources that enable patients to access and sometimes manage their health information, and they are often a component of physicians' electronic health record (EHR) systems.[1] Stage 2 of the meaningful use regulations for EHR systems establishes the following core objectives, among others: (1) "Provide patients the ability to view online, download and transmit their health information" and (2) "Use secure electronic messaging to communicate with patients on relevant health information."[2] PHRs are a key mechanism by which to achieve both goals.

While PHR use has lagged behind EHR system adoption, it is now becoming increasingly common. In 2014, 22 percent of patients viewed test results online, and in 2015, 16 percent of physicians could exchange secure messages with patients as well as enable patients to electronically view, download, and transmit their medical records to third parties.[3] A much higher percentage had some but not all of these capabilities. Optimists forecast that by 2020, over 75 percent of health care providers will implement fully functioning PHRs.[4]

---

[*] For another work by the author on this topic, see Sharona Hoffman, Electronic Health Records and Medical Big Data: Law and Policy (2016).
[1] See Hoffman, supra note *, pt. I.
[2] Ctrs. for Medicare & Medicaid Servs. (CMS), Stage 2 Overview Tipsheet (last updated August 2012), www.cms.gov/regulations-and-guidance/legislation/ehrincentiveprograms/downloads/stage2over view_tipsheet.pdf; 42 C.F.R. § 495.22 (e)(8) & (9) (2016). The regulations include specific requirements as to how many patients must utilize these capabilities.
[3] The Office of the Nat'l Coordinator for Health Info. Tech., Quick Stats, https://dashboard.healthit.gov /quickstats/quickstats.php (last visited December 29, 2016). See also David P. Miller et al., Primary Care Providers' Views of Patient Portals: Interview Study of Perceived Benefits and Consequences, 18 J. Med. Internet Res. e8 (2016), www.ncbi.nlm.nih.gov/pmc/articles/PMC4733220/ (reporting that "only 10% of veterans had authenticated their patient portal account within the Veterans Health Administration system," that in large commercial health systems, typically less than 30-40% of patients activate their online access, and that "in clinics serving primarily disadvantaged populations, portal use has been less than 10%.").
[4] Eric W. Ford et al., Personal Health Record Use in the United States: Forecasting Future Adoption Levels, 18 J. Med. Internet Res. e73 (2016), www.jmir.org/2016/3/e73/.

As PHR implementation accelerates, it is essential that all stakeholders understand PHRs' advantages and risks. Moreover, health care providers must develop thoughtful policies and regulations to address PHR concerns and promote their efficacy.

I. WHAT ARE PHRS?

A PHR can be defined as "an electronic application through which individuals can access, manage and share their health information ... in a private, secure, and confidential environment."[5] There are two types of PHRs.

First, stand-alone PHRs consist of software that enables patients to enter information from their medical records and to store it on their computer or the Internet. Patients may add data about their diet, exercise, or other matters that will help them track their progress and take better care of themselves. Some stand-alone PHRs can also accept entries from external sources, such as laboratories, pharmacies, or insurers, and the patient can decide to share the PHR with loved ones or caregivers.[6] In the alternative, patients may opt for portable, interoperable stand-alone PHRs that are stored on smart cards, cellular phones, or USB-compatible devices.[7]

The second type of PHR is tethered to health care providers' EHR systems. These PHRs, which are also called "patient portals," are tied to the EHR system and are automatically populated with information from the EHR, including test results, clinical summaries, appointment schedules, problem lists, allergies, and more.[8] In some cases, patients may also be allowed to enter information into the PHR, such as results of blood sugar tests, blood pressure checks, or other procedures that they conduct on their own at home.[9] Patients may also be able to order prescriptions through the PHR and exchange secure messages with clinicians.[10] This chapter focuses primarily on tethered PHRs.

---

[5] Paul C. Tang et al., Personal Health Records: Definitions, Benefits, and Strategies for Overcoming Barriers to Adoption, 13 J. Am. Med. Inform. Assoc. 121, 122 (2006); see also Matthew Wynia & Kyle Dunn, Dreams and Nightmares: Practical and Ethical Issues for Patients and Physicians Using Personal Health Records, 38 J.L. Med. & Ethics 64, 65 (2010) (offering a variety of other definitions).

[6] N. Archer et al., Personal Health Records: A Scoping Review, 18 J. Am. Med. Inform. Assoc. 515, 515 (2011); HealthIT.gov, Are There Different Types of Personal Health Records (PHRs)? (last updated March 3, 2016), www.healthit.gov/faq/are-there-different-types-personal-health-records-phrs-0.

[7] Wynia & Dunn, supra note 5, at 65.

[8] Julie A. Dooling, It's About the Patient: Engagement Through Personal Health Records and Patient Portals, 14 J. Health Care Compliance 33, 34 (2012); HealthIT.gov, supra note 6.

[9] Taya Irizarry et al., Patient Portals and Patient Engagement: A State of the Science Review, 17 J. Med. Internet Res. e148 (2015).

[10] Morgan J. Thompson et al., Work System Barriers to Patient, Provider, and Caregiver Use of Personal Health Records: A Systematic Review, 54 Applied Ergonomics 218, 219 (2016).

II. PHR BENEFITS

Studies in the United States and abroad show that patients are often enthusiastic about PHRs. PHRs hold significant promise for health care improvements and increased medical transparency.[11]

A. Greater Information Access and Better Health Outcomes

PHRs enhance medical transparency because they enable patients to access their data and help them feel more empowered in their relationships with health care providers. The HIPAA Privacy Rule has always mandated that patients have access to their health information, but it allows health care providers to take as long as thirty (or even sixty) days to respond to patient requests.[12] By contrast, PHRs furnish patients with real-time access to their data.

Rather than having to call medical offices for test results, patients can log onto their PHRs and easily view them. Those who cannot recall details from their office visit can look them up and find them in their record rather than remain confused or ignorant. Ideally, patients should also be able to transmit information to other clinicians or caregivers.[13]

All of these capabilities should increase patient satisfaction. They should also enable patients to obtain better care from their physicians and to be more active participants in their own care. Patients who can see their medication lists, test outcomes, and further appointments on their PHRs may find it easier to adhere to their treatment plans. More extensive information should also help patients formulate questions for their physicians so that they better understand their conditions and therapies. In addition, patients can refer to their PHRs when communicating with other providers from whom they seek second opinions or specialized care and thus provide them with more accurate information.[14]

B. Improved Communication

Secure messaging enables patients to communicate directly with their doctors without having to schedule an appointment or call the office receptionist.[15] While ordinary email can easily be sent or copied to the wrong person, secure messaging is

---

[11] Simon de Lusignan et al., Patients' Online Access to Their Electronic Health Records and Linked Online Services: A Systematic Interpretative Review, 4 BMJ Open e006021 (2014), http://bmjopen.bmj.com/content/4/9/e006021.full; Kim M. Nazi et al., Evaluating Patient Access to Electronic Health Records: Results from a Survey of Veterans, 51 Med. Care S52 (2013).

[12] 45 C.F.R. §164.524(b)(2) (2018).

[13] Miller et al., supra note 3.

[14] See id.

[15] Melissa Lester et al., Personal Health Records: Beneficial or Burdensome for Patients and Healthcare Providers?, 13 Perspect. Health Info. Mgmt. (2016), www.ncbi.nlm.nih.gov/pmc/articles/PMC4832132/pdf/phimoo13-0001h.pdf.

less vulnerable to privacy breaches.[16] Electronic communication can increase clinicians' accessibility and make patients feel that their doctors are responsive to them. Thus, online contact can enhance the clinician–patient relationship and improve patients' engagement, trust, and satisfaction.[17]

C. Enhanced Efficiency

Patient portals may save medical offices time by reducing the volume of phone calls and requests for in-person appointments. First, patients who can look up their test results or request medication renewals electronically will not need to call their doctors' offices for these reasons. Second, staff can often prioritize and respond to secure messages much more quickly than they can answer or return phone calls. Finally, doctors who receive a detailed narrative from a patient regarding a question may be able to respond electronically without having to dedicate an office visit to the matter.[18]

D. Increased Data Accuracy

Patients' medical records may become more complete and comprehensive with the help of PHRs. If patients add data about their diet, exercise, and medical monitoring activities (for example, blood pressure or blood sugar checks), physicians will be able to gain a deeper understanding of patients' health status.

PHRs may also enable patients to detect errors in their medical records and to request that they be corrected. Patients who scrutinize their PHR data may notice that their medication lists, medical histories, problem descriptions, or other data are incorrect. The HIPAA Privacy Rule empowers individuals to request that their health information be amended and requires covered entities to comply with such requests when the information is in fact inaccurate or incomplete.[19] Although currently patients rarely initiate requests for amendment,[20] they could contribute

---

[16] Patricia R. Recupero, E-mail and the Psychiatrist-Patient Relationship, 33 J. Am. Acad. Psychiatry L. 465, 468 (2005) (explaining that "[t]he chance of misdirection and interception on ... [a] secure network is substantially less than in the case of email accounts hosted by Internet service providers.").

[17] Yi Yvonne Zhou et al., Patient Access to an Electronic Health Record with Secure Messaging: Impact on Primary Care Utilization, 13 Am. J. Managed Care 418, 424 (2007) (concluding that patients using electronic messaging had 6.7 percent to 9.7 percent fewer outpatient primary care visits than others); Kim M. Nazi, The Personal Health Record Paradox: Health Care Professionals' Perspectives and the Information Ecology of Personal Health Record Systems in Organizational and Clinical Settings, 15 J. Med. Internet Res. e70 (2013); J. Herman Blake et al., The Patient-Surgeon Relationship in the Cyber Era: Communication and Information, 22 Thoracic Surgery Clinics 531, 532–33 (2012).

[18] Miller et al., supra note 3.

[19] 45 C.F.R. § 164.526(a) (2018).

[20] David A. Hanauer et al., Patient-Initiated Electronic Health Record Amendment Requests, 21 J. Am. Med. Inform. Assoc. 992, 992 (2014) (finding that "[a]mong all of the patients requesting a copy of their chart, only a very small percentage (approximately 0.2%) submitted an amendment request").

an important layer of data quality control if they more regularly did so. Patient portals could make it easier for patients to request corrections and for clinicians to process these requests.[21]

PHRs may help elucidate the truth in the context of litigation as well. If patients communicate with physicians through secure messaging, there will be a complete record of the conversations' contents.[22] By contrast, phone calls generally are not recorded, and controversies regarding them may entail significant uncertainty and "he said, she said" assertions. Secure messaging, therefore, may be very useful for purposes of discovery.[23]

III. PHR SHORTCOMINGS

PHRs have not been greeted with uniform enthusiasm. Ironically, PHRs' strengths can transform into vulnerabilities if handled inappropriately. The technology's detractors point to several potential disadvantages.

A. Disruption of the Physician–Patient Relationship

PHRs can adversely affect the physician–patient relationship and thus undermine transparency in several ways. First, patients who send secure messages to their doctors may expect immediate responses. Doctors who do not check their messages frequently or do not have time to answer all of them in a given day may find that their patients are frustrated and disappointed.[24]

Second, PHRs may induce patients to avoid scheduling appointments even when they would benefit from an in-person visit. Patients may prefer to have many of their health questions answered electronically without the hassle or expense of a doctor's appointment. Yet, in many cases, an old-fashioned examination would be a much more effective diagnostic or follow-up tool, and doctors who merely provide a brief answer in a message would not serve their patients well.[25]

Finally, data release policies pose a particularly significant challenge for physicians. Some medical practices believe that all health information belongs to the patient and should be released as soon as possible, even if it is bad news.[26] Indeed, a patient who can digest upsetting news on her own, receive emotional support from family and friends, research her condition, and devise appropriate questions before

---

[21] Dooling, supra note 8 (noting that "in some organizations, this process is being accomplished using portal technology").
[22] Miller et al., supra note 3.
[23] See Hoffman, supra note *, at 95–96 (discussing discovery).
[24] Miller et al., supra note 3.
[25] Id.
[26] Sarah A. Collins et al., Policies for Patient Access to Clinical Data via PHRs: Current State and Recommendations, 18 J. Am. Med. Informatics Assoc. Suppl. 1, i2, 25 (2011).

seeing her doctor might have a much more productive discussion during the office visit.

On the other hand, patients who learn of abnormal test results or serious diagnoses by logging into the computer at home rather than through a conversation with a clinician could be traumatized, misunderstand information, or feel angry or hopeless. Such patients might be too frightened to pursue appropriate medical care, become discouraged, fail to comply with their treatment protocols, and suffer medical setbacks.[27]

In fact, some individuals do not welcome pressure to become active members of their own medical team. Humorist Dave Barry typified this approach when he wrote, "I don't WANT to be an informed medical consumer. I liked it better when my only medical responsibility was to stick out my tongue."[28]

Consequently, some health care providers are more paternalistic and post test results selectively. However, if physicians decide to screen and withhold certain information from PHRs, patients who are eager to receive any and all information immediately may be resentful and lose trust in their doctors. In addition, patients who are unaware of physicians' data release practices may be misled by the absence of information. They may think that they are well because no bad news was posted, when in fact data was withheld because they are gravely ill.

Furthermore, if providers share candid and complete progress notes, including personal impressions, with patients, patients who are unhappy with their physicians' conclusions could become less cooperative or trusting of their doctors.[29] If patients become acutely aware that what they tell their doctor becomes part of their documentation, they may also become less open with their doctors. They may avoid disclosing embarrassing or unflattering information that they would not want recorded in their permanent medical charts.

Doctors' behavior may itself be influenced by the fact that patients can see their notes. They may keep their audience very much in mind in the process of documentation and compose more guarded, "watered-down" notes than they otherwise would.[30] The opposite may also be true, however, as doctors who know that patients will read their notes may be more thoughtful and responsible about what they write.

---

[27] Thompson et al., supra note 10, at 228 (stating that "[a]nother recurring theme was fear of accessing unwanted or frightening information.").

[28] Dave Barry, Good for What Ails You, Miami Herald, June 21, 1998, www.miamiherald.com/living/liv-columns-blogs/dave-barry/article2532166.html.

[29] John Halamka, et al., Early Experiences with Personal Health Records, 15 J. Am. Med. Informatics Ass'n 1, 3–5 (2008).

[30] Jan Walker et al., The Road Toward Fully Transparent Medical Records, 370 N. Eng. J. Med. 6, 6–8 (2014).

B. Increased Workload and Decreased Income for Physicians

PHRs can increase clinicians' workload and adversely affect their earnings. They may find that they spend a lot of time answering secure messages, especially if patients abuse the privilege and inundate their doctors with questions.[31] Because time spent on electronic communication is not reimbursed by insurers,[32] this activity may come at the cost of more lucrative pursuits, such as more patient appointments. In addition, patients may often resort to messaging their doctors in order to obtain free care rather than request office visits, and this tendency can further diminish physicians' earnings.[33]

It should be noted that to date there is little evidence that PHRs have added significantly to physicians' work obligations.[34] This may be attributable to the limited uptake of PHR technology thus far.[35] Yet, while physicians express concern about the eventual workload consequences of PHRs, their fears may be exaggerated.

C. Exacerbated Health Disparities

PHRs have the potential to be health equalizers by making more information available to all patients. In reality, however, they may exacerbate health disparities.

Patients who are not highly educated or skilled in computer use may not feel comfortable using patient portals.[36] Commentators have noted that in clinics with underserved patient populations, portal use is particularly low.[37] Likewise, people with disabilities and the elderly may be unable to take advantage of PHRs because of physical or mental limitations. If physicians rely on PHRs to communicate with patients, those who do not use them (often members of vulnerable populations) will be significantly disadvantaged.

D. Compromised Data Accuracy

Some PHRs enable patients to enter information such as home monitoring activities into the system themselves. However, patient-generated information may be

---

[31] Taylor Pressler Vydra et al., Diffusion and Use of Tethered Personal Health Records in Primary Care, 12 Perspect. Health Info. Mgmt. (2015), www.ncbi.nlm.nih.gov/pmc/articles/PMC4696089/pdf/phimoo12-0001c.pdf.
[32] Id.
[33] Miller et al., supra note 3.
[34] Pressler Vydra et al., supra note 31 (stating that "the effect of PHRs on physician workload is currently unestablished"); Lynn E. Keplinger et al., Patient Portal Implementation: Resident and Attending Physician Attitudes, 45 Fam. Med. 335, 335 (2013) (reporting that a small study at a single institution revealed that only 13 percent of respondents felt that their workload had increased).
[35] See supra notes 3–4 and accompanying text.
[36] Lester et al., supra note 15 (stating that "[l]imitations of health literacy and competency have been a paramount concern affecting the use of PHRs").
[37] Miller et al., supra note 3.

incomplete or inaccurate.[38] Patients may misunderstand instructions regarding data entry, measure values incorrectly, or have confusion or dementia that affects their ability to work with PHRs. Physicians who rely on self-entered information to make treatment decisions must keep these uncertainties in mind.

An additional problem is that contemporary EHR systems often are not interoperable.[39] This means that systems operated by different medical practices cannot communicate with each other or integrate each other's records. Without interoperability, patients' records are fragmented and pieces of them are operated upon and stored by a number of different facilities.[40] Such PHRs will not provide patients with a comprehensive view of their health and may be confusing, incomplete, and even inconsistent.

E. Diminished Data Security

PHRs can render patient data less secure if patients are not security conscious. Patients who too freely reveal their passwords or do not store them in a safe place may render their medical information accessible to people with whom they would prefer not to share it.

In addition, patient portals are an entryway to EHR systems. If they are hacked, all the records in the providers' system may be vulnerable to disclosure.[41] It should be noted that nontethered PHRs may be particularly vulnerable to attack if they are not subject to the security mandates of the HIPAA Security Rule. HIPAA governs only health care providers, health insurers, health care clearinghouses, and their business associates.[42] PHRs operated by commercial entities that do not fall into any of these categories may have lax security measures.[43]

F. Added Liability Concerns

Health care providers have expressed anxiety that PHR use can lead to legal liability.[44] Indeed, those who are not careful in implementing PHRs may face legal claims.

[38] Norm Archer et al., Personal Health Records: a Scoping Review, 18 J. Am. Med. Inform. Assoc. 515, 516 (2011).
[39] Hoffman, supra note *, at 54–55 (discussing interoperability).
[40] Lester et al., supra note 15 (stating that "[i]nteroperability is a substantial issue that needs to be addressed for seamless use of PHRs among providers and patients").
[41] David Daglish & Norm Archer, Electronic Personal Health Record Systems: A Brief Review of Privacy, Security, and Architectural Issues, in Proceedings of the 2009 World Congress on Privacy, Security, Trust, and the Management of E-Business, 110–20 (2009); Kyungsook Kim & Eun-shim Nahm, Benefits of and Barriers to the Use of Personal Health Records (PHR) for Health Management among Adults, 16 Online J. Nurs. Informatics 16 (2012), http://ojni.org/issues/?p=1995; Hoffman, supra note *, at 56–79 (discussing data security and the HIPAA Security Rule).
[42] 45 C.F.R. §§ 160.102-160.103 (2018); 42 U.S.C. §17934 (2010).
[43] Wynia & Dunn, supra note 5, at 70.
[44] Lester et al., supra note 15, at 12; Jana Studeny & Alberto Coustasse, Personal Health Records: Is Rapid Adoption Hindering Interoperability?, 11 Persps. in Health Info. Mgmt (2014), http://perspectives.ahima.org/personal-health-records-is-rapid-adoption-hindering-interoperability/.

Online Communication. Mishandling secure messaging can lead to patient harm and ultimately to litigation.[45] A patient, for example, might send a message to her doctor stating that she is experiencing difficulty breathing. If the physician does not quickly respond, the patient might incorrectly assume that the doctor does not think her condition is potentially serious and conclude that she does not need urgent medical attention. If the patient is in fact having a medical emergency, her reliance on electronic communication and unrealistic belief that her doctor is checking it constantly might have catastrophic consequences. Clinicians who do not educate patients about proper and improper secure messaging use, whose patients do not comply with such instructions, or who do not have qualified staff members read messages frequently, might thus face malpractice claims.[46]

Doctors who enable patients to use secure messaging but are unresponsive to electronic communication may be more likely to be sued than doctors who do not offer this feature at all. Multiple studies have shown that patients most often decide to sue when they are displeased with the quality of the physician–patient relationship, including their communication experiences.[47]

No reported medical malpractice case arising from secure messaging (or regular email) could be found as of 2016. However, doctors have been sued for failure to respond appropriately to phone calls.[48] It is only a matter of time before similar claims involving electronic communication arise.

Other Bases for Malpractice Claims. Several other PHR pitfalls may generate liability concerns. Individuals who misinterpret their PHR data or become traumatized by posted test results may not seek appropriate care or comply with their treatment plans.[49] Poor outcomes that result from such behavior may lead to malpractice claims that could have been avoided with more personal contact between clinicians and patients. Even if these claims ultimately prove unjustified, they can be distressing and costly for defendants.

Health care providers who rely on patient-entered data (for example, blood pressure or blood sugar levels) for purposes of treatment decisions may make mistakes when the data are inaccurate. Courts may not be receptive to the argument

---

[45] Madhavi R. Patt et al., Doctors Who Are Using E-mail With Their Patients: A Qualitative Exploration, 5 J. Med. Internet Res. e9 (2003) (stating that doctors are concerned about emails reaching them in a timely fashion); Paul Rosen & C. Kent Kwoh, Patient–Physician E-mail: An Opportunity to Transform Pediatric Health Care Delivery, 120 Pediatrics 701, 705 (2007) (stating that email communication might produce anxiety about increased liability).

[46] Daniel Z. Sands, Help for Physicians Contemplating Use of E-mail with Patients, 11 J. Am. Med. Informatics Ass'n 268, 268 (2004).

[47] Beth Huntington & Nettie Kuhn, Communication Gaffes: A Root Cause of Malpractice Claims, 16 Baylor U. Med. Ctr. Proc. 157, 157–60 (2003).

[48] *Kaznowski v. Biesen-Bradley*, No. C063872, 2012 WL 5984491 (Cal. Ct. App. Nov. 30, 2012); *Lemlek v. Israel*, 161 A.D.2d 299, 301 (1990), modified, 577 N.E.2d 1041 (1991).

[49] See supra notes 26–29 and accompanying text.

that resulting harm is the patient's fault and may expect doctors to verify PHR entries.[50]

Similarly, if secure messaging does substantially increase physicians' workloads, doctors may be more rushed and fatigued during their workdays. This too could contribute to medical errors that harm patients.

Data Security. PHRs are a user interface that can be hacked, and therefore, they are another avenue of attack for wrongdoers. Health care providers whose EHR systems' security is compromised through PHRs may face HIPAA enforcement actions and privacy-related tort claims.

The HIPAA Privacy Rule establishes breach notification requirements along with civil and criminal penalties for data breaches.[51] Although the HIPAA Privacy Rule does not feature a private right of action, plaintiffs who believe they suffered privacy harms may turn to state statutory and common law tort theories.[52]

IV. RECOMMENDATIONS

There is no easy answer to the question of how PHRs can best be used. Formulating a comprehensive blueprint for PHR implementation is well beyond the scope of this chapter. The following are a few suggestions for handling some of the key PHR challenges.

A. Secure Messaging Policies

The American Medical Association has issued guidance concerning physicians' use of electronic communication.[53] It advises in relevant part:

a) Uphold professional standards of confidentiality and protection of privacy, security, and integrity of patient information.
b) Notify the patient of the inherent limitations of electronic communication, including possible breach of privacy or confidentiality, difficulty in validating the identity of the parties, and possible delays in response. Such disclaimers do not absolve physicians of responsibility to protect the patient's interests. Patients should have the opportunity to accept or decline electronic communication before privileged information is transmitted. The patient's decision to accept or decline email communication containing privileged information should be documented in the medical record.

---

[50] Tang et al., supra note 5, at 125 (stating that "courts might apply negligence standards in cases where practitioners rely on inaccurate patient-entered PHR information to make suboptimal decisions about care").
[51] 45 C.F.R. §§ 164.400-.414 (2018); 42 U.S.C. §§ 1320d-5 & 1320d-6 (2010).
[52] Hoffman, supra note *, at 75–78, 93–95.
[53] Am. Medical Ass'n, Code of Medical Ethics § 2.3.1, (last accessed January 17, 2017), www.ama-assn.org/sites/default/files/media-browser/code-of-medical-ethics-chapter-2.pdf.

c) Advise the patient of the limitations of these channels when a patient initiates electronic communication.
d) Obtain the patient's consent to continue electronic communication when a patient initiates electronic communication.
e) Present medical information in a manner that meets professional standards.

The British Medical Protection Society adds the following advice:

- Liaise with your IT provider to ensure that appropriate safeguards are in place and information on the clinical system remains secure.
- Have an automated response indicating that the email has been received, when the patient should expect to receive a reply and a recommendation that they should contact the practice directly if the matter is urgent.
- Monitor email enquiries at regular intervals and ensure that they are promptly brought to the attention of the relevant person.
- [Do not] [f]orget that email exchanges are an important part of a patient's medical records.
- [Do not] [f]orget that many of the subtleties of communication, including nonverbal cues, are lost when communicating by email.[54]

All of these recommendations are sound, and clinicians would be wise to adopt them.

B. Data Release Policies

Health care providers must develop thoughtful data release policies for their PHRs and clearly explain them to patients so that patients have realistic and well-informed expectations about data access.[55] One option is to exclude entirely certain types of information, such as test results indicating the presence of serious illness, from PHRs. Another option is for physicians to screen and withhold potentially distressing data for a time in order to communicate with patients about it before it is posted. A third alternative is to release all information as soon as it becomes available and assume that patients value transparency above all.[56] Thus far, no approach has been empirically shown to be superior to others.

Because patients have different preferences, a possibility that is well worth considering is to allow patients to tailor their own access to information. Thus, patients would be able to indicate in advance which types of information they would like to see and whether they would want it released immediately or only after speaking with

---

[54] Med. Prot. Soc'y, Communicating with Patients by Fax and Email (2014), www.medicalprotection.org/docs/default-source/pdfs/factsheet-pdfs/england-factsheet-pdfs/communicating-by-fax-and-email.pdf?sfvrsn=7.

[55] Michael A. Bruno et al., The "Open Letter": Radiologists' Reports in the Era of Patient Web Portals, 11 J. Am. College Radiology 863, 863 (2014).

[56] Collins et al., supra note 26, at 15.

their clinicians.[57] Meaningful use regulations[58] could require that providers ask patients for their preferences. Likewise, EHR system certification regulations[59] could require that PHR technology facilitate this type of flexibility, in part by enabling patients to indicate their access choices and alerting clinicians to them each time they post data.

C. Error Correction Policies

Health care providers should encourage patients to use PHRs as a means to identify errors in their medical records and request corrections. Patients should be able to ask for changes easily through secure messaging or a separate PHR feature, and providers must be obligated to review and respond to these requests. When providers determine that a request for amendment is unjustified (for example, because the original information is actually correct), they are permitted by law to deny it.[60]

Researchers have found very high error rates in EHRs because it is easy to mistype information, check or select wrong menu items, copy and paste data that is not updated, and make a variety of other mistakes.[61] Patients are often in the best position to detect such errors and can play a key role in safeguarding the integrity of their medical records.

D. Patient Education Initiatives

Patients who are elderly, disabled, economically disadvantaged, or simply disinterested in technology may have poor computer literacy and find it very difficult to use and navigate PHRs.[62] Consequently, providers should offer PHR tutorials through videos or classes that help patients learn to use the technology.[63] In addition, such tutorials could emphasize the importance of PHR security and of double-checking data accuracy for patients who will enter their own health information. They could also furnish guidance concerning appropriate use of secure messaging and requests for error corrections. Though such tutorials will not be effective for all individuals, they would constitute an important step toward increasing patients' comfort and facility with PHR technology.

[57] Thompson et al., supra note 10, at 229 (noting that "a minimum waiting period under certain circumstances may be advisable").
[58] See supra note 2 and accompanying text.
[59] 45 CFR § 170.314 (2018).
[60] 45 C.F.R. § 164.526(a)(2) (2018).
[61] Hoffman, supra note *, at 23–27.
[62] Lester et al., supra note 15 (stating that "[l]imitations of health literacy and competency have been a paramount concern affecting the use of PHRs").
[63] Id.; Thompson et al., supra note 10, at 229.

V. CONCLUSION

Physicians' PHR policies and data disclosure practices can have wide-ranging impacts on the physician–patient relationship. PHRs can contribute significantly to medical transparency, health record integrity, and patient satisfaction, but they can also do the opposite. For some patients, PHRs will be abstruse and frustrating or even erode their confidence in their doctors. PHRs are a key communication tool for clinicians, and their implementation must be carefully thought out. PHRs raise significant legal, ethical, and policy questions that have yet to be fully explored and addressed. These challenges deserve careful consideration from the health care community, information technology professionals, and health policy authorities.

18

Nontransparency in Electronic Health Record Systems

Jim Hawkins, Barbara J. Evans, and Harlan M. Krumholz

In response to incentives created by the Health Information Technology for Economic and Clinical Health (HITECH) Act,[1] electronic health record (EHR) systems have become a central part of the medical information ecosystem. Because they are relatively new, the business and ethical norms that surround EHR systems are still evolving. What is clear is that EHR systems lack transparency, or engage in information blocking, in many key areas because the contracts that govern the relationships between health care providers, their business associates, and EHR vendors contain provisions that block or obscure important information.

Transparency in the context of EHR systems encompasses several distinct concepts. These include the business concept of transparency as a "lack of hidden agendas"[2] that would hide facts to advance the interests of the nondiscloser. They also more broadly encompass the notion that free and open exchange of information is instrumental to other desirable goods such as collaborative problem-solving, good system governance, patient safety, or respect for the right of persons to access their own information.[3] Information blocking takes "many forms, from express policies that prohibit sharing information to more subtle business, technical, or organizational practices that make doing so more costly or difficult" and can prevent authorized persons – including patients – from accessing, exchanging, and using the information these systems hold.[4]

The contracts governing EHR systems cultivate nontransparency expressly (for example, gag clauses) and indirectly (for example, allocating tort liability in ways that disable the revealing effects of pretrial discovery). Health systems may violate patients' rights by blocking their abilities to view, download, and transmit key portions of their records, images, and bills – even as the functionality resides within

---

[1] See Pub. L. 111-5, Div. A, Title XIII, Div. B, Title IV, 123 Stat. 226, 467 (Feb. 17, 2009).
[2] For the definition of "transparency," see Transparency, Business Dictionary, www.businessdictionary.com/definition/transparency.html (last visited Aug. 22, 2017).
[3] See id.
[4] Office of the National Coordinator of Health Information Technology, Report on Health Information Blocking 10 (4/2015).

the EHR systems. This chapter navigates the complexity of transparency in the EHR context by organizing its discussion into sections discussing two important types of harm that may flow from a lack of transparency in EHR systems: harms to patient safety and harms to data privacy. After introducing each problem, the discussion turns to the main topic: what are the legal pathways for improving the transparency of EHR systems?

HARMS TO PATIENT SAFETY

The substantive provisions in EHR vendor contracts prevent information relevant to patient safety from being disclosed to or discussed with health care providers who are considering purchasing EHR systems. Because of this opacity, problems with these systems that compromise patient safety are not corrected by the market, leaving patients at risk.

Safety issues related to EHR dominate concerns about information technology among health care providers. There is an obvious potential for patient injuries if an EHR system malfunctions or fails to deliver timely, accurate information at the point of care when care providers need it.[5] Sharona Hoffman recently described a case in which a health care provider gave an infant 60 times the appropriate amount of sodium because a technician mistyped information into an EHR.[6] In one study, researchers analyzed 100 investigations into information technology patient safety issues from Veterans Affairs facilities. They found that three-quarters related to unsafe technology, and one-quarter related to unsafe EHR use.[7]

Some of the substantive provisions that impede transparency work *directly* to stop health care providers from sharing concerns such as gag clauses and confidentiality and nondisclosure clauses. Others, however, work *indirectly* to undermine transparency by stopping information flow through the litigation process, including clauses providing self-help remedies, arbitration, and limitations on liability.

Concerning direct barriers to transparency, some EHR vendor contracts require that health care providers keep some information about the EHR system confidential.[8] The definition of confidential information can be very expansive, as demonstrated by the following definition in an EHR vendor contract:

---

[5] See Westat, UHC, ECRI Institute. Health Information Technology Adverse Event Reporting: An Analysis of Two Databases (11/24/2015).
[6] See Sharona Hoffman, Electronic Health Records and Medical Big Data 80 (2016).
[7] See Derek W. Meeks et al., An Analysis of Electronic Health Record-related Patient Safety Concerns, 21 J. Am. Med. Inform. Assoc. 1053 (2014)
[8] See Office of the National Coordinator of Health Information Technology, EHR Contracts Untangled 12 (9/2016); see also Office of the National Coordinator of Health Information Technology, Report on Health Information Blocking: Report to Congress 31–32 (April 2015); Darius Tahir, Doctors Barred from Discussing Safety Glitches in US-funded Software, Politico (9/11/15), www.politico.com/story/2015/09/doctors-barred-from-discussing-safety-glitches-in-us-funded-software-213553.

"Confidential Information", means any information concerning our business and includes all data, materials, products, technology, computer programs, specifications, manuals, business plans, software, trade secrets, workflows, customers, source code, data models, marketing plans, methods of operation, financial information, and other information disclosed or submitted, orally or in writing, or through the licensed programs and services or by any other media from one party to another pursuant to this Agreement or any other information that is treated or designated by us as confidential or proprietary, or would reasonably be viewed as confidential or as having value to our competitors.[9]

In a study of eleven contracts between major EHR vendors and health care providers, a Politico reporter found that ten had gag clauses.[10] The prevalence of these clauses is troubling because if a health care provider discovers a problem with an EHR system that affects patient safety, gag clauses and confidentiality clauses prevent disclosure of this information to other potential buyers, leaving the safety issue unchecked.

Market-based solutions to the problem of gag clauses are unlikely to work. Government sources report that industry "best practices" discourage gag clauses,[11] and the government urges clinics to object to gag clauses in their EHR vendor contracts.[12] These statements both suggest that health care providers could play a role in eliminating gag clauses. The problem, however, with this market-based solution is that individual clinics would likely have to pay the EHR vendor to eliminate the contract term because under modern contract theory, each contract term has a corresponding price.[13] Clinics objecting to gag clauses may internalize the cost of eliminating the gag clause through paying a higher price. Yet, the clinics would fully externalize the benefits of contracts without gag clauses because the clinics do not benefit from being able to disclose unsafe features of the EHR system – other prospective buyers who learn more about the product through health care providers' candid reviews benefit from having better information before entering an EHR transaction. Thus, economically, it makes little sense for individual health care providers to object to gag clauses, suggesting this market-based solution is fanciful. Also, if all vendors have gag clause requirements then it is hard to push the market.

Another potential market-based solution is for health care practices that discover defects that could affect patient safety to abandon their EHR vendor in favor of a better system. Economically, however, this choice is often infeasible because the

---

[9] EHR Vendor Contract 1 (on file with authors). In another EHR vendor contract, the agreement defines confidential information as "information or materials about the other Party, its business activities and operations, its technical information and trade secrets, inclusive of the [EHR Vendor] Template." EHR Vendor Contract 2 (on file with authors).
[10] See Tahir, supra note 8.
[11] See EHR Untangled, supra note 8, at 12.
[12] See id. at 13.
[13] See Michael I. Meyerson, The Efficient Consumer Form Contract: Law and Economics Meets the Real World, 24 Ga. L. Rev. 583, 589–90 (1990).

switching costs in this market are substantial.[14] If a clinic selects a new EHR vendor, that new vendor's software may not be interoperable with the old vendor's software,[15] and the clinic with incur all of the start-up costs another time.[16] Even more directly, vendor contracts discourage switching. Some contracts do not even have a plan for winding up service,[17] and others contain liquidated damages clauses that impose fees for switching to competitors' products.[18] Thus, regulators cannot rely on clinics to vote with their feet to fix safety issues in this market.

In contrast to gag clauses, some contract provisions affect patient safety by limiting transparency indirectly. The primary indirect mechanisms for limiting transparency are clauses that discourage litigation or that shroud information learned during litigation. For instance, a variety of clauses in vendor contracts discourage health care providers who have experienced patient safety issues from suing the vendor because the vendor limits its liability for injuries caused by the EHR system.[19] If health care providers have no ability to obtain money from vendors or if the damages are limited, the providers will not sue. As one report notes, "[l]imitations of liability are a common business practice to limit the financial risk of the EHR technology developer for claims that might arise from problems with the EHR system. EHR technology developers often suggest that, without limitations of liability, prices would increase."[20] Some specific ways vendors limit their liability is by stating that financial credits are the sole and exclusive remedy for downtime[21] or by putting limits on the amount of damages the vendor has to pay for lost data,[22] even if that downtime or lost data cause patients harm. One EHR vendor's clause provides an example:

> In no event shall either party be liable for any indirect, incidental, special or consequential damages, or damages for loss of profits, revenue, data or use, incurred by either party or any third party, whether in an action in contract or tort, even if the other party has been advised of the possibility of such damages. [The EHR Vendor's] liability for damages hereunder shall in no event exceed the amount of fees paid by Client under the Agreement for the most recent three (3) month period. The provisions of the Agreement allocate the risks between [the EHR Vendor] and Client. The parties agree that [the EHR Vendor's] pricing and other terms and

[14] See EHR Untangled, supra note 8, at 6, 29, 50; Report on Health Information Blocking, supra note 8, at 15, 17.
[15] See Hoffman, supra note 6, at 36.
[16] See id. at 40.
[17] See Westat, EHR Contracts: Key Contract Terms for Users to Understand 19 (June 25, 2013) ("Despite the potential need to transition between EHR technologies, some standard EHR technology developer contracts fail to provide for termination and wind down services.").
[18] See Report on Health Information Blocking, supra note 8, at 17–18.
[19] See EHR Untangled, supra note 8, at 37.
[20] Key Contract Terms, supra note 17, at 12.
[21] See EHR Untangled, supra note 8, at 17.
[22] See id. at 42.

conditions of the Agreement reflect the allocation of risk and the limitation of liability specified herein.[23]

Another powerful piece of leverage vendors have over health care providers who may want to sue is that the vendor can prevent the health care provider from using the EHR system. Vendor contracts often do not say that the vendor will continue service during a dispute,[24] leaving the health care provider suing the vendor without access to the EHRs. Moreover, vendors can use self-help remedies if they determine the health care provider has breached its contract by suing the vendor. EHR vendors may have electronic means of disabling EHR software in case of a dispute.[25] Modern contract law disfavors such self-help remedies,[26] but these remedies provide substantial leverage for the party that can use them. In this case, that leverage can prevent lawsuits that could otherwise produce transparency about patient safety concerns.[27]

Even if a health care provider is willing to sue, arbitration clauses in EHR vendor contracts can prevent any information from becoming public. EHR vendor contracts frequently include alternative dispute resolution procedures.[28] Arbitration is unlike the standard trial process in America because the discovery is limited, and the proceedings are confidential.[29] Thus, even in the unlikely event of legal action, there is the risk that no information about patient safety concerns will emerge.

The upshot of these limits on liability and powerful self-help remedies is that few lawsuits have been filed against EHR vendors.[30] Without complaints being interrogated through the litigation process, the EHR systems remain opaque.

[23] EHR Vendor Contract 3 (on file with authors).
[24] See Key Contract Terms, supra note 17, at 17 ("Therefore, you should understand whether the contract: Requires the EHR technology developer to continue to perform even if it has not been fully paid (such as because of a dispute over quality or the amount due) or if other disputes have arisen so there is no interruption in access or service that could reduce care to patients. Allows you to withhold payment of disputed amounts until the dispute is resolved (for example, disputes about how a rate schedule was applied); and Permits you to withhold all or a portion of payments for poor service. An EHR technology developer form contract will often not give you the rights described above so they would need to be negotiated.").
[25] See EHR Untangled, supra note 8, at 1, 25, 32–33. For a general description of electronic self-help, see Robert A. Hillman & Maureen A. O'Rourke, Principles of the Law of Software Contracts: Some Highlights, 84 Tul. L. Rev. 1519 (2010). For an example of a self-help remedy in an EHR vendor contract, see EHR Vendor Contract 1 ("We may suspend access to the Programs or the Services by you or any member of your Workforce immediately pending your cure of any breach of this Agreement, or in the event we determine in our sole discretion that access to or use of the Programs or Services by you or the member of your Workforce may jeopardize the Programs or Services or the confidentiality, privacy, security, integrity or availability of information ... ") (emphasis added).
[26] See Richard R.W. Brooks & Alexander Stremitzer, Remedies on and Off Contract, 120 Yale L.J. 690, 726 (2011).
[27] See Report on Health Information Blocking, supra note 8, at 35–36.
[28] See e.g. EHR Vendor Contract 1.
[29] See Richard M. Alderman, Pre-Dispute Mandatory Arbitration in Consumer Contracts: A Call for Reform, 38 Hous. L. Rev. 1237, 1250 (2001).
[30] See Hoffman, supra note 6, at 83, 92.

SOLUTIONS

Various regulatory solutions could enhance reporting of EHR-related adverse events. EHR contracts are wrongly framed as matters of private contract that exclusively affect the interests of an EHR vendor and purchaser. The Supreme Court noted long ago that private property

> becomes clothed with a public interest when it is used in a manner to make it of public consequence, and affect the public at large. When, therefore, one devotes his property to a use in which the public has an interest, he, in effect, grants the public an interest in that use, and must submit to be controlled by the public for the common good.[31]

This idea that private property can be "affected with a public interest" in truth dates back much further, to *Munn v. Illinois*[32] in 1877 and to the earlier English cases it drew upon. There is a "boundary between that which is private, and that in which the public has an interest."[33] What vast lapse in policymaking insight led HHS to conceive EHR contracts as purely private affairs? Vendors and purchasers can be left to slice and dice their interests with no thought to the public – vulnerable patients – whose data can be held hostage, frozen, made unavailable, or erased as needed to gain strategic advantage in disputes between vendors and purchasers. Both the vendors and purchasers can be oblivious to the lives they unwittingly (or indifferently) hold in the balance. Regulation of these contracts, without question, is in order.

The question is which regulator is best positioned to protect patients whose data are caught up in EHR contract disputes? EHR systems are in the nature of infrastructure, and the United States has a long history of regulating privately held infrastructure utilities in ways that force service providers to be mindful of their service obligations to the public. Examples are the Interstate Commerce Act of 1887,[34] subsequently mirrored in the interstate shipping,[35] stockyard,[36] telephone,[37] telegraph,[38]

---

[31] *Charles Wolff Packing Co. v. Court of Indus. Relations*, 262.U.S. 522, 540 (Taft, J.) (quoting *Munn v. People of State of Illinois*, 94 U.S. 113, 126 (1876).
[32] *Munn v. Illinois*, 94 U.S at 126.
[33] Letter from Chief Justice Waite to James Sheldon (Mar. 30, 1877), quoted in G. Edward White, Historicizing Judicial Scrutiny, 57 S.C. L. Rev. 1, 43–44 (2005).
[34] See Interstate Commerce Act, ch. 104, 24 Stat. 379 (1887) (codified as amended in scattered sections of 49 U.S.C. app.).
[35] See Shipping Act of 1916, ch. 451, 39 Stat. 728, 733–35 (1916) (codified as amended at scattered sections of 46 U.S.C. app.).
[36] See Packers and Stockyards Act of 1921, ch. 64, 42 Stat. 159 (codified as amended at 7 U.S.C. §§ 181–229b (2006)).
[37] See Communications Act of 1934, ch. 652, 48 Stat. 1064 (codified as amended at 47 U.S.C.A. §§ 151–614 (West 2001 & Supp. 2008)).
[38] See id.

trucking,[39] electricity,[40] natural gas,[41] and aviation[42] industries.[43] Common situations where governmental regulatory intervention is required are: (1) when barriers – for example, economic or legal – are blocking private-sector development of the needed infrastructure (which is not the case here), or (2) when unregulated private infrastructure operation poses problems, such as abuse of vulnerable persons, that are not adequately addressed by general law[44] (very much the case here). Yet the health care sector flees from the suggestion that health care displays public utility characteristics, leaving Food and Drug Administration (FDA), a medical-product safety regulator, as perhaps the public's last, best hope. Unfortunately, the 21st Century Cures Act of 2016 expressly stripped the FDA of jurisdiction to regulate various categories of medical software, including EHR software that merely stores data without crossing the line into interpreting or analyzing the data for the purpose of diagnosing and treating disease.[45] This left the FDA with only limited jurisdiction to impose adverse-event reporting[46] and other transparency-enhancing measures as part of its safety regulation of medical software.

HARMS TO DATA PRIVACY

Nontransparency in the context of EHRs also threatens patient data privacy. EHRs, by their very nature, facilitate new and more extensive forms of data sharing that patients may not have authorized, may not approve of, and may never know occurred. Two common vehicles for this nontransparent sharing are (1) business associate agreements (BAAs) between health care providers and business associates and (2) EHR vendor contracts.

HIPAA governs covered entities, which includes "(1) A health plan; (2) A health care clearinghouse; [and] (3) A health care provider who transmits any health information in electronic form in connection with a transaction covered by [HIPAA]."[47] A business associate is an organization or person that receives protected

---

[39] See Motor Carrier Act of 1935, ch. 498, 49 Stat. 543 (codified as amended in scattered sections of 49 U.S.C.).

[40] See Public Utility Act of 1935, ch. 687, 49 Stat. 838 (codified as amended at scattered sections of 16 U.S.C.).

[41] See Natural Gas Act of 1938, ch. 556, 52 Stat. 821 (codified as amended at 15 U.S.C. §§ 717–717w (2006)).

[42] See Civil Aeronautics Act of 1938, ch. 601, 52 Stat. 973 (codified as amended and before repeal at scattered sections of 49 U.S.C.).

[43] See Joseph D. Kearney & Thomas W. Merrill, The Great Transformation of Regulated Industries Law, 98 Colum. L. Rev. 1323, 1333–34 (1998).

[44] See Charles F. Phillips, Jr., The Regulation of Public Utilities 172–73 (3d ed. 1993).

[45] See 21st Century Cures Act, Pub. L No. 114–255, § 3060(a), 130 Stat. 1033 (2016) (amending § 520 of the Food, Drug, and Cosmetic Act (21 U.S.C. § 360j) to exclude several categories of medical software from the Act's definition of "medical device" at (21 U.S.C. § 321(h)).

[46] Medical Device Reporting, United States Department of Health and Human Services, at www.fda.gov/medicaldevices/safety/reportaproblem/default.htm (last visited Aug. 22, 2017).

[47] 45 C.F.R. § 160.103.

health information from a covered entity in order to perform services for the covered entity, such as providing legal services, claims administration, data analysis, utilization review, quality improvement and patient-safety studies, or even a EHR services.[48] Covered entities include health plans, health care clearinghouses, and health care providers who conduct certain financial and administrative transactions electronically. Business associates can only use or disclose protected health information in accordance with their BAA or as required by law.[49] The Privacy Rule sets certain required parameters, or "implementation specifications," for BAAs.[50] These specifications give covered entities a great deal of discretion to establish – via law of contract – the ground rules that govern business associates' use of patients' sensitive health information.[51]

One area of concern is the sharing and use of de-identified data, which is facilitated by nontransparent relationships between health care providers and EHR vendors. De-identification involves "the removal, modification, or obfuscation of personal information from data that are collected, used, archived, and shared, with the goal of preventing or limiting informational risks to individuals, protected groups, and establishments."[52] The Privacy Rule provides two methods by which data can be deemed "de-identified"[53] although it is widely understood that neither method precludes the possibility that data may subsequently be reidentified.[54] Once data have been de-identified using one of the two allowed methods, the Privacy Rule no longer considers the data to be protected health information.[55] De-identified data are therefore outside the Privacy Rule's protections and can be used and disclosed without patients' authorization or knowledge.[56]

Business associates and EHR vendors may come into possession of de-identified data in two ways: (1) by receiving de-identified data from health care providers in the course of performing work under a contract (such as a contract that engages a business associate to conduct quality improvement studies for a health care provider) or (2) by receiving data in identifiable form to perform work for the health care provider and then de-identifying the data themselves. The contracts that business associates and vendors sign with health care providers often allow them

[48] Id.
[49] 45 C.F.R. § 164.502(a)(3).
[50] 45 C.F.R. § 164.504(e)(2).
[51] Id.
[52] Simson L. Garfinkel, De-identifying Government Datasets, National Institute of Standards and Technology 800–188 at 3 (Dec. 2016), https://csrc.nist.gov/csrc/media/publications/sp/800-188/draft/documents/sp800_188_draft2.pdf.
[53] See 45 C.F.R. §§ 164.514(b)(1), (2).
[54] See National Committee on Vital and Health Statistics, Letter to the Honorable Thomas E. Price, Secretary Department of Health and Human Services at 3 (Feb. 23, 2017).
[55] See 45 C.F.R. § 160.103 [defining "health information," "individually identifiable health information," and "protected health information"].
[56] See 45 C.F.R. § 164.502 [setting general rules for use and disclosure that extend the Privacy Rule's protections to protected health information].

to use de-identified data for their own, secondary purposes, including various commercial ones. Such contracts create a potential for harm to patients because other people may be able to reidentify the de-identified data, directly undermining patient privacy, and because patients lose autonomy over the use and economic value of their de-identified data.

Health care providers frequently are entering contracts that allow business associates and EHR vendors to exploit de-identified data. The Department of Health and Human Services (HHS) has a standard form BAA that health care providers and business associates can use.[57] In this contract template, HHS anticipates that BAAs will allow BAs to de-identify data and use it. The annotated sample contract explains:

> In addition to other permissible purposes, the parties should specify whether the business associate is authorized to use protected health information to de-identify the information in accordance with 45 CFR 164.514(a)-(c). The parties also may wish to specify the manner in which the business associate will de-identify the information and the permitted uses and disclosures by the business associate of the de-identified information.[58]

Similarly, other contracts we found contained a clause explicitly providing business associates with the right to use de-identified data: "Notwithstanding the provisions of this Agreement, Business Associate and its subcontractors may disclose nonpersonally identifiable information provided that the disclosed information does not include a key or other mechanism that would enable the information to be identified."[59] While this provision does not use the term de-identified data, it is clear that is what the clause is discussing because it forbids BAs from providing a key that could reidentify the data.

In addition to BAs, health care providers frequently give this same right in EHR contracts to the EHR vendors. According to industry lawyers, almost all EHR vendor contracts contain clauses allowing the EHR vendor to de-identify and use the data.[60] As an example, one EHR vendor includes the following clause in its vendor contracts: "[Vendor] maintains the right to de-identify personal information placed on its Internet site, and to use, disclose, sell and otherwise commercialize de-identified information without restriction."[61] Another EHR vendor's contract states:

---

[57] Business Associate Contracts, United States Department of Health and Human Services, at www.hhs.gov/hipaa/for-professionals/covered-entities/sample-business-associate-agreement-provisions/index.html (last visited Aug. 22, 2017).
[58] Id.
[59] See BBA Agreement 1 on file with authors.
[60] See Ken Terry, Patient Records: The Struggle for Ownership, Medical Economics, Dec. 10, 2015, at http://medicaleconomics.modernmedicine.com/medical-economics/news/patient-records-struggle-ownership?page=0%2C3.
[61] Tame Your Practice, The Blog, at https://tameyourpractice.com/blog/does-your-ehr-vendor-sell-your-patients-data (last visited Aug. 22, 2017).

Provided that [the EHR Vendor] implements appropriate de-identification criteria in accordance with the Standards for Privacy of Individually Identifiable Health Information set forth in 45 C.F.R. §164.514(b), Client acknowledges and agrees that de-identified information is not Protected Health Information as defined in the applicable regulations and that [the EHR Vendor] may use such de-identified information for any lawful purpose.[62]

The normal safeguard for patient privacy is the Privacy Rule, but in the case of de-identified data, the Privacy Rule does nothing to stop business associates or EHR vendors from sharing patients' information without their authorizations or knowledge. As noted earlier, HIPAA's concept of protected health information excludes de-identified data: "Health information that does not identify an individual and with respect to which there is no reasonable basis to believe that the information can be used to identify an individual is not individually identifiable health information."[63] Thus, the Privacy Rule's protections, such as a patient's right to receive an accounting for data disclosures,[64] do not apply to disclosures of de-identified data.

Disclosure of de-identified data by business associates and EHR vendors creates a risk of harm to patients because other parties may be able to use the data to reidentify patients. Under HIPAA, to de-identify data, a party can either obtain an expert determination that the risk of reidentification is very small or it can take out all the information specified in the safe harbor section of the statute.[65] As the National Committee on Vital and Health Statistics recently pointed out, however, "[t]hese methods do not necessarily protect against future uses of data that may result in re-identifying or inferring the identity of individuals, protected groups, or establishments."[66] On the first approach, there are no minimum qualifications for an "expert" and no definition of what risks are "very small."[67] Indeed, "[c]urrently there are no performance standards, certification, or third-party testing programs available for de-identification software."[68] Another glaring problem with the safe harbor is that it is a one-size-fits-all approach.[69] In the technical world of data de-identification, there are numerous approaches that apply in different contexts.[70] For instance, records that contain only laboratory results may require different de-identification strategies than records that contain demographic data or patient narratives, but HIPAA's safe harbor is unvarying. As big data sets become more

---

[62] EHR Vendor Contract 2.
[63] See 45 CFR § 164.514.
[64] See 45 CFR 164.528(a)(1) ("An individual has a right to receive an accounting of disclosures of protected health information made by a covered entity") (emphasis added).
[65] See 45 CFR § 164.514(b).
[66] National Committee on Vital and Health Statistics, Letter to the Honorable Thomas E. Price, Secretary Department of Health and Human Services at 3 (Feb. 23, 2017).
[67] Id. at 5–6.
[68] Garfinkel, supra note 52, at x.
[69] See National Committee on Vital and Health Statistics, supra note 66, at 8.
[70] See generally Garfinkel, supra note 52, for technical details.

common and accessible to more people, HIPAA's rules written more than a decade ago will have increasingly little effect.[71] All of these issues make it more likely that de-identified data obtained through EHR vendor relationships will used to reidentify patients.

In addition to the risk of reidentification, disclosure of de-identified data undermines patient autonomy. Patients may dislike their data contributing to research to which they object for moral reasons, or they may be adverse to certain commercial enterprises exploiting their data to increase sales.[72] The Privacy Rule affords individuals a right to have health care providers give them an accounting for disclosures of their data.[73] Unfortunately, this right only applies to disclosures of their protected health information – in other words, not to disclosures of their de-identified data. Because the use of de-identified data is nontransparent, patients lose the freedom to object to its use. Also, by using de-identified data without patient knowledge, business associates and EHR vendors capture considerable value from the data, despite the fact that the health care provider assembled it and the patient ultimately was the source of the data. This practice allows many uses of patients' data to remain hidden from them. In addition to undermining the economic freedoms of patients and providers, it creates an environment of nontransparency both about the extent of data uses that are occurring and the privacy and reidentification risks to which patients are exposed. Trust may be undermined by such actions.

SOLUTIONS

In addition to the federal government enforcing existing laws, three relatively simple legal interventions could improve patient privacy in this context. First, HIPAA's accounting for disclosure provision[74] could be amended to require tracking and accounting for disclosures of de-identified information. The current provision only applies to protected health information, but an amendment could broaden the scope of this provision so patients could understand where their data are going. This would greatly improve the transparency of use of de-identified information from the perspectives of patients and potentially even health care providers, who may not know how EHR vendors ultimately use these data sets.

Second, HHS could issue new standard provisions for BAAs that discourage covered entities from allowing business associates to make secondary use of de-identified data. Such provisions likely would be unpopular: business associates that currently gain value by re-using de-identified data presumably would charge covered

---

[71] See National Committee on Vital and Health Statistics, supra note 66, at 7.
[72] See Bonnie Kaplan, Selling Health Data: De-Identification, Privacy, and Speech, 24 *Cambridge Quarterly of Healthcare Ethics* 8, www.cambridge.org/core/journals/cambridge-quarterly-of-healthcare-ethics/article/selling-health-data/A7F20A5EA198A30064FF524861766AEF
[73] See 45 C.F.R. § 164.524.
[74] See 45 C.F.R. § 164.528.

entities higher fees for the services they provide, absent this benefit. However, the current situation in effect is forcing patients to provide a subsidy (in the form of assuming greater privacy risks) to the cost of services that covered entities purchase from their BAs. This subsidy is particularly problematic because patients are unaware that they are providing it. Because data-sharing provisions are not transparent to patients, patients involuntarily subsidize covered entities' costs for EHR systems. Given these economics, reform is unlikely to occur spontaneously. Currently, government entities seem to presume broad use of de-identified data, but policymakers could curtail this practice by setting a different default.

A final potential solution that could help address this concern is to require health care providers to disclose to patients in plain language (1) the terms of their BAAs and EHR vendor contracts and (2) the health care providers', their business associates', and their EHR vendors' practices regarding use, disclosure, and sale of de-identified data.[75] If patients understand that that their sensitive health data are being used and disclosed for secondary commercial or research purposes, the patients may not necessarily "vote with their feet" because many patients are in health plans that constrain their selections of health care providers. Nevertheless, patients would have an opportunity to complain if such uses were objectionable and this might add pressure for regulatory reforms. In reality, many patients may be comfortable with the current practices, but since there is little transparency in regard to these practices, they do not have the freedom to choose.[76]

CONCLUSION

The expanding use of EHR systems presents a number of transparency issues: EHR contracts impede transparency directly through gag clauses and indirectly through clauses that discourage litigation. This nontransparency threatens patient safety by stifling the dissemination of information about harms related to EHR products. Without this knowledge the market cannot drive improvement and innovation is not drawn to mitigate or neutralize the harm. In addition to these patient safety concerns, EHR contracts threaten patient privacy by routinely allowing vendors and health care providers' business associates to use identified data for commercial purposes and de-identified data without restriction, and without transparently disclosing these uses to patients. These de-identified data pose risks to patients who may find their data have been re-identified without their consent or lead to uses that the patient would not have authorized. In both the case of gag clauses and the case of clauses permitting business associates to use de-identified data, the problems stem

---

[75] For a similar recommendation, see National Committee on Vital and Health Statistics, supra note 66, at 4 ("Recommendation 8: HHS should use the vehicle of the Model Notice of Privacy Practices to inform individuals that their data may be de-identified and used for other purposes, and the range of downstream uses for de-identified data.").

[76] See Kaplan, supra note 72, at 20.

from the contracts themselves. EHR providers have created contracts that undermine transparency, and the law should step in to foster more limpid transactions. A hopeful sign is that the 21st Century Cures Act included measures to address information blocking,[77] although implementing regulations still had not been promulgated as this chapter went to press in mid-2018. Even after the information blocking regulations come into force, the transparency challenges that surround EHR systems, which are multifaceted, will likely require more comprehensive oversight than has yet been proposed. Ultimately the interests of the patients should be central to any solutions that are developed.

[77] See 21st Century Cures Act, Pub. L. No. 114–255, § 4004, 130 Stat. 1033 (2016).

19

Transparency Challenges in Reproductive Health Care

Dov Fox*

INTRODUCTION

More than ten percent of Americans of childbearing age have received medical treatment for infertility, including over a hundred thousand cycles of assisted reproduction every year for over a decade.[1] Almost two percent of all babies born in the United States today are conceived using assisted reproductive technology (ART) such as *in vitro* fertilization (IVF).[2] Despite its ubiquity and importance, ART operates largely in the shadows. A 1992 law requires ART providers to report pregnancy rates to the Centers for Disease Control (CDC),[3] while others voluntarily report information to the Society for Assisted Reproductive Technology (SART). Yet the most comprehensive analysis of ART data between 2005 and 2010 reveals transparency deficits, including between 3.3 percent to 7.4 percent of all initiated cycles whose outcomes were excluded from the data.[4]

This missing information about reproductive medicine is not primarily about health and safety. The CDC's federally mandated National ART Surveillance System (NASS) reports for 94 percent of cycles on complications that lead to infection, hemorrhage, ovarian hyperstimulation, hospitalization, or even death.[5] Omitted data can be difficult to interpret or operationalize. Average ART success rates do not account for the patient characteristics. So it is not clear whether clinics with higher success rates are simply treating patients whose age, fertility diagnosis,

---

* My thanks to USD students Taini Adhikary, Pat Denton, and Veneeta Jaswal for excellent research assistance and to Professors Barbara Evans, Ann Marie Marciarille, Daniel Stretch, George Taffet, and David Weimer for especially helpful comments.
[1] See Ctrs. for Disease Control & Prevention, ART Success Rates, www.cdc.gov/art/reports/index.html.
[2] See Ctrs. for Disease Control & Prevention, Reproductive Health, www.cdc.gov/reproductivehealth/index.html.
[3] See Fertility Clinic Success Rate and Certification Act of 1992, Pub. L. No. 102–493, 106 Stat. 3146 (2012).
[4] Vitaly A. Kushnir et al., The Status of Public Reporting of Clinical Outcomes in ART, 100 Fertility & Sterility 736, 737–39 (2013).
[5] Jennifer F. Kawwass et al., Safety of Assisted Reproductive Technology in the U.S.: 2000–2011, 313 JAMA 88, 89 (2015).

and medical history make them more likely to bring home a baby. Likewise, the incidence of multiple-birth deliveries, while generally associated with worse maternal and infant health compared to singletons, neglects potential justifications for transferring multiple embryos at once based on patients' age, health, medical history, financial resources, and particular personal values.

And these transparency issues in assisted reproduction obscure a potentially deeper problem that has received little attention to date. This unnoticed problem is the range of uncontroversially adverse ART outcomes for which systematic evidence is altogether absent. There is no available information – not by government or professional association – that reports how often or which providers destroy, contaminate, or switch reproductive materials in ways that devastate patients' dreams to have children. That CDC and SART data do not cover any ART subfields or procedures such as the genetic screening of embryos for genetic anomalies, for example, means that misdiagnosis and misimplantation escape disclosure entirely. These mistakes might sound far-fetched. Yet a recent anonymous survey of nearly 200 American fertility clinics found that one in five reported errors in the testing, labeling, or handling of gametes and embryos.[6]

Most troubling among clinical and clerical errors are those that disrupt reproductive outcomes in ways that undo patients' efforts to have the children they long for and pay handsomely to make possible.[7] Lost embryos, switched samples, and misdiagnosed gametes cannot be chalked up to the inevitable slip of the hand or reasonable mistake in judgment. These preventable and serious errors are instead the product of outmoded procedures, uncalibrated equipment, unsanitized laboratories, and unreliable quality controls that range from screening measures prone to erroneous results to paper-and-pen labeling of reproductive specimens and recording for their storage, transfer, or use. These ART never events, as I refer to them, represent the most pressing challenge for transparency in reproductive medicine and technology.

A. NEVER EVENTS

The National Quality Forum developed the concept of "never events" to describe the most preventable and serious kinds of medical errors The three most common categories of never events in health care practice involve the wrong patient, wrong procedure, or wrong body part.[8] Since the Centers for Medicare and Medicaid

---

[6] Susannah Baruch et al., Practices and Perspectives of U.S. In Vitro Fertilization Clinics, 89 Fertility & Sterility 1053, 1055 (2008).

[7] See, e.g., Tamar Lewin, Sperm Banks Accused of Losing Samples and Lying About Donors, N.Y. Times, July 21, 2016, www.nytimes.com/2016/07/22/us/sperm-banks-accused-of-losing-samples-and-lying-about-donors.html.

[8] Healthcare Research & Quality, Patient Safety Primers: Never Events, http://psnet.ahrq.gov/primer .aspx?primerID=3; Nat'l Quality Forum, List of SREs (2015), www.qualityforum.org/Topics/SREs/List_of_SREs.aspx.

Services stopped reimbursing for such events and associated corrective treatment in 2008,[9] more than half of states have adopted requirements for reporting them.[10] But none of this applies to similarly egregious and avoidable transgressions by procreation specialists.

Following the designation of never events in other areas of medicine, I define ART never events as comprising three broad categories of plainly deficient care with acute aftermaths for patient well-being. First is the *mishandling* of materials like sperm, egg, and embryos that includes their loss, destruction, or contamination. Mishandling errors deprive fertility patients of whatever chances competent reproductive care would have given them to have genetically related children. The other two error types lead patients to have children they might not have, or to have ones with different genetic traits than those they selected. Second are material *misinformation* errors that include the misrepresentation of nontrivial donor traits or misdiagnosis of nontrivial attributes in gametes or embryos. Third are *misconception* errors that involve mix-ups and switches such as fertilizing with the wrong sperm or implanting the wrong embryo.

The first category of ART never events involves the destruction or misplacement of reproductive materials that patients cryopreserved in anticipation of or response to their apparent inability to conceive without intervention. These errors include loss or damage in transport to the lab or when specimens are centrifuged, incubated, tested on, or stored. For example, cancer survivors who store sperm or eggs prior to chemotherapy have been informed that their material has been inadvertently thawed.[11] In another class of these cases, fertility clinic technicians appear to have dropped the tray containing a couple's embryos.[12] ART providers have also rendered gametes or embryos unusable in other ways as by contaminating them with chemicals that "cause a fatal neurological disorder in humans."[13] The mishandling of reproductive materials in these cases deny patients the chances they otherwise had to have biologically related children.

The next category of ART never events involves the mis(sed)diagnosis of reproductive patients or materials. This includes false positives and negatives based on mistakes in warranted screening or testing or the misinterpretation or

---

[9] Changes to the Hospital Inpatient Prospective Payment Systems for Acute Care Hospitals, 74 Fed. Reg. 43,754 (Aug, 27, 2009) (to be codified at 42 C.F.R. pts. 412, 413, 415, 485, 489); Ctrs. for Medicare & Medicaid Servs., Readmissions Reduction Program (2015), www.cms.gov/Medicare/Medicare-Fee-for-Service-Payment/AcuteInpatientPPS/Readmissions-Reduction-Program.html.

[10] See Healthcare Research & Quality, supra note 8.

[11] See, e.g., *Hollman v. Saadat*, No. BC555411 (Cal. Super. Ct. Aug. 21, 2014); *Saleh v. Hollinger*, 335 S.W.3d 368 (Tex. App. 2011); *Witt v. Yale-New Haven Hospital*, 977 A.2d 779 (Conn. 2008).

[12] See, e.g., *Miller v. Am. Infertility Grp.*, 897 N.E.2d 837, 839–40 (Ill. App. Ct. 2008); *Jeter v. Mayo Clinic*, 121 P.3d 1256 (Ariz. Ct. App. 2005); *Frisina v. Women & Infants Hosp. of R.I.*, 2002 WL 1288784 (R.I. Super. Ct., May 30, 2002).

[13] *Doe v. Irvine Scientific Sales*, 7 F. Supp. 2d 737, 739 (E.D. Va. 1998).

miscommunication of results, besides failure to order testing or report results.[14] Many of these mistakes involve failures to detect a disease patients had sought testing for as carriers.[15] In one such case, a couple risked passing along a devastating X-linked disorder to a son (but not a daughter), and so screened out male embryos; a testing error led to the birth of a male with that X-linked disorder.[16] Misinformation cases can cause a child born with a debilitating condition instead of one who is healthy.[17] False negatives based on erroneous diagnoses of prenatal risk also lead some would-be parents to discard embryos or terminate pregnancies they would have wanted to keep.[18] The results in these misinformation cases range from the imposition of unwanted parenthood to its deprivation when it is wanted desperately

The third and final category of ART never events are misconception cases, in which reproductive specialists combine sperm or egg with the wrong sample or place genetic materials into the wrong person. In such cases, clinics or sperm banks have fertilized eggs with the sperm from a donor instead of a spouse,[19] or from a different donor than the one that the patients selected,[20] or specialists implant embryos from one couple into another.[21] Misconception cases most often come to light when they involve intended and genetic parents of different races, or sick children whose blood types could only have come from a person other than their mother or father. The most plausible cause of such errors involve obsolete pen-and-paper systems for labeling materials, preparation of multiple specimens at once, and failure to maintain a signed record sheet before storing, transferring, or using samples. As with the faulty quality control practices or risk assessment and prevention policies that are the most likely cause of mishandling and misinformation errors, it stands to reason that the misconception category of ART never events are also readily avoidable.

B. CROWDSOURCING

There is no reporting system to track ART never events. One reason may have to do with the fact that such services are usually paid for out of pocket. Americans who have health insurance for other medical treatment tend to delegate considerations of cost and quality to insurers. This leaves little appetite to address these concerns once

---

[14] See, e.g., *D.D. v. Idant Labs.*, 374 F. App'x 319, 320 (3d Cir. 2010); *Coggeshall v. Reprod. Endocrine Assoc. of Charlotte*, 655 S.E.2d 476 (S.C. 2007); *Paretta v. Med. Offices for Human Reprod.*, 760 N.Y.S. 2d 639 (N.Y. Sup. Ct. 2003).
[15] See, e.g., *Grossbaum v. Genesis Genetics Inst.*, No. 07-1359, 2011 WL 2462279 (D. N.J. June 10, 2011).
[16] See, e.g., *Bergero v. Univ. of S. Cal. Keck Sch. of Med.*, No. B200595, 2009 WL 946874, at *14 (Cal. App. Apr. 9, 2009).
[17] See, e.g., *Khadim v. Lab. Corp. of Am.*, 838 F.Supp.2d 448 (W.D. Va. 2011).
[18] See *Alger v. Univ. of Rochester Med. Ctr.*, 980 N.Y.S.2d 200 (App. Div. 2014)).
[19] See, e.g., *Maher v. Vaughn, Silverberg & Assocs.*, 95 F. Supp. 3d 999, 1003-04 (W.D. Tex. 2015).
[20] See, e.g., Meredith Rodriguez, Lawsuit: Wrong Sperm Delivered to Lesbian Couple, Chi. Tribune, Oct. 1, 2014.
[21] See, e.g., *Walterspiel v. Jain*, No. BC467123 (Cal. Super. Ct. Aug. 17, 2011).

the intermediary of insurance is removed. Another reason is the complex politics of reproductive health care. Practices involving the creation, destruction, and selection of human life invoke charged values that divide voters not just across constituencies, but within them.[22]

And when unregulated reproductive activity does result in injury, practitioners resist liability for even the most blameworthy mistakes.[23] Courts do not deny that specialists are to blame. They find little basis in the law, however, to recognize disrupted family planning as a harm that is worthy of protection. Mishandling errors that deprive people of procreation – for example, dropped embryos – rarely cause the kinds of physical or economic injury that the tort system generally requires as a condition of monetary recovery. When misinformation errors impose procreation on people who would with full information have avoided it, courts more often than not insist that any burdens of parenthood are offset by its countervailing joys and blessings. And when misconception errors frustrate plans for a child of a particular type, courts typically deny compensation for fear that it will send a message that disparages the value of an existing child's life. As a result, these errors are virtually immune to the after-the-fact protections that tort law affords similar mistakes in other areas of medicine. This makes the disclosure of ART never events all the more critical.

Can the market succeed where public law, private law, and professional associations have failed to bring transparency to reproductive health care?[24] Among the deficiencies of data collection by the CDC and SART are that self-reporting attracts bias and that there is no tracking of never events whatsoever. It is worth considering a neutral platform – sponsored by no patient or provider group – to crowdsource reviews of reproductive medicine. Its purposes would be to provide prospective patients with more and better information, and through better choices induce higher-quality care. This platform would solicit reflections from those who access reproductive services about the care they received. What should we make of a market-based platform on which past patients report on the incidence of ART never events?

At its best, a user-generated system to record ART never events could help patients obtain better reproductive care, namely, by steering them away from error-prone providers, discouraging misconduct, and identifying areas for improvement. In theory, these reviews would advantage providers that deliver high-quality care through recognition within the user-generated system that prospective patients may rely on in deciding on a particular clinic or procedure. The platform also runs

---

[22] See Dov Fox, Interest Creep, 82 Geo. Wash. L. Rev. 273, 352 (2014) (referring to reproduction as "a site of contestation about the ... relationship between men and women, parents and children, individuals and government, humans and nature").

[23] See Dov Fox, Reproductive Negligence, 117 Colum. L. Rev. 149, 168–70 (2017).

[24] See Kristin M. Madison, The Law and Policy of Health Care Quality Reporting, 31 Campbell L. Rev. 215 (2009).

serious risks, however, such as reducing the quality of care or diminishing access to it. As with similar ratings systems in other areas of medicine based on statistical or anecdotal data, its merits in the reproductive context depend on both the quality of information that it provides and the balance of its implications for both patients and providers.[25]

A user-generated ART reporting system promises to arm patients with information that materially informs their decisions about creating the families they long for. Knowledge about the incidence of ART never events based on patient and procedure profiles helps those seeking similar reproductive services to select a provider who delivers quality care relevant to their circumstances. The system could extrapolate this kind of case-specific anecdotal information to disclose statistically significant incidence data. Access to such aggregated never event data may empower reproductive patients with decisional autonomy, in the sense of helping them choose more freely to undertake important life experiences of their own making. It also holds the promise to promote their well-being, in that those choices help them lead lives they value more or fulfill those preferences for procreation and parenthood that are more likely to make them happy.

On the other hand, reviews could also risk worsening reproductive care by publicizing inaccurate, misleading, or quality-neutral measures that some patients might nevertheless associate with quality. The focus on never events, however, means that patients would not measure the quality of care in superficial or subjective terms of wait-time music, lobby appearance, or parking convenience. The mark of quality reproductive care would instead be medical outcomes. Some might worry that it is difficult for patients to know whether a doctor diagnosed a condition correctly, for example, or applied a clinically sound course of treatment. Yet for never events, demonstrable outcomes – reproductive materials were preserved or destroyed, a child was born with or without a prenatally tested disease, related to a spouse or stranger – will usually leave patient reviewers with credible evidence about whether the provision of reproductive care resulted in a mishandling, misinformation, or misconception error. And so they are well equipped to report true and pertinent information about the incidence of ART never events in their own experiences.

Could even high-quality reporting prompt defensive deviations from sound practice by leading review-conscious providers to order tests or recommend procedures that confer marginal clinical value? Might reproductive providers, fearful of bad reviews, overtreat patients in ways that not only yield too many side effects, but also make ART more costly? A related concern is that sensitivity to favorable reviews could drive ART specialists to select patients based less on their relative reproductive needs and benefits than on risk profiles that suggest straightforwardly successful outcomes. Might providers, in the wide discretion they exercise over which patients

[25] Cf. Daniel Strech, Ethical Principles for Physician Rating Sites, 13 J. Med. Internet Res. e113 (2011).

to treat, accordingly deny access to reproductive services to those with poor health or low income?[26] Studies show that patient selection in other areas of medicine has led to racial and ethnic disparities based on data suggesting that excluding government-funded insurance patients, for example, tends to improve clinical outcomes and patient reviews.[27] In reproductive medicine, studies indicate worse ART outcomes among black women as compared with others, due in part to higher rates of tubal-factor and uterine-factor infertility.[28] Turning away patients perceived to be at risk of poor reproductive outcomes could, in this case, deepen the racial disparities in access to health care.[29]

It is less obviously problematic for providers to decline treatment where factors like age or body mass so lower the prospects of success that the risks of treatment outweigh its benefits.[30] Reproductive providers today are too willing to indulge optimistic hopes such patients may harbor. Women over forty-four, for example, or men who have no working sperm count have such low potential to have biological children that even the best care is unlikely to help them have the children they seek.[31] Accordingly, for them to undergo costly and risky reproductive procedures may do them a disservice at the expense of the clinic's scarce resources. And it does not seem disquieting to deny futile treatment to patients, even if it overrides their preferences and appears motivated by self-serving aversion to unfavorable reviews. The key is designing a ratings system that informs patients by providing honest information about high risks and low benefits, while discouraging provider refusal except where reproductive success is improbable. Self-reported statistics about reproductive success should include details that put them in proper context.

C. ART REVIEWS

What should a ratings system for ART never events look like? What features should it borrow from databases like HealthGrades, Vitals, and ZocDoc in other areas of medicine that solicit information about the quality of care from patients/consumers rather than industry experts or academics? And what features should distinguish a Yelp-like platform to report never events in the context of reproductive care? Since reproductive services are rarely covered by insurance, reviews would influence

---

[26] Doctors are generally free to deny ART treatment except in states with antidiscrimination laws barring refusal for certain categories of patients. See N. Coast Women's Care Med. Grp. v. San Diego Cty. Superior Court, 189 P.3d 959, 962 (Cal. 2008).
[27] Rachel M. Werner et al., Racial Profiling: The Unintended Consequences of Coronary Artery Bypass Graft Report Cards, 111 Circulation 1257 (2005)(study showing report cards associated with increased racial disparity in use of bypass surgery).
[28] Alicia Armstrong & Torie C. Plowden, Ethnicity and Assisted Reproductive Technologies, 9 Clinical Practice 651 (2012).
[29] Inst. of Med., Confronting Racial and Ethnic Disparities in Health Care 3 (2002).
[30] See Armstrong & Plowden, supra note 28.
[31] See Ian Sample, Changes of IVF Success 'Futile' for Women over 44, Says Study, Guardian, June 16, 2015.

provider reputation among consumer-patients rather than subsidy or reimbursement rates, as in some other areas of medicine. To maximize access and quality and quantity of data, the transparency platform would ideally operate at no cost to reviewers or the prospective patients who would rely on their evaluations. To guard against outlier reviews from overzealous patients or unrepresentative inferences from too-small sample sizes, a minimum number of reviews about a particular clinic should be required before making them public.[32]

So early reviews should be solicited prior to releasing their results until data is reliable and meaningful.

Reviews should capture dimensions of care like ART never events of greatest concern to patients. For example, reproductive services are expensive and typically ineligible for insurance coverage, making patients in this area more sensitive than in many others to the cost of care beyond its quality. The content, structure, and ordering of questions posed could be informed by consultation with patients and providers.[33] They might ask about experiences with doctors, nurses, embryologists, or billing departments; "success" using particular courses of treatment; cost; the number and diversity of donor samples available; and adoption of known quality-control processes. Assuming a prominent place among these will be questions about whether a provider lost, switched, misdiagnosed, or contaminated patients' reproductive materials. Third-party administrators should screen reports of ART never events for hyperbole or hearsay. Before posting, they might hand-read reviews for credible and convincing information or evidence that samples had gone missing, that a newborn has a screened-for condition, or a parent and child lack genetic ties.

Each review should incorporate basic information about the reviewer so that prospective patients can consider it by reference to their own risks, needs, and preferences. That means disclosing reviewer information like age, sex, income, medical history, fertility diagnosis, demographic profile, and treatment type relevant to other people with a range of priorities, perspectives, and circumstances. Making this data public risks discouraging participation out of concerns for patient privacy. In few other areas of medicine do patients routinely hesitate to report even egregious mistakes for fear that disclosing them might reveal that they had sought such care.[34] Stigma associated with nontraditional family formation through fertility treatment and offspring selection confounds the recruitment of reviewers if they could be singled out.

So the platform should not display personally identifiable information about individual reviewers like name, birth date, or email address. This kind of anonymity

---

[32] Samir K. Trehan & Aarin Daluiski, Online Patient Ratings: Why They Matter and What They Mean, 41 J. Hand Surgery Am. 316, 318 (2016).

[33] Yann B. Ferrand, et al., Patient Satisfaction with Healthcare Services: A Critical Review, 23 QMJ 6, 8 (2016).

[34] See P. Slade et al., The Relationship Between Perceived Stigma, Disclosure Patterns, Support and Distress in New Attendees at an Infertility Clinic, 22 Human Reproduction 2309, 2309 (2007).

comes with limits and costs, however. The location of any reproductive practitioner would still tie patients fairly closely to a particular region. That geographical link, combined with patient age and other disclosed data, could risk reidentification. And the removal of overt identifiers could invite fraudulent review by biased friends, family members, competitors, or paid promoters. The platform should accordingly verify the authenticity of the reviews it publishes by requiring nonpersonal proof, like a receipt, that a reviewer was in fact a patient at the clinic that he or she is reviewing. This individually identifiable health information, voluntarily disclosed, would be used exclusively for verification purposes. That means that this information should not be publicly displayed to platform users. Nor, ideally, should it be accessible in litigation that arises about related events, though anonymous reporting systems may have trouble avoiding discovery in court proceedings.

The ART reporting platform should organize reviews into diversity portfolios based on traits shared by prospective patients. The incidence of never events should be risk adjusted and reported as a function of favorable outcomes, not only at a particular doctor or clinic, but also as compared with the rates of never events at relevantly similar facilities in terms of location, costs, available procedures, or reproductive risk. Data could still be posted before it becomes statistically significant on these points. But it would framed to provide patients with the most accurate and accessible information possible.

Providers should also have an opportunity to reply with comments to explain the existence, cause, and circumstances of reported adverse events together with measures taken to prevent similar outcomes in the future. This would of course have to be done in a way that would not violate patients' privacy rights. And providers may not need patient-specific information to figure out what went wrong and respond to it. Such replies would also be sensitive to implications for potential liability litigation. With these concerns and caveats in mind, providers might, by responding to aggrieved patients, stand to gain positive publicity about updates to their reproductive clinic policies and practices for quality control, risk assessment, or prevention, and could include improvements to training, staffing, procedures, techniques, and equipment.[35]

For *mishandling errors*, for example, providers might mention newly adopted protections against samples having been extracted or transported off-site; unsafe environments to maintain cells or tissues or the mediums and cultures in which they are grown or preserved; uncalibrated temperature or pH levels; and power failures or unsanitized equipment.[36] For *misinformation errors*, a clinic could note improved reliability testing or interpretation of genetic results as through

---

[35] Sharon Mortimer & David Mortimer, Quality and Risk Management in the IVF Laboratory (2d ed. 2015); Matts Wikland & Cecilia Sjöblom, The Application of Quality Systems in ART Programs, 166 Molecular & Cellular Endocrinology 3, 5 (2000).

[36] Amjad Hossain et al., Human Sperm Bioassay for Reprotoxicity Testing in Embryo Culture Media: Some Practical Considerations in Reducing the Assay Time, 2010 Advances in Urology (2010).

interlaboratory comparison programs.[37] Popular FISH-based methods of embryo screening that look at just five to nine of forty-six chromosomes, for example, are susceptible to false negatives since abnormalities can be present on untested chromosomes.[38] Clinics could highlight adoption of diagnostically superior tools that enable comprehensive screening of risk markers for spontaneous abortion, multiple pregnancy, and chromosomal disorders before selecting which embryos to implant.[39] And for *misconception errors*, providers might highlight their reliable methods of labeling materials such as barcode tagging or radio-frequency identification, or that they now prepare specimens one at a time and maintain signed record sheets before storing, transferring, or using them.[40] Availability of reliable quality-control information would dramatically enhance transparency in ART.

D. CONCLUSION

There is no reporting system for the lost embryos, switched samples, and misdiagnosed gametes that comprise the three categories of ART never events. Mishandling, misinformation, and misconception errors go virtually undeterred and uncompensated. This chapter has proposed and analyzed a Yelp-like, user-generated platform to address this absence of transparency in reproductive medicine. ART reviews have the potential to help patients get better outcomes by steering them away from error-prone providers, discouraging misconduct, and identifying ways to improve the quality of reproductive care.

I argued that these reviews should be organized into diversity portfolios based on factors such as age, income, medical history, and fertility treatment, so prospective patients could use that information to obtain the care best suited to their risks, needs, and preferences. But ART reviews should still be anonymous to encourage patients to disclose the positive or negative outcomes that would reveal that they had sought often-stigmatizing care. This anonymity in turn invites risk of biased or fraudulent reviews that warrants requiring submission of nonpersonal evidence like a receipt to verify authenticity as well as screening for hyperbole or hearsay. Requiring a minimum number of reviews about a particular reproductive provider before making them public would guard against overzealous outliers or unrepresentative

---

[37] See J. P. W. Vermeiden, Laboratory-Related Risks in Assisted Reproductive Technologies, Assisted Reproductive Technologies: Quality and Safety 127, 128–29 (Jan Gerris, Francois Olivennes & Petra De Sutter eds., 2004).
[38] See Cristina Gutiérrez-Mateo et al., Validation of Microarray Comparative Genomic Hybridization for Comprehensive Chromosome Analysis of Embryos, 95 Fertility & Sterility 953, 955 (2011).
[39] See William B. Schoolcraft et al., Clinical Application of Comprehensive Chromosomal Screening at the Blastocyst Stage, 94 Fertility & Sterility 1700, 1700 (2010).
[40] Sergi Novo et al., Barcode Tagging of Human Oocytes and Embryos to Prevent Mix-Ups in Assisted Reproduction Technologies, 29 Hum. Reprod. 18 (2014).

inferences from small sample sizes. Even reliable reporting could lead providers to selectively deny services to patients whose statistically lower chances for success might be thought to make them less likely to write favorable reviews. But it is not obviously problematic to refuse treatment on the basis of bleak reproductive prospects.

PART VI

Challenges in Promoting and Measuring Transparency in Health Care

Introduction to Part VI

I. Glenn Cohen

The four chapters in this section all focus on transparency initiatives in health care and the challenges they face, but at a first glance the chapters seem quite disparate. They differ regarding whose disclosure is at issue – that of Institutional Review Boards (IRBs) (Chapter 22, Holly Fernandez Lynch); of pharmacy benefit managers (PBMs) (Chapter 20, Erin C. Fuse Brown and Jaime S. King, and Chapter 23, David A. Hyman and William E. Kovacic); of drugmakers (Chapter 21, Jennifer E. Miller); or of health care providers and health plans (Chapter 20, Fuse Brown and King). They also identify different sources of pressure toward transparency – coming from state regulators (Chapter 23, Hyman and Kovacic, and Chapter 20, Fuse Brown and King); from the federal government (Chapter 21, Miller); from industry self-regulation (Chapter 21, Miller and, depending on how "industry" is defined, perhaps Chapter 22, Lynch); and, finally, from ethical considerations and academic goals (Chapter 21, Miller, and Chapter 22, Lynch). There are also distinctions between the chapters as *to whom* the pertinent information would be disclosed – to the public, to researchers interested in studying the behavior of firms that apply for permission, or to regulated entities.

What unites them? One way of organizing the chapters is to see them as transparency initiatives being attempted at multiple points of a particular product's lifecycle, the main product being pharmaceuticals. Miller and Lynch are concerned with the product development phase. In Chapter 21, Miller focuses on transparency around clinical trials and their results, while Lynch is concerned with transparency of the decision making of the relevant IRBs in Chapter 22. Fuse Brown and King and Hyman and Kovacic, by contrast, focus on the marketing phase – more specifically, the regulation of sharing of information about how PBMs, one of the most important intermediaries in pharmaceutical purchasing, handle things like rebates, substitution of one medication for another, and so forth – in Chapters 20 and 23, respectively.[1]

---

[1] To be sure, while this organization captures a good deal that is in these chapters it does not capture everything. Fernandez Lynch is concerned with IRBs inside and outside the pharmaceutical space; Fuse Brown and King look not only at pharmacy benefit managers, but also at all-payers claims databases and other engines of transparency.

Viewed as such, one can see the possibility that "upstream" and "downstream" transparency regulation of a product can be complements or substitutes. This insight is particularly important because these chapters do a very nice job of cataloging many key obstacles to successful transparency initiatives – noncompliance, industry capture of disclosure programs, federal pre-emption of state initiatives, financial costs, and the need to avoid imposing unfunded mandates. These obstacles are more salient for some disclosure "pressure points" than others.

Another theme that runs throughout these chapters, most emphasized by Chapter 23, are the political economic considerations that make disclosure mandates so attractive to regulators. They want to do "something" about the problem, but directly regulating an area is complex and costly. Regulated constituencies can effectively make a public case against certain direct regulations, but disclosure mandates are much harder to oppose – who can be against providing more information? For those on the pro-regulatory side, disclosure mandates may threaten to defang more robust forms of regulation and allow the legislator to appear as though he or she is doing something, even if that something is of significant less effectiveness than alternatives. For those on the antiregulatory side, the concern is precisely the opposite – about a rush to embrace disclosure mandates in the absence of market failures requiring more disclosure. Which side one falls in this divide will color how one reads the chapters that follow – are the obstacles faced by disclosure regimes welcome "speed bumps" or problematic inhibitors to sensible health care policy?

20

ERISA as a Barrier for State Health Care Transparency Efforts

Erin C. Fuse Brown and Jaime S. King

I. INTRODUCTION

To improve health care market dynamics and reduce costs, many states have passed legislation to promote transparency in health care for consumers, regulators, and employers. Significant state-led initiatives include building price transparency tools using data from state all-payer claims databases (APCDs), requiring pharmacy benefit managers (PBMs) to report drug markups and pricing methodologies, increasing provider network transparency, and limiting surprise medical bills from out-of-network providers.

Effective transparency laws are essential for consumer protection, particularly as the national debate over the Affordable Care Act indicates policymakers' interest in increasing consumer "skin in the game" through wider use of health savings accounts and high-deductible health plans.[1] Beyond consumer protection, states need accurate, detailed, and comprehensive health care price, utilization, and quality data to understand and oversee their own health care markets.[2]

Despite robust and salutary state innovation in consumer health care transparency, the federal Employee Retirement Income Security Act's (ERISA) growing preemptive sweep prevents these state laws from benefitting a growing percentage of health care consumers – those covered by self-funded employee health plans, in which the employer retains the financial or insurance risk for its employees' health benefits. Self-funded employee plans cover more than 60 percent of all workers with employer-based health insurance.[3] Due to ERISA pre-emption, private self-funded plans are beyond the reach of state law, accountable only to the federal Department of Labor, which administers ERISA.

---

[1] Stuart Butler, Repeal and Replace Obamacare: What Could It Mean?, 317 JAMA 244 (2017).
[2] Erin C. Fuse Brown & Jaime S. King, The Double-Edged Sword of Health Care Integration: Consolidation and Cost Control, 92 Indiana L. J. 55, 81 (2017).
[3] Kaiser Family Found., Employer Health Benefit Survey 2016, Section 10, Plan Funding. http://kff.org/report-section/ehbs-2016-section-nine-section-ten-plan-funding/.

In *Gobeille v. Liberty Mutual*, the Supreme Court dramatically broadened ERISA's pre-emptive reach to include state laws imposing data-reporting requirements on self-funded plans.[4] The expanding scope of ERISA pre-emption fundamentally limits the ability of states to protect their citizen-consumers and oversee rising health care costs through health care transparency laws, namely price transparency through APCDs, drug price transparency for PBMs, and transparency about when a patient may incur a surprise medical bill. As a result, many now call for the federalization of health care transparency and consumer protection, tasks for which states may be better suited or more legislatively inclined. For transparency initiatives to achieve their maximal effect at the state level, lawmakers must make changes at the federal level. A federal solution could take many forms, ranging from narrow-issue administrative rulemaking to amending ERISA to exempt state transparency laws from pre-emption. Although federal policy may be necessary for health care transparency efforts to reach all consumers, such a policy should be crafted to preserve state flexibility and innovation.

II. STATE HEALTH CARE TRANSPARENCY LAWS

We highlight three types of health care transparency laws pursued by states to protect consumers and control health care costs: price transparency through APCDs, transparency of PBMs' drug pricing methods, and increased provider network transparency and disclosure of surprise medical bills from out-of-network providers.

A. All-Payer Claims Databases (APCDs)

State APCDs form the foundation of the most robust tools for health care price and quality transparency. APCDs collect provider-specific claims data, which reflect population health, health care utilization, and the notoriously opaque *amounts paid* by various payers, as opposed to the less meaningful *amounts charged*. APCDs aim to promote transparency as a cost-containment tool, while managing the risks of collusion and price increases from unfettered price transparency. Without APCDs, comprehensive data on health care prices, utilization, and quality are kept secret by nondisclosure clauses in contracts between plans and providers and are further obscured by the sheer complexity of a system where each service has different prices and methods of calculating rates depending on the payer.[5] The best state price transparency tools make provider- and plan-specific price and quality data available to consumers via a searchable, public website that allows comparisons among a wide range of

---
[4] *Gobeille v. Liberty Mutual Ins. Co.*, 136 S. Ct. 936 (2016).
[5] Morgan A. Muir, Stephanie Alessi & Jaime S. King, Clarifying Costs: Can Increased Price Transparency Reduce Healthcare Spending?, 4 Wm. & Mary Pol'y Rev. 319 (2013).

providers.[6] Examples of states with consumer-friendly price transparency websites built on ACPD data are Colorado, Maine, New Hampshire, and Oregon.[7] Twenty states have adopted laws to establish APCDs and provide critical and otherwise inaccessible data to consumers, state regulators, and health researchers about the cost and quality of health care services.[8]

B. Drug Price Transparency from Pharmacy Benefit Managers

As prescription drug prices soar, states have also pursued policies to shine a light on the factors contributing to consumers' drug costs, including markups and rebates for pharmacy benefit managers (PBMs) and others along the pharmaceutical supply chain.[9] When a patient receives a prescription drug, the patient's cost-sharing and the amount paid by the patient's health plan for the drug are determined in confidential negotiations between the PBM, the drug manufacturer, and the pharmacy, with an array of invisible rebates, fees, and markups.[10] Typically, consumers, purchasers, and state regulators have no way of knowing a PBM's markup over its manufacturer price or the various intermediaries' financial incentives. To counter this opacity, states have pursued requirements for PBMs to disclose their pricing methodologies to state regulators and purchasers.

C. Measures to Address Surprise Out-of-Network Bills

States have enacted laws to protect patients from surprise medical bills through transparency and disclosure as well as substantive limits on this financially harmful billing practice. Surprise medical bills arise when an insured patient involuntarily and inadvertently receives care from an out-of-network provider, which often occurs in an emergency or when the facility is in-network, but physicians are not.[11]

Narrowing provider networks increase the likelihood of surprise medical bills. In response, several states have enacted measures to increase the transparency and accuracy of provider networks by requiring health plans to update and make available timely and accurate lists of in-network providers to

---

[6] Francois De Brantes & Suzanne Delbanco, Catalyst for Payment Reform, Report Card on State Price Transparency Laws 6 (July 2016).
[7] See Colorado Center for Improving Value in Health Care, http://www.civhc.org/shop-for-care/; CompareMaine: Health Costs & Quality, http://www.comparemaine.org/; Health Costs for Consumer, N.H. HealthCost, http://nhhealthcost.nh.gov/health-costs-consumers; Oregon Hospital Guide, http://oregonhospitalguide.org/.
[8] APCD Council, State Efforts, www.apcdcouncil.org/state/map (last accessed Feb. 27, 2017).
[9] Ameet Sarpatwari, Jerry Avorn & Aaron S. Kesselheim. State Initiatives to Control Medication Costs – Can Transparency Legislation Help?, 374 New Eng. J. Med. 2301 (2016).
[10] See Ameet Sarpatwari, Jerry Avorn & Aaron S. Kesselheim, Chapter 8.
[11] Karen Pollitz, Kaiser Family Foundation Issue Brief: Surprise Medical Bills (March 2016), http://kff.org/private-insurance/issue-brief/surprise-medical-bills/.

consumers.[12] Updated and accurate provider directories are necessary for consumers to select in-network providers and plans, and for regulators to assess network adequacy.

A few states, including New York, Connecticut, Florida, California, Texas, and Illinois, go further to shield patients from surprise bills more directly.[13] To counter the involuntary and unanticipated nature of surprise medical bills, these laws rely on transparency by requiring providers to disclose out-of-network status to patients and to obtain informed consent from patients (disclosure/ informed consent). If the patient does not consent to the out-of-network service after full disclosure, the laws impose one or more of the following requirements: (1) limit balance-billing and amounts that out-of-network providers may collect from patients, usually to in-network payment levels (limit charges/balance-billing);[14] (2) require health plans to ensure that patients will not be responsible for paying more than in-network cost-sharing for surprise bills and count all such cost-sharing toward in-network deductibles and out-of-pocket limits (hold harmless); or (3) provide mechanisms to determine how much plans will owe out-of-network providers through dispute resolution or statutory caps. Thus, these state laws attempt to make it more transparent when a patient will receive out-of-network services at an in-network facility and impose substantive limits on patients' payment obligations when the patient involuntarily and inadvertently receives out-of-network care.

III. ERISA PRE-EMPTION OF STATE HEALTH CARE TRANSPARENCY LAWS

A. Background on ERISA Pre-emption

ERISA's pre-emptive effects are extraordinarily far-reaching. Of particular relevance to state health care transparency laws, Section 514 of ERISA expressly pre-empts state laws that "relate to any employee benefit plan."[15] This provision has been construed broadly to displace a swath of state health care laws because of their impermissible connection to employee health

---

[12] See, e.g., S.B. 302, 153rd Gen. Assemb. (Ga. 2016) (signed into law Apr. 26, 2016, to be codified at O.C.G.A. § 33-20C-1 et seq.); Md. H.B. 131, 436th Gen. Assemb. (Md. 2016) (signed into law Apr. 26, 2016).

[13] N.Y. Ins. Law § 3241(c); N.Y. Fin. Servs. Law Art. 6; Conn. Gen. Stat. 38a-591a; § 20-7f; Cal. Health & Safety Code § 1371.71; Cal. Ins. Code § 10112.82; Fla. Stat. § 627.64194; Tex. Ins. Code § 1467.05; 215 Ill. Comp. Stat. 5/356z.3a. See Mark A. Hall, Chapter 11.

[14] See Carol K. Lucas & Michelle A. Williams, The Rights of Nonparticipating Providers in a Managed Care World: Navigating the Minefields of Balance Billing and Reasonable and Customary Payments, 3 J. Health & Life Sci. L. 132, 147 (2009) ("The term 'balance billing' refers to the practice of out-of-network medical providers billing a patient the difference between the reimbursement made by an enrollee's health plan and the amount the provider contends it is owed for the services rendered.").

[15] ERISA § 514(a); 29 U.S.C. § 1144(a).

plans.[16] The result is that state laws that impose transparency requirements on health plans cannot be applied to many ERISA plans, including laws requiring reporting or disclosure of claims data, drug pricing methodology, or the out-of-network status and billing implications for patients. Not all state laws that have some effect on ERISA plans "relate to an employee benefit plan." Notably, state laws that are primarily directed at health care *providers* and have only an incidental effect on ERISA plans do not "relate to" employee benefit plans and, therefore, do not trigger ERISA's express pre-emption.[17]

Under an exception created by ERISA's "savings clause," state health care transparency laws that regulate insurance escape pre-emption.[18] These insurance laws will apply to traditional "fully insured" employee health plans, where the employer contracts with an insurance company to assume the financial risk for employees' health care costs in exchange for premiums.[19] A state law regulates insurance if the state law is "specifically directed towards entities engaged in insurance," and the state law "substantially affect[s] the risk pooling arrangement between the insurer and the insured."[20] A state statute will satisfy the second requirement when it "alters the scope of permissible bargains between insurers and insured."[21] The applicability of the savings clause is relevant to determining whether a state transparency law will be invalidated as to *all* ERISA plans, or only those that are self-funded. This is because ERISA's "deemer clause" creates an exception from the savings clause, pre-empting all state laws that relate to *self-funded* group health plans, which are not deemed to be in the business of insurance.[22] ERISA will even pre-empt state insurance laws that apply to fully insured plans via the savings clause insofar as they apply to self-funded employee health plans.

In sum, Section 514 pre-empts state laws that relate to employee benefit plans if they either (1) do not qualify as insurance regulation; or (2) relate to self-funded employee health plans. Thus, despite the burgeoning efforts by states to

---

[16] For example, state laws relate to ERISA plans if they (i) mandate ERISA plans to cover certain benefits, *Shaw v. Delta Air Lines, Inc.*, 463 U.S. 85, 96–97 (1983); (ii) interfere with nationally uniform plan administration, *Gobeille*, 136 S. Ct. at 943; or (iii) intrude on the relationship between ERISA plans, beneficiaries, and administrators, *Self-Insurance Inst. of Am., Inc. v. Snyder*, 827 F.3d 549, 559 (6th Cir. 2016).

[17] *De Buono v. NYSA-ILA Med. & Clinical Servs. Fund*, 520 U.S. 806, 815–16 (1997); *N.Y. St. Conf. of Blue Cross & Blue Shield Plans v. Travelers Ins. Co.*, 514 U.S. 645, 658–59; *Retail Indus. Leaders Ass'n v. Fielder*, 475 F.3d 180, 191 (4th Cir. 2007) (citing *DeBuono* and *Travelers* to conclude, "States continue to enjoy wide latitude to regulate healthcare providers.").

[18] ERISA § 514(b)(2)(A); 29 U.S.C. § 1144(b)(2)(A); *Ky. Ass'n of Health Plans v. Miller*, 538 U.S. 329, 338–39 (2003).

[19] Approximately 39 percent of workers who are covered by employer-based plans are in fully insured plans. Kaiser Family Found., Employer Health Benefit Survey 2016, Section 10, Plan Funding, http://kff.org/report-section/ehbs-2016-section-nine-section-ten-plan-funding/

[20] *Miller*, 538 U.S. at 341–42.

[21] *Id.* at 338–39.

[22] 29 U.S.C. § 1144(b)(2)(B).

improve health care transparency, ERISA excludes about a third of the nonelderly U.S. population[23] from the benefits of these state transparency initiatives because of its sweeping pre-emptive effect with respect to self-funded employee health plans.

B. Pre-emption of State Health Care Transparency Laws

1. APCD Reporting Laws

In 2016, the Supreme Court undercut state APCDs in *Gobeille v. Liberty Mutual*, holding that ERISA pre-empts Vermont's APCD reporting law with respect to self-funded employee health plans.[24] The Vermont law required all payers to report health care claims information, including utilization, provider reimbursement rates, and other information related to health care services, to the state APCD. The Court concluded that the APCD reporting requirements had an impermissible connection with an ERISA plan because they interfered with the reporting and disclosure functions under ERISA that are central to "nationally uniform plan administration."[25]

The Court reasoned that because ERISA required health plans to report financial information, which goes to the heart of ERISA's original purpose of ensuring solvency in employee benefit plans, ERISA would pre-empt any state law requiring ERISA plans to report any information. While Justices Ginsburg and Sotomayor,[26] as well as the federal government,[27] recognized the distinction between the detailed claim information Vermont collected and the financial data ERISA plans generally report to the Department of Labor, the majority did not. Instead, its rote analysis of ERISA pre-emption applied the very "uncritical literalism" it professed to reject, with sweeping and potentially devastating implications for state health care transparency efforts.

Notably, the Court did not discuss the applicability of ERISA's savings clause in its analysis, as the question was not before the Court in *Gobeille* because respondent Liberty Mutual was a self-insured ERISA plan. However, the savings clause will likely enable state APCD requirements to avoid pre-emption with respect to fully insured employee benefit plans. Practically, this means that state APCDs could include data about nearly 40 percent of the employer-based insurance market, which remains crucial because it would be the only employer-based data

---

[23] In 2015, 56 percent of the nonelderly population was enrolled in employer-sponsored coverage. Of these, 61 percent are enrolled in self-funded plans. So (56% * 61% = 34%). Kaiser Family Found., Employer Health Benefit Survey 2016.
[24] *Gobeille*, 136 S. Ct. 936.
[25] Id. at 945.
[26] Id. at 954–55 (Ginsburg, J., dissenting).
[27] Brief for the United States, as Amicus Curiae in Support of Petitioner, at 10–11, *Gobeille v. Liberty Mutual*, 136 S.Ct. 936 (2016) (No. 14–181).

represented in the database. Determining if APCD reporting requirements for fully insured plans are saved from pre-emption depends on whether they constitute insurance regulation by "alter[ing] the scope of permissible bargains between the insurer and insured."[28] APCDs provide the raw data that permit states to operate consumer price transparency tools and regulate insurance company premiums through rate review, among other functions. APCDs thus arguably alter the scope of permissible bargains between insurers and insureds by providing enrollees with benefits such as price comparison tools, by regulating premiums, and by helping plans steer enrollees to high-value providers through cost-sharing incentives.

Significant consequences flow from the *Gobeille* decision for state health care transparency efforts. First, the decision means APCD data may exclude a large segment of privately insured individuals, who are covered by self-funded plans. This exclusion can skew the data within the APCD, because self-funded plans may differ in systematic ways from other populations. For example, those who get their insurance through employers tend to be healthier than those covered by public payers.[29] Further, different industries, sizes of employers, and geographic regions have different rates of self-insurance, and thus estimates based on remaining data may not fully represent the health care market of the state as a whole.

Second, and perhaps most significantly, the *Gobeille* decision extends beyond APCDs to threaten a broad swath of state health care transparency measures, as discussed below. The reasoning in *Gobeille* – that reporting and disclosure are central functions of plan administration – has been taken to mean that states cannot require transparency or data reporting of almost any sort from self-funded ERISA plans or their third-party administrators. This shift threatens the efficacy of numerous state efforts to improve price and quality transparency to protect consumers and control health care costs.

2. Pre-emption of PBM Transparency Laws

ERISA also limits state attempts to control pharmaceutical drug prices by pre-empting state reporting laws that apply to PBMs that administer drug benefits for self-funded employers. In 2017, the Eighth Circuit struck down Iowa's drug pricing transparency law as applied to PBMs acting as third-party administrators for ERISA plans.[30] The state law required, among other provisions, PBMs to report their drug pricing methodology to the state insurance commissioner.[31] Citing *Gobeille*, the court reasoned that ERISA pre-empts a state law requiring disclosure from PBMs that administer drug benefits for ERISA plans because it

---

[28] *Miller*, 538 U.S. at 341–42.
[29] Brief for the Harvard Law School Center for Health Law & Policy et al., as Amici Curiae in support of Petitioner, at 19–20, *Gobeille v. Liberty Mutual Ins. Co.*, 136 S.Ct. 936 (2016) (No. 14–181).
[30] *Pharm. Care Mgmt. Ass'n v. Gerhart*, 852 F.3d 722, 731 (8th Cir. 2017).
[31] Iowa Code § 510B.8.

"intrudes upon a matter central to plan administration and interferes with nationally uniform plan administration."[32] This straightforward application of *Gobeille* illustrates the broad and destructive consequences of that case – ERISA prevents any state requirement for data reporting or disclosure, the heart of any transparency initiative, from being imposed on self-funded employer-based health plans or any entity that administers such a plan, whether it is a third-party administrator or PBM.

3. Pre-emption of Surprise Billing Laws

The expanding sweep of ERISA pre-emption after *Gobeille* also impedes states' efforts to improve the transparency of provider networks and limit surprise medical bills. To the extent they regulate *health plans*, as opposed to *providers*, state laws on network adequacy or surprise billing are subject to ERISA pre-emption. As a result, none of the state law requirements for health plans apply to self-funded ERISA plans, including state requirements for network transparency or accurate provider directories. Further, a patient with self-funded coverage could not expect the plan to hold her harmless from a provider's out-of-network balance-bill or participate in dispute resolution, even if her state passed a surprise medical billing law with these requirements.

The Supreme Court's expansive view that ERISA pre-empts state law reporting requirements for ERISA plans has far-reaching consequences for state health care transparency efforts that center upon information reporting and disclosure from health plans. For consumers, the availability of the protections provided by these state health care transparency laws hinges on whether their employer offers a self-funded health plan, which is itself opaque. Relatively few employees know whether their employer self-funds their health plan, because the plan is administered by what appears to be a health insurance company, such as Aetna or Cigna, but is really a third-party administrator, acting on behalf of the employer.

IV. THE NEED FOR A FEDERAL SOLUTION

The growing sweep of ERISA pre-emption significantly limits the reach of state transparency laws aimed at protecting health care consumers and constraining rising health care costs. For state transparency efforts to achieve their fullest effect, changes are required at the federal level. A federal solution could take a couple forms. First, the Department of Labor could provide guidance or rulemaking to establish federal standards on health care transparency applicable to ERISA plans or, better yet, work with states in a hybrid approach. Second, Congress could amend ERISA to protect state efforts to improve health care transparency from ERISA's pre-emptive reach.

---

[32] *Gerhart*, 852 F.3d at 730–31.

Although federal action is necessary for health care transparency efforts to reach all consumers, the federal government should craft its solution in a manner that preserves state flexibility and innovation.

A. Federal Rules from the Department of Labor

The Department of Labor regulates employee health plans under ERISA, so the Department could issue rules for ERISA plans to establish federal requirements for price transparency, drug price transparency, provider network transparency, and surprise medical bills, provided it has the requisite statutory authority to establish each substantive federal standard. In some areas, such as price transparency reporting requirements, the Department currently has the statutory authority to regulate. In others, including surprise billing and network adequacy, the Department's authority is less clear, as discussed below. Where substantive consumer protections extend beyond the Department's statutory authority under ERISA, Congress would need to pass additional legislation for the rulemaking solution to work.[33]

1. Health Care and Drug Price Transparency Regulations

To require ERISA plans to report health care and drug utilization and price information, the Department of Labor could independently create federal regulations governing health care transparency, or it could work with state or private entities to coordinate those efforts. To do so, the Department could use its existing authority under the Affordable Care Act (ACA) and ERISA to require self-funded health plans and their administrators to report a standardized set of data about health care claims and drug pricing to the Department.[34] The statutory authority for the Department to require ERISA plans to submit health care claims data derives from Public Health Service Act (PHSA) § 2715A, which authorizes collection of data on health care costs and payments,[35] and PHSA § 2717, which authorizes collection of data on health care quality.[36] Both provisions were among those health insurance reforms created by the ACA and applied to group health plans by ERISA § 715.[37] In addition, the Department of Labor has authority to collect data under the provisions of ERISA §§ 104 and 505, which authorize the Department to promulgate regulations and require any

---

[33] See Mark A. Hall et al., Solving Surprise Medical Bills, The Schaeffer Initiative for Innovation in Health Policy, A Brookings Institution-USC Schaeffer Center Partnership 24 (Oct. 2016), www.brookings.edu/wpcontent/uploads/2016/10/sbb1.pdf.

[34] See Nat'l Acad. for State Health Policy, Comments on Department of Labor Notice of Proposed Rulemaking (Sep. 20, 2016), www.dol.gov/sites/default/files/ebsa/laws-and-regulations/rules-and-regulations/public-comments/1210-AB63/00030.pdf.

[35] 42 U.S.C. § 300gg-15a.

[36] 42 U.S.C. § 300gg-17.

[37] 29 U.S.C. § 1185d.

information or data from plans as necessary to carry out the purposes of the statute.[38]

While it may have the authority to require ERISA plans to report health care and drug claims data, the Department of Labor may lack the resources necessary to collect, store, analyze, and distribute the information to states, policymakers, and researchers. Alternatively, under ERISA § 506, the Department could partner with states, and potentially private entities, to facilitate collection, analysis, and distribution of self-funded ERISA plans' claim and PBM drug pricing data.[39] Under this partnership model, the Department could require ERISA plans to report such data to a state-run APCD[40] or to a private entity contracted to perform the functions of an APCD for states without an APCD, similar to the federal exchanges under the ACA. Under this model, regulators and health services researchers would have access to standardized ERISA plan claims data from across the nation, and more consumers could benefit from price transparency and quality transparency tools powered by this data. In short, this model would close the transparency and information gap created by *Gobeille* for self-funded ERISA plans. Importantly, several states with existing APCDs as well as payers have agreed to a standardized "common data layout" that could form the basis for a federal standard and address the burden identified by the Court in *Gobeille* from ERISA plans having to comply with inconsistent state reporting requirements.[41] Thus, the Department has options to work with states and private entities to coordinate and utilize health care claims data in ways that can alleviate the costs and administrative burdens of doing so.

2. Surprise Billing and Network Adequacy Laws

In contrast to price transparency, the Labor Department's statutory authority to issue substantive rules on network transparency and surprise medical bills is a bit more ambiguous. The Department could interpret its network adequacy standards to require ERISA plans to count surprise bills toward annual out-of-pocket maximums.[42] Under the ACA § 1311 and PHSA § 2715A, which require transparency of cost-sharing and out-of-network payments of health plans, the Department could require ERISA plans to disclose to enrollees: (1) the fact they are about to receive care from an out-of-network provider at an in-network facility; and (2) how much it

---

[38] 29 U.S.C. §§ 1024(a)(2)(B), 1135.
[39] 29 U.S.C. § 1136.
[40] See Nat'l Acad. for State Health Policy, supra note 35.
[41] See APCD Council, Standards, www.apcdcouncil.org/standards (last visited Mar. 28, 2017).
[42] 42 U.S.C. § 300gg-6(b); Mark Hall, How the Department of Labor Can Help End Surprise Medical Bills, Brookings, Dec. 14, 2016, www.brookings.edu/2016/12/14/how-the-department-of-labor-can-help-end-surprise-medical-bills/; Dep'ts of Labor, Health & Human Servs., Treasury, FAQ About Affordable Care Act Implementation (Part XXI), Oct. 10, 2014, www.dol.gov/sites/default/files/ebsa/about-ebsa/our-activities/resource-center/faqs/aca-part-xxi.pdf.

will cost the enrollee to see the out-of-network provider.[43] Such information, by itself, would not provide much assistance to a patient who is unable to avoid an out-of-network provider, such as in an emergency, under anesthesia, or when no in-network providers are available, as is often the case in surprise billing cases. Unfortunately, it remains unclear whether the Labor Department has the existing statutory authority to directly *require* ERISA plans to hold beneficiaries harmless from surprise bills. Mark A. Hall has suggested that where the Department lacks the authority to mandate protections by group health plans, it could incentivize voluntary protections by creating a safe harbor that would shield employers from claims that they breached their fiduciary duties to enrollees under ERISA if the employer complied with provisions protecting enrollees from surprise medical bills.[44] Such a safe harbor could establish a federal standard for protections against surprise bills, including holding enrollees harmless from surprise bills, participating in dispute resolution, or abiding by out-of-network payment limits. In addition, the Department of Labor could also clarify through rules or guidance that states retain the authority to regulate *providers*, such as capping providers' out-of-network rates, prohibiting surprise billing by providers, and limiting providers' collection practices. To be clear, states have the authority to regulate providers with or without such a clarification from the Department of Labor. Moreover, even if states enforce their surprise medical billing laws only against providers to avoid ERISA pre-emption, health plans must be included in the regulation for these protections to really work, by obligating plans to hold patients harmless or deciding how to count surprise bills toward deductibles or cost-sharing limits. Federal rules on surprise medical bills would provide additional transparency for patients to help them avoid surprise bills, but more limited substantive protections once the bill was incurred.

The Department of Labor's uncertain authority under ERISA to promulgate comprehensive health care transparency rules underscores the enormity of the black hole created by ERISA: ERISA pre-emption means that states cannot enforce health care transparency requirements against self-funded ERISA plans, but the Department may not have the authority under ERISA to promulgate parallel federal requirements of self-funded plans. In these areas, no one – neither the states nor the Department of Labor – has the authority to regulate self-funded health plans.

B. Amend ERISA

Alternatively, Congress could amend ERISA to carve out state health care transparency laws that require participation of health plans (for example, state APCD

---

[43] 42 U.S.C. § 18031 (setting forth cost-sharing transparency requirements for Exchange plans); 42 U.S.C. § 300gg-15a (requiring group health plans to provide the information required of Exchange plans in 42 U.S.C. § 18031); 29 U.S.C. § 1185d (incorporating the ACA's market reforms for Exchange and other health insurance plans into ERISA with respect to group health plans).

[44] See Hall, supra note 34.

reporting laws, PBM transparency laws, or surprise medical billing protections) from ERISA's pre-emptive scheme, replacing broad pre-emption with ordinary conflict pre-emption.[45] Under conflict pre-emption, state laws are only pre-empted if they conflict with federal law, as opposed to ERISA's broader pre-emption scheme that pre-empts all state laws if they relate to employee benefit plans, whether or not they conflict with ERISA. This change would permit states to experiment with additional or different consumer protections, but allow federal standards to be established where desired.

The challenge here is largely political. Even though ERISA has strayed far beyond its original scope, the current political climate appears generally deregulatory and may favor business interests – the self-funded plan sponsors and their third-party administrators – over the interests of individual consumers or even states. Continued ERISA pre-emption serves business interests by promoting national uniformity of standards for employers sponsoring benefit plans, as well as minimizing regulation to entice multistate employers to continue to offer employee benefits. Nevertheless, such employers continue to have strong incentives to offer health benefits owing to preferred tax treatment and labor market demands. Moreover, much of the current rhetoric in health policy favors giving states more responsibility and flexibility for their health care systems and increasing consumerism to reign in health care spending. These themes could swing political support in favor of limited carve-outs to ERISA that open the door for state health transparency efforts.

If state flexibility and consumer responsibility represent current ideology in health policy, then a measure to exempt state health care transparency and consumer protection laws from ERISA pre-emption would serve these principles better than seeking issue-specific federal regulation from the Department of Labor on each of these health care transparency measures.

C. What States Can Do to Promote Transparency

In the meantime, states can take a few steps to avoid ERISA pre-emption of their health care transparency efforts. First, states can promulgate measures that require disclosure and participation from non-ERISA entities, such as health care providers or drug manufacturers. These requirements do not relate to an employee benefit plan, and thus do not implicate ERISA pre-emption. Second, states can continue to require transparency of plans other than self-insured ERISA plans, including fully insured plans, state employee health plans, nongroup plans, and Medicaid plans. Third, states can encourage voluntary participation by self-funded ERISA plans by demonstrating to employers the benefits of transparency, including enabling more value-based provision of health care for their employees

---

[45] See Elizabeth Y. McCuskey, Body of Preemption: Health Law Traditions and the Presumption Against Preemption, 89 Temp. L. Rev. 95, 103 (2016).

and providing employers with analyses of the cost-drivers of their employee health plans. These efforts do not entirely fill the gap created by *Gobeille*, but for states that have expended resources to implement APCDs, proceeding with a more limited set of data may still be possible. Finally, states may still require incidental reporting of data pursuant to a tax on health plans, including ERISA plans, such as taxes to fund Medicaid or high-risk pools. A post-*Gobeille* court decision held that such assessments on employer-based plans are *not* pre-empted by ERISA, and that incidental reporting of data pursuant to a tax on health plans would be permitted.[46] This Sixth Circuit decision preserves states' ability to levy taxes on payers, including ERISA plans, to finance health programs. In addition, the decision opens up an avenue for states to gather some data from ERISA plans and escape pre-emption, by collecting the data incidentally to an exercise of traditional state regulation.[47]

V. CONCLUSION

ERISA has grown far beyond its intended purpose as a federal law regulating employee pension and retirement plans into a pre-emptive black hole that is increasingly consuming the field of state health and safety regulation. The expanding scope of ERISA pre-emption significantly limits the ability of consumers and purchasers to have all the information they need to be active and effective purchasers, even while policymakers contemplate an increasing reliance on health savings accounts, consumerism, and state flexibility to deliver health care and reign in health care costs. In its current state, ERISA pre-emption of state transparency laws cripples state attempts to protect their citizen-consumers and oversee rising health care costs. ERISA pre-emption excludes a large and growing number of individuals and families insured by self-funded employer health plans from the benefits of state health care transparency laws. Despite meaningful state innovation and leadership, fixing the ERISA black hole requires a federal solution to protect all health care consumers from medical-bill related financial harms. However, the federal government should work with states to craft a solution that achieves states' transparency goals while preserving state flexibility and innovation.

---

[46] See *Self-Ins. Inst. of Am., Inc. v. Snyder*, 827 F.3d 549 (6th Cir. 2016), cert. denied, No. 16-593, 2017 WL 69264 (U.S. Jan. 9, 2017).
[47] See Case Comment, Sixth Circuit Holds that ERISA Does Not Preempt Michigan Medicaid Tax Law: Self Insurance Institute of America v. Snyder, 130 Harv. L. Rev. 1512, 1520–21 (2017).

21

Transparency and Data Sharing in Clinical Research and Big Pharma

*Jennifer E. Miller**

INTRODUCTION

The importance of clinical trial transparency for patient care, protecting research participants, and health care innovation, is now widely established and consensus based. However, there remain debates around how to define, measure, and practice appropriate levels of clinical trial transparency. Academics, researchers, regulators, nongovernmental agencies (NGOs), industry trade associations, medical societies, and pharmaceutical companies[1] often differ in their definitions and practices.[2] Additionally, their standards and practices have been evolving, trending toward greater openness, over the last twenty years and continue to evolve as this chapter is being written.

This heterogeneity and mutability in standards and practices result in confusion around exactly which trials should be subject to information sharing, the typology of information that should be shared, when and where to disclose information, as well as who is ultimately responsible for reporting, publishing, and sharing trial information.

Accordingly, this chapter describes three categories of prominent definitions for clinical trial transparency that have emerged in practice and guidance documents. It also shows how new drugs approved by the FDA and large drug companies are performing relative to these definitions. Because industry is the largest sponsor of

---

* The author thanks Nolan Ritcey for his research contributions to this chapter.
[1] Charles Piller, Failure to Report: A STAT Investigation of Clinical Trials Reporting, STAT, Dec. 13 2015, www.statnews.com/2015/12/13/clinical-trials-investigation/; Ruijun Chen et al., Publication and Reporting of Clinical Trial Results: Cross Sectional Analysis Across Academic Medical Centers, 352 BMJ i637 (2016).
[2] Joseph S. Ross et al., Trial Publication after Registration in ClinicalTrials.Gov: A Cross-Sectional Analysis, 6 PLoS Med. e1000144 (2009); Christopher W. Jones et al., Non-Publication of Large Randomized Clinical Trials: Cross Sectional Analysis, 347 BMJ f6104 (2013); Kirby Lee et al., Publication of Clinical Trials Supporting Successful New Drug Applications: A Literature Analysis, 5 PLoS Med. e191 (2008); Joseph S. Ross et al., Publication of NIH-Funded Trials Registered in ClinicalTrials.gov: Cross Sectional Analysis, 344 BMJ d7292 (2012); Kay Dickersin & Drummond Rennie, Registering Clinical Trials, 290 JAMA 2545 (2003); Monique L. Anderson et al., Compliance with Results Reporting at ClinicalTrials.gov, 372 N. Engl. J. Med. 1031 (2015).

clinical research, accounting for 90 percent of total clinical research spending for investigational drugs and devices[3] and, more generally, 58 percent of all United States biomedical research spending,[4] this paper focuses on the transparency practices of pharmaceutical and biotechnology companies.

DEFINING CLINICAL TRIAL TRANSPARENCY

Current clinical trial transparency practices and definitions can be classified into three categories: (1) baseline U.S. legal requirements, (2) middle-tier standards that go beyond legal requirements and are generally reflected in industry trade association codes of conduct and prominent multi-stakeholder guidance documents, and (3) newer more demanding standards recommended by forward-thinking funders and NGOs and implemented by a few field leaders.

Baseline Standards: U.S. Legal Requirements

The Food and Drug Administration Modernization Act (FDAMA), enacted in 1997, was one of the earlier U.S. regulations on clinical trial transparency. It mandated the creation of a clinical trial registry, or databank, to be maintained by the National Institutes of Health (NIH). It also newly required the registration of trials for *serious* or *life-threatening* diseases and conditions in the NIH databank within twenty-one days of the approval of the trial's protocol. As part of registration, researchers were to disclose various trial information, including the purpose of the experimental drug, participation eligibility criteria, trial site location, and who to contact to enroll in the trial. The act stressed registration language should be "in a form that can be readily understood by members of the public,"[5] in other words, in *lay language*.

Ten years later, the movement toward formalized transparency requirements was further solidified into law in 2007 by the Food and Drug Administration Amendments Act (FDAAA), Section 801. FDAAA extended registration requirements beyond just trials for serious and life-threatening conditions to include all types of conditions and diseases. It also added new *results reporting* requirements.[6]

More recently, the NIH issued a Final Rule with respect to FDAAA, which went into effect on January 18, 2017. The Final Rule clarifies language ambiguities in FDAAA and further expands reporting requirements to include more types of trials for both FDA-approved and *unapproved* indications. Additionally, expanded access

---

[3] Kenneth A. Getz, Sizing Up the Clinical Research Market, Applied Clinical Trials (Mar. 1, 2010), www.appliedclinicaltrialsonline.com/sizing-clinical-research-market.

[4] E. Ray Dorsey et al., Funding of US Biomedical Research, 2003–2008, 303 JAMA 137 (2010).

[5] Food and Drug Administration Modernization Act of 1997, Pub. L. No. 105–115 (1997), www.fda.gov/RegulatoryInformation/LawsEnforcedbyFDA/SignificantAmendmentstotheFDCAct/FDAMA/FullTextofFDAMAlaw/default.htm.

[6] Food and Drug Administration Amendments Act of 2007, H.R. 3580, 110th Cong. § 801(j)(1)(A)(ix) (I–II) (2007), www.govtrack.us/congress/bills/110/hr3580.

trials are now required to be registered.[7] Phase I trials conducted in healthy volunteers, trials conducted entirely outside the United States, and trials for drugs manufactured outside the United States are generally *not* required to be reported for industry-sponsored trials, under the Final Rule. However, they are for NIH-sponsored trials, arguably creating a double standard for publicly versus privately funded trials.[8]

About 17–24 percent of trials conducted to gain regulatory approval of a new drug are subject to mandatory results reporting under FDAAA.[9] While it is too early to calculate the exact percentage of trials in New Drug Applications (NDA) that will be covered by the Final Rule, it is likely fair to estimate that the percentage will be about the same as under FDAAA.

Middle-Tier Standards: Trade Associations and Prominent Guidance Documents

Around 2009, the industry trade association Pharmaceutical Research and Manufacturers of America (PhRMA) and individual drug companies committed to a slightly more robust definition of clinical trial transparency than what was mandated in FDAAA. PhRMA committed its member companies to disclose results for *all* trials conducted in *patients* for *approved* drugs "by the *latter* of twelve months after the trial ends or within thirty days after approval of the drug."[10] This definition is slightly broader than FDAAA, as it does not explicitly exclude trials conducted entirely outside the United States, uncontrolled trials, or trials for drugs manufactured outside the United States. The 2009 industry definition for clinical trial transparency covers about 32 percent of trials in a successful NDA.[11]

Other prominent guidance documents, such as The World Medical Association's (WMA) Declaration of Helsinki and the World Health Organization (WHO) Joint statement on public disclosure of results from clinical trials, recommend still more expansive transparency standards. In 2013, the WMA recommended that *all* human subjects research be registered and have public results.[12] In May of 2017, the WHO

---

[7] Deborah A. Zarin et al., Trial Reporting in ClinicalTrials.gov – The Final Rule, 375 N. Eng. J. Med. 1998 (2016).

[8] Id.; NIH Policy on the Dissemination of NIH-Funded Clinical Trial Information (Sep. 16, 2016), https://grants.nih.gov/grants/guide/notice-files/NOT-OD-16–149.html.

[9] Jennifer E. Miller et al., Clinical Trial Registration, Reporting, Publication and FDAAA Compliance: A Cross-Sectional Analysis and Ranking of New Drugs Approved by the FDA in 2012, 5 BMJ Open e009758 (2015), http://bmjopen.bmj.com/content/5/11/e009758.

[10] PhRMA, Principles on Conduct of Clinical Trials: Communication of Clinical Trial Results (2009), http://phrma-docs.phrma.org/sites/default/files/pdf/042009_clinical_trial_principles_final.pdf.

[11] Jennifer E. Miller et al., Measuring Clinical Trial Transparency: An Empirical Analysis of Newly Approved Drugs and Large Pharmaceutical Companies, BMJ Open 2017;0:e017917 (2017).

[12] World Medical Association, WMA Declaration of Helsinki – Ethical Principles for Medical Research Involving Human Subjects (Oct. 19, 2013), www.wma.net/policies-post/wma-declaration-of-helsinki-ethical-principles-for-medical-research-involving-human-subjects/.

along with twenty other organizations, including the Bill and Melinda Gates Foundation and Wellcome Trust, signed a joint statement affirming the WMA's guidelines and adding compliance deadlines.

The WHO recommends research results should be both reported in a public registry and published in the medical literature. Registry reporting should occur by twelve months after a study's primary completion date (the last visit of the last subject for collection of data on the primary outcome). Publication in a medical journal is recommended within twenty-four months of a trial's completion.[13] The WHO also recommends that trial protocols be made publicly available no later than the time of summary results reporting. Interestingly, the statement is rather silent on the issue of sharing patient-level trial data. It merely states that it supports the concept and the development of ethics and legal frameworks to govern data use and sharing.

The WMA and WHO conceptualizations of clinical trial transparency are far more robust than FDAAA requirements, as they recommend the reporting of *all* trial results. This includes Phase I trials, trials in healthy volunteers, trials conducted entirely outside the United States, trials for drugs manufactured in any country, and perhaps most noteworthy – trials for unapproved drugs – all of which are excluded from FDAAA. This standard applies to about 71–92 percent of trials in an NDA.[14] It does not apply to 100 percent of trials at the time the FDA approves a drug or even a year later, because many trials in an NDA are still ongoing or not yet at least one year past their completion date at those points.

Emerging Standards

More demanding standards for clinical trial transparency – beyond registration, reporting summary results, and publishing trials in the medical literature – are emerging. Now, several funders, NGOs, and companies are advocating for sharing of patient-level trial data.[15] Patient-level trial data can involve two elements: the analysis-ready data set and trial metadata. Metadata are generally contained in the Clinical Study Report. Alternatively, the elements of metadata are fourfold. They include the data set dictionary, the study protocol, the statistical analysis plan, and the Clinical Study Report synopsis.

---

[13] World Health Organization, Joint statement on public disclosure of results from clinical trials (2017), www.who.int/ictrp/results/jointstatement/en/index1.html.

[14] Miller et al., supra note 9.

[15] Darren B. Taichman et al., Sharing Clinical Trial Data: A Proposal from the International Committee of Medical Journal Editors, 13 PLoS Med. e1001950 (2016); Deborah A. Zarin, Participant-Level Data and the New Frontier in Trial Transparency, 369 N. Eng. J. Med. 468 (2013); Peter Doshi et al., The Imperative to Share Clinical Study Reports: Recommendations from the Tamiflu Experience, 9 PLoS Med. e1001201 (2012); Joseph S. Ross & Harlan M. Krumholz, Ushering in a New Era of Open Science Through Data Sharing: The Wall Must Come Down, 309 JAMA 1355 (2013).

Motivations to request and share such data are twofold: (1) advocates believe sharing patient-level data better honors the people who participate in trials by ensuring their data maximally contribute to generalizable knowledge,[16] and (2) access to patient-level data, as opposed to summary trial results, may allow scientists to innovate new cures more quickly, conserve resources, and better replicate and reproduce existing studies.[17]

Data sharing standards are much newer and still evolving compared to those for trial registration, which date back to at least 1997. The National Academies of Medicine (NAM) (formerly, the IOM) released its principles for data sharing in 2015. The guidelines apply to trials initiated after January 14, 2015.[18] PhRMA and EFPIA (the European counterpart to PhRMA) released data sharing principles for its member companies to implement starting on January 1, 2014.[19] Around 2014, two large pharmaceutical companies, GlaxoSmithKline[20] and Johnson and Johnson (J&J), took leads in data sharing, publicly committing to sharing patient-level data for large trials supporting FDA-approved drugs.[21]

GSK shares data via ClinicalStudyDataRequest.com (CSDR), which is now a multi-sponsor platform also used by Astellas, Bayer, Boehringer Ingelheim, Daiichi Sankyo, Eisai, Lilly, Novartis, Roche, Sanofi, Takeda, UCB, and ViiV Healthcare.[22] J&J, on the other hand, partnered with Yale University to form the

[16] Howard Bauchner et al., Data Sharing: An Ethical and Scientific Imperative, 315 JAMA 1237 (2016); Jane Kaye et al., From Patients to Partners: Participant-centric Initiatives in Biomedical Research, 13 Nat. Revs. Genetics 371 (2012); Peter C. Gøtzsche, Why We Need Easy Access to All Data From All Clinical Trials and How to Accomplish it, 12 Trials 249 (2011); Sharon F. Terry & Patrick F. Terry, Power to the People: Participant Ownership of Clinical Trial Data, 3 Sci. Translational Med. 69cm3 (2011); Andrew J. Vickers, Whose Data Set is it Anyway? Sharing Raw Data from Randomized Trials, 7 Trials 15 (2006).
[17] Dimitri A. Christakis & Frederick J. Zimmerman, Rethinking Reanalysis, 310 JAMA 2499 (2013); Mark Walport & Paul Brest, Sharing Research Data to Improve Public Health, 377 The Lancet 537 (2011); Taichman et al., supra note 15; Bauchner et al., supra note 16; PhRMA, Principles for Clinical Trial Data Sharing (2017), www.phrma.org/codes-and-guidelines/phrma-principles-for-responsible-clinical-trial-data-sharing1.
[18] Nat'l Acads. of Sci., Eng'g, & Med., Health & Med. Div., Sharing Clinical Trial Data: Maximizing Benefits, Minimizing Risk (Jan. 14, 2015), www.nationalacademies.org/hmd/Reports/2015/Sharing-Clinical-Trial-Data.aspx.
[19] PhRMA, Principles for Responsible Clinical Data Sharing (2013), http://phrma-docs.phrma.org/sites/default/files/pdf/PhRMAPrinciplesForResponsibleClinicalTrialDataSharing.pdf.
[20] Perry Nisen & Frank Rockhold, Access to Patient-level Data from GlaxoSmithKline Clinical Trials, 369 N. Eng. J. Med. 475 (2013); Clinical Study Data Request Home Page, https://clinicalstudydatarequest.com/ (last accessed Oct. 25, 2017).
[21] PhRMA, Press release: EFPIA-PhRMA Rules for Clinical Trial Data Sharing Active (Jan. 1, 2014), www.phrma.org/press-release/joint-efpia-phrma-principles-for-responsible-clinical-trial-data-sharing-become-effective-today.
[22] Lisa Henderson, Behind ClinicalStudyDataRequest.com in Pharma Transparency, Applied Clinical Trials, May 22, 2014, www.appliedclinicaltrialsonline.com/behind-clinicalstudydatarequestcom-pharma-transparency.

YODA Platform, also used by Medtronic and SI-BONE, Inc.[23] Subsequently, other companies followed suit,[24] including Bristol-Myers Squibb, who partnered with Duke University to form the SOAR initiative, and NovoNordisk, who shares data on their own corporate website managed by an independent review panel of academics.

While similar in mission, the data sharing systems differ significantly. CSDR, for example, allows companies *veto power*. That is, a company can deny access to data despite an independent review panel recommending sharing is appropriate.[25] NovoNordisk and YODA, in contrast, do not generally allow vetoes to their independent review panel decisions. Additionally, under CSDR, each participating data holder can set their own data sharing policy. Therefore, trial sponsors vary on which trials they provide data for and the timelines for sharing. For example, Astellas, one of CSDR's participants, makes data available for Phase 1 to 4 clinical trials completed after January 2010. In contrast, Roche shares only Phase 2 and 3 studies, but will share older studies dating back to 1999. Smaller platforms like YODA are more likely to have a single homogenous policy for all data-holder participants. CSDR and YODA both provide public metrics about the types of data requests they receive and how the requests were handled.

NAM (IOM) and the PhRMA-EFPIA standards vary as well. NAM is specific on its deadlines for sharing data, whereas the trade associations are not. NAM urges research sponsors to share data by the *latter* of thirty days after FDA and EMA approval of a drug, eighteen months after the primary completion date of a trial, or six months after the publication of a trial. In contrast, the trade associations ask that companies share within a *reasonable* period of time. While more specific, the NAM guidelines may have a loophole; if a sponsor does not publish its trial results, it may not have to share trial data.

They also vary in the types of data they recommend for sharing. NAM recommends that both the analysis ready data set and trial metadata be shared. For NAM, metadata includes four elements: the statistical analysis plan, study protocol, clinical study report (CSR), and analytic code. PhRMA and EFPIA commit member companies to sharing the analysis ready data set and only two parts of metadata: the study protocol and CSR – not the statistical analysis plan or analytics code. NAM is generally silent about which trials should be subject to data sharing, stating mainly

---

[23] Harlan M. Krumholz et al., A Historic Moment for Open Science: The Yale University Open Data Access Project and Medtronic, 158 Annals Intern. Med. 910 (2013); Yale University Open Data Access (YODA), Policies & Procedures to Guide External Investigator Access to Clinical Trial Data, http://yoda.yale.edu/policies-procedures-guide-external-investigator-access-clinical-trial-data (last visited Oct. 25, 2017).

[24] Brian L. Strom et al., Data Sharing, Year 1—Access to Data from Industry-Sponsored Clinical Trials, 371 N. Eng. J. Med. 2052 (2014); Ann Marie Navar et al., Use of Open Access Platforms for Clinical Trial Data, 315 JAMA 1283 (2016); Vinay Rathi et al., Sharing of Clinical Trial Data Among Trialists: A Cross Sectional Survey, 345 BMJ e7570 (2012).

[25] Brian L. Strom et al., Data Sharing – Is the Juice Worth the Squeeze?, 375 N. Eng. J. Med. 1608 (2016).

that it is those initiated after January 14, 2016. In contrast, the trade associations generally consider data sharing appropriate for trials in *patients* for products *approved* in both the United States and EU after January 1, 2014.

There remain some ethical concerns around the broad sharing of patient-level data. For example, many guidance documents express patient privacy concerns for trials with small enrollment numbers and for diseases affecting small populations. Both NAM (IOM) and PhRMA exclude rare diseases, diseases affecting less than 200,000 patients in the United States at any given time, from data sharing, noting that small populations can make reidentification of patients easier.

Also, some companies and trade associations claim certain types of trial data and information are proprietary and trade secrets. PhRMA argues providing access to some trial data could allow competitors a "free ride" off the investments of their member companies. They note,

> ... discovering and developing new medicines is a long, complex, and costly process. For every 5,000 to 10,000 experimental compounds considered, typically only one will gain FDA approval, after 10 to 15 years of research and development costing an average of $1.2 billion ... only two out of every 10 medicines will recoup the money spent on their development.[26]

Exact definitions for trade secrets and proprietary commercial information are hard to pin down, but in general they seem to involve information that could help a competitor "gain approval of a competing medicine."[27]

In my personal conversations with companies, it seems aspects of the *statistical analysis code* for trials are also considered proprietary by some. Arguments from companies for not sharing this code include that it likely will not work outside the environment in which it was created, that they do not generally receive requests for code, and that one can replicate a study by following the statistical analysis plan and therefore the code is not needed for replication. You can see this position reflected in PhRMA's code of conduct for data sharing; it does not require sharing the statistical analysis code, like the NAM (IOM) guidelines suggest.

My sense is that it is not the code, per se, that is considered proprietary, but the *macros* that inform the code. Companies may be willing to share the code, but it is likely useless without the macros. A *macro* can be defined as a fragment of code that has been given a name such that whenever the name is used, it is replaced by the contents of the macro.[28] Macros can be *object-like* macros resembling data objects or *function-like* macros resembling function calls.[29]

---

[26] PhRMA, supra note 21.
[27] Id.
[28] Macros, The C Preprocessor: Macros, https://gcc.gnu.org/onlinedocs/cpp/Macros.html (last visited Oct. 25, 2017).
[29] Id.

While there is growing momentum for trial sponsors to share patient-level trial data, the practice remains nescient. Academia and small companies are especially behind in setting and implementing data sharing policies. Additionally, not many trials in NDAs for recently approved drugs are subject to data sharing yet, because of the late application dates of the guidelines and initiatives (that is, 2015 and 2014).

Lastly, there is growing momentum to return aggregate or individual trial results, in lay language, to patients participating in trials. Motivations for returning results to research participants include fostering trust in the clinical research system, honoring their participation, helping patients better understand the nature of what they participated in and clinical research more generally, and perhaps even using these data to advance their own personal health.

Pfizer states it was the first drug company to return "lay-language clinical trial data to patients."[30] The company piloted the return process in 2009 with four trials and has since expanded the program. It aims to provide "Blue Button" technology to its U.S. trial participants.

Blue Button is a national project, started around 2009, so patients can access the health information collected about them from third parties like "doctors' offices, hospitals, drug stores and health insurance companies."[31] Today, the button symbolizes "that an organization has a way for you to access your health records electronically."[32] In the case of Pfizer and lay summaries, it "enables the secure electronic delivery of medical information gathered in a study directly to trial participants and allows integration into electronic medical records."[33]

Below is a summary table of the above discussed transparency standards (Table 1).

MEASURING CLINICAL TRANSPARENCY

The Measures

While there has been a plethora of academic studies[34] over the years measuring clinical trial transparency using various definitions, only two groups have emerged to

---

[30] Pfizer, Returning Clinical Data to Patients, www.pfizer.com/science/clinical_trials/trial_data_and_results/data_to_patients (last visited Oct. 25, 2017).
[31] HealthIT.gov, Blue Button, www.healthit.gov/patients-families/your-health-data (last visited Oct. 25, 2017).
[32] Id.
[33] Pfizer, supra note 30.
[34] Joseph S. Ross et al., Trial Publication after Registration in ClinicalTrials.Gov: A Cross-Sectional Analysis, 6 PLoS Med. e1000144 (2009), http://journals.plos.org/plosmedicine/article?id=10.1371/journal.pmed.1000144; Jones et al., supra note 2; Sally Hopewell et al., Publication Bias in Clinical Trials Due to Statistical Significance or Direction of Trial Results, 1 Cochrane Database of Systematic Revs. MR000006 (2009), http://onlinelibrary.wiley.com/doi/10.1002/14651858.MR000006.pub3/full; K. Dickersin et al., Publication Bias and Clinical Trials, 8 Controlled Clinical Trials 343 (1987), www.sciencedirect.com/science/article/pii/0197245687901553; Kirby Lee et al., Publication of Clinical Trials Supporting Successful New Drug Applications: A Literature Analysis, 5 PLoS Med. e191 (2008); Ross et al., supra note 2; Anderson et al., supra note 2.

Tiers of Definitions	Source of Definition	Covered Trials	Trial Elements to Share	Deadline for Sharing Trial Elements
Tier 1: Baseline Standards	Legal requirements defined in FDAAA	FDAAA: Registration and summary results reporting in a public trial registry of interventional non-phase I trials for **approved products** only. This generally excludes trials conducted entirely outside the US and trials for drugs manufactured outside the US	Summary trial results	By **30** days after FDA approval of drug
Tier 2: Middle-tier Standards	PhRMA Principles on conduct of clinical trials: communication of clinical trial results	Registration and summary results reporting in a public registry for trials conducted in **patients** for **approved products**. Generally, excludes phase I trials in healthy volunteers	Summary trial results	By the **latter** of **12** months after the trial ends or within **30** days after FDA approval of the drug
	Prominent guidance documents, like the Declaration of Helsinki and WHO joint statement	Results for **all** clinical trials, including trials in healthy volunteers, should be publicly available in a registry or the medical literature	Summary trial results with trial protocol and publication in medical journal	By **12** months post a trial's primary completion date (PCD) and **24** months post publication in a medical journal.

Tier 3: More demanding emerging standards and practices	NAM (IOM) report	Clinical trials initiated after 1/14/2015, excludes trials with high risk of reidentification, i.e., *rare disease* trials	1. Analysis-ready dataset
			2. Metadata: including all of below:
			  a. Statistical analysis plan
			  b. Protocol
			  c. Analytic code
			  d. CSR
				By **30** days after drug approval, **18** months post trials' PCD, or **6** months after publication, whichever is later

	PhRMA and EFPIA principles for data sharing	Trials in **patients** for *approved* drugs submitted for approval in the US and EU after 1/1/2014, excludes trials with high risk of reidentification, i.e., *rare disease* trials	1. Analysis-ready dataset
			2. Metadata: including all of below:
			  a. Protocol
			  b. CSR
				Within a reasonable period, post drug approval

	Company practices, particular Pfizer, the first to implement this standard.	Phase IIb & Phase III studies initiated in or after 2014, in countries where regulations will allow it.	The above plus summary trial results, in easy-to-read, nontechnical language for trial participants, including: 1. Why study was done 2. How it was done 3. Results	Unclear

consistently benchmark the transparency performance of research sponsors: AllTrials and Bioethics International. AllTrials created the TrialTracker and Bioethics International created the Good Pharma Scorecard.

While differing in their scopes and methods, both initiatives aim to track clinical trial transparency performance and progress over time, recognize best practices, and incent reform where needed. AllTrials debuted TrialsTracker in November of 2016, to track whether registered trials on ClinicalTrials.Gov have reported or published results by two years after the end of the trial. They generally analyze interventional non-Phase 1 clinical trials, excluding trials with "a formal request to delay results."[35] The project also ranks the reviewed trial sponsors on those metrics. The process is mostly automated, so authors warn research sponsors that they must "ensure the trial ID is in their PubMed entry" to get credit for their publication.[36] AllTrials was founded in 2013 in the UK. It codeveloped TrialsTracker with academics from the University of Oxford in 2016.[37]

Bioethics International (BEI), founded in 2005, began creating the Good Pharma Scorecard (GPS) around 2007, publicly debuting the project in 2009 at a multi-stakeholder meeting hosted by Goodwin Procter in New York City.[38] Currently, the GPS is an index that evaluates and ranks both new FDA-approved drugs and pharmaceutical companies on their clinical trial transparency performance annually. The process involves identifying all trials conducted to gain regulatory approval of a drug and assessing whether those trials are registered, report results in any of its forty-plus reviewed registries (not just ClinicalTrials.Gov), are published in PubMed or EMBASE journals, share a CSR synopsis, and comply with U.S. legal disclosure requirements. We assess three samples of trials (all trials in an NDA, patient trials, and FDAAA-applicable trials) and evaluate transparency at multiple time points (at FDA approval of the drug and at three, six, and thirteen months post-approval as well as by FDAAA timelines). All data are sent to NDA sponsors for validation to help ensure accuracy. From 2012 to 2015, the GPS system was piloted at Harvard University (in 2015, Duke University's Kenan Center for Ethics also supported the pilot). The first set of rankings was published in BMJ Open in 2015. Today, the scorecard is supported by the Laura and John Arnold Foundation and led by investigators from NYU School of Medicine, Yale University, and Stanford University. Subsequent rankings include metrics assessing companies' patient-level data sharing practices.

[35] TrialsTracker, Who's Not Sharing Their Clinical Trial Results?, https://trialstracker.ebmdatalab.net /#/ (last visited Oct. 25, 2017).
[36] Id.
[37] AllTrials, Launch of new TrialsTracker (Nov. 3, 2016), www.alltrials.net/news/trialstracker/.
[38] The author is a co-founder of BEI and the GPS.

Companies' Compliance with Legal Requirements

Many large pharmaceutical companies are generally now meeting *legal* transparency requirements reflected in FDAAA. At least three studies found that a median of 100 percent of trials for each new drug approved by the FDA in 2012 and 2014, sponsored by a large company, were FDAAA compliant (IQR 88–100 percent for 2012 drugs; 75–100 percent for 2014 drugs).[39]

Strikingly, most previous studies showed that companies were largely failing to meet FDAAA requirements.[40] What changed? One big change is how the FDAAA requirements are now interpreted since the passing of the Final Rule. Previous studies, including one I co-authored and a prominent NEJM study by Anderson and colleagues (which included former FDA commissioner Robert Califf as an author), used more demanding interpretations of the law.

When FDAAA was originally passed in 2007, many experts interpreted it to require results reporting for applicable trials within *one year of a trial's primary completion date* (PCD), unless a certificate of delay was submitted to the NIH requesting an extension of time to report results. The issuance of the Final Rule last year clarified that FDAAA only applies to trials for *approved* drugs. Additionally, results for initial drug approvals are not due until *thirty days* post-FDA approval, not one year after a trial's completion.[41]

Interestingly, the Final Rule, which goes into effect this year, requires results reporting for both approved and unapproved drugs. In many ways, the Final Rule reporting requirements resemble how many of us originally interpreted FDAAA requirements back around 2007. It remains to be seen how companies will comply with the new Final Rule requirements.

Companies' Compliance with Trade Association Standards

In general, companies are close to meeting trade association requirements, but there is room for improvement. Our study of drugs approved by the FDA in 2014 found that a median of 65 percent (IQR 50–73 percent) of trials conducted in patients, for each drug, were publicly available at the time of FDA approval and 85 percent (IQR 67–100 percent) were publicly available by three months post-approval. This study did not specifically measure disclosures at thirty days post-FDA approval as required by PhRMA guidelines. However, since I was a co-author on the study and have the

---

[39] Scott M. Lassman et al., Clinical Trial Transparency: A Reassessment of Industry Compliance with Clinical Trial Registration and Reporting Requirements in the United States, 7 BMJ Open e015110 (2017); Jennifer E. Miller et al., supra note 11; Jennifer E. Miller et al., Letter in Response: Clinical Trial Transparency: A Reassessment of Industry Compliance with Clinical Trial Registration and Reporting Requirements in the United States, 7 BMJ Open e015110 (Sep. 25, 2017).

[40] A. P. Prayle et al., Compliance with Mandatory Reporting of Clinical Trial Results on ClinicalTrials.gov: Cross Sectional Study, 344 BMJ d7373 (2012), www.bmj.com/content/344/bmj.d7373; Anderson et al., supra note 2.

[41] Food and Drug Administration Amendments Act of 2007, supra note 6, at § 801(j)(3)(E)(iv).

raw data, we were able to reanalyze it for this chapter, finding that (IQR 65–100 percent) of trials, per drug, meet PhRMA requirements to report summary results by *one* year after a trial is over or *thirty* days post-regulatory approval of a drug.

These finding are supported in a study by Rawal and colleagues that found that 90 percent of company-sponsored trials conducted in *patients*, for each new medicine approved by the European Medicines Agency (EMA) in 2012, had publicly available trial results "within twelve months of the later of either first regulatory approval or trial completion."[42] Compliance with PhRMA guidelines would be lower than 90 percent, as the Rawal et al. study gave companies eleven extra months after the PhRMA deadline to report results.

Companies' Implementation of Other Guidelines

Companies are not generally meeting guidelines set by multi-stakeholder or nonindustry groups, like those in the Declaration of Helsinki and WHO Joint Statement, which call for results disclosures for *all* human subjects research, including trials in healthy volunteers, by around one year after a trial is over. Only 13.4 percent of trials reported summary results within twelve months after trial completion, according to a study by Anderson and colleagues.[43] The percentage of trials meeting these guidelines is likely even lower than 13 percent, as the Anderson et al. study excluded phase 1 trials and other trials that should be reported under the Helsinki Declaration and WHO joint statement.

It is not yet clear whether companies are consistently meeting the newer IOM and Pharma-EFPIA guidelines around patient-level data sharing. Empirical analysis is needed in this area. However, a study by Goldacre and colleagues that reviewed large companies' commitments to data sharing found that 96 percent committed to sharing CSRs and individual patient data (IPD).[44] Companies clearly have policies for data sharing. However, it remains to be measured whether their commitments have been well operationalized.

RECOMMENDATIONS

As the founder of the Good Pharma Scorecard, I have fairly set views on what is needed for the pharmaceutical industry regarding clinical trial transparency. I think an independent third-party governance system, like the Good Pharma Scorecard, is needed to help set and communicate harmonized standards for the global industry

---

[42] Bina Rawal & Bryan R. Deane, Clinical Trial Transparency Update: An Assessment of the Disclosure of Results of Company-Sponsored Trials Associated with New Medicines Approved in Europe in 2012, 31 Current Med. Res. & Opinion 1431 (2015).
[43] Anderson et al., supra note 2.
[44] Ben Goldacre et al., Pharmaceutical Companies' Policies on Access to Trial Data, Results, and Methods: Audit Study, 358 BMJ j3334 (2017).

as well as monitor, incent, and recognize their implementation and help rebuild trust into the system. Such a system should be based on multi-stakeholder dialogue. In the case of the Good Pharma Scorecard, for example, we are creating a convening system where major stakeholders in clinical trial transparency have a voice in setting standards, particularly patients. Each year we aim to host one to two round tables with each category of stakeholders (that is, with patients, industry, clinicians, regulators, academics, and the like) and one conference where all stakeholders can come together.

There are not enough opportunities for this type of dialogue. For example, companies have complained that the IOM standards were developed with consultation from only one pharma company. Additionally, it is not clear the industry standards were developed in concert with any patients.

Second, a discussion is needed about the appropriateness of having double standards for industry versus publicly funded trials. Should ownership structures and funding sources matter when it comes to reaping the public health benefits of clinical trial transparency? Publicly funded trials (that is, NIH-funded trials) are held to more demanding standards than privately funded industry trials. Part of the reason is that each sector has its own definition for clinical research. The FDA defines clinical research as

> ... any experiment that involves a test article and one or more human subjects, and that either must meet the requirements for prior submission to the FDA ... or the results of which are intended to be later submitted to, or held for inspection by, the FDA as part of an application for a research or marketing permit.[45]

In contrast, the U.S. Department of Health and Human Services (HHS) defines clinical research, "as a systematic investigation, including research development, testing and evaluation, designed to develop or contribute to generalizable knowledge."[46] This definition hails from the Belmont Report.[47] Only this definition suggests research should contribute to generalizable knowledge.

One can argue that it is not ethical to expose people to risks in trials and experiment on them without the potential for advancing generalizable knowledge and the common good. Additionally, many people sign up for trials because of altruism, that is, because of the potential to contribute to generalizable knowledge and all the potential benefits that may materialize. Therefore, these two definitions for research should likely be harmonized.

Second, and perhaps most importantly, clinical trial transparency is but one issue when it comes to fostering integrity and trustworthiness in the pharmaceutical

---

[45] U.S. Food & Drug Admin., Comparison of FDA and HHS Human Subject Protection Regulations, www.fda.gov/scienceresearch/specialtopics/runningclinicaltrials/educationalmaterials/ucm112910.htm (last updated Mar. 10, 2009).
[46] Id.
[47] Dep't of Health, Educ., & Welfare, Office for Human Research Prots., The Belmont Report (Apr. 18, 1979), www.hhs.gov/ohrp/regulations-and-policy/belmont-report/index.html.

sector. Attention is also needed on other issues, such as how clinical trials are designed. There are, for example, concerns about inclusivity in clinical trial enrollment. One worry is that drugs are often tested in healthy, young, white, males and therefore not enough minorities have access to clinical trials and the knowledge about how drugs may work for them. Other concerns involve the reproducibility of trials, whether companies complete FDA-required Phase 4 post-marketing studies, drug pricing, and the like.

I highly recommend that an ethical framework be developed for the pharmaceutical industry that comprehensively addresses all key bioethics issues. This framework should be developed in consultation with multiple stakeholders and based on a review of existing standards and expert recommendations. We have significant literature, school curricula, and attention on value and supply chains, why not on an *ethics chain* for pharmaceutical companies?

CONCLUSION

The ethics of clinical trial transparency remains a central point of discussion in research ethics. With the shift in the discussion of clinical trial transparency moving in the direction of transparency in sharing patient-level data, clinical trial sponsors face the arduous task of readying trial data for distribution and managing access to these data. In terms of research ethics, this reintroduces key questions of patient privacy, as well as issues of proprietary rights of pharmaceutical companies. The prospect of improving the pace and quality of medical research highlights the importance of answering difficult ethical questions about patient-level data sharing and addressing the logistical challenges with sharing large amounts of sensitive data. Benchmarking programs, such as those discussed, can identify common practices and measure progress toward the goal of transparency. The benchmarks can also function as quality improvement mechanisms by motivating improvement in subpar performance and illustrating the impact and feasibility of best practices from industry leaders.

22

Promoting IRB Transparency

About What, To Whom, Why, and How?

Holly Fernandez Lynch*

Researchers seeking to collect data through "intervention or interaction" with human beings, through the use of their "identifiable private information,"[1] or as part of "clinical investigations"[2] will typically find their work subject to oversight by one or more Institutional Review Boards (IRBs). IRBs are responsible to oversee research with human participants funded by U.S. government dollars or for submission to U.S. regulatory authorities; many other countries have similar systems. IRBs have the authority to approve, require modifications to, or disapprove research activities based on a number of regulatory criteria.[3] Despite this hefty responsibility and its potential impact on researchers, participants, and the public, IRB processes (in the United States and elsewhere) are largely opaque.[4] The virtues of transparency have been extolled in many other settings, however, from court decisions to allocation of health resources to clinical trial data to the FDA approval process. Is transparency a good that we ought to demand of IRBs, too? In this chapter, I argue that the answer is yes.

---

* Thank you to Mark Satta for excellent research assistance, and to Laura Odwazny, Emily Largent, and I. Glenn Cohen for insightful comments. The views reflected in this chapter are my own, and should not be attributed to any organization with which I am affiliated. The chapter is based on a longer article: Holly Fernandez Lynch, Opening Closed Doors: Promoting IRB Transparency, 46(1) J. L. Med. & Ethics 145–158 (2018).

[1] 45 C.F.R. § 46.102(f) (2016). In January 2017, Final Regulations were published to update the "Common Rule." 82 Fed. Reg. 7149 (Jan. 19, 2017). The general compliance date for these new requirements has been delayed several times; as of September 2018, the general compliance date is set for January 21, 2019. 83 Fed. Reg. 28497 (June 19, 2019). Given the transition, in this chapter, citations will be provided both to the pre-2019 regulatory provisions, as well as the regulatory sections as they will be modified under the revised Common Rule. In the revised Common Rule, this particular regulatory provision will be found at 45 C.F.R. 46.102(e) (2019).

[2] 21 C.F.R. § 50.3(c) (2016). The FDA regulations have not yet undergone revision to harmonize with the revised Common Rule.

[3] See 45 C.F.R. § 46.109(a), 46.111 (2016)(2019); 21 C.F.R. §§ 56.109(a), 56.111 (2016).

[4] See E. S. Dove, B. M. Knoppers & M. H. Zawati, Towards an Ethics Safe Harbor for Global Biomedical Research, 1 J. L. & Biosciences 3, 12 (2014); S. McMurphy, J. Lewis & P. Boulos, Extending the Olive Branch: Enhancing Communication and Trust between Research Ethics Committees and Qualitative Researchers, 8 J. Empir. Res. Hum. Res. Ethics 29, 33 (2013).

WHAT DO WE MEAN BY TRANSPARENCY?

When thinking about IRB transparency, it is important to be specific: transparency to whom, about what, and by what mechanisms? Recognizing what it is not – namely, a mandate to use or do anything with the information obtained – is also helpful. In this regard, transparency is best viewed as a means to other ends, such as trust, efficiency, and quality, as explored below.

To Whom?

The most obvious type of IRB transparency refers to accessibility to and openness with investigators and sponsors whose research protocols are under review. But other stakeholders also have a clear interest in IRB decisions and decision making, including the research participants whose interests IRBs are charged with protecting and the institutions hosting research studies who will bear the legal brunt of any IRB shortcomings. IRBs at other institutions may also have an interest in transparency among their peer boards, because they are engaged in collaborative research or because they seek to benchmark behavior of other IRBs as a learning exercise. Regulators, of course, need to know what IRBs are doing for compliance purposes.

The public in general also has a claim to transparency. IRBs are often deciding whether and how publicly funded research may proceed, they are overseeing compliance with public laws and regulations, they may be approving research that will affect the public, and they may play an important role in promoting public trust in the research enterprise.

A final stakeholder group is comprised of researchers who wish to study IRBs. As others have recognized, the transparency needed to conduct such research – on questions related to how IRBs balance risks and benefits, assess social value, handle uncertainty, view their responsibilities, explain their decisions to investigators, navigate substantive and procedural obligations, and measure their own success or failure, just to name a few examples – has traditionally been lacking,[5] but is sorely needed.[6]

About What?

Each of these stakeholders may have a desire (or need) for transparency regarding different aspects of IRB operations and outcomes. Investigators need transparency about IRB determinations regarding their protocols, as well as the underlying rationale; knowing how and why decisions were reached can be important for

---

[5] B. Bozeman, C. Slade & P. Hirsch, Understanding Bureaucracy in Health Science Ethics: Toward a Better Institutional Review Board, 99 Am. J. Public Health 1549, 1554 (2009).
[6] L. Abbott & C. Grady, A Systematic Review of the Empirical Literature Evaluating IRBs: What We Know and What We Still Need to Learn, 6 J. Empir. Res. Hum. Res. Ethics 3, 8 (2011).

compliance purposes, crafting amendments, and designing future research such that it will be approved as expeditiously as possible. Importantly, information about IRB approvals and disapprovals (or deferrals) can be equally valuable, since both provide insight into the IRB's overarching philosophy, its interpretation of relevant regulations, how it is likely to behave in the future, what should be emulated or avoided, and potentially what should be protested and changed.

In addition to the outcome and basis for IRB determinations regarding specific protocols, transparency regarding IRB procedures and policies is also useful. Investigators need to know what to submit, to whom, about what, and by when, and to understand how IRBs are interpreting various regulatory requirements that leave them with substantial discretion. The best (and typically most well-funded and institutionally supported) boards provide such information through easy-to-navigate websites, training sessions, and the like. While some IRBs have a robust library of formal policies covering a wide range of circumstances, it is also often the case that there will be informal policies that have developed over time, which can be difficult to track, circulate, and understand. There is also wide variability as to whether written IRB policies and procedures are available on an institution's public website – available for all to see, learn from, and analyze.

Finally, IRBs may have and maintain a variety of information about their own work, for example how many protocols they review, on what timeline, and of what nature, and they may have mechanisms in place for self-assessment, quality improvement, and the like. Ideally, IRBs will analyze data across these various parameters on a systematic basis, use it to adjust their own approaches, and publish it for the benefit of others. This is not technically within the IRB's regulatory purview, however, and many boards simply lack adequate resources to conduct these additional activities.

By What Mechanisms?

In terms of the mechanisms of IRB transparency, this can be achieved in a variety of ways depending on the goal to be achieved and stakeholder of interest. Some information may be provided verbally, for example through informal conversation between investigators and IRB staff, or in writing. Another mechanism might be to open IRB meetings to the team of investigators whose protocol is under review (as some IRBs already do) – or more broadly to any investigator at the institution, to other IRBs, to researchers interested in studying IRBs, to potential or current participants, or to members of the public more generally. Alternatively or in addition, IRBs might share their meeting minutes with any of these stakeholders. And similarly, IRBs could choose to make their determinations (and rationales) available beyond the affected investigator. Of course, in any of these scenarios, appropriate confidentiality requirements would need to be established.

Transparency to whom	About what	By what mechanisms
• Investigators • Sponsors • Research participants • Research institution • Other IRBs • Regulators • The public • Researchers of IRBs	• Source of authority • Protocol approvals, disapprovals, requests for modification (and rationale) • Specific regulatory, and other underlying, IRB determinations (and rationale) • Deliberations • Correspondence • Policies • Board statistics/data	• Verbal communication • Written communication • Open IRB meetings • Accessible meeting minutes • Accessible IRB determinations • Accessible IRB websites and training tools

Figure 1. Defining IRB transparency parameters

CURRENT REGULATORY REQUIREMENTS

Transparency across each of the parameters described above would be an ideal case but it is far from reality. Under the current regulatory structure, what must IRBs actually do when it comes to transparency? At present, not very much. The Federal Policy for the Protection of Human Subjects (the "Common Rule"), which governs most research conducted or supported by federal agencies, and regulations for research under the purview of the Food and Drug Administration (FDA), do address transparency generally, but they leave wide latitude for IRBs. An IRB is required to have (but not necessarily publish or share) policies for "reporting its findings and actions to the investigator and the institution,"[7] and the regulations require it to "notify investigators and the institution in writing of its decision to approve or disapprove the proposed research activity, or of modifications required to secure IRB approval of the research activity."[8] In the event the IRB decides to disapprove a research activity (which is exceedingly rare – deferrals until amendments are made are much more common), "it shall include in its written notification a statement of the reasons for its decision and give the investigator an opportunity to respond in person or in writing."[9] Similarly, if an IRB suspends or terminates a protocol's approval, it must provide the "investigator, appropriate institutional officials, and

---

[7] 45 C.F.R. § 46.103(b)(4) (2016) and 45 C.F.R. § 46.108(a)(3)(i) (2019); 21 C.F.R. 56.108(a)(1).
[8] 45 C.F.R. § 46.109(d) (2016) (2019); 21 C.F.R. § 56.109(e).
[9] Id.

the department or agency head" a statement of reasons.[10] Ultimately, the regulations require transparency about the bare outcome of the IRB's deliberation in all cases and transparency about the IRB's rationale in only some; indeed, empirical evidence suggests that IRBs frequently fail to justify the stipulations they impose on research as a condition of approval, often leaving ethical and regulatory concerns implicit in correspondence with investigators.[11] Even when transparency is required, however, the requirement is limited at most to the investigator, institution, and regulators.

By comparison, sharing IRB meeting minutes could generate much more substantial insight. By regulation, minutes must be "in sufficient detail to show ... actions taken by the IRB; the vote on these actions including the number of members voting for, against, and abstaining; the basis for requiring changes in or disapproving research; and a written summary of the discussion of controverted issues and their resolution."[12] Regulatory guidance further specifies that meeting minutes include documentation of findings, "including protocol-specific information justifying each IRB finding," regarding specific regulatory provisions governing consent and research with special populations,[13] as well as documentation of certain other details and determinations.[14] Although regulatory guidance acknowledges that IRB minutes are intended to "provide information to persons not present at the meeting (e.g., investigators, institutional officials, regulators, IRB members who could not attend),"[15] meeting minutes are not required to be shared with anyone, including the investigator. Instead, they must simply be maintained with IRB records and made available for review by regulators. The overarching theme is obvious: "IRBs are rarely required to explain or justify their decisions."[16]

CURRENT IRB PRACTICE

In terms of what happens in practice, there is wide variety in what IRBs communicate to whom and how. At the front end, some IRBs provide substantial outreach and education to help investigators understand what they are looking for and how to avoid common mistakes.[17] This requires resources, however – personnel, time, and

---

[10] 45 C.F.R. § 46.113 (2016) (2019); 21 C.F.R. § 56.113.
[11] Justin T. Clapp, Katherine A. Gleason & Steven Joffe, Justification and Authority in Institutional Review Board Letters, 194 Soc. Sci. Med. 25 (2017).
[12] 45 C.F.R. § 46.115(a)(2) (2016) (2019); 21 C.F.R. § 56.115.
[13] Office for Human Research Prots., Guidance: Written IRB Procedures (2011), www.hhs.gov/ohrp/minutes-institutional-review-board-irb-meetings-guidance-institutions-and-irbs.html-0 (last visited Oct. 1, 2018).
[14] Office for Human Research Prots. and Food & Drug Admin., Guidance for Institutions and IRBs: Minutes of Institutional Review Board (IRB) Meetings (2017), www.hhs.gov/ohrp/minutes-institutional-review-board-irb-meetings-guidance-institutions-and-irbs.html-0 (last visited Sept. 27, 2017).
[15] Id.
[16] C. H. Coleman, Rationalizing Risk Assessment in Human Subject Research, 46 Ariz. L. Rev. 1, 14 (2004).
[17] S. T. Fiske, Institutional Review Boards: From Bane to Benefit, 4 Persp. on Psych. Sci. 30, 31 (2009).

money.[18] In many cases, IRB "deliberations are conducted behind closed doors, and minutes of meetings are made available to outsiders only under limited circumstances."[19] Little is known about the issues that IRBs "consider important to their decisions or about the substance of IRB deliberations."[20] Beyond deliberations, decisions themselves are generally kept private, shared only with the particular investigators whose research is affected. How IRBs communicate their decisions to investigators is also variable. Some IRBs write "lengthy memos to [principal investigators] in response to submitted protocols, assisting these PIs in rewriting studies" and some try to point out the specific regulations and ethical principles behind their decisions.[21] But again, this is resource-intensive, and seems to be the exception not the rule.[22] Finally, although some information is shared at conferences, in journals, and through email listservs aimed at IRB professionals, as well as through various training opportunities, there are no systematic mechanisms in place for IRBs to learn laterally from one another's experiences, or to facilitate and promote such learning.[23]

Ultimately, we lack empirical data about actual levels of IRB transparency across different parameters, but what we know is that the regulations are permissive of relative nontransparency, which is also common in practice. Typically, IRBs are not writing opinions justifying their actions, meeting minutes may cover little of substance (especially when a protocol is approved),[24] and entire swaths of stakeholders may be unable to access key information.

A PUSH FOR IRB TRANSPARENCY

Given the benefits of transparency described below, and the protections that can be put in place to avoid potential negative consequences, the present level of IRB nontransparency is unacceptable – and good reasons for nontransparency in particular contexts are likely to be few and far between.

General Benefits of Transparency

Consider, for example, the litigation system and court decisions, agency rulemaking through notice-and-comment processes, and agency review decisions, such as those made by the FDA in approving new medical products. All entail processes that are

---

[18] R. Klitzman, From Anonymity to 'Open Doors': IRB Responses to Tensions with Researchers, 347 BMC Res. Notes 5, 6 (2012).
[19] Coleman, supra note 16, at 14. See also L. Stark, Behind Closed Doors (2011); J. Katz, Toward a Natural History of Ethical Censorship, Legality, Social Research, and the Challenge of Institutional Review Boards, 41 L. & Soc. Rev. 797, 800 (2007); R. Klitzman, The Ethics Police?: IRBs' Views Concerning Their Power, 6 PLoS One e28773 (2011).
[20] Abbott & Grady, supra note 6, at 6.
[21] Klitzman, supra note 18.
[22] Clapp et al., supra note 11.
[23] Coleman, supra note 16, at 15, 50.
[24] Id. at 14, 40.

more transparent than IRB oversight of research, and have in common not only analysis of applicable issues and arguments, but also detailed written evaluations that are made available to the public beyond the immediate parties at issue to explain the outcome and rationale. This forces development of articulable and defensible reasons, helps to provide a foundation for future analyses, and facilitates external oversight.[25] These are each important generalized benefits of a transparent system of decision making, which the current IRB system fails to capitalize on. By contrast, when decisions are not made transparently, there is not only a lack of accountability, but also the possibility of confusion and uncertainty for affected parties, inconsistency between decision makers, ad hoc decision making and poor reasoning, and even abuse of power.[26]

Benefits of Transparency to the Public

Beyond these baseline considerations in favor of transparency, it is important to recognize the impact of IRB decisions on the public. Given their gatekeeping authority, IRBs can play a critical role in promoting scientific advancement, for example facilitating and speeding the approval of useful research. Conversely, they can stand in the way and slow things down, beyond the appropriate impediment of scientifically or ethically unsound projects. Both approaches have real implications for the public, such that it is appropriate for the public to demand to be given access to understand the how and why of IRB determinations in order to gauge whether the gatekeeper is striking the right balance and promoting the right priorities and to permit public calls for change where needed. Relatedly, given that many IRBs are reviewing government-funded research, the public has an interest in understanding the impact of IRB review on their tax dollars and is aggrieved by being shut out of the process. In addition to these reasons supporting transparency directly to the public, the public's interest in medical and scientific advancement means that they also have an interest in improving IRB transparency to other stakeholders as well, given the benefits of such transparency described below.

Benefits of Transparency to Investigators

Investigators have a more direct interest in IRB transparency, on at least two grounds. First, there is some indication that the present lack of transparency, real or perceived, can lead investigators to distrust IRBs, or even to "demonize" them.[27] This can result in a variety of problems, from failure to engage IRBs about research questions early on to dismissal of the IRB process as illegitimate, which in the

---

[25] Id. at 41–43.
[26] See, e.g., D. C. Vladeck & M. Gulati, Judicial Triage: Reflections on the Debate over Unpublished Decisions, 62 Wash. & Lee L. Rev. 1667, 1676–81 (2005).
[27] Klitzman, supra note 18.

extreme may spur disrespect of ethical rules. If investigators are helped to understand the goals of IRBs, why certain questions are asked, on what grounds modifications are requested, the ways in which IRBs can help support research, timelines for review, IRB processes, and the like, this can avoid misunderstandings, assuage feelings of arbitrariness, and improve investigator trust in IRBs.[28] This is even more likely if IRBs can transparently demonstrate to investigators that they are being treated fairly in relation to other investigators and projects. Transparency should improve the essential relationship between IRBs and investigators, and facilitate weeding out IRB activities that are overly conservative.

The second basis for investigator interest in IRB transparency is simple efficiency. When investigators are uncertain why the IRB is imposing various requirements or reaching particular outcomes, they are in a poor position to submit approvable protocols from the start or to make appropriate adjustments. Similarly, when investigators are unclear as to how previous protocols have fared (and why), they may undertake unnecessarily duplicative work, for example justifying methods that the IRB may already be comfortable with or tracking down new approaches that the IRB might have already decided to be problematic. In short, "[w]ell-considered, thoughtful reviews could ... serve as exemplars and educational tools."[29]

Relatedly, to the extent that investigators fear that IRBs will slow down their research or behave conservatively,[30] they may self-censor what they submit for review in hopes of getting approval as quickly and painlessly as possible. While substantial empirical evidence of such behavior is lacking, anecdotal evidence is abundant.[31] If, rather than guessing, investigators had a better sense of what really would impede IRB approval, and what would not, detrimental self-censoring could be minimized or avoided.

Benefits of Transparency to IRBs

Efficiency concerns are also relevant in support of IRB transparency with other IRBs, as well as systems to promote transparency within IRBs over time, that is, preservation of institutional memory via easily accessible and searchable records of prior

---

[28] Id.; McMurphy et al., supra note 4; Dove et al., supra note 4; S. G. Henry, P. S. Romano & M. Yarborough, Building Trust Between Institutional Review Boards and Researchers, 31 J. Gen. Intern. Med. 987 (2016).

[29] A. M. Mascette et al., Are Central Institutional Review Boards the Solution? The National Heart, Lung, and Blood Institute Working Group's Report on Optimizing the IRB Process, 87 Acad. Med. 1710 (2012); see also Katz, supra note 19, at 806; M. Tolich & E. Tumilty, Making Ethics Review a Learning Institution: The Ethics Application Repository Proof of Concept – tear.otago.ac.nz, 14 Qualitative Res. 201, 202–03 (2014).

[30] See, e.g., S. N. Whitney et al., Principal Investigator Views of the IRB System, 5 Int. J. Med. Sci. 68 (2008).

[31] See, e.g., J. Kempner, J.F. Merz & C.L. Bosk, Forbidden Knowledge: Public Controversy and the Production of Nonknowledge, 26 Soc. F. 475, 487 (2011).

decisions. When IRBs are unable to learn from each other (and themselves), the research enterprise suffers; resources may be wasted and research slowed.

A related concern is that a lack of transparency between IRBs, including failure to share policies, determination letters, and meeting minutes, for example, can contribute to variability between them. Sharing these materials and rationales will not automatically lead to consistency, but it can help minimize thoughtless or ill-conceived variation. This is also not to suggest that IRBs should blindly "go with the crowd" once it becomes apparent what others are doing. Sometimes, independent judgment will be needed, and just as there may be majority and minority rules in different legal jurisdictions, it may be that there is no obvious "right" answer when it comes to certain issues raised before IRBs, even with transparency. The key is to have sufficient grounding to know whether any differences are considered and purposeful, and to avoid accidental difference simply out of ignorance to the behavior and decisions of peers. In this way, transparency can help lay the foundation for a system of IRB precedent,[32] or at the very least generation of best practices.

Benefits of Transparency to Research Participants

When considering the benefits of IRB transparency, we cannot overlook a primary beneficiary: research participants. While participants would benefit from many of the various advantages already described with regard to transparency to other stakeholders, helping potential participants understand as part of the consent process why an IRB found regulatory criteria to be satisfied – direct risks and benefits balanced, for example – could reasonably be relevant to the decision whether to participate.[33] And in the event that an IRB determines the regulatory criteria have not been satisfied, this may be relevant to patient communities who stand to benefit from research and may have been willing to participate, and who can potentially help provide the IRB with additional information or help researchers address IRB concerns, for example.[34] Empirical study would be valuable to assess how prospective participants and patient groups would respond to IRB transparency, for example whether it could improve trust in research to have a better sense of the IRB's role or whether it might have the opposite effect by virtue of exposing debates, disagreements, and some of the "sausage-making" aspects of research.

---

[32] Dove et al., supra note 4, at 39–40.
[33] This information need not be provided as a matter of course in informed consent materials, which are already too lengthy. But it could be provided in a link to more information, for example, for participants who are interested in learning more.
[34] L. Stark, Gaps in Medical Research Ethics, L.A. Times, Oct. 8, 2010 (calling on the regulators to "empower research participants by posting the results of ethics reviews online").

Additional Benefits

There are at least two additional benefits to IRB transparency that span a variety of stakeholders. First, under the status quo of nontransparency, it is difficult to hold IRBs accountable for their decisions. This is most obviously because many stakeholders may simply not know what IRBs are doing, and therefore may not know to object, appeal, or push for change. But at a more subtle level, when IRB materials are not shared or available, and in particular, when IRB decisions are not presented in written form with analysis, IRBs can more easily fall back on "gut feelings" or intuition.[35] In an alternate scenario in which IRB activities are made accessible to others, IRBs are more likely to be compelled to articulate reasons and provide precise (or any) justifications for their decisions. And when reasons are provided, they can be assessed, analyzed, critiqued, praised, adjusted, and the like.[36] Moreover, the process of articulating reasons may cause IRBs to reassess their own views; perhaps they are less well supported than initially "felt," and alternative approaches are warranted.[37] Ultimately, IRB transparency should improve the quality of IRB decisions, just as publication of judicial decisions has been correlated with higher quality.[38]

A second benefit of IRB transparency is that transparent decisions, policies, and practices can be studied empirically. Empirical evaluation of IRBs is essential, given the resources devoted and impact on scientific advancement, and important work has been done already.[39] But this sort of work can be challenging, with important limitations, for example relying on IRBs to voluntarily provide information, which some may deny, or relying on investigators to pass along their correspondence, which may be incomplete. More robust analysis via greater IRB transparency will provide important insights into the bases for IRB decisions (for example, regulations, institutional policy, ethical principles, and so forth); areas of focus (for example, informed consent, trial design issues, and privacy); goals (for example, participant protection and institutional liability avoidance); consistency (within and between IRBs); and overall approaches (helpful or detached). It will allow assessment of whether IRBs are being too conservative, too permissive, too bureaucratic, too conflicted, too resource intensive – and what they are doing well, adding value to the research enterprise and participant protection. Evidence-based policymaking, in turn, will allow the IRB system to focus its energies on areas where it can be most effective.

[35] Dove et al., supra note 4, at 12; Coleman, supra note 16, at 14.
[36] Katz, supra note 19, at 798.
[37] "The discipline of providing written reasons ... often will show weaknesses or inconsistencies in the intended decision that may compel a change in the rationale or even in the ultimate result." William L. Reynolds & William M. Richman, An Evaluation of Limited Publication in the United States Courts of Appeals: The Price of Reform, 48 Univ. Chi. L. Rev. 573, 603 (1981).
[38] Id. at 598–604 (demonstrating that a large fraction of unpublished judicial opinions failed to satisfy basic standards of quality, such as providing a rationale for the judgment).
[39] See Abbott & Grady, supra note 6.

General	To the public	To investigators	To IRBs	To participants
• Accountability • Defensible reasons • Clarity and certainty • Foundation for precedent – or justification of inconsistency • Empirical study	• Check on gate-keepers • Interest in publicly-funded research • Open government	• Trust in IRBs • Use of IRBs as a resource • Dispel myths • Avoid unnecessary self-censoring • Efficient protocol development	• Efficiency (not reinventing the wheel) • Avoid inappropriate variation • Self-reflection	• Trust in research enterprise • Challenge IRB protectionism, as needed

Figure 2. Benefits of IRB transparency

OBJECTIONS AND RESPONSES

In light of these benefits of IRB transparency, why has greater transparency not yet been adopted – what are the downsides? One concern has to do with confidentiality. IRBs are reviewing protocols that may contain sensitive information, including commercially valuable information about new products or even the investigator's trial design and study description. In a world of lucrative drugs and devices, in which even a few months difference can result in significant market advantage, and in the realm of academic research, in which investigators' careers hinge on publications and funding awards, the inclination to wall off commercial and intellectual competitors is understandable.[40]

While this rationale may suggest caution with regard to who is allowed to attend IRB meetings (which could at least partially be addressed via confidentiality agreements), there is a relatively simple solution when it comes to IRB minutes and decisions: redact them.[41] Moreover, this sort of confidentiality concern is no reason not to be more transparent about IRB policies, rather than protocol-specific decisions, nor is it a reason not to be entirely forthcoming and direct with investigators about the IRB's decision and rationale related to their own submissions.

It is possible that greater IRB transparency could have a range of unintended consequences. For example, perhaps IRBs would become even more conservative if they fear that their activities will be subject to outside scrutiny or if they discover that their board is not as conservative as others, or perhaps the candor of IRB deliberations would be negatively affected on a more transparent approach.[42] IRBs may actually be inclined to document and disclose *less* if they fear opening themselves up to litigation.[43] And it is also possible that increased transparency will result in more "IRB shopping" by sponsors and investigators seeking the most lenient boards.

While these are reasonable worries, they need not be insurmountable. First, given the general benefits of IRB transparency described above, *possible* bad outcomes seem inadequate to support the status quo. In particular, with regard to litigation, there have been relatively few lawsuits stemming from research studies,[44] and there is so much discretion in the applicable regulations that IRBs likely need not worry so

---

[40] L. Stark, IRBs and the Problem of "Local Precedents," in Human Subjects Research Regulation: Perspectives on the Future 182 (I. G. Cohen & H. Fernandez Lynch, eds., 2014); Coleman, supra note 16, at 14, n. 84.

[41] Klitzman, supra note 18. Another option might be delayed publication of IRB "cases" so that they are available for reference later on, at some point when confidentiality may be less important.

[42] Coleman, supra note 16, at 14, n. 84.

[43] Id. at 15, n. 90.

[44] In the early 2000s, there was a flurry of clinical trials litigation, including suits naming IRBs and individual members, much of which was spearheaded by a single attorney, Alan Milstein. See S. Silverstein, Clinical Trial Litigation, www.sskrplaw.com/clinical-trial-litigation.html (last visited May 27, 2017). This trend has not continued, however. Today, research litigation does happen, but, for a variety of reasons including lack of a private right of action in the applicable regulations, is relatively infrequent.

long as they are behaving reasonably. Moreover, transparency can help build an IRB "standard of care" based on what others are doing in similar contexts. Second, these are empirical questions: we could pilot test different approaches to transparency to see how they work and what impact they have. And third, it is also possible that IRB transparency will have the salutary effect of facilitating more liberal approaches as IRBs see others adopting creative solutions to facilitate research. In this regard, if there is "IRB shopping," it may not be a bad thing, so long as IRBs at the more lenient end of the spectrum are satisfying regulatory standards and complying with best practices.

Probably the most important argument against IRB transparency is not that transparency itself is undesirable, but rather that it is costly. Many IRBs are already woefully under-resourced,[45] so asking them to write out and share robust determinations and policies is an added burden, which could ultimately result in delay. Nonetheless, if this is the argument against transparency, there are even greater concerns – namely that IRBs are inadequately resourced to render justifiable determinations in the first place. Clearly, this cannot stand.

With appropriate protection against conflict of interest, IRB user fees may be a part of the solution, as some institutions have recognized, at least for industry-sponsored research. It is also possible that new requirements for single-IRB review of multisite research will lead to certain efficiency gains and more resources for reviewing IRBs. Finally, note that some types of IRB transparency will be less costly than others, such as making existing policies more freely available, such that cost cannot be an unqualified defense of nontransparency.

To the extent that time is itself a resource, a related worry is that if one goal of transparency is to allow IRBs to learn from each other, IRBs need to have time to review the cases that came before, as well as some mechanism for sorting and searching them. This might be addressed by relying more heavily on IRB staff and administrators to help find and summarize relevant materials. Bioethics researchers interested in IRB issues can also help distill key points of learning from their own empirical analyses, which can be provided to IRBs through various training and continuing education opportunities.

RECOMMENDATIONS

While it is certainly not the case across the board, the default rule – permitted by the regulations governing IRBs and demonstrated by the practices of many – has been for IRBs to be closed-door, relatively secretive bodies. Given the clear benefits of IRB transparency in terms of accountability, consistency, trust, and efficiency, the question is not whether to push for improved transparency or why, but rather how and along which parameters.

---

[45] C. Grady, Institutional Review Boards: Purpose and Challenges, 148 *Chest* 1148, 1150–51 (2015).

One option is regulatory change. The regulations could, for example, impose more specificity with regard to IRB minutes, set expectations in favor of open meetings, flesh out the requirements for the content of determination letters, and specify that these materials be shared beyond institutional and regulatory audits. Regulatory change is procedurally difficult, but regulatory agencies could nonetheless offer guidance to this effect. Regulators could also make selected real-world cases available for training and guidance, facilitate research on IRB decision making, and conduct their own analyses of trends and approaches demonstrated by the records they have exclusive access to in order to develop best practices.

IRBs (and staff of institutional human research protection programs) can also voluntarily accept the responsibility to promote transparency, and in many ways have begun to do so, as noted above, through investigator-oriented websites, as well as listservs, conferences, journals, and other venues to share information between themselves.[46] Note, however, that individuals likely face institutional restrictions and confidentiality requirements, such that they may not be able to promote transparency without institutional support and permission.

Even if IRBs fail to embrace transparency, however, investigators could drive a movement themselves by sharing the materials they have access to, for example publishing decision letters, sharing protocols as they looked before and after the IRB process, and the like. Indeed, one such initiative has already launched in New Zealand, where "The Ethics Application Repository" (TEAR) serves as a voluntary digital archive of IRB applications and related materials in which researchers from any institution around the world can post their IRB's requested changes and ultimate decisions.[47] The hope is that both researchers and IRBs will learn from what came before.

CONCLUSION

No one ought to prefer a black box system in which the relevant stakeholders lack access to information that can improve efficiency, quality, and accountability. We ought to promote a new approach – one that supports transparency about a wide range of IRB activity to the wide range of stakeholders who stand to be affected. We can begin with stepwise progress, first addressing low-hanging fruit, like thin explanation of IRB actions to investigators and closed-door IRB meetings, while working steadily toward the goal of full transparency in this endeavor with such high stakes.

---

[46] Z. Schrag, A Plea for "Networked Learning," Instit. Rev. Blog, Jun. 26, 2010, www.institutionalreviewblog.com/2010/06/plea-for-networked-learning.html (last visited May 27, 2017).

[47] Tolich & Tumilty, supra note 29.

23

Using Disclosure to Regulate PBMs

The Dark Side of Transparency

David A. Hyman and William E. Kovacic

Perhaps no group of people has been so much maligned in recent years as the middlemen. It has been said that there are too many middlemen; that many of them are speculators, pure and simple; that they are inefficient; that they are avaricious profiteers; and that they carry on their businesses at too heavy expense to both producers and consumers.[1]

Transparency is popular across the political spectrum. As Professor William Sage accurately noted in an article in the *Columbia Law Review*, "because disclosure laws influence private transactions without substituting direct government regulation, they illuminate all parts of the political spectrum, appealing equally to conservatives, who applaud 'market facilitation' and 'bootstrapping,' and to liberals, who favor 'empowerment' and the 'right to know.'"[2] Unsurprisingly, transparency has become a favored regulatory tool in multiple policy domains, including health care. Indeed, most of the chapters in this book are singing from the same hymnal on the benefits of transparency in the medical marketplace.

In fairness, there is broad agreement that health care could benefit from more transparency. Most patients know little about their newly diagnosed conditions – let alone understand their treatment options and the extent to which those options are supported by actual evidence of efficacy and cost effectiveness. Similarly, it is difficult (if not impossible) for patients to obtain good information on the performance statistics for providers (for example, is this physician better or worse than any other physician?). And, for almost everyone, the cost of care and the extent to which that care will be covered as an in-network benefit remains a mystery until long after the services have been rendered.

That said, transparency can have anticompetitive consequences – and any sensible accounting of the costs and benefits of transparency should take account of these effects. In addition, transparency can be ineffective, or it can cause harms for

---

[1] Paul D. Converse, Middlemen: Who They Are and How They Operate, 11 (1922), https://archive.org/details/middlemenwhotheyooconv.
[2] William M. Sage, Regulating Through Information: Disclosure Laws and American Health Care, 99 Colum. L. Rev. 1701, 1825–26 (1999).

reasons other than its effects on competition. Those possibilities, which also counsel for caution in the use of transparency initiatives, are beyond the scope of this chapter, which focuses on transparency initiatives affecting pharmacy benefit managers (PBMs). Multiple states have enacted legislation requiring PBMs to disclose details about their contractual arrangements with counterparties. Legislation seeking to impose similar requirements on PBMs contracting with public payers (such as Medicare Part D, TRICARE, and the FEHPB) is currently pending in Congress.[3] The Patient Protection and Affordable Care Act (PPACA) also includes a provision imposing greater transparency on PBMs.[4]

Building on our earlier work in this space, we show that transparency initiatives can have significant anticompetitive consequences, resulting in higher spending on pharmaceuticals.[5] The primary beneficiaries of such legislation are pharmacies – which explains why they are enthusiastic supporters of these reforms. Consumers, who bear the costs of these "protections," should be considerably less enthusiastic.

Our analysis helps make it clear that transparency is neither a cure-all nor magic bullet. Instead, it is a tool that works well for some problems and poorly (or not at all) for others. Our findings argue for greater skepticism about the utility of transparency as a regulatory strategy – particularly given the "bootleggers and Baptists" dynamics that underlie many legislative initiatives, including the ones we describe in this chapter.[6]

Part I of this chapter describes the market for pharmaceuticals. Part II analyzes legislative efforts to increase PBM transparency regarding contracts with counterparties. Part III discusses the implications of our findings. Part IV concludes.

I. THE MARKET FOR PHARMACEUTICALS

The market for pharmaceuticals is complex, highly regulated, and exceedingly nontransparent.[7] Prescription pharmaceuticals come in two principal types: branded and generic. Approval by the Food and Drug Administration (FDA) is necessary to sell branded drugs and generics in the United States. Branded drugs are typically subject to patent protection, but generics are not. The FDA lists approved pharmaceuticals, their generic equivalents, and all associated patents in what is commonly known as the "Orange Book."[8] Generics must be shown to be bioequivalent to the branded drug to appear in the Orange Book.

[3] See, e.g., Creating Transparency to Have Drug Rebates Unlocked Act of 2017, S. 637 (115th Cong. 2017); Prescription Drug Price Transparency Act, H.R. 1316, (115th Cong. 2017).
[4] Patient Protection & Affordable Care Act, § 6005.
[5] David A. Hyman & William E. Kovacic, Health Care Competition Law in the Shadow of State Action: Minimizing MACS, 48 Loyola L. Rev. 757 (2017), https://ssrn.com/abstract=2829769.
[6] Bruce Yandle, Bootleggers and Baptists in Retrospect, 22 *Regulation* 5 (1999).
[7] See Health Mgmt. Assocs., Study of the Pharmacy Chain of Supply (2017), www.insurance.wa.gov/sites/default/files/2017-06/pharmacy-supply-chain-study_0.pdf [hereinafter "HMA/OIC Report"].
[8] The technical name for the "Orange Book" is "Approved Drug Products with Therapeutic Equivalence Evaluations." U.S. Food & Drug Admin., Approved Drug Products with Therapeutic Equivalence Evaluations (Orange Book), www.fda.gov/Drugs/InformationOnDrugs/ucm129662.htm.

Branded drugs capture most of the media attention, and are responsible for a heavily disproportionate share of drug spending – but generic prescriptions account for more than 85 percent of filled prescriptions.[9] On a per-unit basis, generic drugs are significantly cheaper than branded drugs – but in recent years, generic drug prices have trended upward – sometimes sharply.[10] Like any other product, drug pricing is affected by both supply-side and demand-side factors.[11]

Pharmaceutical manufacturers do not sell their products directly to patients. Instead, their products are sold to wholesalers (for example, Amerisource Bergen, Cardinal, and McKesson), who sell in turn to pharmacies. Chain pharmacies often deal direct with manufacturers, in which case the wholesaler handles distribution, but does not take title.

When pharmacies dispense prescription pharmaceuticals to insured individuals, they are paid either solely by the consumer, solely by a plan sponsor/PBM, or by both. Most insurers contract with a PBM to handle their prescription drug coverage. PBMs are quintessential middlemen, in that they help structure the market for the administration of prescription drug benefits by processing and paying prescription drug claims; creating networks of pharmacies at which prescriptions will be filled for a specified price; creating formularies; and negotiating for discounts or rebates.[12] Insurers and employers that want to offer a prescription drug benefit must either handle such tasks themselves or contract with a PBM to have them done (that is, they must "make" or "buy" such services).

Contracting for PBM services is complex. Contracts must specify the amount that plan sponsors will pay per dispensed prescription for each covered drug, and the charges for the PBM services that plan sponsors utilize. PBMs use formularies (which list PBM-approved drugs for treating various diseases and conditions) to control the price that health plans and enrollees pay and affect the use of various drugs and the mix of drugs dispensed. Generic substitution and therapeutic interchange help lower drug spending.

PBMs use the promise of being included in the formulary (and the threat of exclusion) to encourage pharmaceutical manufacturers to pay rebates. Depending on the contract, these rebates are either paid to the plan sponsor, retained by the PBM, or shared between.[13]

There are three large independent, full-service PBMs with national scope: CVS Health, Express Scripts, and United Health. These three PBMs are major players in most markets, but there are many smaller PBMs that compete to provide the same

---

[9] Aria A. Razmaria, Generic Drugs, 315 JAMA 2746 (2016).

[10] Ana Vega et al., Commentary on Current Trends in Rising Drug Costs and Reimbursement Below Cost, Managed Care (2016), www.managedcaremag.com/archives/2016/4/commentary-current-trends-rising-drug-costs-and-reimbursement-below-cost.

[11] See Jonathan D. Alpern, William M. Stauffer & Aaron S. Kesselheim, High-Cost Generic Drugs – Implications for Patients and Policymakers, 371 New Eng. J. Med. 1859 (2014).

[12] Patricia Danzon, 2014 ERISA Advisory Council PBM Compensation and Fee Disclosure (2014), www.dol.gov/sites/default/files/ebsa/about-ebsa/about-us/erisa-advisory-council/ACDanzon061914.pdf.

[13] Fed. Trade Comm'n, Pharmacy Benefit Managers: Ownership of Mail-Order Pharmacies (Aug. 2005), www.ftc.gov/sites/default/files/documents/reports/pharmacy-benefit-managers-ownership-mail-order-pharmacies-federal-trade-commission-report/050906pharmbenefitrpt_0.pdf

services in particular markets. The FTC concluded in a 2004 analysis that competition between PBMs for contracts with plan sponsors was "vigorous."[14] Despite this (now somewhat dated) finding, many commentators have expressed concern about concentration in the market for PBM services and disparities in bargaining power between individual pharmacies and PBMs. That sentiment is an important part of the political economy story behind the transparency initiatives we describe in Part II.

What about the contracts between pharmacies and PBMs? PBMs must assemble a network of pharmacies willing and able to dispense pharmaceuticals to covered plan beneficiaries. Pharmacies want to be sure they are paid enough to justify participation in the proposed network. But neither knows in advance which medications will be dispensed – or in what amounts. To achieve their joint objectives, PBMs and pharmacies enter into contracts (called participating pharmacy agreements or PPAs) that specify a formula for payment for each dispensed pharmaceutical, and provide a dispute resolution mechanism in the event the pharmacy is unhappy with the amount it receives.

To enhance their negotiating leverage in dealing with PBMs, independent pharmacies often join together under the umbrella of a pharmacy services administrative organization (PSAO). PSAOs assist in negotiating contracts and handling disputes with PBMS. PSAOs can also negotiate with group purchasing organizations (GPOs) on behalf of pharmacies, allowing them to concentrate their purchases with one or more preferred vendors. Figure 1 illustrates the web of contractual relationships among the various entities that are active in this space.

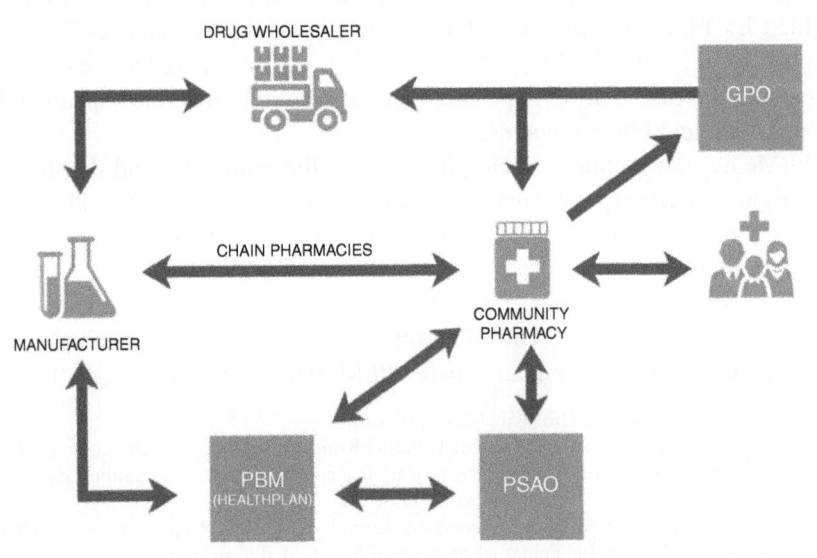

FIGURE 1: The web of contractual relationships[15]

[14] Fed. Trade Comm'n, Statement In the Matter of Caremark Rx, Inc./AdvancePCS (Feb. 11, 2004), www.ftc.gov/os/caselist/0310239/040211ftcstatement0310239.pdf.
[15] HMA/OIC Report, supra note 7, at 14.

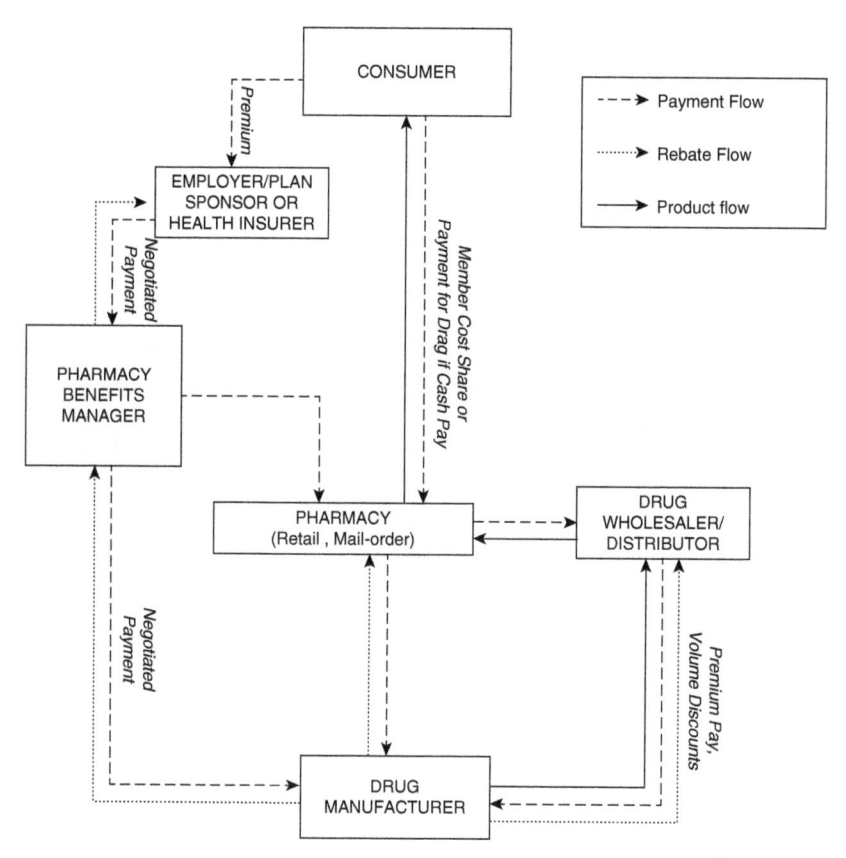

FIGURE 2: Flow of payments, rebates, and pharmaceuticals[16]

Figure 1 shows that there are multiple contractual arrangements, but it does not indicate the flow of payments, rebates, and pharmaceutical products. Figure 2 presents that information, while omitting several of the players in Figure 1.

In Part II, we describe two disputes that have arisen in this policy space. In both, transparency has been offered or implemented as the "solution."

II. THE WAR OVER PBM TRANSPARENCY

As PBMs became significant players in the market for pharmaceuticals, pharmacies felt squeezed, and looked for ways to push back. The initial campaign involved efforts to force PBMs to disclose financial information, including the details of their rebate arrangements with pharmaceutical manufacturers. A subsequent campaign involves (ongoing) efforts to force PBMs to disclose details regarding their

---

[16] Health Strategies Consultancy, Follow the Pill: Understanding the U.S. Commercial Pharmaceutical Supply Chain, http://avalere.com/research/docs/Follow_the_Pill.pdf.

methodology for determining how much to pay pharmacies for dispensing generics (that is, maximum allowable cost, or MAC). We describe each campaign in turn.

A. The Initial Campaign

As noted previously, pharmaceutical manufacturers pay rebates to induce PBMs to include their (branded) pharmaceuticals on drug formularies. Depending on the contract, these rebates are either retained by the PBM, shared with the plan sponsor, or passed through to the plan sponsor in their entirety. Rebate programs help intensify competition in the market for branded pharmaceuticals and are an important tool with which to lower drug spending. Indeed, Medicaid has relied on a similar rebate program since 1990.

Pharmacists were exceedingly unhappy that they were being financially squeezed at the same time PBMs were collecting millions in rebates – even though PBMs did not necessarily retain these rebates.[17] Pharmacists also disliked being put in the middle when a formulary did not cover a prescribed drug. In response, pharmacists lobbied for various transparency initiatives that they believed would make life more difficult for PBMs. California Assembly Bill 1960 (AB 1960) is a representative example. This legislation, which was under consideration in 2004, would have required PBMs to disclose a laundry list of information to purchasers and prospective purchasers of PBM services, including information regarding rebates and drug utilization.[18] AB 1960 also would have required PBMs to disclose certain information to prescribers and patients before seeking to substitute one medication for another.

The FTC was quite critical of the transparency provisions in AB 1960:

> If pharmaceutical manufacturers learn the exact amount of the rebates offered by their competitors ... then tacit collusion among manufacturers is more feasible. Consequently, the required disclosures may lead to higher prices for PBM services and pharmaceuticals.
>
> Inclusion in a PBM formulary offers pharmaceutical manufacturers the prospect of substantially increased sales opportunities. Whenever PBMs have a credible threat to exclude pharmaceutical manufacturers from their formulary, manufacturers have a powerful incentive to bid aggressively. Willingness to bid aggressively, however, is affected by the degree of transparency with respect to the terms that pharmaceutical companies offer PBMs. Whenever competitors know the actual prices charged by other firms, tacit collusion – and thus higher prices – may be more likely.[19]

---

[17] See supra note 14 and accompanying text.
[18] See Fed. Trade Comm'n, Letter to Assemb. Greg Aghazarian (Sept. 7, 2004), www.ftc.gov/be/ V040027.pdf. One of the authors signed the letter as Special Counsel to the FTC.
[19] Id.

The FTC also criticized the fact that the transparency initiatives in AB 1960 were likely to increase the costs of drug substitution and might cause distortions in the market for PBM services. Far from helping consumers, the FTC argued that AB 1960 was "likely to increase costs to consumers without providing any countervailing benefits," and would therefore likely cause "an increase in the number of Americans who do without pharmaceuticals and/or health insurance."[20]

The California legislature enacted the proposed bill, but it was vetoed by Governor Schwarzenegger, who cited the FTC's analysis to support his conclusion "that enactment of this legislation will limit competition and significantly increase the cost of prescription drugs."[21]

The FTC subsequently submitted similar advocacy letters involving PBM transparency legislation in Virginia (2006)[22] and Mississippi (2011).[23] Both letters recapitulated the themes in the earlier letter. The Mississippi letter observed that transparency initiatives could undermine "competition between pharmacies to be included in PBM networks and between pharmaceutical manufacturers to offer discounts to PBMs. Both outcomes could raise prescription drug prices for consumers."[24] Virginia did not pass the proposed legislation, but Mississippi did.[25] Other states have considered (and in some instances enacted) similar legislation. In 2014, an Advisory Council to the Department of Labor recommended that similar requirements should be imposed on all PBM contracts.[26] As noted above, federal legislation is currently pending.[27]

Branded pharmaceutical manufacturers have also joined in, launching a publicity campaign, arguing that a portion of their (high) "list" prices are rebated to PBMs and payers, and calling for a pass-through of those savings to patients with high-deductible plans.[28] Depending on how this proposal is implemented, it might also require compelled disclosure of information by PBMs and could have similar effects to those warned of by the FTC.

As our discussion suggests, any evaluation of transparency initiatives that does not take competitive effects into account is likely to give a distorted impression of the

---

[20] Id.
[21] See Veto Statement of Governor Schwarzenegger, on file with author.
[22] See Fed. Trade Comm'n, Letter to Del. Terry G. Kilgore (Oct. 2, 2006), www.ftc.gov/be/V060018.pdf.
[23] See Fed. Trade Comm'n, Letter to Rep. Mark Formby (Mar. 22, 2011), www.ftc.gov/policy/policy-actions/advocacy-filings/2011/03/ftc-staff-letter-honorable-mark-formby-mississippi.
[24] Id.
[25] See 2011 Miss. Laws SB 2445 ("Mississippi Pharmacy Practice Act") (enacted Apr. 26, 2011), http://billstatus.ls.state.ms.us/2011/pdf/history/SB/SB2445.xml.
[26] See, e.g., ERISA Advisory Council, PBM Compensation and Fee Disclosure (Nov. 2014), www.dol.gov/sites/default/files/ebsa/about-ebsa/about-us/erisa-advisory-council/2014ACreport1.pdf.
[27] See supra note 3.
[28] See Jared S. Hopkins & Zachary Tracer, Blame Game Over High Drug Prices Escalates With New Ad, Bloomberg, Apr. 6, 2017, https://www.bloomberg.com/news/articles/2017-04-06/blame-game-over-high-drug-prices-gets-worse-with-lobby-s-new-ad; see also Pharm. Research & Mfrs. of Am., Share the Savings, www.phrma.org/discounts (last visited Sep. 27, 2017).

potential costs and benefits. We return to this issue below. We now turn to the second campaign, which involved an issue that was much more central to pharmacy profitability.

B. The Second Campaign

The second campaign involved an obscure corner of the pharmaceutical reimbursement market – MAC schedules. Medicaid and PBMs use MACs to reimburse pharmacies for dispensing generic drugs. MACs were pioneered by state Medicaid programs, and then adopted by PBMs. But in the past few years, MACs have become the focal point of heated controversies between PBMs and pharmacies – triggering legislative action in thirty-eight states and Puerto Rico.

MACs emerged in the Medicaid program as a tool to pay pharmacies their reasonable acquisition costs for the drugs they dispensed. Before MACs were developed, reimbursement generally involved paying the lesser of the estimated acquisition cost (EAC) plus a reasonable dispensing fee or the providers' usual and customary charges to the general public. The EAC was typically determined based on published list prices – including the Average Wholesale Price (AWP).

At one time, the AWP reflected pharmacists' acquisition costs, but it quickly became apparent that there was considerable divergence between the AWP and pharmacists' true acquisition costs, particularly as generic drugs became more prevalent. Once this fact became clear, it was necessary to modify Medicaid's reimbursement formula to ensure the amounts paid reflected pharmacists' actual costs (that is, the acquisition cost plus the costs associated with dispensing the pharmaceutical).

In 1987, the federal government responded by requiring states to implement an aggregate payment limit for specific drugs.[29] The payment limit (known as a "FUL," for "Federal Upper Limit") was determined mechanically.[30] Pursuant to this payment limit, the dispensing pharmacy was paid a flat amount for acquiring the dispensed drug, *irrespective of its actual acquisition cost*. However, some state Medicaid program directors believed they were still overpaying for many drugs. Those states responded by adopting MAC programs, which were similar to FULs, but applied to a far broader array of drugs and set lower reimbursement levels.[31] Medicaid MACs are calculated based on aggregate figures that reflect pharmacies' average acquisition cost for a given pharmaceutical product. As of January 12, 2012, all states used FULs and approximately forty-five states used MACs in their Medicaid programs.[32]

[29] 42 C.F.R. § 447.301 et seq. (1987).
[30] PPACA modified the formula for calculating a payment limit. The federal government is still in the process of implementing this change.
[31] Richard G. Abramson et al., Generic Drug Cost Containment in Medicaid: Lessons from Five State MAC Programs, 25 Health Care Fin. Rev. 25 (2004).
[32] Office of Inspector Gen., Medicaid Drug Pricing in State Maximum Allowable Cost Programs (Aug. 29, 2013), https://oig.hhs.gov/oei/reports/oei-03-11-00640.asp.

For drugs not subject to FULs and MACs, states implemented additional cost-control measures, including paying pharmacies based on published wholesale acquisition costs (WACs) and applying a standardized discount to published AWPs. In combination, these measures brought the amounts paid for pharmaceuticals closer to the actual acquisition costs incurred by pharmacies – and created an incentive for pharmacies to search for the lowest-priced drugs.

PBMs adopted these strategies and incorporated them into their PPAs. However, pharmacies insisted that PBMs were underpaying them by setting MAC levels too low and failing to update them quickly enough when acquisition costs increased. Pharmacies argued that the resulting shortfalls in payment placed considerable financial pressure on independent pharmacies (particularly those in rural areas) – causing closures and more limited access to pharmacy services. PBMs insisted that they were paying the correct amounts – and pharmacies that were losing money on dispensed generic prescriptions were either paying higher acquisition costs than they needed to; were mistaken about the transactions in question; or did not realize that MACs were intended to average out across all the generic prescriptions dispensed by a well-run pharmacy, with overpayments on some drugs compensating for underpayments on others.

Pharmacies were unpersuaded, and aggressively lobbied for legislation. In short order, thirty-eight states and Puerto Rico responded. Although the specifics varied from state to state, the general approach was to require public disclosure of each PBMs' MACs and the methodology for arriving at the amounts that will be paid; limit the circumstances in which MACs may be used (for example, by requiring a certain number of A-rated equivalents); require the submission of proprietary information regarding MACs to public authorities; specify particular methods and timeframes for MAC appeals and payment adjustments, including requiring retroactive payments; and in a few instances, requiring PBMs to reimburse the actual acquisition costs that are incurred, even if a cheaper alternative was available in the marketplace.

As we have detailed elsewhere, none of these initiatives are likely to improve the performance of the pharmaceutical market, and most seem quite likely to make things worse from a competition-oriented perspective.[33] Restrictive state-specific criteria undermine the flexibility of PBMs to develop and implement MACs. Mandatory public disclosure of MACs and the specifics of underlying methodologies are unlikely to benefit consumers, since the disclosure will probably lead to less intensive competition and higher prices. Forced disclosure of MAC methodologies means that PBMs will be unable to obtain a competitive advantage by developing more effective MACs. That may undermine PBMs' incentive to invest in such efforts (since other PBMs will be able to free-ride). In that environment, PBMs will be less likely to innovate – meaning that MACs will be less effective than they could be.

[33] Hyman & Kovacic, supra note 5.

Stated differently, and as we found with the first campaign against PBMs, compelled disclosure can create a risk to competition that is likely to result in higher prices for consumers.

Attempts to "score" the costs of such state-level regulation of MACs have been limited. One study, done by Visante, estimated that spending on the affected pharmaceuticals would increase by 31–56 percent, with a nationwide impact of $6.2 billion increased spending annually.[34] A second study performed by the Washington Health Care Authority concluded that the proposed legislation would make MAC lists much less effective and would dramatically reduce pharmacies' incentive to acquire generic drugs at the lowest possible cost, "significantly increasing" costs for public employee benefits.[35] Finally, the HMA/OIC Report concluded that MACs in Washington State appeared to be set at a level that paid pharmacies "fairly" (meaning at or above the average ingredient cost, using a variety of benchmarks). The HMA/OIC findings certainly do not indicate that there are no problems with MACs, but they do suggest that many of the complaints by pharmacies were overblown.

II. IMPLICATIONS/ DISCUSSION

A. Does Transparency "Fit" the Problem?

Transparency initiatives make sense if they map onto a form of market failure that can be "fixed" through information disclosure. But most forms of market failure problems cannot be "fixed" through information disclosure. For example, transparency initiatives are unlikely to have any effect on market failures attributable to force, fraud, duress, monopoly, externalities, and so on. Unfortunately, transparency initiatives are routinely deployed in circumstances that have little to do with the core problem information disclosure is intended to address. But even if transparency initiatives are being deployed to deal with informational asymmetries, it is important to understand that they may not have the desired effect – or any effect whatsoever.[36]

Given these dynamics, it is not entirely obvious why transparency initiatives are so popular. Perhaps transparency initiatives are the only ground for compromise between legislators who prefer to do nothing and legislators who want to use coercive top–down command and control strategies. Alternatively, transparency initiatives may be appealing because they satisfy the felt necessity of "doing something" about a problem, even if legislators do not actually understand either the problem or the list of available remedies. Legislators who are rationally ignorant of such details

---

[34] Visante, Proposed MAC Legislation May Increase Costs of Affected Generic Drugs by More Than 50 Percent (Jan. 2015), on file with author.
[35] WHCA Fiscal Note, SSB – 5857.
[36] Omri Ben-Shahar & Carl Schneider, More Than You Wanted to Know: The Failure of Mandated Disclosure (2014).

might reasonably view transparency initiatives as all upside, since they are as American as apple pie.

But as our analysis indicates, transparency is not a panacea. Instead, it is a tool that may work well for some problems and poorly (or not at all) for others. The best way to sort out whether any given transparency initiative will improve on the status quo is to employ a three-part strategy:

- Conduct an *ex ante* analysis of the nature of the underlying market failure;
- Structure the reform to address the specific type of market failure that has been identified and to minimize collateral competitive consequences, keeping in mind the likelihood any given reform is likely to prove sticky – which is often not a good thing, particularly in a dynamic industry;
- Conduct an *ex post* evaluation to ensure that the transparency initiative is achieving the desired objectives and that collateral consequences are minimized. Depending on the results, revisit the first two steps in the analysis and decide whether to continue, extend, revise, or scrap the transparency initiative.

B. The Political Economy of Anti-PBM Transparency Initiatives

As Professor Jack Balkin memorably observed, the justification for governmental action almost always has a nice version and a naughty version.[37] So far, we have mostly credited the nice version of the fight over PBM transparency – but there is a lot to be said for the naughty version. In health care, every dollar of health care spending is a dollar of income for some health care provider. To the extent PBMs are effective at reducing pharmaceutical spending, they reduce the amounts that pharmacies receive for dispensing those same drugs. Pharmacists are understandably aggrieved that their services are not being compensated at the handsome level that they believe their expertise and professionalism justifies – and they lobby for relief from the hardships imposed by competitive markets.

Consider a few salient facts. Although chains account for a near-majority of pharmacies in most states, the protection of small independent local pharmacies from the depredations of large out-of-state PBMs was the basis of the lobbying campaign. The flames were fanned by references to the rebates that PBMs were receiving from drug companies – even though the rebates had nothing whatsoever to do with the price at which generics were dispensed.[38] Given these dynamics, it is not surprising that we went from *no* states with anti-MAC legislation at the beginning of

---

[37] Jack Balkin, The Footnote, 83 Nw. U. L. Rev. 275, 291 (1989).
[38] Rebates are paid on branded drugs – not generics. It is difficult to see the relevance of rebates paid on branded drugs by a third party to a dispute over whether PBMs are paying pharmacies the "right" amount for dispensing generic drugs. And the fact that PBMs may have multiple sources of revenue does not translate into a legal or ethical obligation to share any of that revenue with pharmacies.

2013 to thirty-eight states having anti-MAC legislation only three and a half years later.

Second, in thirty-six of the thirty-eight states that adopted anti-MAC legislation, the state Medicaid program is excluded from the requirements imposed by the statute.[39] Many of these states also exclude state employees from the "consumer protections" contained in the MAC statutes. The only thing these two groups have in common is that the costs of their health coverage are on-budget expenses, borne (either in whole or in part) by the state in its sovereign capacity. By excluding these populations from the scope of MAC legislation, state legislators made it clear that they thought that the supposed consumer protections were worth doing – right up until the moment the state would bear the costs of doing so.[40] This pattern provides a useful (albeit underinclusive) signal of legislation that would never be enacted if the costs of reform were internalized.

Although the legislative campaign was built around the protection of independent (mostly rural) pharmacies, state anti-MAC statutes were not so limited. Instead, in all of these jurisdictions, every single pharmacy – including chain drugstores in urban locations – receives the benefits of the legislation. This strategy means the anti-MAC legislation is not well targeted to address the supposed problem that it is allegedly remedying. Stated differently, anti-MAC legislation puts money in the pockets of all pharmacies in a state, whether they were being "underpaid" or not. Indeed, that was the whole point of the exercise – and any attempt to target the fix more precisely would have probably fragmented the coalition supporting "reform."

Finally, in some states, the legislative history casts light on whose interests are actually being protected. When Iowa was considering anti-MAC legislation, one overly enthusiastic legislator stated that the legislation was necessary because the lack of regulation was "eroding local pharmacies." Another Iowa legislator explained that legislation was necessary because PBMs were engaging in "unfair business practices that hurt community pharmacies and their patients." Similarly, when Washington enacted anti-MAC legislation, the OIC was instructed to conduct a study that would inter alia "discuss suggestions that recognize the unique nature of small and rural pharmacies and possible options that support a viable business model that do not increase the cost of pharmacy products."[41] An *ex ante* legislative declaration that certain businesses are "unique" or "special" will quite predictably be the source of no end of mischief.[42]

Instead, competitive dynamics determine how much PBMs must pay to induce pharmacies to enter into a PPA.

[39] The exceptions are Mississippi and Texas.
[40] See also David A. Hyman, Drive-Through Deliveries: Is Consumer Protection Just What the Doctor Ordered?, 78 N.C. L. Rev. 5 (1999) (noting that majority of the states that enacted prohibitions on drive-through deliveries excluded state employees and Medicaid beneficiaries from the statute).
[41] Washington S.B. 5857 (2016).
[42] Richard Epstein, Why is Health Care Special?, 40 U. Kan. L. Rev. 307, 310 (1992).

As these facts make clear, the fight over PBM transparency is merely the latest act in a long-running show, where governmental action is the result of an unsavory alliance of Bootleggers and Baptists[43] conspiring against the public interest to favor "the concentrated interests of incumbent providers ... "[44] It is commonplace to complain about market failures, but anti-PBM transparency legislation is all about governmental failure.

That said, even a stopped clock is right twice a day. PBMs can misbehave.[45] When they do they should be punished to deter future misconduct. The key question is whether transparency initiatives are an effective prophylactic measure against such misconduct. That question cannot be answered with a throwaway invocation of Justice Brandeis's observation that "sunlight is the best of disinfectants." Instead, one must grapple with the complications and trade-offs of disclosure remedies, including their potential impact on competition and on the price and quality of the goods or services in question.

C. Regulatory Nontransparency?

People are quick to deploy transparency initiatives when they believe people don't understand what private sellers are offering – and wouldn't want it if they were better informed. But shouldn't we feel the same way when the government is the one doing the selling? Consider Professor Jonathan Gruber's memorable description of the importance of nontransparency in getting Obamacare through Congress:

> Transparent financing? Let's have transparent financing and transparent spending. This bill was written in a tortured way to make sure CBO [the Congressional Budget Office] did not score the mandate as taxes. If CBO scored the mandate as taxes, the bill dies. Okay. So it was written to do that. In terms of risk-rated subsidies, if you had a law which said healthy people are going to pay in – if you made it explicit that healthy people pay in sick people get money it would not have passed. Okay.
>
> Lack of transparency is a huge political advantage, and basically, call it the stupidity of the American voter or whatever, but basically that was really, really critical for getting the thing to pass.[46]

If we are going to commit to transparency, it should be apply to both private and public sector activities. Indeed, the whole point of the Freedom of Information Act

---

[43] See Yandle, supra note 6.
[44] See David A. Hyman, Getting the Haves to Come out Behind: Fixing the Distributive Injustices of American Health Care, 69 L. & Contemp. Probs. 265 (2006); see also David A. Hyman, Regulating Managed Care: What's Wrong With A Patient Bill of Rights, 73 S. Cal. L. Rev. 221 (2000).
[45] See generally PBM Watch, Federal and State Litigation Regarding Pharmacy Benefit Managers, www.pbmwatch.com/pbm-litigation-overview.html (last visited Sep. 27, 2017).
[46] Ian Schwartz, Obamacare Architect: Lack Of Transparency Is A Huge Political Advantage, Real Clear Pol., Nov. 10, 2014, www.realclearpolitics.com/video/2014/11/10/obamacare_architect_lack_of_transparency_is_a_huge_political_advantage.html.

was to make information about the federal government available to the citizenry – who, after all, are footing the bill. Sauce for the gander, anyone?

III. CONCLUSION

Transparency is popular and middlemen are unpopular. This simple syllogism encapsulates the logic of forcing PBMs to disclose details about their contractual arrangements with counterparties. But, popularity (or the lack thereof) provides an exceedingly unreliable foundation on which to build legislation. Transparency initiatives are not costless, even when they are effective – and the effects are not always what supporters promise, let alone hope for. Transparency only fits a subset of market failure problems – and even when it is deployed to address such problems, one should worry about collateral consequences and governmental failure. These factors counsel for greater caution in deploying transparency as a cure-all for what ails the medical marketplace.